THE COSMOLOGY OF A.N. WHITEHEAD

Alfred North Whitehead (1861–1947) began his career writing primarily on mathematics and logic. His book *Principia Mathematica* (with Bertrand Russell) is widely considered one of the most important texts in mathematical logic of the twentieth century. Later turning to the philosophy of science and metaphysics, he pioneered process philosophy, which looks at reality as a constantly evolving, interconnected web of events and processes rather than a collection of fixed substances. *Adventures of Ideas* and *Science and the Modern World* reflect on the power of general ideas – about humanity, God, and the universe – to shape the course of civilization, the latter book focusing particularly on the influence of science.

Anirudh Sridhar completed his D.Phil. from the University of Oxford in 2020. His work involved the philosophy of science, mathematics, and poetry. His book *Agon* (2025) explores the contest between poetry and mathematics in the quest for truth. He has an MA from the University of Freiburg, and a B.Sc. in Environmental Law from the State University of New York. He is currently pursuing a second bachelor's degree in Pure Mathematics from The Open University, UK. He is also dean at Alliance University, where he set up the School of Liberal Arts. He also pursues his interests in climate law as senior fellow in the Grantham Centre at London School of Economics.

THE COSMOLOGY OF A.N. WHITEHEAD

Two celebrated works under one cover

Science and the Modern World • Adventures of Ideas

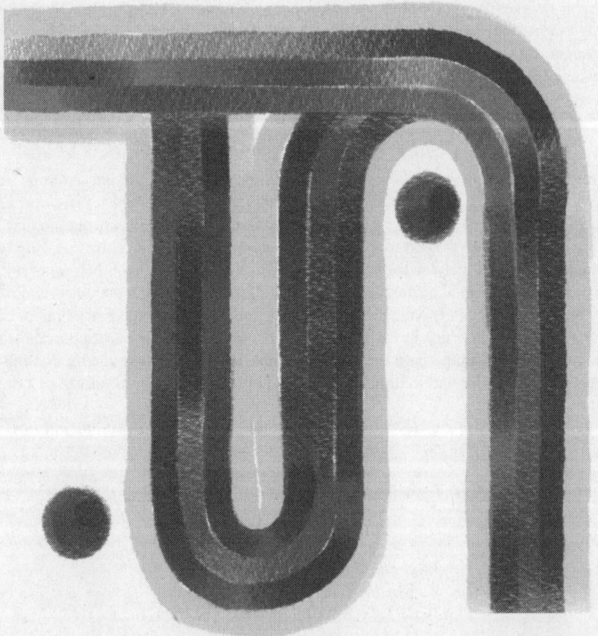

With an Introduction by Anirudh Sridhar

Adventures of Ideas by Alfred North Whitehead
First printed and published in the UK by Cambridge University Press
and in the US by Macmillan Company in 1933.

Science and the Modern World by Alfred North Whitehead
First printed and published in the US by Macmillan Company in 1926.

This edition published in paperback in 2026 by Hachette India
(Registered name: Hachette Book Publishing India Pvt. Ltd)
An Hachette UK company
www.hachetteindia.com

1

Image credit for images on pages 25 and 263: GDJ/pixabay.com

ISBN: 978-93-5731-734-4

Hachette Book Publishing India Pt. Ltd
4th/5th Floors, Corporate Centre,
Plot No. 94, Sector 44, Gurugram 122003, India

Typeset in Adobe Garamond Pro 11.5/16
by Content Respondus
New Delhi

Printed and bound in India
by Manipal Technologies Limited

CONTENTS

INTRODUCTION

Anirudh Sridhar[1]

THE LAST PHILOSOPHER IN the speculative tradition declared it his purpose to 'frame a coherent, logical, necessary system of general ideas in terms of which every element of our experience can be interpreted'.[2] Such ambition would only be fantasy, even for a solitary genius, after Alfred North Whitehead retired his pen because science had come to declare what is true in nearly every domain of knowledge. If a philosopher today is to propose a system of ideas through which all elements of experience can be interpreted, he must be able to stand above the disciplines of modern science to then put them in their place: a task that Whitehead was the last to attempt, and a near-impossible one now given the continually multiplying and specializing character of the empirical sciences.

Born in 1861, he began as a mathematician at Cambridge University in the late nineteenth century but came to write works of a philosophic nature only when he was nearing 50, around 1910. Whitehead becomes a philosopher around 250 years after the publication of Newton's *Principia*, and in the intervening centuries, the elements of our experience had been gradually annexed by science—until, as the logician Ernest Gellner observed,

1. I am most grateful to Arkady Plotnitsky (Purdue University) and Adam Jones (Cambridge University) for lending me their expertise in mathematics and keen editorial eye.
2. A.N. Whitehead, *Process and Reality: An Essay in Cosmology* (New York: The Macmillan Company, 1929), p. 4.

it came to be generally agreed that 'when one determines whether or not something is "scientific", one is *ipso facto* deciding whether or not it has a certain legitimate claim on our attention, and perhaps even on our credence'.[3] From the seventeenth century onwards, science had posited its methods to be exclusively suited to uncovering the one true picture of reality. The technology that the sciences made possible had, in a brute fashion, reconfigured the rhythm and texture of lived experience in the nineteenth century, in what is called the first age of machines. In society at large, science became sovereign over mind not only by offering a plausible picture of reality, but principally through the techne whose development it enabled—chiefly electricity, the internal combustion engine, and the telegraph—which had altered modes of labour, reshaped human interaction, and demoted the primacy of the body in the material upkeep of civilization. It is above all because nature appeared pliant to its techne that science was able to proclaim its picture of the world as 'objective' and thereby overrule other understandings of the natural world: ones emerging from our embodied perspective rather than measuring instruments. In the early twentieth century, most 'movements' in philosophy gave up attempting to posit an independent picture of the world and instead clamoured to conform, even reform, their traditions to the methods and findings of science. An exception is phenomenology, which attempted to rescue the body from obsolescence in our collective understanding of reality. Husserl and Heidegger are the ones most remembered today. But they failed to intellectually domesticate the civilizational authority of science, in great part because they could not account for the tremendous success the sciences had in describing aspects of nature sufficiently to successfully manipulate it. An intellectual rebellion that did not step into the weeds and hack at the dogmas of science could

3. Ernest Gellner, 'The Scientific Status of the Social Sciences', *International Social Science Journal*, 36.4 (1984), 567–86, p. 570.

not hope to undermine it in an electro-mechanical age, however hypnotic its call to reason may have been. Husserl and Heidegger exhibit an ambition akin to Whitehead's—but their writings have been primarily absorbed into the humanities, as have been those of their successors, such as the existentialists, who are at times propagated as much by literary studies.

In 1910, Whitehead—one might say, the logician in Whitehead—collaborated with Bertrand Russell to produce the rather unmodestly named *Principia Mathematica*. It became a foundational text in the development of logic in the twentieth century.[4] Its framework of formal logic would be used by David Hilbert, Kurt Gödel, and Alan Turing: a line of influence that would lead to the theoretical foundations of the first digital computer.[5] But Whitehead rarely recalled its ideas in his subsequent works and, in fact, seemed to abjure its legacy in later life as the enterprise of philosophy came to acquire for him an amplitude seldom witnessed among philosophers since the triumph of science in the nineteenth century. As he grew from logician to metaphysician, Whitehead began to appreciate more thoroughly than most before him the desperate poverty in the scientific account of phenomena. In a series of lectures he delivered at Cambridge in 1919 titled *The Concept of Nature*, he says, 'any theory of nature which for one moment loses sight of the great basic facts of experience is simply silly'.[6] Throughout the 1920s, he points to ways in which science had lost touch with what is plainly available before experience in its attempt to construct a complete picture of reality. The world

4. Alfred N. Whitehead and Bertrand Russell, *Principia Mathematica, vol. 1* (Cambridge: Cambridge University Press, 1910).

5. See Robert Constable, *The Triumph of Types: Principia Mathematica's Impact on Computer Science*. Proceedings of the 10th Annual Oregon Programming Languages Summer School, July 16 2011 (Cornell University Computing and Information Science Technical Report).

6. A.N. Whitehead, *The Concept of Nature* (Cambridge: Cambridge University Press 1964), p. 40.

physics describes is only composed of measurable parts, which is a very small slice of experienced reality. While such regular patterns of behaviour as science models are undeniably visible in nature, spontaneous activity—what was once understood as 'life'—is as prevalent and yet seems to have no plausible place in a mathematically determined scheme of reality. Observing these deficiencies, he finds the philosophy of organism and the vitalism of the French philosopher Bergson more plausible, wherein life is as natural a part of phenomena as inert substance—as naturally represented in theory without the extraordinary strain with which a materialist science must derive *anima* from matter. In an organicist view, even matter is not sterile but is rather engaged with its environment, which is in turn 'concerned'—to use Whitehead's favourite Quaker word—with its denizens.[7]

Science and the Modern World is a collection of eight lectures delivered at Harvard University in 1925. It runs the reader through the salient developments of modern science from an organicist perspective of a philosopher well on his way, by then, to becoming the mystic who would, at the close of the decade, write *Process and Reality*—Whitehead's magnum opus. These lectures present one of the most startling views of reality in Western philosophy—at least since the great Rationalists of the seventeenth century, Leibniz and Spinoza, after whom the mainstream of philosophy seldom departs too glaringly from the world as presented by science. In introducing Whitehead, it is difficult to reword his ideas without producing a poor copy of his own inimitable prose: so integral is his doings with words to what gets said. Yet the reader must be prepared for the strangeness of its doctrine. Whitehead conjures a diametrically opposite picture of reality from that of science. The world posited by science consists of matter composed of atoms

---

7. See pages 294 and 463 in *Adventures of Ideas.*

in space; in Whitehead, the world is a collection of interacting events that are composed of primary occasions.[8] An occasion is a *momentary becoming* that synchronizes with other such becomings to form an event, as opposed to the lifeless atom that agglutinates into the matter we can see and touch. Our minds have come to reflexively receive reality as a collection of things: of physical stuff. All things either lie upon or are contained within an abstract and unbounded surface called 'space'. This surface—or 'stage', so to put it, for the adventures of matter—is infinitesimally divisible and continuous: a dogma that seems to agree with the idea of substance as divisible into microscopic pieces taken to be the fundamental particles of existence. But Whitehead attempts to persuade his reader that the fundamentality of matter is an illusion sustained only by our habits of mind: a 'fallacy of misplaced concreteness'.[9] It is activity that is truly fundamental, while objects only come and go. What we perceive as an object is merely a period of cooperation among smaller objects, which are themselves the expressions of more fundamental activity. The things that consciousness holds onto as concrete—people, furniture, trees, mountains—are actually events in themselves participating with each other to become larger events. In other words, the permanent objects that our nouns name are in actuality only recurring patterns of solidity—one might even say *solidarity* amongst occasions. The thing captured by our word 'tree', for instance, is only a consequence of collaboration between different activities within the tree and without. As Yeats asks, 'O chestnut tree, great rooted blossomer,/ Are you the leaf, the blossom or the bole?'[10] For Whitehead, the tree is but the

8. Wittgenstein also described the world in terms of events as opposed to things, but in a different sense from Whitehead.
9. See page 89 in *Science and the Modern World.*
10. W.B. Yeats, "Among School Children" in *The Collected Poems of W.B. Yeats* (London: St Martin's Press, 1958).

enduring residue of a great swell of activity from ground to sky that continually sustains it as the object our imagination grasps. If we wish to twist the famous closing of the poem, we might say that it is not the dancer who dances but the dance that reveals a dancer. While the scientific outlook isolates objects and breaks them down to their material components, an organic view of what is beheld gives us a 'prehensive unity':[11] an integration of the *aspects* of a situation—a soil nourishing, root absorbing, bole conveying, blossom expressing, cloud showering, and sun vivifying, altogether limning the event we have named tree.

It seems impossible for us to sustain for long such a view of reality. The daily activities that order our life require the assumption of things that act, not acts that thing. But this may only be a parochial view of a technological civilization reared and ordered under the intellectual government of science. Let us entertain the possibility of a society remote from ours that instinctively takes activity as fundamental. The narrator in a Borges *ficcion* finds an encyclopaedia describing the world of Tlön: a fictional planet conjured by the people of an ambiguously located region called Uqbar. For the people of Tlön,

> The world is not a concourse of objects through space, but a heterogenous series of independent events: their world is successive and temporal, not spatial. There are no substantives in the conjectural *ursprache* of Tlön, from which its recorded languages and dialects derive: there are impersonal verbs only, qualified by monosyllabic suffixes and prefixes adverbial in value. There is, for example, no word there corresponding to 'moon': but there is a verb which might be Englished as 'enlune' or 'lunate'. '*The moon rose over the river*' is to be said '*hlör u fang axaxaxas mlö*': or in the order proper to it: '*upward behind durant-flowing*

11. See page 101 in *Science and the Modern World.*

there lunated'. Xul Solar transcribes succinctly: *upa tras perfluye lunó*: *upward behind the onstreaming it mooned.*[12]

The possibility of an event-based notion of reality is kept sufficiently fantastical in Borges within the invented language of a fictional realm, Tlön, imagined by the legendary people of Uqbar, whose exploits are recorded in an encyclopaedia of questionable authenticity. But Whitehead proposes a not-so-different picture of reality than is conjured in the *ursprache* of Tlön as a serious alternative to the scientific world-picture—all the while trying to make a career among physicists, applied mathematicians, and logical positivists.

The reader may have already come to regard Whitehead's worldview to be too counter-intuitive to form the basis for a shared understanding of reality—perhaps it can only be sustained in tantric meditation. Aspects change. Events are finished before they can be grasped. Metaphysics is fundamentally a conservative enterprise, seeking what is permanent beneath the flux of things. But Whitehead would reply that permanence, just like change, is just another part of our experience. Indeed, the very idea of permanence is given not in space but *time*. If it is through time that we divine what is always, then we should not be so nervous

---

12. Translation of *Tlön, Uqbar, Orbis Tertius* effected by the mathematician and philosopher Hans Mathews (personal correspondence). Here is the original passage in Spanish: El mundo para ellos no es un concurso de objetos en el espacio; es una serie heterogénea de actos independientes. Es sucesivo, temporal, no espacial. No hay sustantivos en la conjetural *Ursprache* de Tlön, de la que proceden los idiomas "actuales" y los dialectos: hay verbos impersonales, calificados por sufijos (o prefijos) monosilábicos de valor adverbial. Por ejemplo: no hay palabra que corresponda a la palabra *luna*, pero hay un verbo que sería en español *lunecer* o *lunar*. *Surgió la luna sobre el río* se dice *hlör u fang axaxaxas mlö* o sea en su orden: hacia arriba (*upward*) detrás duradero-fluir lunerció. (Xul Solar traduce con brevedad: upa tras perfluyue lunó. *Upward, behind the onstreaming it mooned.*) (Jorge Luis Borges, *"Tlön, Uqbar, Orbis Tertius." Revista Sur*, no. 68, [May 1940])

about the change that in fact discloses to us time as such, for we grasp the forward march of time only through the succession of occasions, not from a floating clock in the sky. Whitehead would grant that in the course of hammering a nail, the hammer, nail, and board have to be treated as objects to carry out the task effectively. But such a picture of things then only complements the scale of our daily lives and the nature of our technical and material culture: a hunting society may be better off perceiving activity and colour as primary and objects as secondary. If we step back from the immediate press of life, we will recognize that time will spread discord, eventually, even among the most abiding patterns of solidarity: cliffs will erode, rocks will fall, and glaciers will melt. For Whitehead, the only aspects of phenomena that seem invulnerable to time are those that science had relegated to 'secondary qualities'. Descartes had said of colour, for instance, that 'we are not aware of their being anything other than various arrangements of the size, figure, and motions of the parts of these objects which make it possible for our nerves to move in various ways'.[13] Mind conjured these phantoms, in other words, under stress of the primary stuff of existence: matter in motion. The reader might be shocked, then, to find that colour is raised above matter in Whitehead's cosmological hierarchy:

> The mountain endures. But when after ages it has been worn away, it has gone. If a replica arises, it is yet a new mountain. A colour is eternal. It haunts time like a spirit. It comes and it goes. But where it comes, it is the same colour. It neither survives nor does it live. It appears when it is wanted.[14]

While he thus shows how the world-picture of science picks and chooses what is primary based on its methodological limitations and doctrinal requirements, Whitehead does not suggest that we

---

13. René Descartes, *Principles of Philosophy*, trans. Valentine Rodger Miller and Reese P. Miller (London: Kluwer Academic Publishers, 1982), p. 282.
14. See page 127 in *Science and the Modern World*.

all become impressionists in response. Colour is eternal but not the foundation of nature. Eternality is simply another part of our experience of nature, alongside change and endurance. When reading Whitehead, the uncanny world he thus conjures seems just plausible enough, despite the investing savour of fantasy. The prose seems to seek and even win agreement from our embodied selves by recruiting the powers latent in the common tongue that English still was in the 1920s, before slowly losing its facilities in the Standard American that became the global lingua franca after the Second World War.

'Nature is a process,' declares Whitehead, 'as in the case of everything directly exhibited in sense-awareness, there can be no explanation of this characteristic of nature. All that can be done is to use language which may speculatively demonstrate it'.[15] The common tongue emerges from and orders daily experience, and is thereby the medium wherein reality as experienced can be 'speculatively demonstrated'. Whitehead's prose is a high point in the mid-twentieth century style—matched perhaps only by Bradley and Cornford. The scope of Victorian writing, the novel particularly, had, over the course of the liberal nineteenth century, shrunken into the dollhouse of English class society. It seldom, if ever, confronted the larger truths of England—naval empire, colonial expansion, and the electrification and automation of daily life, to name a few. By the end of the nineteenth century, English prose had—not unlike its subject-matter—folded into itself through play and wit; there were exceptions beyond the world of fiction, like Richard Burton, but his prose is already charged with nostalgic romance. In general, the world of letters into which Whitehead comes of age is constrained by the temperamental inhibitions of educated English society. The capacities of English prose to produce grand summations of human doings in the space of a sentence had died with Gibbon, just as the ability to pithily

15. Whitehead, *Concept of Nature*, p. 54.

capture the full circumference of a complex subject within a paragraph had done a century before with Bacon.[16] Men of letters hoping once more to confront their material reality after the Victorian sophistication—domestication even—of English had almost to invent their own ways of talking to recover the resources of Gibbon and Bacon while surrendering their magisterial pitch and Ciceronian syntax for a more sober age. Whitehead thus fashions out of the common tongue a language that pitches mind as if into the very condition of experience.

Unlike the ostensibly 'objective' view of science, prehension incorporates the vantage of the observing organism. This does not render the scene a solipsistic illusion of subjective consciousness or reduce it to impulses in the optic nerve. All elements of a scene, animate and inanimate, are afforded a perspective and feature as *aspects* furnishing the perspective field of others. The beholder is involved in the event but becomes thereby merely one among its interacting aspects, thus folding him, as if into an ecclesiastical fraternity of aspects within 'the *community of occasions* which constitutes our metaphysical situation'.[17] Roughly, we might conceive a scene as composed of interacting aspects, obviating the need for an investing 'space', and the event as realized through simultaneous and successive occasions, from which science derives its fictional time of serialized 'instants'. Among the various ways in which we attempt to grasp reality—through science, history, or art—such a view of the world was, for Whitehead, disclosed mainly in nature poetry. The almost chemical interaction of words with words, the interplay of a personal and impersonal register, and the communication of primal energy through rhythm and rhyme grant to poetic form a greater power than mere conveyance of thought: a power to grasp and display the prehensive unities in nature. For Whitehead, it is in poetry that events find their

16. Ruskin is the great exception of the nineteenth century.

17. See page 58 in *Science and the Modern World.*

scriptural vindication. He quotes an exemplary passage from Wordsworth's *The Prelude*:[18]

> Ye Presences of Nature in the sky
> And on the earth! Ye Visions of the hills!
> And Souls of lonely places! can I think
> A vulgar hope was yours when ye employed
> Such ministry, when ye through many a year
> Haunting me thus among my boyish sports,
> On caves and trees, upon the woods and hills,
> Impressed upon all forms the characters
> Of danger or desire; and thus did make
> The surface of the universal earth
> With triumph and delight, with hope and fear,
> Work like a sea?...[19]

It takes a great poet to say what seems obvious once it has been said. What is ultimately present to us are the *presences of Nature*: presences in immediate conversation and—as perspective wanders lonely above the clouds—distant communion; a verbal disclosure which discovers to the prehending reader the world itself as a great roiling event. This is not a vision of reality that the reasoning mind can model. It is rather impressed upon the embodied reader through energies released in poetic words. Notice, for instance, how the plenary image conjured by the word 'sea' is prepared by the 'presences' *impressed* upon 'form', which *haunt* the poet as he gambols across creation. The poem shows things in nature not as inert shapes for observing subjects: they haunt us and are, in a sense, haunted by us. 'In thus citing Wordsworth', he says,

> The point which I wish to make is that we forget how strained and paradoxical is the view of nature which modern science imposes

18. See page 123 in *Science and the Modern World.*
19. See William Wordsworth, *The Prelude or, Growth of a Poet's Mind; An Autobiographical Poem* (London: Edward Moxon, Dover Street, 1850), p. 18.

> on our thoughts. Wordsworth, to the height of genius, expresses the concrete facts of our apprehension, facts which are distorted in the scientific analysis. Is it not possible that the standardized concepts of science are only valid within narrow limitations, perhaps too narrow for science itself?[20]

Much of this poetic power cannot be harnessed in a prose ungoverned by rhythm and perlocution. But at times, words in *Science and the Modern World* cease to be mere vehicles and modify each other as they do in verse. To take a simple instance, an event is described as the 'grasping into unity of a pattern of aspects'.[21] Notice how the bodily memory of grasping is evoked but the suggestion of individual agency is elided by the gerund form functioning as a noun. A grasping is a physical forcing together: but the brute act is modified by the abstract sense of a pattern, which yet suggests a mutual connection between ordered things—say, in the way the vertices of a polygon are determined by one another's position. But *only* the aspects of things are involved with one another—a circumstance which forestalls suggestions of continuous connection or material causation. The concentration of a grand metaphysics thus in an eight-word line prompts us to describe Whitehead's prose as 'poetic'—with due apologies for the cliché; and appropriately so, as an organic philosophy is in a sense doing the opposite of technical scientific description, attempting to communicate not the inert and separate but the active and intervolved nature of things. Instantaneous velocity might be ingeniously approximated by the derivate of distance over time, but in truth, 'what we perceive as present is the vivid fringe of memory tinged with anticipation'.[22]

20. See page 124 in *Science and the Modern World.*
21. See page 163 in *Science and the Modern World.*
22. Whitehead, *Concept of Nature*, p. 88.

His language is itself an apprehending of prehension, we might say: an apprehension that lapses from consciousness once we stop reading him, leaving the body to its animal prehending and restoring to mind the inherited picture of things. Beyond an agreeable thought experiment, it may thus be difficult for us to take seriously the notion that there are no fundamental particles—that even the electron is only an event. But in an ironic twist of fate, the very development of science had, in the twentieth century, led to a contradiction in its doctrine: its picture of the world as finally composed of atoms in continuous space. The measuring instruments upon whose testimony science had built its edifice from the seventeenth century on seemed at the turn of the twentieth century to display 'entities' that flickered into existence here, went out there, and resumed elsewhere. Whitehead says,

> This discontinuous existence in space, thus assigned to electrons, is very unlike the continuous existence of material entities which we habitually assume as obvious. The electron seems to be borrowing the character which some people have assigned to the Mahatmas of Tibet. These electrons, with the correlative protons, are now conceived as being the fundamental entities out of which the material bodies of ordinary experience are composed. Accordingly, if this explanation is allowed, we have to revise all our notions of the ultimate character of material existence. For when we penetrate to these final entities, this startling discontinuity of spatial existence discloses itself.[23]

Physicists are thus left to talk of electrons as *particles* where picked up by measurement: but as *waves* of probable existence in between measurements, because they do not seem to traverse the intervening 'space' between their points of detection.[24] To conceive

23. See page 69 in *Science and the Modern World*.
24. For a clear exposition of the wave-particle duality, see Richard Feynman, *QED: The Strange Theory of Light and Matter* (Princeton: Princeton University Press, 1985); for the famous Copenhagen interpretation of the duality, see Werner Heisenberg, *Physics and Philosophy: The Revolution in Modern Science* (New York: Harper & Brothers, 1958)

the fundamental units of reality as discontinuous particles *and* probabilistic waves will surely try imagination more than conceiving them as events. But the contradiction has not shaken the collective faith that science provides the one true picture of reality. This is in great part because such representations of quantum behaviour as we have sufficed in designing the techne that sustains modern life: transistors and semiconductors, particularly, that underwrite computers and smartphones. The scientific process is often eulogized by its historians through the narrative of theory borne out over time by practical success. But machines that manage quantum energy might, on a different interpretation, be seen as only a natural progression of the experimental tradition and heroic craftsmanship which produced the subtle instruments that were first capable of measuring quantum activity—a teleological evolution of techne from photoelectric cathodes and crystal detectors to transistors and semiconductors.[25] In other words, rather than corroborating a 'picture of the world', technical success may be seen as merely exhibiting a certain consistency in our instruments, which require no organizing gospel in order to function.

From the diagrams and pictures we encounter in our high school textbooks, it is natural to assume experimental physicists are observing little particles jumping here and there as if in a miniaturized *Looney Tunes*. The actual indications of supposedly fundamental particles, however, come in the form of tracks and clicks from which the counts necessary for calculation can be gathered:[26] Whitehead might describe them as the residue of an encounter between a recording instrument and a focusing instrument through which some aspect in nature is isolated for perception. Scientific education often elides the process by which

25. The foundations for such a view of a 'formal' evolution of instruments can be found in Peter Galison, *Image and Logic: A Material Culture of Microphysics* (Chicago: University of Chicago Press, 1997).

26. See chapters 2 and 6 of Galison, *Image and Logic*.

the complex thing called scientific fact is fabricated: one where pointer readings on sophisticated instruments are accommodated into the best mathematical tools available at a given time.[27] Without developments in the Fourier analysis, Hilbert spaces, and probability theory, for instance, a quantum wavefunction could not have been conceived as assigning probabilities to the outcomes of measurements.[28] 'Discussions on the method of science wander off onto the topic of experiment,' says Whitehead, 'but experiment is nothing else than a mode of cooking the facts for the sake of exemplifying the law.'[29] Any 'picture of reality' that emerges thereafter is a metaphysical interpretation of this highly provisional process of fitting numericized data into elegant formulae. Whitehead thinks himself justified, therefore, in offering an alternate interpretation of the apparent discontinuity of quantum particles in the terms of his own system of ideas. Armed with a concept of nature as events circumscribed by duration, and matter as the temporary intimacy of occasions, Whitehead is able, he thinks, to explain away the seemingly profound mystery:

> There is no difficulty in explaining the paradox, if we consent to apply to the apparently steady undifferentiated endurance of matter the same principles as those now accepted for sound and light. A steadily sounding note is explained as the outcome of vibrations in the air: a steady colour is explained as the outcome of vibrations in ether. If we explain the steady endurance of matter on the same principle, we shall conceive each primordial element as a vibratory ebb and flow of an underlying energy, or activity. Suppose we keep to the physical idea of energy: then each primordial element will be an organized system of vibratory streaming of energy. Accordingly there will be a definite period

27. See Arthur Eddington, *The Nature of the Physical World* (Cambridge: Cambridge University Press, 1928), p. 48-52.
28. See Paul Dirac, *The Principles of Quantum Mechanics* (Oxford University Press, 1930).
29. See page 366 in *Adventures of Ideas.*

> associated with each element; and within that period the stream-system will sway from one stationary maximum to another stationary maximum,—or, taking a metaphor from the ocean tides, the system will sway from one high tide to another high tide. This system, forming the primordial element, is nothing at any instant. It requires its whole period in which to manifest itself. In an analogous way, a note of music is nothing at an instant, but it also requires its whole period in which to manifest itself.[30]

Such a view is not entirely at odds with the metaphysics of modern science. In their own way, quantum physicists have been reconciled to involving agency—the measuring act—in their definition of phenomena: that is indeed why this branch of physics seems to appeal to Whitehead. The passage is a demonstration, rather, of how Whitehead's system of ideas provides the terms for a complete interpretation of existing findings. We do not have to accept Whitehead's view of reality to recognize that under its framework, the findings of modern science are not merely baffling. That they, in some coherent way, rescue those findings from the aporias of scientific doctrine.[31] But we must ask if it is wise for Whitehead to tie his philosophy down just so to the happenstance theories of a current scientific paradigm. Although his system does not depend

---

30. See pages 69-70 in *Science and the Modern World.* Even when one assumes a physical reality of quantum waves (not everyone does: Bohr and Heisenberg did not, Schrödinger did, initially, and Whitehead partly follows Schrödinger's view, simplifying it) the waves would not work as Whitehead suggests. But this will not concern Whitehead because he is not attempting to add to the science or influence the development of experiment and techne in any way.

31. Of course, it is an aporia only if one maintains that science offers us an objective picture of reality independent of agency. Classical physics and relativity are both based on the idea that one can neglect or control the role of agencies of observation in observing the phenomena considered: because we can observe them without appreciably affecting them. This is admitted to be impossible in quantum physics. Nevertheless the science does not offer a coherent picture of reality where it would be natural to expect the anomalies of the quantum realm, as does the organic vision that Whitehead presents us with.

in any way on the findings of quantum mechanics, in arguing that they are not paradoxical under his system there seems to be some calculation on his part that the instruments will not disclose something contrary in the coming centuries—an assumption for which history has not given us compelling reasons.

The performance of such an argument shows us that Whitehead's cosmology seeks not to simply rebel against science: he is rather testing its capacity to coherently accommodate—and thereby, in a sense, subordinate—its world-picture. Perhaps Whitehead intuited that the English intelligentsia was, by the 1920s, too straitjacketed by their technical sophistication to entertain a mystical vision of the whole and sensed that the Americans yet retained in some small way that spirit of Emerson that could welcome a true philosopher. Entering into his 60s, the mature sage made voyage to the New World to see if his ideas might find an audience there. *Adventures of Ideas* collects lectures delivered on a variety of topics—from politics to sociology to aesthetics—across American universities in the 1920s and 30s. The Protestant temper of his audience received his ideas as a program for social reform more than a metaphysical challenge to the reigning world-picture. The sociologist Lewis Mumford would, in the 1930s, theorize the city as an organism, for instance, and politics as a process with a telos.[32] Charles Hartshorne, Whitehead's student at Harvard, would adapt organicism into a 'process theology' in the 1940s.[33] Both Mumford and Hartshorne went on to influence debates in ecology, which later gained prominence in American politics. In the 1950s and 60s, the then-famous poet Charles Olson, who set out on a rather grandiose project to reform the American soul through verse, attempted to elaborate Whitehead's view of reality

32. See Lewis Mumford, *Technics and Civilization* (New York: Harcourt, Brace & Company, 1934).
33. See Charles Hartshorne, *The Divine Relativity: A Social Conception of God* (New Haven: Yale University Press, 1948).

through his strange poetics. His so-called 'projective verse' sought to recover in an American sensibility blunted by technocracy a sense of nature as pure activity.[34]

Whitehead's philosophical system thus had implications across the domains of life. If science is taken to provide the only licit picture of reality, a clear hierarchy emerges in our shared understanding of matter, life, and human doing. It is with incredible stress that a method designed to calculate planetary motions accommodates living organisms and political life. Yet owing to the reflected prestige of physics and chemistry enjoyed by biology and the social sciences, we have become reconciled to a dim and hazy view of life and society that their inferior modes have attempted to adumbrate. The advantage of an organicist philosophy is that it provides a common framework, a language for understanding the human and natural world on equal terms. Amidst a continual tendency to chaos, organicism shows things mingling and cooperating for a time: the prehensive unities amongst aspects disclose the objects, people, relationships, experiences, and ideas that constitute our experience. It is through the community of occasions, this mutual standing of things to one another, that things are rescued from randomness and 'value' consequently emerges—it is not difficult to imagine an ethics and politics emerging from this view of things. Whitehead argues that the material and discursive success of the sciences have, in the last three centuries, insidiously reordered the social and political world to mirror its own distorted designs. The laws binding the organization of men have inevitably come to reflect the dogmas of science. The scientific world-picture began from individuated matter in space moving through time. Concurrently, the Enlightenment conjured the State as the backdrop of a society composed of self-sufficient individuals contracting with each

34. I discuss how Whitehead's ideas are reflected in Olson's poetry in Chapter 4, section 4.2.3 in Anirudh Sridhar, *Agon: Poetry's resistance to the mathematization of reality* (Oxford: Oxford University Press, 2025).

other as free agents. Individuals thus became the atoms of society. Whitehead says, scientific

> laws are the outcome of the character of the behaving things: they are the 'communal customs' of which Clement spoke [...] What we know of external nature is wholly in terms of how the various occasions in nature contribute to each other's natures. The whole environment participates in the nature of each of its occasions [...] Also the laws which condition each environment merely express the general character of the occasions composing that environment.[35]

From birth into adulthood, individuals are always members of communities. Their actions are seldom if ever 'original' but conform to conventions even when modifying them. Their labour, their games, and even their conversations are governed by custom. The very language with which individuals in society seek to understand themselves and others is a communal and historical possession of all. Religious laws for Whitehead reflected this understanding that men stood with one another as communities.[36] But in a modern society undergirded by individual rights, there is a pervasive fiction that the solitary individual sits in his study devising novel contrivances to advance mankind, which he sells as 'intellectual property' in the free marketplace of ideas. Under the organicist conception, the laws of mankind would not begin from idealistic fictions of atomized individuals contracting into a State, *ex nihilo*, but would rather emerge from the mutually dependent condition in which things always are, *in media res*. Law would express how civilizations might endure amidst the restless flux of activity underlying the cosmos.

Men seek with and through their fellows to satisfy their appetites. In the process, they speculate on the ideal ways to organize themselves for enduring association. Any political

35. See page 313 in *Adventures of Ideas*.
36. See page 313 in *Adventures of Ideas*.

structure that will sustain the ever-expanding desires of men must, for Whitehead, first acknowledge the nature of their predicament, the social reality within which they seek to advance themselves.

> The self-sufficing independent man, with his peculiar property which concerns no one else, is a concept without any validity for modern civilization. Unfortunately this notion [...] has reappeared tingeing western political theory in the commercial epoch immediately succeeding the decay of mediaeval feudalism. But it is not the practicable alternative to a slave society. The problem of social life is the problem of the coordination of activities, including the limits of such coordination.[37]

It is evident that the modern liberal order, whose template was set out by Locke, is deeply unsatisfactory for Whitehead. The atomism of science, he notes, pervades and refashions our understanding of everything from ecology to society.[38] In the nineteenth century, Darwin described organic life as engaged in 'universal warfare'.[39] At the same time, John Ruskin said,

> [I]n a plant, the taking away of any one part [...] injure[s] the rest. Hurt or remove any portion of the sap, bark, or pith, the rest is injured. If any part enters into a state in which it no more assists the rest, and has thus become 'helpless', we call it 'dead'. The power which causes the several portions of the plant to help each other, we call life. Much more is this so in an animal.[40]

Yet we think of the fundamental disposition of life in nature not in terms of help but of strife, a conception consonant with a society ostensibly based upon competition amongst autonomous

---

37. See page 297 in *Adventures of Ideas.*
38. See page 142 in *Adventures of Ideas.*
39. Charles Darwin, *On the Origin of Species by Means of Natural Selection or The Preservation of Favoured Races in the Struggle for Life* (London: John Murray, 1859), p. 65.
40. John Ruskin, *Modern Painters vol. V* (London: George Allen, 1888), p. 159.

individuals. If nature is not ultimately atomic, the foundation of the political cosmos for Whitehead is not the individual. Just as objects in nature are merely the expressions of a community of occasions, it is as a community that men realize their nature as self-seeking political animals.

Even the notion of 'freedom' undergirding the Enlightenment constitution is only a parochial one. Anglo-Saxon civilization saw liberty as the individual's freedom *from* the interference of his fellows.[41] But for Whitehead, such a concept ignores how freedom is experienced in daily life. The confusion emerges from the fact that the 'intellectuals' who theorize politics and draft constitutions are seldom involved in the labour and war that erects and maintains civilization. He says,

> When we think of freedom, we are apt to confine ourselves to freedom of thought, freedom of the press, freedom for religious opinions. Then the limitations to freedom are conceived as wholly arising from the antagonisms of our fellow men. This is a thorough mistake. The massive habits of physical nature, its iron laws, determine the scene for the sufferings of men. Birth and death, heat, cold, hunger, separation, disease, the general impracticability of purpose, all bring their quota to imprison the souls of women and of men. Our experiences do not keep step with our hopes […] The essence of freedom is the practicability of purpose.[42]

Men seek to tame nature in pursuit of daily needs and wants. Freedom is the experience of nature yielding to their cunning. The opposite of freedom is not censorship but the frustration of purpose, which may come in the form of 'a drought, a wet summer, a bad harvest, a cattle disease, a raid of pirates'.[43] Civilization is then

41. Quentin Skinner, *Liberty as Independence: The Making and Unmaking of a Political Ideal* (Cambridge: Cambridge University Press, 2025).
42. See page 342 in *Adventures of Ideas.*
43. See page 343 in *Adventures of Ideas.*

to be understood as the banding together of men to coordinate their activities in order to make their purposes practicable. The experience of freedom is possible only together, while the notion of individual rights upon which public law is often based sees in the collective primarily the limitation rather than the realization of freedom.

Although Whitehead's philosophy does not argue for a well-rounded political philosophy, it requires political order to be premised upon the 'basic facts of experience',[44] which show civilization as built upon communities attempting to realize their purpose together more than individuals protecting their range of choice from the collective. But competition is very much also a feature of civilization: one that cannot be erased, for Whitehead, as the communists sought to do.[45] It is from the at-times-contradictory facts of experience that philosophy must intuit the ideal Republic. Unlike historiography, philosophy does not restrict itself to mere description and often rushes ahead to project what human beings can be if well disposed. Even 'impracticable ideals', for Whitehead, whether in religion or philosophy, can over time become the spur to action and 'a program for reform'.[46] The two engines of civilization are the conflict among individuals and with Nature, on the one hand, and the harmony toward which men strive together, on the other. He says,

> Strife is at least as real a fact in the world as Harmony. If you side with Francis Bacon and concentrate on the efficient causes, you can interpret large features of the growth of structure in terms of 'strife'. If, with Plato, you fix attention on the end, rationally worthy, you can interpret large features in terms of 'harmony'.[47]

---

44. Whitehead, *Concept of Nature*, p. 40.
45. See pages 305 and 329 in *Adventures of Ideas.*
46. See page 313 in *Adventures of Ideas.*
47. See page 302 in *Adventures of Ideas.*

Competition among individuals is an inevitable part of coexistence that must not be ignored by political constitution, but it must be remembered that individuality only gains its effectiveness from coordination. A dissipation of activity has no value for mind, we can only 'analyze' things that somehow hang together. Just so, a 'welter of rapine' has no value for civilization[48]—we can only pursue our ends by harmonizing activity. If there is one consistent idea in Whitehead, it is that 'value'—moral, political or intellectual—ultimately lies in prehension.

Despite the overreach of intellectuals, philosophical speculation plays for Whitehead an indispensable part in civilization. His own speculative philosophy gropes at the very source of harmony in the cosmos, which he, unlike the scientist, does not attempt to capture but to demonstrate. His language seeks to grasp creation and is valuable to the extent that it becomes briefly part of it; an outward reverberation or echo of what goes rumbling on in mind and world. The arc of human duration is just so joined onto the disinterested cosmos of science that, through Whitehead, philosophy in the twentieth century becomes for a final time properly 'epic'. The dialogues of Plato, written to the citizen soldiers of Athens, preserved by the Romans, incorporated into Christianity, lost in the Middle Ages, and recovered among the Florentines, finish their odyssey in remaking the world, but in the age of the household refrigerator, such mad ambition as Whitehead's was never to see practical success. But in the last, for the philosopher, truth must be its own reward:

> There is a freedom lying beyond circumstance, derived from the direct intuition that life can be grounded upon its absorption in what is changeless amid change. This is the freedom at which Plato was groping, the freedom which Stoics and Christians obtained as the gift of Hellenism. It is the freedom of that virtue directly

48. See page 296 in *Adventures of Ideas*.

derived from the source of all harmony. For it is conditioned only by its adequacy of understanding. And understanding has this quality that, however it be led up to, it issues in the soul freely conforming its nature to the supremacy of insight. It is the reconciliation of freedom with the compulsion of the truth. In this sense the captive can be free, taking as his own the supreme insight, the indwelling persuasion towards the harmony which is the height of existence.[49]

49. See page 344 in *Adventures of Ideas*.

Science and the Modern World

PREFACE

The present book embodies a study of some aspects of Western culture during the past three centuries, in so far as it has been influenced by the development of science. This study has been guided by the conviction that the mentality of an epoch springs from the view of the world which is, in fact, dominant in the educated sections of the communities in question. There may be more than one such scheme, corresponding to cultural divisions. The various human interests which suggest cosmologies, and also are influenced by them, are science, aesthetics, ethics, religion. In every age each of these topics suggests a view of the world. In so far as the same set of people are swayed by all, or more than one, of these interests, their effective outlook will be the joint production from these sources. But each age has its dominant preoccupation; and, during the three centuries in question, the cosmology derived from science has been asserting itself at the expense of older points of view with their origins elsewhere. Men can be provincial in time, as well as in place. We may ask ourselves whether the scientific mentality of the modern world in the immediate past is not a successful example of such provincial limitation.

Philosophy, in one of its functions, is the critic of cosmologies. It is its function to harmonise, refashion, and justify divergent intuitions as to the nature of things. It has to insist on the scrutiny of the ultimate ideas, and on the retention of the whole of the evidence in shaping our cosmological scheme. Its business is to render explicit, and—so far as may be—efficient, a process which otherwise is unconsciously performed without rational tests.

Bearing this in mind, I have avoided the introduction of a variety of abstruse detail respecting scientific advance. What is wanted, and what I have striven after, is a sympathetic study of main ideas as seen from the inside. If my view of the function of philosophy is correct, it is the most effective of all the intellectual pursuits. It builds cathedrals before the workmen have moved a stone, and it destroys them before the elements have worn down their arches. It is the architect of the buildings of the spirit, and it is also their solvent:—and the spiritual precedes the material. Philosophy works slowly. Thoughts lie dormant for ages; and then, almost suddenly as it were, mankind finds that they have embodied themselves in institutions.

This book in the main consists of a set of eight Lowell Lectures delivered in the February of 1925. These lectures with some slight expansion, and the subdivision of one lecture into Chapters VII and VIII, are here printed as delivered. But some additional matter has been added, so as to complete the thought of the book on a scale which could not be included within that lecture course. Of this new matter, the second chapter—"Mathematics as an Element in the History of Thought"—was delivered as a lecture before the Mathematical Society of Brown University, Providence, R. I.; and the twelfth chapter—"Religion and Science"—formed an address delivered in the Phillips Brooks House at Harvard, and is to be published in the August number of the *Atlantic Monthly* of this year (1925). The tenth and eleventh chapters—"Abstraction" and "God"—are additions which now appear for the first time. But the book represents one train of thought, and the antecedent utilisation of some of its contents is a subsidiary point.

There has been no occasion in the text to make detailed reference to Lloyd Morgan's *Emergent Evolution* or to Alexander's *Space, Time and Deity*. It will be obvious to readers that I have found them very suggestive. I am especially indebted to Alexander's great work. The wide scope of the present book makes it impossible to acknowledge in detail the various sources of information or of ideas. The book is the product of thought and reading in past years, which were not undertaken with any anticipation of utilisation for the present purpose. Accordingly it would now be impossible for me to give reference to my sources for details, even if it were desirable so to do. But there is no need: the facts which are relied upon are simple and well known. On the philosophical side, any consideration of epistemology has been entirely excluded. It would have been impossible to discuss that topic without upsetting the whole balance of the work. The key to the book is the sense of the overwhelming importance of a prevalent philosophy.

My most grateful thanks are due to my colleague Mr Raphael Demos for reading the proofs and for the suggestion of many improvements in expression.

Harvard University,
29 *June* 1925

Chapter I

THE ORIGINS OF MODERN SCIENCE

THE PROGRESS OF CIVILISATION is not wholly a uniform drift towards better things. It may perhaps wear this aspect if we map it on a scale which is large enough. But such broad views obscure the details on which rest our whole understanding of the process. New epochs emerge with comparative suddenness, if we have regard to the scores of thousands of years throughout which the complete history extends. Secluded races suddenly take their places in the main stream of events: technological discoveries transform the mechanism of human life: a primitive art quickly flowers into full satisfaction of some aesthetic craving: great religions in their crusading youth spread through the nations the peace of Heaven and the sword of the Lord.

The sixteenth century of our era saw the disruption of Western Christianity and the rise of modern science. It was an age of ferment. Nothing was settled, though much was opened—new worlds and new ideas. In science, Copernicus and Vesalius may be chosen as representative figures: they typify the new cosmology and the scientific emphasis on direct observation. Giordano Bruno was the martyr; but the cause for which he suffered was not that of science, but that of free imaginative speculation. His death in the year 1600 ushered in the first century of modern science in the strict sense of the term. In his execution there was an unconscious symbolism: for the subsequent tone of scientific thought has contained distrust of his type of general speculativeness. The Reformation, for all its importance, may be considered as a domestic affair of the European races. Even the Christianity of the East viewed it with profound disengagement. Furthermore, such disruptions are no new phenomena in the history of Christianity or of other religions. When we project this great revolution upon the whole history of the Christian Church, we cannot look upon it as introducing a new principle into human life. For good or for evil, it was a great transformation of religion; but it was not the coming of religion. It did not itself claim to be so. Reformers maintained that they were only restoring what had been forgotten.

It is quite otherwise with the rise of modern science. In every way it contrasts with the contemporary religious movement. The Reformation was a popular uprising, and for a century and a half drenched Europe in blood. The beginnings of the scientific movement were confined to a minority among the intellectual élite. In a generation which saw the Thirty Years' War and remembered Alva in the Netherlands, the worst that happened to men of science was that Galileo suffered an honourable detention and a mild reproof, before dying peacefully in his bed. The way in which the persecution of Galileo has been remembered is a tribute to the quiet commencement of the most intimate change in outlook which the human race had yet encountered. Since a babe was born in a manger, it may be doubted whether so great a thing has happened with so little stir.

The thesis which these lectures will illustrate is that this quiet growth of science has practically recoloured our mentality so that modes of thought which in former times were exceptional, are now broadly spread through the educated world. This new colouring of ways of thought had been proceeding slowly for many ages in the European peoples. At last it issued in the rapid development of science; and has thereby strengthened itself by its most obvious application. The new mentality is more important even than the new science and the new technology. It has altered the metaphysical presuppositions and the imaginative contents of our minds; so that now the old stimuli provoke a new response. Perhaps my metaphor of a new colour is too strong. What I mean is just that slightest change of tone which yet makes all the difference. This is exactly illustrated by a sentence from a published letter of that adorable genius, William James. When he was finishing his great treatise on the *Principles of Psychology*, he wrote to his brother Henry James, "I have to forge every sentence in the teeth of irreducible and stubborn facts."

This new tinge to modern minds is a vehement and passionate interest in the relation of general principles to irreducible and stubborn facts. All the world over and at all times there have been practical men, absorbed in 'irreducible and stubborn facts': all the world over and at all times there have been men of philosophic temperament who have been absorbed in the weaving of general principles. It is this union of passionate interest in the detailed facts with equal devotion to abstract generalisation which forms the novelty in our present society. Previously it had appeared sporadically and as if by chance. This balance of mind has now become part of the tradition which infects cultivated thought. It is the salt which keeps life sweet. The main business of universities is to transmit this tradition as a widespread inheritance from generation to generation.

Another contrast which singles out science from among the European movements of the sixteenth and seventeenth centuries, is its universality. Modern science was born in Europe, but its home is the whole world. In the last two centuries there has been a long and confused impact of Western modes upon the civilisation of Asia. The wise men of the East have been puzzling, and are puzzling, as to what may be the regulative secret of life which can be passed from West to East without the wanton destruction of their own inheritance which they so rightly prize. More and more it is becoming evident that what the West can most readily give to the East is its science and its scientific outlook. This is transferable from country to country, and from race to race, wherever there is a rational society.

In this course of lectures I shall not discuss the details of scientific discovery. My theme is the energising of a state of mind in the modern world, its broad generalisations, and its impact upon other spiritual forces. There are two ways of reading history, forwards and backwards. In the history of thought, we require both methods. A climate of opinion—to use the happy phrase of a seventeenth century writer—requires for its understanding the consideration of its antecedents and its issues. Accordingly in this lecture I shall consider some of the antecedents of our modern approach to the investigation of nature.

In the first place, there can be no living science unless there is a widespread instinctive conviction in the existence of an *Order of Things*, and, in particular, of an *Order of Nature*. I have used the word *instinctive* advisedly. It does not matter what men say in words, so long as their activities are controlled by settled instincts. The words may ultimately destroy the instincts. But until this has occurred, words do not count. This remark is important in respect to the history of scientific thought. For we shall find that since the time of Hume, the fashionable scientific philosophy has been such as to deny the rationality of science. This conclusion lies upon the surface of Hume's philosophy. Take, for example, the following passage from Section IV of his *Inquiry Concerning Human Understanding*:

> In a word, then, every effect is a distinct event from its cause. It could not, therefore, be discovered in the cause; and the first invention or conception of it, *à priori*, must be entirely arbitrary.

If the cause in itself discloses no information as to the effect, so that the first invention of it must be *entirely* arbitrary, it follows at once that science is impossible, except in the sense of establishing *entirely arbitrary* connections which are not warranted by anything intrinsic to the natures either of causes or effects. Some variant of

Hume's philosophy has generally prevailed among men of science. But scientific faith has risen to the occasion, and has tacitly removed the philosophic mountain.

In view of this strange contradiction in scientific thought, it is of the first importance to consider the antecedents of a faith which is impervious to the demand for a consistent rationality. We have therefore to trace the rise of the instinctive faith that there is an Order of Nature which can be traced in every detailed occurrence.

Of course we all share in this faith, and we therefore believe that the reason for the faith is our apprehension of its truth. But the formation of a general idea—such as the idea of the Order of Nature—, and the grasp of its importance, and the observation of its exemplification in a variety of occasions are by no means the necessary consequences of the truth of the idea in question. Familiar things happen, and mankind does not bother about them. It requires a very unusual mind to undertake the analysis of the obvious. Accordingly I wish to consider the stages in which this analysis became explicit, and finally became unalterably impressed upon the educated minds of Western Europe.

Obviously, the main recurrences of life are too insistent to escape the notice of the least rational of humans; and even before the dawn of rationality, they have impressed themselves upon the instincts of animals. It is unnecessary to labour the point, that in broad outline certain general states of nature recur, and that our very natures have adapted themselves to such repetitions.

But there is a complementary fact which is equally true and equally obvious:—nothing ever really recurs in exact detail. No two days are identical, no two winters. What has gone, has gone forever. Accordingly the practical philosophy of mankind has been to expect the broad recurrences, and to accept the details as emanating from the inscrutable womb of things, beyond the ken of rationality. Men expected the sun to rise, but the wind bloweth where it listeth.

Certainly from the classical Greek civilisation onwards there have been men, and indeed groups of men, who have placed themselves beyond this acceptance of an ultimate irrationality. Such men have endeavoured to explain all phenomena as the outcome of an order of things which extends to every detail. Geniuses such as Aristotle, or Archimedes, or Roger Bacon, must have been endowed with the full scientific mentality, which instinctively holds that all things great and small are conceivable as exemplifications of general principles which reign throughout the natural order.

But until the close of the Middle Ages the general educated public did not feel that intimate conviction, and that detailed interest, in such an idea, so as to lead to an unceasing supply of men, with ability and opportunity adequate to maintain a coordinated search for the discovery of these hypothetical principles. Either people were doubtful about the existence of such principles, or were doubtful about any success in finding them, or took no interest in thinking about them, or were oblivious to their practical importance when found. For whatever reason, search was languid, if we have regard to the opportunities of a high civilisation and the length of time concerned. Why did the pace suddenly quicken in the sixteenth and seventeenth centuries? At the close of the Middle Ages a new mentality discloses itself. Invention stimulated thought, thought quickened physical speculation, Greek manuscripts disclosed what the ancients had discovered. Finally although in the year 1500 Europe knew less than Archimedes who died in the year 212 B. C., yet in the year 1700, Newton's *Principia* had been written and the world was well started on the modern epoch.

There have been great civilisations in which the peculiar balance of mind required for science has only fitfully appeared and has produced the feeblest result. For example, the more we know of Chinese art, of Chinese literature, and of the Chinese philosophy of life, the more we admire the heights to which that civilization attained. For thousands of years, there have been in China acute and learned men patiently devoting their lives to study. Having regard to the span of time, and to the population concerned, China forms the largest volume of civilization which the world has seen. There is no reason to doubt the intrinsic capacity of individual Chinamen for the pursuit of science. And yet Chinese science is practically negligible. There is no reason to believe that China if left to itself would have ever produced any progress in science. The same may be said of India. Furthermore, if the Persians had enslaved the Greeks, there is no definite ground for belief that science would have flourished in Europe. The Romans showed no particular originality in that line. Even as it was, the Greeks, though they founded the movement, did not sustain it with the concentrated interest which modern Europe has shown. I am not alluding to the last few generations of the European peoples on both sides of the ocean; I mean the smaller Europe of the Reformation period, distracted as it was with wars and religious disputes. Consider the world of the eastern Mediterranean, from Sicily to western Asia, during the period of about 1400 years from the death of Archimedes [in 212 B. C.] to the irruption of the Tartars. There were wars and revolutions and large changes of religion: but nothing much worse than the wars of the sixteenth and seventeenth centuries throughout Europe. There was a great and wealthy civilisation, Pagan, Christian, Mahometan. In that period a great deal was added to science. But on the whole the progress was slow and wavering; and, except in mathematics, the men of the Renaissance practically started from the position which Archimedes had reached. There had been some progress in medicine and some progress in astronomy. But the total advance was very little compared to the marvellous success of the seventeenth century. For example, compare the progress of scientific knowledge from the year 1560, just before the births of Galileo and of Kepler, up to the year 1700, when Newton was in the height of his fame, with the progress in the ancient period, already mentioned, exactly ten times as long.

Nevertheless, Greece was the mother of Europe; and it is to Greece that we must look in order to find the origin of our modern ideas. We all know that on the eastern shores of the Mediterranean there was a very flourishing school of Ionian philosophers, deeply interested in theories concerning nature. Their ideas have been transmitted to us, enriched by the genius of Plato and Aristotle. But, with the exception of Aristotle, and it is a large exception, this school of thought had not attained to the complete scientific mentality. In some ways, it was better. The Greek genius was philosophical, lucid and logical. The men of this group were primarily asking philosophical questions. What is the substratum of nature? Is it fire, or earth, or water, or some combination of any two, or of all three? Or is it a mere flux, not reducible to some static material? Mathematics interested them mightily. They invented its generality, analysed its premises, and made notable discoveries of theorems by a rigid adherence to deductive reasoning. Their minds were infected with an eager generality. They demanded clear, bold ideas, and strict reasoning from them. All this was excellent; it was genius; it was ideal preparatory work. But it was not science as we understand it. The patience of minute observation was not nearly so prominent. Their genius was not so apt for the state of imaginative muddled suspense which precedes successful inductive generalisation. They were lucid thinkers and bold reasoners.

Of course there were exceptions, and at the very top: for example, Aristotle and Archimedes. Also for patient observation, there were the astronomers. There was a mathematical lucidity about the stars, and a fascination about the small numerable band of run-a-way planets.

Every philosophy is tinged with the colouring of some secret imaginative background, which never emerges explicitly into its trains of reasoning. The Greek view of nature, at least that cosmology transmitted from them to later ages, was essentially dramatic. It is not necessarily wrong for this reason: but it was overwhelmingly dramatic. It thus conceived nature as articulated in the way of a work of dramatic art, for the exemplification of general ideas converging to an end. Nature was differentiated so as to provide its proper end for each thing. There was the centre of the universe as the end of motion for those things which are heavy, and the celestial spheres as the end of motion for those things whose natures lead them upwards. The celestial spheres were for things which are impassible and ingenerable, the lower regions for things impassible and generable. Nature was a drama in which each thing played its part.

I do not say that this is a view to which Aristotle would have subscribed without severe reservations, in fact without the sort of reservations which we ourselves would make. But it was the view which subsequent Greek thought extracted from Aristotle and passed on to the Middle Ages. The effect of such an imaginative setting for nature was to damp down the historical spirit. For it was the end which seemed illuminating, so why bother about the beginning? The Reformation and the scientific movement were two aspects of the historical revolt which was the dominant intellectual movement of the later Renaissance. The appeal to the origins of Christianity, and Francis Bacon's appeal to efficient causes as against final causes, were two sides of one movement of thought. Also for this reason Galileo and his adversaries were at hopeless cross purposes, as can be seen from his *Dialogues on the Two Systems of the World.*

Galileo keeps harping on how things happen, whereas his adversaries had a complete theory as to why things happen. Unfortunately the two theories did not bring out the same results. Galileo insists upon "irreducible and stubborn facts," and Simplicius, his opponent, brings forward reasons, completely satisfactory, at least to himself. It is a great mistake to conceive this historical revolt as an appeal to reason. On the contrary, it was through and through an anti-intellectualist movement. It was the return to the contemplation of brute fact; and it was based on a recoil from the inflexible rationality of medieval thought. In making this statement I am merely summarising what at the time the adherents of the old régime themselves asserted. For example, in the fourth book of Father Paul Sarpi's *History of the Council of Trent*, you will find that in the year 1551 the Papal Legates who presided over the Council ordered:

> That the Divines ought to confirm their opinions with the holy Scripture, Traditions of the Apostles, sacred and approved Councils, and by the Constitutions and Authorities of the holy Fathers; that they ought to use brevity, and avoid superfluous and unprofitable questions, and perverse contentions.... This order did not please the Italian Divines; who said it was a novity, and a condemning of School-Divinity, which, in all difficulties, *useth reason*, and because it was not lawful [*i.e.*, by this decree] to treat as St. Thomas [Aquinas], St. Bonaventure, and other famous men did.

It is impossible not to feel sympathy with these Italian divines, maintaining the lost cause of unbridled rationalism. They were deserted on all hands. The Protestants were in full revolt against them. The Papacy failed to support them, and the Bishops of the Council could not even understand them. For a few sentences below the foregoing quotation, we read: "Though many complained here-of [*i.e.*, of the Decree], yet it prevailed but little, because generally the Fathers [*i.e.*, the Bishops] desired to hear men speak with intelligible terms, not abstrusely, as in the matter of Justification, and others already handled."

Poor belated medievalists! When they used reason they were not even intelligible to the ruling powers of their epoch. It will take centuries before stubborn facts are reducible by reason, and meanwhile the pendulum swings slowly and heavily to the extreme of the historical method.

Forty-three years after the Italian divines had written this memorial, Richard Hooker in his famous *Laws of Ecclesiastical Polity* makes exactly the same complaint of his Puritan adversaries.[1] Hooker's balanced thought—from which the appellation "The Judicious Hooker" is derived—, and his diffuse style, which is the vehicle of such thought, make his writings singularly unfit for the process of summarising by a short, pointed quotation. But, in the section referred to, he reproaches his opponents with *Their Disparagement of Reason*; and in support of his own position definitely refers to "The greatest amongst the school-divines," by which designation I presume that he refers to St. Thomas Aquinas.

Hooker's *Ecclesiastical Polity* was published just before Sarpi's *Council of Trent*. Accordingly there was complete independence between the two works. But both the Italian divines of 1551, and Hooker at the end of that century testify to the anti-rationalist trend of thought at that epoch, and in this respect contrast their own age with the epoch of scholasticism.

This reaction was undoubtedly a very necessary corrective to the unguarded rationalism of the Middle Ages. But reactions run to extremes. Accordingly, although one outcome of this reaction was the birth of modern science, yet we must remember that science thereby inherited the bias of thought to which it owes its origin.

The effect of Greek dramatic literature was many-sided so far as concerns the various ways in which it indirectly affected medieval thought. The pilgrim fathers of the scientific imagination as it exists today, are the great tragedians of ancient Athens, Aeschylus, Sophocles, Euripides. Their vision of fate, remorseless and indifferent, urging a tragic incident to its inevitable issue, is the vision possessed by science. Fate in Greek Tragedy becomes the order of nature in modern thought. The absorbing interest in the particular heroic incidents, as an example and a verification of the workings of fate, reappears in our epoch as concentration of

1. *Cf.* Book III, Section VIII.

interest on the crucial experiments. It was my good fortune to be present at the meeting of the Royal Society in London when the Astronomer Royal for England announced that the photographic plates of the famous eclipse, as measured by his colleagues in Greenwich Observatory, had verified the prediction of Einstein that rays of light are bent as they pass in the neighbourhood of the sun. The whole atmosphere of tense interest was exactly that of the Greek drama: we were the chorus commenting on the decree of destiny as disclosed in the development of a supreme incident. There was dramatic quality in the very staging:—the traditional ceremonial, and in the background the picture of Newton to remind us that the greatest of scientific generalisations was now, after more than two centuries, to receive its first modification. Nor was the personal interest wanting: a great adventure in thought had at length come safe to shore.

Let me here remind you that the essence of dramatic tragedy is not unhappiness. It resides in the solemnity of the remorseless working of things. This inevitableness of destiny can only be illustrated in terms of human life by incidents which in fact involve unhappiness. For it is only by them that the futility of escape can be made evident in the drama. This remorseless inevitableness is what pervades scientific thought. The laws of physics are the decrees of fate.

The conception of the moral order in the Greek plays was certainly not a discovery of the dramatists. It must have passed into the literary tradition from the general serious opinion of the times. But in finding this magnificent expression, it thereby deepened the stream of thought from which it arose. The spectacle of a moral order was impressed upon the imagination of classical civilisation.

The time came when that great society decayed, and Europe passed into the Middle Ages. The direct influence of Greek literature vanished. But the concept of the moral order and of the order of nature had enshrined itself in the Stoic philosophy.

For example, Lecky in his *History of European Morals* tells us 'Seneca maintains that the Divinity has determined all things by an inexorable law of destiny, which He has decreed, but which He Himself obeys.' But the most effective way in which the Stoics influenced the mentality of the Middle Ages was by the diffused sense of order which arose from Roman law. Again to quote Lecky, "The Roman legislation was in a two-fold manner the child of philosophy. It was in the first place formed upon the philosophical model, for, instead of being a mere empirical system adjusted to the existing requirements of society, it laid down abstract principles of right to which it endeavoured to conform; and, in the next place, these principles were borrowed directly from Stoicism." In spite of the actual anarchy throughout large regions in Europe after the collapse of the Empire, the sense of legal order always haunted the racial memories of the Imperial populations. Also the Western Church was always there as a living embodiment of the traditions of Imperial rule.

It is important to notice that this legal impress upon medieval civilisation was not in the form of a few wise precepts which should permeate conduct. It was the conception of a definite articulated system which defines the legality of the detailed structure of social organism, and of the detailed way in which it should function. There was nothing vague. It was not a question of admirable maxims, but of definite procedure to put things right and to keep them there. The Middle Ages formed one long training of the intellect of Western Europe in the sense of order. There may have been some deficiency in respect to practice. But the idea never for a moment lost its grip. It was preëminently an epoch of orderly thought, rationalist through and through. The very anarchy quickened the sense for coherent system; just as the modern anarchy of Europe has stimulated the intellectual vision of a League of Nations.

But for science something more is wanted than a general sense of the order in things. It needs but a sentence to point out how the habit of definite exact thought was implanted in the European mind by the long dominance of scholastic logic and scholastic divinity. The habit remained after the philosophy had been repudiated, the priceless habit of looking for an exact point and of sticking to it when found. Galileo owes more to Aristotle than appears on the surface of his *Dialogues*: he owes to him his clear head and his analytic mind.

I do not think, however, that I have even yet brought out the greatest contribution of medievalism to the formation of the scientific movement. I mean the inexpugnable belief that every detailed occurrence can be correlated with its antecedents in a perfectly definite manner, exemplifying general principles. Without this belief the incredible labours of scientists would be without hope. It is this instinctive conviction, vividly poised before the imagination, which is the motive power of research:—that there is a secret, a secret which can be unveiled. How has this conviction been so vividly implanted on the European mind?

When we compare this tone of thought in Europe with the attitude of other civilisations when left to themselves, there seems but one source for its origin. It must come from the medieval insistence on the rationality of God, conceived as with the personal energy of Jehovah and with the rationality of a Greek philosopher. Every detail was supervised and ordered: the search into nature could only result in the vindication of the faith in rationality. Remember that I am not talking of the explicit beliefs of a few individuals. What I mean is the impress on the European mind arising from the unquestioned faith of centuries. By this I mean the instinctive tone of thought and not a mere creed of words.

In Asia, the conceptions of God were of a being who was either too arbitrary or too impersonal for such ideas to have much effect on instinctive habits of mind. Any definite occurrence might be due to the fiat of an irrational despot, or might issue from some impersonal, inscrutable origin of things. There was not the same confidence as in the intelligible rationality of a personal being.

I am not arguing that the European trust in the scrutability of nature was logically justified even by its own theology. My only point is to understand how it arose. My explanation is that the faith in the possibility of science, generated antecedently to the development of modern scientific theory, is an unconscious derivative from medieval theology.

But science is not merely the outcome of instinctive faith. It also requires an active interest in the simple occurrences of life for their own sake.

This qualification "for their own sake" is important. The first phase of the Middle Ages was an age of symbolism. It was an age of vast ideas, and of primitive technique. There was little to be done with nature, except to coin a hard living from it. But there were realms of thought to be explored, realms of philosophy and realms of theology. Primitive art could symbolise those ideas which filled all thoughtful minds. The first phase of medieval art has a haunting charm beyond compare: its own intrinsic quality is enhanced by the fact that its message, which stretched beyond art's own self-justification of aesthetic achievement, was the symbolism of things lying behind nature itself. In this symbolic phase, medieval art energised in nature as its medium, but pointed to another world.

In order to understand the contrast between these early Middle Ages and the atmosphere required by the scientific mentality, we should compare the sixth century in Italy with the sixteenth century. In both centuries the Italian genius was laying the foundations of a new epoch. The history of the three centuries preceding the earlier period, despite the promise for the future introduced by the rise of Christianity, is overwhelmingly infected by the sense of the decline of civilisation. In each generation something has been lost. As we read the records, we are haunted by the shadow of the coming barbarism. There are great men, with fine achievements in action or in thought. But their total effect is merely for some short time to arrest the general decline. In the sixth century we are, so far as Italy is concerned, at the lowest point of the curve. But in that century every action is laying the foundation for the tremendous rise of the new European civilisation. In the background the Byzantine Empire, under Justinian, in three ways determined the character of the early Middle Ages in Western Europe. In the first place, its armies, under Belisarius and Narses, cleared Italy from the Gothic domination. In this way, the stage was freed for the exercise of the old Italian genius for creating organisations which shall be protective of ideals of cultural activity. It is impossible not to sympathise with the Goths: yet there can be no doubt but that a thousand years of the Papacy were infinitely more valuable for Europe than any effects derivable from a well-established Gothic kingdom of Italy.

In the second place, the codification of the Roman law established the ideal of legality which dominated the sociological thought of Europe in the succeeding centuries. Law is both an engine for government, and a condition restraining government. The canon law of the Church, and the civil law of the State, owe to Justinian's lawyers their influence on the development of Europe. They established in the Western mind the ideal that an authority should be at once lawful, and law-enforcing, and should in itself exhibit a rationally adjusted system of organisation. The sixth century in Italy gave the initial exhibition of the way in which the impress of these ideas was fostered by contact with the Byzantine Empire.

Thirdly, in the non-political spheres of art and learning Constantinople exhibited a standard of realised achievement which, partly by the impulse to direct imitation, and partly by the indirect inspiration arising from the mere knowledge that such things existed, acted as a perpetual spur to Western culture. The wisdom of the Byzantines, as it stood in the imagination of the first phase of medieval mentality, and the wisdom of the Egyptians as it stood in the imagination of the early Greeks, played analogous rôles. Probably the actual knowledge of these respective wisdoms was, in either case, about as much as was good for the recipients.

They knew enough to know the sort of standards which are attainable, and not enough to be fettered by static and traditional ways of thought. Accordingly, in both cases men went ahead on their own and did better. No account of the rise of the European scientific mentality can omit some notice of this influence of the Byzantine civilisation in the background. In the sixth century there is a crisis in the history of the relations between the Byzantines and the West; and this crisis is to be contrasted with the influence of Greek literature on European thought in the fifteenth and sixteenth centuries. The two outstanding men, who in the Italy of the sixth century laid the foundations of the future, were St. Benedict and Gregory the Great. By reference to them, we can at once see how absolutely in ruins was the approach to the scientific mentality which had been attained by the Greeks. We are at the zero point of scientific temperature. But the life-work of Gregory and of Benedict contributed elements to the reconstruction of Europe which secured that this reconstruction, when it arrived, should include a more effective scientific mentality than that of the ancient world. The Greeks were over-theoretical. For them science was an offshoot of philosophy. Gregory and Benedict were practical men, with an eye for the importance of ordinary things; and they combined this practical temperament with their religious and cultural activities. In particular, we owe it to St. Benedict that the monasteries were the homes of practical agriculturalists, as well as of saints and of artists and of men of learning. The alliance of science with technology, by which learning is kept in contact with irreducible and stubborn facts, owes much to the practical bent of the early Benedictines. Modern science derives from Rome as well as from Greece, and this Roman strain explains its gain in an energy of thought kept closely in contact with the world of facts.

But the influence of this contact between the monasteries and the facts of nature showed itself first in art. The rise of Naturalism in the later Middle Ages was the entry into the European mind of the final ingredient necessary for the rise of science. It was the rise of interest in natural objects, and in natural occurrences, for their own sakes. The natural foliage of a district was sculptured in out-of-the-way spots of the later buildings, merely as exhibiting delight in those familiar objects. The whole atmosphere of every art exhibited a direct joy in the apprehension of the things which lie around us. The craftsmen who executed the late medieval decorative sculpture, Giotto, Chaucer, Wordsworth, Walt Whitman, and, at the present day, the New England poet Robert Frost, are all akin to each other in this respect. The simple immediate facts are the topics of interest, and these reappear in the thought of science as the "irreducible stubborn facts."

The mind of Europe was now prepared for its new venture of thought. It is unnecessary to tell in detail the various incidents which marked the rise of science: the growth of wealth and leisure; the expansion of universities; the invention of printing; the taking of Constantinople; Copernicus; Vasco da Gama; Columbus; the telescope. The soil, the climate, the seeds, were there, and the forest grew. Science has never shaken off the impress of its origin in the historical revolt of the later Renaissance. It has remained predominantly an anti-rationalistic movement, based upon a naïve faith. What reasoning it has wanted, has been borrowed from mathematics which is a surviving relic of Greek rationalism, following the deductive method. Science repudiates philosophy. In other words, it has never cared to justify its faith or to explain its meanings; and has remained blandly indifferent to its refutation by Hume.

Of course the historical revolt was fully justified. It was wanted. It was more than wanted: it was an absolute necessity for healthy progress. The world required centuries of contemplation of irreducible and stubborn facts. It is difficult for men to do more than one thing at a time, and that was the sort of thing they had to do after the rationalistic orgy of the Middle Ages. It was a very sensible reaction; but it was not a protest on behalf of reason.

There is, however, a Nemesis which waits upon those who deliberately avoid avenues of knowledge. Oliver Cromwell's cry echoes down the ages, "My brethren, by the bowels of Christ I beseech you, bethink you that you may be mistaken."

The progress of science has now reached a turning point. The stable foundations of physics have broken up: also for the first time physiology is asserting itself as an effective body of knowledge, as distinct from a scrap-heap. The old foundations of scientific thought are becoming unintelligible. Time, space, matter, material, ether, electricity, mechanism, organism, configuration, structure, pattern, function, all require reinterpretation. What is the sense of talking about a mechanical explanation when you do not know what you mean by mechanics?

The truth is that science started its modern career by taking over ideas derived from the weakest side of the philosophies of Aristotle's successors. In some respects it was a happy choice. It enabled the knowledge of the seventeenth century to be formularised so far as physics and chemistry were concerned, with a completeness which has lasted to the present time. But the progress of biology and psychology has probably been checked by the uncritical assumption of half-truths. If science is not to degenerate into a medley of *ad hoc* hypotheses, it must become philosophical and must enter upon a thorough criticism of its own foundations.

In the succeeding lectures of this course, I shall trace the successes and the failures of the particular conceptions of cosmology with which the European intellect has clothed itself in the last three centuries. General climates of opinion persist for periods of about two to three generations, that is to say, for periods of sixty to a hundred years. There are also shorter waves of thought, which play on the surface of the tidal movement. We shall find, therefore, transformations in the European outlook, slowly modifying the successive centuries. There persists, however, throughout the whole period the fixed scientific cosmology which presupposes the ultimate fact of an irreducible brute matter, or material, spread throughout space in a flux of configurations. In itself such a material is senseless, valueless, purposeless. It just does what it does do, following a fixed routine imposed by external relations which do not spring from the nature of its being. It is this assumption that I call 'scientific materialism.' Also it is an assumption which I shall challenge as being entirely unsuited to the scientific situation at which we have now arrived. It is not wrong, if properly construed. If we confine ourselves to certain types of facts, abstracted from the complete circumstances in which they occur, the materialistic assumption expresses these facts to perfection. But when we pass beyond the abstraction, either by more subtle employment of our senses, or by the request for meanings and for coherence of thoughts, the scheme breaks down at once. The narrow efficiency of the scheme was the very cause of its supreme methodological success. For it directed attention to just those groups of facts which, in the state of knowledge then existing, required investigation.

The success of the scheme has adversely affected the various currents of European thought. The historical revolt was anti-rationalistic, because the rationalism of the scholastics required a sharp correction by contact with brute fact. But the revival of philosophy in the hands of Descartes and his successors was entirely coloured in its development by the acceptance of the scientific cosmology at its face value. The success of their ultimate ideas confirmed scientists in their refusal to modify them as the result of an enquiry into their rationality. Every philosophy was bound in some way or other to swallow them whole. Also the example of science affected other regions of thought. The historical revolt has thus been exaggerated into the exclusion of philosophy from its proper rôle of harmonising the various abstractions of methodological thought. Thought is abstract; and the intolerant use of abstractions is the major vice of the intellect. This vice is not wholly corrected by the recurrence to concrete experience. For after all, you need only attend to those aspects of your concrete experience which lie within some limited scheme. There are two methods for the purification of ideas. One of them is dispassionate observation by means of the bodily senses. But observation is selection. Accordingly, it is difficult to transcend a scheme of abstraction whose success is sufficiently wide. The other method is by comparing the various schemes of abstraction which are well founded in our various types of experience. This comparison takes the form of satisfying the demands of the Italian scholastic divines whom Paul Sarpi mentioned. They asked that *reason* should be used. Faith in reason is the trust that the ultimate natures of things lie together in a harmony which excludes mere arbitrariness. It is the faith that at the base of things we shall not find mere arbitrary mystery. The faith in the order of nature which has made possible the growth of science is a particular example of a deeper faith. This faith cannot be justified by any inductive generalisation. It springs from direct inspection of the nature of things as disclosed in our own immediate present experience. There is no parting from your own shadow. To experience this faith is to know that in being ourselves we are more than ourselves: to know that our experience, dim and fragmentary as it is, yet sounds the utmost depths of reality: to know that detached details merely in order to be themselves demand that they should find themselves in a system of things: to know that this system includes the harmony of logical rationality, and the harmony of aesthetic achievement: to know that, while the harmony of logic lies upon the universe as an iron necessity, the aesthetic harmony stands before it as a living ideal moulding the general flux in its broken progress towards finer, subtler issues.

Chapter II

MATHEMATICS AS AN ELEMENT IN THE HISTORY OF THOUGHT

THE SCIENCE OF PURE Mathematics, in its modern developments, may claim to be the most original creation of the human spirit. Another claimant for this position is music. But we will put aside all rivals, and consider the ground on which such a claim can be made for mathematics. The originality of mathematics consists in the fact that in mathematical science connections between things are exhibited which, apart from the agency of human reason, are extremely unobvious. Thus the ideas, now in the minds of contemporary mathematicians, lie very remote from any notions which can be immediately derived by perception through the senses; unless indeed it be perception stimulated and guided by antecedent mathematical knowledge. This is the thesis which I proceed to exemplify.

Suppose we project our imaginations backwards through many thousands of years, and endeavour to realise the simple-mindedness of even the greatest intellects in those early societies. Abstract ideas which to us are immediately obvious must have been, for them, matters only of the most dim apprehension. For example take the question of number. We think of the number 'five' as applying to appropriate groups of any entities whatsoever—to five fishes, five children, five apples, five days. Thus in considering the relations of the number 'five' to the number 'three,' we are thinking of two groups of things, one with five members and the other with three members. But we are entirely abstracting from any consideration of any particular entities, or even of any particular sorts of entities, which go to make up the membership of either of the two groups. We are merely thinking of those relationships between those two groups which are entirely independent of the individual essences of any of the members of either group. This is a very remarkable feat of abstraction; and it must have taken ages for the human race to rise to it. During a long period, groups of fishes will have been compared to each other in respect to their multiplicity, and groups of days to each other. But the first man who noticed the analogy between a group of seven fishes and a group of seven days made a notable advance in the history of thought. He was the first man who entertained a concept belonging to the science of pure mathematics. At that moment it must have been impossible for him to divine the complexity and subtlety of these abstract mathematical ideas which were waiting for discovery. Nor could he have guessed that these notions would exert a widespread fascination in each succeeding generation. There is an erroneous literary tradition which represents the love of mathematics as a monomania confined to a few eccentrics in each generation. But be this as it may, it would have been impossible to anticipate the pleasure derivable from a type of abstract thinking which had no counterpart in the then-existing society. Thirdly, the tremendous future effect of mathematical knowledge on the lives of men, on their daily avocations, on their habitual thoughts, on the organization of society, must have been even more completely shrouded from the foresight of those early thinkers. Even now there is a very wavering grasp of the true position of mathematics as an element in the history of thought. I will not go so far as to say that to construct a history of thought without profound study of the mathematical ideas of successive epochs is like omitting Hamlet from the play which is named after him. That would be claiming too much. But it is certainly analogous to cutting out the part of Ophelia. This simile is singularly exact. For Ophelia is quite essential to the play, she is very charming,—and a little mad. Let us grant that the pursuit of mathematics is a divine madness of the human spirit, a refuge from the goading urgency of contingent happenings.

When we think of mathematics, we have in our mind a science devoted to the exploration of number, quantity, geometry, and in modern times also including investigation into yet more abstract concepts of order, and into analogous types of purely logical relations. The point of mathematics is that in it we have always got rid of the particular instance, and even of any particular sorts of entities. So that for example, no mathematical truths apply merely to fish, or merely to stones, or merely to colours. So long as you are dealing with pure mathematics, you are in the realm of complete and absolute abstraction. All you assert is, that reason insists on the admission that, if any entities whatever have any relations which satisfy such-and-such purely abstract conditions, then they must have other relations which satisfy other purely abstract conditions.

Mathematics is thought moving in the sphere of complete abstraction from any particular instance of what it is talking about. So far is this view of mathematics from being obvious, that we can easily assure ourselves that it is not, even now, generally understood. For example, it is habitually thought that the certainty of mathematics is a reason for the certainty of our geometrical knowledge of the space of the physical universe. This is a delusion which has vitiated much philosophy in the past, and some philosophy in the present. This question of geometry is a test case of some urgency. There are certain alternative sets of purely abstract conditions possible for the relationships of groups of unspecified entities, which I will call *geometrical conditions*. I give them this name because of their general analogy to those conditions, which we believe to hold respecting the particular geometrical relations of things observed by us in our direct perception of nature. So far as our observations are concerned, we are not quite accurate enough to be certain of the exact conditions regulating the things we come across in nature. But we can by a slight stretch of hypothesis identify these observed conditions with some one set of the purely abstract geometrical conditions. In doing so, we make a particular determination of the group of unspecified entities which are the *relata* in the abstract science. In the pure mathematics of geometrical relationships, we say that, if *any* group of entities enjoy *any* relationships among its members satisfying *this* set of abstract geometrical conditions, then such-and-such additional abstract conditions must also hold for such relationships. But when we come to physical space, we say that some definitely observed group of physical entities enjoys some definitely observed relationships among its members which do satisfy this above-mentioned set of abstract geometrical conditions. We thence conclude that the additional relationships which we concluded to hold in *any* such case, must therefore hold in *this particular* case.

The certainty of mathematics depends upon its complete abstract generality. But we can have no *à priori* certainty that we are right in believing that the observed entities in the concrete universe form a particular instance of what falls under our general reasoning. To take another example from arithmetic. It is a general abstract truth of pure mathematics that any group of forty entities can be subdivided into two groups of twenty entities. We are therefore justified in concluding that a particular group of apples which we believe to contain forty members can be subdivided into two groups of apples of which each contains twenty members. But there always remains the possibility that we have miscounted the big group; so that, when we come in practice to subdivide it, we shall find that one of the two heaps has an apple too few or an apple too many.

Accordingly, in criticising an argument based upon the application of mathematics to particular matters of fact, there are always three processes to be kept perfectly distinct in our minds. We must first scan the purely mathematical reasoning to make sure that there are no mere slips in it—no casual illogicalities due to mental failure. Any mathematician knows from bitter experience that, in first elaborating a train of reasoning, it is very easy to commit a slight error which yet makes all the difference. But when a piece of mathematics has been revised, and has been before the expert world for some time, the chance of a casual error is almost negligible. The next process is to make quite certain of all the abstract conditions which have been presupposed to hold. This is the determination of the abstract premises from which the mathematical reasoning proceeds. This is a matter of considerable difficulty. In the past quite remarkable oversights have been made, and have been accepted by generations of the greatest mathematicians. The chief danger is that of oversight, namely, tacitly to introduce some condition, which it is natural for us to presuppose, but which in fact need not always be holding. There is another opposite oversight in this connection which does not lead to error, but only to lack of simplification. It is very easy to think that more postulated conditions are required than is in fact the case. In other words, we may think that some abstract postulate is necessary which is in fact capable of being proved from the other postulates that we have already on hand. The only effects of this excess of abstract postulates are to diminish our aesthetic pleasure in the mathematical reasoning, and to give us more trouble when we come to the third process of criticism.

This third process of criticism is that of verifying that our abstract postulates hold for the particular case in question. It is in respect to this process of verification for the particular case that all the trouble arises. In some simple instances, such as the counting of forty apples, we can with a little care arrive at practical certainty. But in general, with more complex instances, complete certainty is unattainable. Volumes, libraries of volumes, have been written on the subject. It is the battle ground of rival philosophers. There are two distinct questions involved. There are particular definite things observed, and we have to make sure that the relations between these things really do obey certain definite exact abstract conditions. There is great room for error here. The exact observational methods of science are all contrivances for limiting these erroneous conclusions as to direct matters of fact. But another question arises. The things directly observed are, almost always, only samples. We want to conclude that the abstract conditions, which hold for the samples, also hold for all other entities which, for some reason or other, appear to us to be of the same sort. This process of reasoning from the sample to the whole species is Induction. The theory of Induction is the despair of philosophy—and yet all our activities are based upon it. Anyhow, in criticising a mathematical conclusion as to a particular matter of fact, the real difficulties consist in finding out the abstract assumptions involved, and in estimating the evidence for their applicability to the particular case in hand.

It often happens, therefore, that in criticising a learned book of applied mathematics, or a memoir, one's whole trouble is with the first chapter, or even with the first page. For it is there, at the very outset, where the author will probably be found to slip in his assumptions. Farther, the trouble is not with what the author does say, but with what he does not say. Also it is not with what he knows he has assumed, but with what he has unconsciously assumed. We do not doubt the author's honesty. It is his perspicacity which we are criticising. Each generation criticises the unconscious assumptions made by its parents. It may assent to them, but it brings them out in the open.

The history of the development of language illustrates this point. It is a history of the progressive analysis of ideas. Latin and Greek were inflected languages. This means that they express an unanalyzed complex of ideas by the mere modification of a word; whereas in English, for example, we use prepositions and auxiliary verbs to drag into the open the whole bundle of ideas involved. For certain forms of literary art,—though not always—the compact absorption of auxiliary ideas into the main word may be an advantage. But in a language such as English there is the overwhelming gain in explicitness. This increased explicitness is a more complete exhibition of the various abstractions involved in the complex idea which is the meaning of the sentence.

By comparison with language, we can now see what is the function in thought which is performed by pure mathematics. It is a resolute attempt to go the whole way in the direction of complete analysis, so as to separate the elements of mere matter of fact from the purely abstract conditions which they exemplify.

The habit of such analysis enlightens every act of the functioning of the human mind. It first (by isolating it) emphasizes the direct aesthetic appreciation of the content of experience. This direct appreciation means an apprehension of what this experience is in itself in its own particular essence, including its immediate concrete values. This is a question of direct experience, dependent upon sensitive subtlety. There is then the abstraction of the particular entities involved, viewed in themselves, and as apart from that particular occasion of experience in which we are then apprehending them. Lastly there is the further apprehension of the absolutely general conditions satisfied by the particular relations of those entities as in that experience. These conditions gain their generality from the fact that they are expressible without reference to those particular relations or to those particular *relata* which occur in that particular occasion of experience. They are conditions which might hold for an indefinite variety of other occasions, involving other entities and other relations between them. Thus these conditions are perfectly general because they refer to no particular occasion, and to no particular entities (such as green, or blue, or trees) which enter into a variety of occasions, and to no particular relationships between such entities.

There is, however, a limitation to be made to the generality of mathematics; it is a qualification which applies equally to all general statements. No statement, except one, can be made respecting any remote occasion which enters into no relationship with the immediate occasion so as to form a constitutive element of the essence of that immediate occasion. By the 'immediate occasion' I mean that occasion which involves as an ingredient the individual act of judgment in question. The one excepted statement is,—If anything out of relationship, then complete ignorance as to it. Here by 'ignorance,' I mean *ignorance*; accordingly no advice can be given as to how to expect it, or to treat it, in 'practice' or in any other way. Either we know something of the remote occasion by the cognition which is itself an element of the immediate occasion, or we know nothing. Accordingly the full universe, disclosed for every variety of experience, is a universe in which every detail enters into its proper relationship with the immediate occasion. The generality of mathematics is the most complete generality consistent with the community of occasions which constitutes our metaphysical situation.

It is further to be noticed that the particular entities require these general conditions for their ingression into any occasions; but the same general conditions may be required by many types of particular entities. This fact, that the general conditions transcend any one set of particular entities, is the ground for the entry into mathematics, and into mathematical logic, of the notion of the 'variable.' It is by the employment of this notion that general conditions are investigated without any specification of particular entities. This irrelevance of the particular entities has not been generally understood: for example, the shape-iness of shapes, *e.g.*, circularity and sphericity and cubicality as in actual experience, do not enter into the geometrical reasoning.

The exercise of logical reason is always concerned with these absolutely general conditions. In its broadest sense, the discovery of mathematics is the discovery that the totality of these general abstract conditions, which are concurrently applicable to the relationships among the entities of any one concrete occasion, are themselves inter-connected in the manner of a pattern with a key to it. This pattern of relationships among general abstract conditions is imposed alike on external reality, and on our abstract representations of it, by the general necessity that every thing must be just its own individual self, with its own individual way of differing from everything else. This is nothing else than the necessity of abstract logic, which is the presupposition involved in the very fact of interrelated existence as disclosed in each immediate occasion of experience.

The key to the pattern means this fact:—that from a select set of those general conditions, exemplified in any one and the same occasion, a pattern involving an infinite variety of other such conditions, also exemplified in the same occasion, can be developed by the pure exercise of abstract logic. Any such select set is called the set of postulates, or premises, from which the reasoning proceeds. The reasoning is nothing else than the exhibition of the whole pattern of general conditions involved in the pattern derived from the selected postulates.

The harmony of the logical reason, which divines the complete pattern as involved in the postulates, is the most general aesthetic property arising from the mere fact of concurrent existence in the unity of one occasion. Wherever there is a unity of occasion there is thereby established an aesthetic relationship between the general conditions involved in that occasion. This aesthetic relationship is that which is divined in the exercise of rationality. Whatever falls within that relationship is thereby exemplified in that occasion; whatever falls without that relationship is thereby excluded from exemplification in that occasion. The complete pattern of general conditions, thus exemplified, is determined by any one of many select sets of these conditions. These key sets are sets of equivalent postulates. This reasonable harmony of being, which is required for the unity of a complex occasion, together with the completeness of the realisation (in that occasion) of all that is involved in its logical harmony, is the primary article of metaphysical doctrine. It means that for things to be together involves that they are reasonably together. This means that thought can penetrate into every occasion of fact, so that by comprehending its key conditions, the whole complex of its pattern of conditions lies open before it. It comes to this:—provided we know something which is perfectly general about the elements in any occasion, we can then know an indefinite number of other equally general concepts which must also be exemplified in that same occasion. The logical harmony involved in the unity of an occasion is both exclusive and inclusive. The occasion must exclude the inharmonious, and it must include the harmonious.

Pythagoras was the first man who had any grasp of the full sweep of this general principle. He lived in the sixth century before Christ. Our knowledge of him is fragmentary. But we know some points which establish his greatness in the history of thought. He insisted on the importance of the utmost generality in reasoning, and he divined the importance of number as an aid to the construction of any representation of the conditions involved in the order of nature. We know also that he studied geometry, and discovered the general proof of the remarkable theorem about right-angled triangles. The formation of the Pythagorean Brotherhood, and the mysterious rumours as to its rites and its influence, afford some evidence that Pythagoras divined, however dimly, the possible importance of mathematics in the formation of science. On the side of philosophy he started a discussion which has agitated thinkers ever since. He asked, "What is the status of mathematical entities, such as numbers for example, in the realm of things?" The number 'two,' for example, is in some sense exempt from the flux of time and the necessity of position in space. Yet it is involved in the real world. The same considerations apply to geometrical notions—to circular shape, for example. Pythagoras is said to have taught that the mathematical entities, such as numbers and shapes, were the ultimate stuff out of which the real entities of our perceptual experience are constructed. As thus boldly stated, the idea seems crude, and indeed silly. But undoubtedly, he had hit upon a philosophical notion of considerable importance; a notion which has a long history, and which has moved the minds of men, and has even entered into Christian theology. About a thousand years separate the Athanasian Creed from Pythagoras, and about two thousand four hundred years separate Pythagoras from Hegel. Yet for all these distances in time, the importance of definite number in the constitution of the Divine Nature, and the concept of the real world as exhibiting the evolution of an idea, can both be traced back to the train of thought set going by Pythagoras.

The importance of an individual thinker owes something to chance. For it depends upon the fate of his ideas in the minds of his successors. In this respect Pythagoras was fortunate. His philosophical speculations reach us through the mind of Plato. The Platonic world of ideas is the refined, revised form of the Pythagorean doctrine that number lies at the base of the real world. Owing to the Greek mode of representing numbers by patterns of dots, the notions of number and of geometrical configuration are less separated than with us. Also Pythagoras, without doubt, included the shape-iness of shape, which is an impure mathematical entity. So to-day, when Einstein and his followers proclaim that physical facts, such as gravitation, are to be construed as exhibitions of local peculiarities of spatio-temporal properties, they are following the pure Pythagorean tradition. In a sense, Plato and Pythagoras stand nearer to modern physical science than does Aristotle. The two former were mathematicians, whereas Aristotle was the son of a doctor, though of course he was not thereby ignorant of mathematics. The practical counsel to be derived from Pythagoras, is to measure, and thus to express quality in terms of numerically determined quantity. But the biological sciences, then and till our own time, have been overwhelmingly classificatory. Accordingly, Aristotle by his Logic throws the emphasis on classification. The popularity of Aristotelian Logic retarded the advance of physical science throughout the Middle Ages. If only the schoolmen had measured instead of classifying, how much they might have learnt!

Classification is a halfway house between the immediate concreteness of the individual thing and the complete abstraction of mathematical notions. The species take account of the specific character, and the genera of the generic character. But in the procedure of relating mathematical notions to the facts of nature, by counting, by measurement, and by geometrical relations, and by types of order, the rational contemplation is lifted from the incomplete abstractions involved in definite species and genera, to the complete, abstractions of mathematics. Classification is necessary. But unless you can progress from classification to mathematics, your reasoning will not take you very far.

Between the epoch which stretches from Pythagoras to Plato and the epoch comprised in the seventeenth century of the modern world nearly two thousand years elapsed. In this long interval mathematics had made immense strides. Geometry had gained the study of conic sections and trigonometry; the method of exhaustion had almost anticipated the integral calculus; and above all the Arabic arithmetical notation and algebra had been contributed by Asiatic thought. But the progress was on technical lines. Mathematics, as a formative element in the development of philosophy, never, during this long period, recovered from its deposition at the hands of Aristotle. Some of the old ideas derived from the Pythagorean-Platonic epoch lingered on, and can be traced among the Platonic influences which shaped the first period of evolution of Christian theology. But philosophy received no fresh inspiration from the steady advance of mathematical science. In the seventeenth century the influence of Aristotle was at its lowest, and mathematics recovered the importance of its earlier period. It was an age of great physicists and great philosophers; and the physicists and philosophers were alike mathematicians. The exception of John Locke should be made; although he was greatly influenced by the Newtonian circle of the Royal Society. In the age of Galileo, Descartes, Spinoza, Newton, and Leibniz, mathematics was an influence of the first magnitude in the formation of philosophic ideas. But the mathematics, which now emerged into prominence, was a very different science from the mathematics of the earlier epoch. It had gained in generality, and had started upon its almost incredible modern career of piling subtlety of generalization upon subtlety of generalization; and of finding, with each growth of complexity, some new application, either to physical science, or to philosophic thought. The Arabic notation had equipped the science with almost perfect technical efficiency in the manipulation of numbers. This relief from a struggle with arithmetical details (as instanced, for example, in the Egyptian arithmetic of B. C. 1600) gave room for a development which had already been faintly anticipated in later Greek mathematics. Algebra now came upon the scene, and algebra is a generalisation of arithmetic. In the same way as the notion of number abstracted from reference to any one particular set of entities, so in algebra abstraction is made from the notion of any particular numbers. Just as the number '5' refers impartially to any group of five entities, so in algebra the letters are used to refer impartially to any number, with the proviso that each letter is to refer to the same number throughout the same context of its employment.

This usage was first employed in equations, which are methods of asking complicated arithmetical questions. In this connection, the letters representing numbers were termed 'unknowns.' But equations soon suggested a new idea, that, namely, of a function of one or more general symbols, these symbols being letters representing any numbers. In this employment the algebraic letters are called the 'arguments' of the function, or sometimes they are called the 'variables.' Then, for instance, if an angle is represented by an algebraical letter, as standing for its numerical measure in terms of a given unit, Trigonometry is absorbed into this new algebra. Algebra thus develops into the general science of analysis in which we consider the properties of various functions of undetermined arguments. Finally the particular functions, such as the trigonometrical functions, and the logarithmic functions, and the algebraic functions, are generalised into the idea of 'any function.' Too large a generalisation leads to mere barrenness. It is the large generalisation, limited by a happy particularity, which is the fruitful conception. For instance the idea of any *continuous* function, whereby the limitation of continuity is introduced, is the fruitful idea which has led to most of the important applications. This rise of algebraic analysis was concurrent with Descartes' discovery of analytical geometry, and then with the invention of the infinitesimal calculus by Newton and Leibniz. Truly, Pythagoras, if he could have foreseen the issue of the train of thought which he had set going would have felt himself fully justified in his brotherhood with its excitement of mysterious rites.

The point which I now want to make is that this dominance of the idea of functionality in the abstract sphere of mathematics found itself reflected in the order of nature under the guise of mathematically expressed laws of nature. Apart from this progress of mathematics, the seventeenth century developments of science would have been impossible. Mathematics supplied the background of imaginative thought with which the men of science approached the observation of nature. Galileo produced formulae, Descartes produced formulae, Huyghens produced formulae, Newton produced formulae.

As a particular example of the effect of the abstract development of mathematics upon the science of those times, consider the notion of periodicity. The general recurrences of things are very obvious in our ordinary experience. Days recur, lunar phases recur, the seasons of the year recur, rotating bodies recur to their old positions, beats of the heart recur, breathing recurs. On every side, we are met by recurrence. Apart from recurrence, knowledge would be impossible; for nothing could be referred to our past experience. Also, apart from some regularity of recurrence, measurement would be impossible. In our experience, as we gain the idea of exactness, recurrence is fundamental.

In the sixteenth and seventeenth centuries, the theory of periodicity took a fundamental place in science. Kepler divined a law connecting the major axes of the planetary orbits with the periods in which the planets respectively described their orbits: Galileo observed the periodic vibrations of pendulums: Newton explained sound as being due to the disturbance of air by the passage through it of periodic waves of condensation and rarefaction: Huyghens explained light as being due to the transverse waves of vibration of a subtle ether: Mersenne connected the period of the vibration of a violin string with its density, tension, and length. The birth of modern physics depended upon the application of the abstract idea of periodicity to a variety of concrete instances. But this would have been impossible, unless mathematicians had already worked out in the abstract the various abstract ideas which cluster round the notions of periodicity. The science of trigonometry arose from that of the relations of the angles of a right-angled triangle, to the ratios between the sides and hypotenuse of the triangle. Then, under the influence of the newly discovered mathematical science of the analysis of functions, it broadened out into the study of the simple abstract periodic functions which these ratios exemplify. Thus trigonometry became completely abstract; and in thus becoming abstract, it became useful. It illuminated the underlying analogy between sets of utterly diverse physical phenomena; and at the same time it supplied the weapons by which any one such set could have its various features analysed and related to each other[1].

---

1. For a more detailed consideration of the nature and function of pure mathematics *cf.* my *Introduction to Mathematics*, Home University Library, Williams and Norgate, London.

Nothing is more impressive than the fact that, as mathematics withdrew increasingly into the upper regions of ever greater extremes of abstract thought, it returned back to earth with a corresponding growth of importance for the analysis of concrete fact. The history of the seventeenth century science reads as though it were some vivid dream of Plato or Pythagoras. In this characteristic the seventeenth century was only the forerunner of its successors.

The paradox is now fully established that the utmost abstractions are the true weapons with which to control our thought of concrete fact. As the result of the prominence of mathematicians in the seventeenth century, the eighteenth century was mathematically minded, more especially where French influence predominated. An exception must be made of the English empiricism derived from Locke. Outside France, Newton's direct influence on philosophy is best seen in Kant, and not in Hume.

In the nineteenth century, the general influence of mathematics waned. The romantic movement in literature, and the idealistic movement in philosophy were not the products of mathematical minds. Also, even in science, the growth of geology, of zoology, and of the biological sciences generally, was in each case entirely disconnected from any reference to mathematics. The chief scientific excitement of the century was the Darwinian theory of evolution. Accordingly, mathematicians were in the background, so far as the general thought of that age was concerned. But this does not mean that mathematics was being neglected, or even that it was uninfluential. During the nineteenth century pure mathematics made almost as much progress as during all the preceding centuries from Pythagoras onwards. Of course progress was easier, because the technique had been perfected. But allowing for that, the change in mathematics between the years 1800 and 1900 is very remarkable. If we add in the previous hundred years, and take the two centuries preceding the present time, one is almost tempted to date the foundation of mathematics somewhere in the last quarter of the seventeenth century. The period of the discovery of the elements stretches from Pythagoras to Descartes, Newton, and Leibniz, and the developed science has been created during the last two hundred and fifty years. This is not a boast as to the superior genius of the modern world; for it is harder to discover the elements than to develop the science.

Throughout the nineteenth century, the influence of the science was its influence on dynamics and physics, and thence derivatively on engineering and chemistry. It is difficult to overrate its indirect influence on human life through the medium of these sciences. But there was no direct influence of mathematics upon the general thought of the age.

In reviewing this rapid sketch of the influence of mathematics throughout European history, we see that it had two great periods of direct influence upon general thought, both periods lasting for about two hundred years. The first period was that stretching from Pythagoras to Plato, when the possibility of the science, and its general character, first dawned upon the Grecian thinkers. The second period comprised the seventeenth and eighteenth centuries of our modern epoch. Both periods had certain common characteristics. In the earlier, as in the later period, the general categories of thought in many spheres of human interest, were in a state of disintegration. In the age of Pythagoras, the unconscious Paganism, with its traditional clothing of beautiful ritual and of magical rites, was passing into a new phase under two influences. There were waves of religious enthusiasm, seeking direct enlightenment into the secret depths of being; and at the opposite pole, there was the awakening of critical analytical thought, probing with cool dispassionateness into ultimate meanings. In both influences, so diverse in their outcome, there was one common element— an awakened curiosity, and a movement towards the reconstruction of traditional ways. The pagan mysteries may be compared to the Puritan reaction and to the Catholic reaction; critical scientific interest was alike in both epochs, though with minor differences of substantial importance.

In each age, the earlier stages were placed in periods of rising prosperity, and of new opportunities. In this respect, they differed from the period of gradual declension in the second and third centuries when Christianity was advancing to the conquest of the Roman world. It is only in a period, fortunate both in its opportunities for disengagement from the immediate pressure of circumstances, and in its eager curiosity, that the Age-Spirit can undertake any direct revision of those final abstractions which lie hidden in the more concrete concepts from which the serious thought of an age takes its start. In the rare periods when this task can be undertaken, mathematics becomes relevant to philosophy. For mathematics is the science of the most complete abstractions to which the human mind can attain.

The parallel between the two epochs must not be pressed too far. The modern world is larger and more complex than the ancient civilization round the shores of the Mediterranean, or even than that of the Europe which sent Columbus and the Pilgrim Fathers across the ocean. We cannot now explain our age by some simple formula which becomes dominant and will then be laid to rest for a thousand years. Thus the temporary submergence of the mathematical mentality from the time of Rousseau onwards appears already to be at an end. We are entering upon an age of reconstruction, in religion, in science, and in political thought. Such ages, if they are to avoid mere ignorant oscillation between extremes, must seek truth in its ultimate depths. There can be no vision of this depth of truth apart from a philosophy which takes full account of those ultimate abstractions, whose interconnections it is the business of mathematics to explore.

In order to explain exactly how mathematics is gaining in general importance at the present time, let us start from a particular scientific perplexity and consider the notions to which we are naturally led by some attempt to unravel its difficulties. At present physics is troubled by the quantum theory. I need not now explain[2] what this theory is, to those who are not already familiar with it. But the point is that one of the most hopeful lines of explanation is to assume that an electron does not continuously traverse its path in space. The alternative notion as to its mode of existence is that it appears at a series of discrete positions in space which it occupies for successive durations of time. It is as though an automobile moving at the average rate of thirty miles an hour along a road, did not traverse the road continuously; but appeared successively at the successive milestones, remaining for two minutes at each milestone.

In the first place there is required the purely technical use of mathematics to determine whether this conception does in fact explain the many perplexing characteristics of the quantum theory. If the notion survives this test, undoubtedly physics will adopt it. So far the question is purely one for mathematics and physical science to settle between them, on the basis of mathematical calculations and physical observations.

But now a problem is handed over to the philosophers. This discontinuous existence in space, thus assigned to electrons, is very unlike the continuous existence of material entities which we habitually assume as obvious. The electron seems to be borrowing the character which some people have assigned to the Mahatmas of Tibet. These electrons, with the correlative protons, are now conceived as being the fundamental entities out of which the material bodies of ordinary experience are composed. Accordingly, if this explanation is allowed, we have to revise all our notions of the ultimate character of material existence. For when we penetrate to these final entities, this startling discontinuity of spatial existence discloses itself.

There is no difficulty in explaining the paradox, if we consent to apply to the apparently steady undifferentiated endurance of matter the same principles as those now accepted for sound and

2. *Cf.* Chapter VIII.

light. A steadily sounding note is explained as the outcome of vibrations in the air: a steady colour is explained as the outcome of vibrations in ether. If we explain the steady endurance of matter on the same principle, we shall conceive each primordial element as a vibratory ebb and flow of an underlying energy, or activity. Suppose we keep to the physical idea of energy: then each primordial element will be an organized system of vibratory streaming of energy. Accordingly there will be a definite period associated with each element; and within that period the stream-system will sway from one stationary maximum to another stationary maximum,—or, taking a metaphor from the ocean tides, the system will sway from one high tide to another high tide. This system, forming the primordial element, is nothing at any instant. It requires its whole period in which to manifest itself. In an analogous way, a note of music is nothing at an instant, but it also requires its whole period in which to manifest itself.

Accordingly, in asking where the primordial element is, we must settle on its average position at the centre of each period. If we divide time into smaller elements, the vibratory system as one electronic entity has no existence. The path in space of such a vibratory entity—where the entity is *constituted by* the vibrations—must be represented by a series of detached positions in space, analogously to the automobile which is found at successive milestones and at nowhere between.

We first must ask whether there is any evidence to associate the quantum theory with vibration. This question is immediately answered in the affirmative. The whole theory centres round the radiant energy from an atom, and is intimately associated with the periods of the radiant wave-systems. It seems, therefore, that the hypothesis of essentially vibratory existence is the most hopeful way of explaining the paradox of the discontinuous orbit.

In the second place, a new problem is now placed before philosophers and physicists, if we entertain the hypothesis that the ultimate elements of matter are in their essence vibratory. By this

I mean that apart from being a periodic system, such an element would have no existence. With this hypothesis we have to ask, what are the ingredients which form the vibratory organism. We have already got rid of the matter with its appearance of undifferentiated endurance. Apart from some metaphysical compulsion, there is no reason to provide another more subtle stuff to take the place of the matter which has just been explained away. The field is now open for the introduction of some new doctrine of organism which may take the place of the materialism with which, since the seventeenth century, science has saddled philosophy. It must be remembered that the physicists' energy is obviously an abstraction. The concrete fact, which is the organism, must be a complete expression of the character of a real occurrence. Such a displacement of scientific materialism, if it ever takes place, cannot fail to have important consequences in every field of thought.

Finally, our last reflection must be, that we have in the end come back to a version of the doctrine of old Pythagoras, from whom mathematics, and mathematical physics, took their rise. He discovered the importance of dealing with abstractions; and in particular directed attention to number as characterizing the periodicities of notes of music. The importance of the abstract idea of periodicity was thus present at the very beginning both of mathematics and of European philosophy.

In the seventeenth century, the birth of modern science required a new mathematics, more fully equipped for the purpose of analysing the characteristics of vibratory existence. And now in the twentieth century we find physicists largely engaged in analysing the periodicities of atoms. Truly, Pythagoras in founding European philosophy and European mathematics, endowed them with the luckiest of lucky guesses—or, was it a flash of divine genius, penetrating to the inmost nature of things?

Chapter III

THE CENTURY OF GENIUS

THE PREVIOUS CHAPTERS WERE devoted to the antecedent conditions which prepared the soil for the scientific outburst of the seventeenth century. They traced the various elements of thought and instinctive belief, from their first efflorescence in the classical civilisation of the ancient world, through the transformations which they underwent in the Middle Ages, up to the historical revolt of the sixteenth century. Three main factors arrested attention,—the rise of mathematics, the instinctive belief in a detailed order of nature, and the unbridled rationalism of the thought of the later Middle Ages. By this rationalism I mean the belief that the avenue to truth was predominantly through a metaphysical analysis of the nature of things, which would thereby determine how things acted and functioned. The historical revolt was the definite abandonment of this method in favour of the study of the empirical facts of antecedents and consequences. In religion, it meant the appeal to the origins of Christianity; and in science it meant the appeal to experiment and the inductive method of reasoning.

A brief, and sufficiently accurate, description of the intellectual life of the European races during the succeeding two centuries and a quarter up to our own times is that they have been living upon the accumulated capital of ideas provided for them by the genius of the seventeenth century. The men of this epoch inherited a ferment of ideas attendant upon the historical revolt of the sixteenth century, and they bequeathed formed systems of thought touching every aspect of human life. It is the one century which consistently, and throughout the whole range of human activities, provided intellectual genius adequate for the greatness of its occasions. The crowded stage of this hundred years is indicated by the coincidences which mark its literary annals. At its dawn Bacon's *Advancement of Learning* and Cervantes' *Don Quixote* were published in the same year (1605), as though the epoch would introduce itself with a forward and a backward glance. The first quarto edition of *Hamlet* appeared in the preceding year, and a slightly variant edition in the same year. Finally Shakespeare and Cervantes died on the same day, April 23, 1616. In the spring of this same year Harvey is believed to have first expounded his theory of the circulation of the blood in a course of lectures before the College of Physicians in London. Newton was born in the year that Galileo died (1642), exactly one hundred years after the publication of Copernicus' *De Revolutionibus*. One year earlier Descartes published his *Meditationes* and two years later his *Principia Philosophiae*. There simply was not time for the century to space out nicely its notable events concerning men of genius.

I cannot now enter upon a chronicle of the various stages of intellectual advance included within this epoch. It is too large a topic for one lecture, and would obscure the ideas which it is my purpose to develop. A mere rough catalogue of some names will be sufficient, names of men who published to the world important work within these limits of time: Francis Bacon, Harvey, Kepler, Galileo, Descartes, Pascal, Huyghens, Boyle, Newton, Locke, Spinoza, Leibniz. I have limited the list to the sacred number of twelve, a number much too small to be properly representative. For example, there is only one Italian there, whereas Italy could have filled the list from its own ranks. Again Harvey is the only biologist, and also there are too many Englishmen. This latter defect is partly due to the fact that the lecturer is English, and that he is lecturing to an audience which, equally with him, owns this English century. If he had been Dutch, there would have been too many Dutchmen; if Italian, too many Italians; and if French, too many Frenchmen. The unhappy Thirty Years' War was devastating Germany; but every other country looks back to this century as an epoch which witnessed some culmination of its genius. Certainly this was a great period of English thought; as at a later time Voltaire impressed upon France.

The omission of physiologists, other than Harvey, also requires explanation. There were, of course, great advances in biology within the century, chiefly associated with Italy and the University of Padua. But my purpose is to trace the philosophic outlook, derived from science and presupposed by science, and to estimate some of its effects on the general climate of each age. Now the scientific philosophy of this age was dominated by physics; so as to be the most obvious rendering, in terms of general ideas, of the state of physical knowledge of that age and of the two succeeding centuries. As a matter of fact, these concepts are very unsuited to biology; and set for it an insoluble problem of matter and life and organism, with which biologists are now wrestling. But the science of living organisms is only now coming to a growth adequate to impress its conceptions upon philosophy. The last half century before the present time has witnessed unsuccessful attempts to impress biological notions upon the materialism of the seventeenth century. However this success be estimated, it is certain that the root ideas of the seventeenth century were derived from the school of thought which produced Galileo, Huyghens and Newton, and not from the physiologists of Padua. One unsolved problem of thought, so far as it derives from this period, is to be formulated thus: Given configurations of matter with locomotion in space as assigned by physical laws, to account for living organisms.

My discussion of the epoch will be best introduced by a quotation from Francis Bacon, which forms the opening of Section (or 'Century') IX of his *Natural History*, I mean his *Silva Silvarum*. We are told in the contemporary memoir by his chaplain, Dr. Rawley, that this work was composed in the last five years of his life, so it must be dated between 620 and 1626. The quotation runs thus:

> It is certain that all bodies whatsoever, though they have no sense, yet they have perception; for when one body is applied to another, there is a kind of election to embrace that which is agreeable, and to exclude or expel that which is ingrate; and whether the body be alterant or altered, evermore a perception precedeth operation; for else all bodies would be like one to another. And sometimes this perception, in some kind of bodies, is far more subtile than sense; so that sense is but a dull thing in comparison of it: we see a weatherglass will find the least difference of the weather in heat or cold, when we find it not. And this perception is sometimes at a distance, as well as upon the touch; as when the loadstone draweth iron; or flame naphtha of Babylon, a great distance off. It is therefore a subject of a very noble enquiry, to enquire of the more subtile perceptions; for it is another key to open nature, as well as the sense; and sometimes better. And besides, it is a principal means of natural divination; for that which in these perceptions appeareth early, in the great effects cometh long after.

There are a great many points of interest about this quotation, some of which will emerge into importance in succeeding lectures. In the first place, note the careful way in which Bacon discriminates between *perception*, or *taking account of*, on the one hand, and *sense*, or *cognitive experience*, on the other hand. In this respect Bacon is outside the physical line of thought which finally dominated the century. Later on, people thought of passive matter which was operated on externally by forces. I believe Bacon's line of thought to have expressed a more fundamental truth than do the materialistic concepts which were then being shaped as adequate for physics. We are now so used to the materialistic way of looking at things, which has been rooted in our literature by the genius of the seventeenth century, that it is with some difficulty that we understand the possibility of another mode of approach to the problems of nature.

In the particular instance of the quotation which I have just made, the whole passage and the context in which it is embedded, are permeated through and through by the experimental method, that is to say, by attention to "irreducible and stubborn facts", and by the inductive method of eliciting general laws. Another unsolved problem which has been bequeathed to us by the seventeenth century is the rational justification of this method of Induction. The explicit realisation of the antithesis between the deductive rationalism of the scholastics and the inductive observational methods of the moderns must chiefly be ascribed to Bacon; though, of course, it was implicit in the mind of Galileo and of all the men of science of those times. But Bacon was one of the earliest of the whole group, and also had the most direct apprehension of the full extent of the intellectual revolution which was in progress. Perhaps the man who most completely anticipated both Bacon and the whole modern point of view was the artist Leonardo Da Vinci, who lived almost exactly a century before Bacon. Leonardo also illustrates the theory which I was advancing in my last lecture, that the rise of naturalistic art was an important ingredient in the formation of our scientific mentality. Indeed, Leonardo was more completely a man of science than was Bacon. The practice of naturalistic art is more akin to the practice of physics, chemistry and biology than is the practice of law. We all remember the saying of Bacon's contemporary, Harvey, the discoverer of the circulation of the blood, that Bacon "wrote of science like a Lord Chancellor." But at the beginning of the modern period Da Vinci and Bacon stand together as illustrating the various strains which have combined to form the modern world, namely, legal mentality and the patient observational habits of the naturalistic artists.

In the passage which I have quoted from Bacon's writings there is no explicit mention of the method of inductive reasoning. It is unnecessary for me to prove to you by any quotations that the enforcement of the importance of this method, and of the importance, to the welfare of mankind, of the secrets of nature to be thus discovered, was one of the main themes to which Bacon devoted himself in his writings. Induction has proved to be a somewhat more complex process than Bacon anticipated. He had in his mind the belief that with a sufficient care in the collection of instances the general law would stand out of itself. We know now, and probably Harvey knew then, that this is a very inadequate account of the processes which issue in scientific generalisations. But when you have made all the requisite deductions, Bacon remains as one of the great builders who constructed the mind of the modern world.

The special difficulties raised by induction emerged in the eighteenth century, as the result of Hume's criticism. But Bacon was one of the prophets of the historical revolt, which deserted the method of unrelieved rationalism, and rushed into the other extreme of basing all fruitful knowledge upon inference from particular occasions in the past to particular occasions in the future. I do not wish to throw any doubt upon the validity of induction, when it has been properly guarded. My point is, that the very baffling task of applying reason to elicit the general characteristics of the immediate occasion, as set before us in direct cognition, is a necessary preliminary, if we are to justify induction; unless indeed we are content to base it upon our vague instinct that of course it is all right. Either there is something about the immediate occasion which affords knowledge of the past and the future, or we are reduced to utter scepticism as to memory and induction. It is impossible to over-emphasise the point that the key to the process of induction, as used either in science or in our ordinary life, is to be found in the right understanding of the immediate occasion of knowledge in its full concreteness. It is in respect to our grasp of the character of these occasions in their concreteness that the modern developments of physiology and of psychology are of critical importance. I shall illustrate this point in my subsequent lectures. We find ourselves amid insoluble difficulties when we substitute for this concrete occasion a mere abstract in which we only consider material objects in a flux of configurations in time and space. It is quite obvious that such objects can tell us only that they are where they are.

Accordingly, we must recur to the method of the school-divinity as explained by the Italian medievalists whom I quoted in the first lecture. We must observe the immediate occasion, and *use reason* to elicit a general description of its nature. Induction presupposes metaphysics. In other words, it rests upon an antecedent rationalism. You cannot have a rational justification for your appeal to history till your metaphysics has assured you that there is a history to appeal to; and likewise your conjectures as to the future presuppose some basis of knowledge that there *is* a future already subjected to some determinations. The difficulty is to make sense of either of these ideas. But unless you have done so, you have made nonsense of induction.

You will observe that I do not hold Induction to be in its essence the derivation of general laws. It is the divination of some characteristics of a particular future from the known characteristics of a particular past. The wider assumption of general laws holding for all cognizable occasions appears a very unsafe addendum to attach to this limited knowledge. All we can ask of the present occasion is that it shall determine a particular community of occasions, which are in some respects mutually qualified by reason of their inclusion within that same community. That community of occasions considered in physical science is the set of happenings which fit on to each other—as we say—in a common space-time, so that we can trace the transitions from one to the other. Accordingly, we refer to *the* common space-time indicated in our immediate occasion of knowledge. Inductive reasoning proceeds from the particular occasion to the particular community of occasions, and from the particular community to relations between particular occasions within that community. Until we have taken into account other scientific concepts, it is impossible to carry the discussion of induction further than this preliminary conclusion.

The third point to notice about this quotation from Bacon is the purely qualitative character of the statements made in it. In this respect Bacon completely missed the tonality which lay behind the success of seventeenth century science. Science was becoming, and has remained, primarily quantitative. Search for measurable elements among your phenomena, and then search for relations between these measures of physical quantities. Bacon ignores this rule of science. For example, in the quotation given he speaks of action at a distance; but he is thinking qualitatively and not quantitatively. We cannot ask that he should anticipate his younger contemporary Galileo, or his distant successor Newton. But he gives no hint that there should be a search for quantities. Perhaps he was misled by the current logical doctrines which had come down from Aristotle. For, in effect, these doctrines said to the physicist *'classify'* when they should have said *'measure.'*

By the end of the century physics had been founded on a satisfactory basis of measurement. The final and adequate exposition was given by Newton. The common measurable element of *mass* was discerned as characterising all bodies in different amounts. Bodies which are apparently identical in substance, shape, and size have very approximately the same mass: the closer the identity, the nearer the equality. The force acting on a body, whether by touch or by action at a distance, was [in effect] defined as being equal to the mass of the body multiplied by the rate of change of the body's velocity, so far as this rate of change is produced by that force. In this way the force is discerned by its effect on the motion of the body. The question now arises whether this conception of the magnitude of a force leads to the discovery of simple quantitative laws involving the alternative determination of forces by circumstances of the configuration of substances and of their physical characters. The Newtonian conception has been brilliantly successful in surviving this test throughout the whole modern period. Its first triumph was the law of gravitation. Its cumulative triumph has been the whole development of dynamical astronomy, of engineering, and of physics.

This subject of the formation of the three laws of motion and of the law of gravitation deserves critical attention. The whole development of thought occupied exactly two generations. It commenced with Galileo and ended with Newton's *Principia*; and Newton was born in the year that Galileo died. Also the lives of Descartes and Huyghens fall within the period occupied by these great terminal figures. The issue of the combined labours of these four men has some right to be considered as the greatest single intellectual success which mankind has achieved. In estimating its size, we must consider the completeness of its range. It constructs for us a vision of the material universe, and it enables us to calculate the minutest detail of a particular occurrence. Galileo took the first step in hitting on the right line of thought. He noted that the critical point to attend to was not the motion of bodies but the changes of their motions. Galileo's discovery is formularised by Newton in his first law of motion:—"Every body continues in its state of rest, or of uniform motion in a straight line, except so far as it may be compelled by force to change that state."

This formula contains the repudiation of a belief which had blocked the progress of physics for two thousand years. It also deals with a fundamental concept which is essential to scientific theory; I mean, the concept of an ideally isolated system. This conception embodies a fundamental character of things, without which science, or indeed any knowledge on the part of finite intellects, would be impossible. The 'isolated' system is not a solipsist system, apart from which there would be nonentity. It is isolated as within the universe. This means that there are truths respecting this system which require reference only to the remainder of things by way of a uniform systematic scheme of relationships. Thus the conception of an isolated system is not the conception of substantial independence from the remainder of things, but of freedom from casual contingent dependence upon detailed items within the rest of the universe. Further, this freedom from casual dependence is required only in respect to certain abstract characteristics which attach to the isolated system, and not in respect to the system in its full concreteness.

The first law of motion asks what is to be said of a dynamically isolated system so far as concerns its motion as a whole, abstracting from its orientation and its internal arrangement of parts. Aristotle said that you must conceive such a system to be at rest. Galileo added that the state of rest is only a particular case, and that the general statement is "either in a state of rest, or of uniform motion in a straight line." Accordingly, an Aristotelean would conceive the forces arising from the reaction of alien bodies as being quantitatively measurable in terms of the velocity they sustain, and as directively determined by the direction of that velocity; while the Galilean would direct attention to the magnitude of the acceleration and to its direction. This difference is illustrated by contrasting Kepler and Newton. They both speculated as to the forces sustaining the planets in their orbits. Kepler looked for tangential forces pushing the planets along, whereas Newton looked for radial forces diverting the directions of the planets' motions.

Instead of dwelling upon the mistake which Aristotle made, it is more profitable to emphasise the justification which he had for it, if we consider the obvious facts of our experience. All the motions which enter into our normal everyday experience cease unless they are evidently sustained from the outside. Apparently, therefore, the sound empiricist must devote his attention to this question of the sustenance of motion. We here hit upon one of the dangers of unimaginative empiricism. The seventeenth century exhibits another example of this same danger; and, of all people in the world, Newton fell into it. Huyghens had produced the wave theory of light. But this theory failed to account for the most obvious facts about light as in our ordinary experience, namely, that shadows cast by obstructing objects are defined by rectilinear rays. Accordingly, Newton rejected this theory and adopted the corpuscular theory which completely explained shadows. Since then both theories have had their periods of triumph. At the present moment the scientific world is seeking for a combination of the two. These examples illustrate the danger of refusing to entertain an idea because of its failure to explain one of the most obvious facts in the subject matter in question. If you have had your attention directed to the novelties in thought in your own lifetime, you will have observed that almost all really new ideas have a certain aspect of foolishness when they are first produced.

Returning to the laws of motion, it is noticeable that no reason was produced in the seventeenth century for the Galilean as distinct from the Aristotelian position. It was an ultimate fact. When in the course of these lectures we come to the modern period, we shall see that the theory of relativity throws complete light on this question; but only by rearranging our whole ideas as to space and time.

It remained for Newton to direct attention to *mass* as a physical quantity inherent in the nature of a material body. Mass remained permanent during all changes of motion. But the proof of the permanence of mass amid chemical transformations had to wait for Lavoisier, a century later. Newton's next task was to find some estimate of the magnitude of the alien force in terms of the mass of the body and of its acceleration. He here had a stroke of luck. For, from the point of view of a mathematician, the simplest possible law, namely the product of the two, proved to be the successful one. Again the modern relativity theory modifies this extreme simplicity. But luckily for science the delicate experiments of the physicists of to-day were not then known, or even possible. Accordingly, the world was given the two centuries which it required in order to digest Newton's laws of motion.

Having regard to this triumph, can we wonder that scientists placed their ultimate principles upon a materialistic basis, and thereafter ceased to worry about philosophy? We shall grasp the course of thought, if we understand exactly what this basis is, and what difficulties it finally involves. When you are criticising the philosophy of an epoch, do not chiefly direct your attention to those intellectual positions which its exponents feel it necessary explicitly to defend. There will be some fundamental assumptions which adherents of all the variant systems within the epoch unconsciously presuppose. Such assumptions appear so obvious that people do not know what they are assuming because no other way of putting things has ever occurred to them. With these assumptions a certain limited number of types of philosophic systems are possible, and this group of systems constitutes the philosophy of the epoch.

One such assumption underlies the whole philosophy of nature during the modern period. It is embodied in the conception which is supposed to express the most concrete aspect of nature. The Ionian philosophers asked, What is nature made of? The answer is couched in terms of stuff, or matter, or material,—the particular name chosen is indifferent—which has the property of simple location in space and time, or, if you adopt the more modern ideas, in space-time. What I mean by matter, or material, is anything which has this property of *simple location*. By simple location I mean one major characteristic which refers equally both to space and to time, and other minor characteristics which are diverse as between space and time.

The characteristic common both to space and time is that material can be said to be *here* in space and *here* in time, or *here* in space-time, in a perfectly definite sense which does not require for its explanation any reference to other regions of space-time. Curiously enough this character of simple location holds whether we look on a region of space-time as determined absolutely or relatively. For if a region is merely a way of indicating a certain set of relations to other entities, then this characteristic, which I call simple location, is that material can be said to have just these relations of position to the other entities without requiring for its explanation any reference to other regions constituted by analogous relations of position to the same entities. In fact, as soon as you have settled, however you do settle, what you mean by a definite place in space-time, you can adequately state the relation of a particular material body to space-time by saying that it is just there, in that place; and, so far as simple location is concerned, there is nothing more to be said on the subject.

There are, however, some subordinate explanations to be made which bring in the minor characteristics which I have already mentioned. First, as regards time, if material has existed during any period, it has equally been in existence during any portion of that period. In other words, dividing the time does not divide the material. Secondly, in respect to space, dividing the volume does divide the material. Accordingly, if material exists throughout a volume, there will be less of that material distributed through any definite half of that volume. It is from this property that there arises our notion of density at a point of space. Anyone who talks about density is not assimilating time and space to the extent that some extremists of the modern school of relativists very rashly desire. For the division of time functions, in respect to material, quite differently from the division of space.

Furthermore, this fact that the material is indifferent to the division of time leads to the conclusion that the lapse of time is an accident, rather than of the essence, of the material. The material is fully itself in any sub-period however short. Thus the transition of time has nothing to do with the character of the material. The material is equally itself at an instant of time. Here an instant of time is conceived as in itself without transition, since the temporal transition is the succession of instants.

The answer, therefore, which the seventeenth century gave to the ancient question of the Ionian thinkers, "What is the world made of?" was that the world is a succession of instantaneous configurations of matter,—or of material, if you wish to include stuff more subtle than ordinary matter, the ether for example.

We cannot wonder that science rested content with this assumption as to the fundamental elements of nature. The great forces of nature, such as gravitation, were entirely determined by the configurations of masses. Thus the configurations determined their own changes, so that the circle of scientific thought was completely closed. This is the famous mechanistic theory of nature, which has reigned supreme ever since the seventeenth century. It is the orthodox creed of physical science. Furthermore, the creed justified itself by the pragmatic test. It worked. Physicists took no more interest in philosophy. They emphasized the anti-rationalism of the Historical Revolt. But the difficulties of this theory of materialistic mechanism very soon became apparent. The history of thought in the eighteenth and nineteenth centuries is governed by the fact that the world had got hold of a general idea which it could neither live with nor live without.

This simple location of instantaneous material configurations is what Bergson has protested against, so far as it concerns time and so far as it is taken to be the fundamental fact of concrete nature. He calls it a distortion of nature due to the intellectual 'spatialisation' of things. I agree with Bergson in his protest: but I do not agree that such distortion is a vice necessary to the intellectual apprehension of nature. I shall in subsequent lectures endeavour to show that this spatialisation is the expression of more concrete facts under the guise of very abstract logical constructions. There is an error; but it is merely the accidental error of mistaking the abstract for the concrete. It is an example of what I will call the 'Fallacy of Misplaced Concreteness.' This fallacy is the occasion of great confusion in philosophy. It is not necessary for the intellect to fall into the trap, though in this example there has been a very general tendency to do so.

It is at once evident that the concept of simple location is going to make great difficulties for induction. For, if in the location of configurations of matter throughout a stretch of time there is no inherent reference to any other times, past or future, it immediately follows that nature within any period does not refer to nature at any other period. Accordingly, induction is not based on anything which can be observed as inherent in nature. Thus we cannot look to nature for the justification of our belief in any law such as the law of gravitation. In other words, the order of nature cannot be justified by the mere observation of nature. For there is nothing in the present fact which inherently refers either to the past or to the future. It looks, therefore, as though memory, as well as induction, would fail to find any justification within nature itself.

I have been anticipating the course of future thought, and have been repeating Hume's argument. This train of thought follows so immediately from the consideration of simple location, that we cannot wait for the eighteenth century before considering it. The only wonder is that the world did in fact wait for Hume before noting the difficulty. Also it illustrates the anti-rationalism of the scientific public that, when Hume did appear, it was only the religious implications of his philosophy which attracted attention. This was because the clergy were in principle rationalists, whereas the men of science were content with a simple faith in the order of nature. Hume himself remarks, no doubt scoffingly, "Our holy religion is founded on faith." This attitude satisfied the Royal Society but not the Church. It also satisfied Hume and has satisfied subsequent empiricists.

There is another presupposition of thought which must be put beside the theory of simple location. I mean the two correlative categories of Substance and quality. There is, however this difference. There were different theories as to the adequate description of the status of space. But whatever its status, no one had any doubt but that the connection with space enjoyed by entities, which are said to be in space, is that of simple location.

We may put this shortly by saying that it was tacitly assumed that space is the locus of simple locations. Whatever is in space is *simpliciter* in some definite portion of space. But in respect to substance and quality the leading minds of the seventeenth century were definitely perplexed; though, with their usual genius, they at once constructed a theory which was adequate for their immediate purposes.

Of course, substance and quality, as well as simple location, are the most natural ideas for the human mind. It is the way in which we think of things, and without these ways of thinking we could not get our ideas straight for daily use. There is no doubt about this. The only question is, How concretely are we thinking when we consider nature under these conceptions? My point will be, that we are presenting ourselves with simplified editions of immediate matters of fact. When we examine the primary elements of these simplified editions, we shall find that they are in truth only to be justified as being elaborate logical constructions of a high degree of abstraction. Of course, as a point of individual psychology, we get at the ideas by the rough and ready method of suppressing what appear to be irrelevant details. But when we attempt to justify this suppression of irrelevance, we find that, though there are entities left corresponding to the entities we talk about, yet these entities are of a high degree of abstraction.

Thus I hold that substance and quality afford another instance of the fallacy of misplaced concreteness. Let us consider how the notions of substance and quality arise. We observe an object as an entity with certain characteristics. Furthermore, each individual entity is apprehended through its characteristics. For example, we observe a body; there is something about it which we note. Perhaps, it is hard, and blue, and round, and noisy. We observe something which possesses these qualities: apart from these qualities we do not observe anything at all. Accordingly, the entity is the substratum, or substance, of which we predicate qualities. Some of the qualities are essential, so that apart from them the entity would not be itself; while other qualities are accidental and changeable. In respect to material bodies, the qualities of having a quantitative mass, and of simple location somewhere, were held by John Locke at the close of the seventeenth century to be essential qualities. Of course, the location was changeable, and the unchangeability of mass was merely an experimental fact except for some extremists.

So far, so good. But when we pass to blueness and noisiness a new situation has to be faced. In the first place, the body may not be always blue, or noisy. We have already allowed for this by our theory of accidental qualities, which for the moment we may accept as adequate. But in the second place, the seventeenth century exposed a real difficulty. The great physicists elaborated transmission theories of light and sound, based upon their materialistic views of nature. There were two hypotheses as to light: either it was transmitted by the vibratory waves of a materialistic ether, or—according to Newton—it was transmitted by the motion of incredibly small corpuscles of some subtle matter. We all know that the wave theory of Huyghens held the field during the nineteenth century, and that at present physicists are endeavouring to explain some obscure circumstances attending radiation by a combination of both theories. But whatever theory you choose, there is no light or colour as a fact in external nature. There is merely motion of material. Again, when the light enters your eyes and falls on the retina, there is merely motion of material. Then your nerves are affected and your brain is affected, and again this is merely motion of material. The same line of argument holds for sound, substituting waves in the air for waves in the ether, and ears for eyes.

We then ask in what sense are blueness and noisiness qualities of the body. By analogous reasoning, we also ask in what sense is its scent a quality of the rose.

Galileo considered this question, and at once pointed out that, apart from eyes, ears, or noses, there would be no colours, sounds, or smells. Descartes and Locke elaborated a theory of primary and secondary qualities. For example, Descartes in his "Sixth Meditation" says[1]: "And indeed, as I perceive different sorts of colours, sounds, odours, tastes, heat, hardness, etc., I safely conclude that there are in the bodies from which the diverse perceptions of the senses proceed, certain varieties corresponding to them, although, perhaps, not in reality like them;…."

Also in his *Principles of Philosophy*, he says: "That by our senses we know nothing of external objects beyond their figure [or situation], magnitude, and motion."

Locke, writing with a knowledge of Newtonian dynamics, places mass among the primary qualities of bodies. In short, he elaborates a theory of primary and secondary qualities in accordance with the state of physical science at the close of the seventeenth century. The primary qualities are the essential qualities of substances whose spatio-temporal relationships constitute nature. The orderliness of these relationships constitutes nature. The orderliness of these relationships constitutes the order of nature. The occurrences of nature are in some way apprehended by minds, which are associated with living bodies. Primarily, the mental apprehension is aroused by the occurrences in certain parts of the correlated body, the occurrences in the brain, for instance. But the mind in apprehending also experiences sensations which, properly speaking, are qualities of the mind alone. These sensations are projected by the mind so as to clothe appropriate bodies in external nature. Thus the bodies are perceived as with qualities which in reality do not belong to them, qualities which in fact are purely the offspring of the mind. Thus nature gets credit which should in truth be reserved for ourselves: the rose for its scent: the nightingale for his song: and the sun for his radiance. The poets are entirely mistaken. They should address their lyrics to themselves, and should turn them into odes of self-congratulation on the

1. Translation by Professor John Veitch.

excellency of the human mind. Nature is a dull affair, soundless, scentless, colourless; merely the hurrying of material, endlessly, meaninglessly.

However you disguise it, this is the practical outcome of the characteristic scientific philosophy which closed the seventeenth century.

In the first place, we must note its astounding efficiency as a system of concepts for the organisation of scientific research. In this respect, it is fully worthy of the genius of the century which produced it. It has held its own as the guiding principle of scientific studies ever since. It is still reigning. Every university in the world organises itself in accordance with it. No alternative system of organising the pursuit of scientific truth has been suggested. It is not only reigning, but it is without a rival.

And yet—it is quite unbelievable. This conception of the universe is surely framed in terms of high abstractions, and the paradox only arises because we have mistaken our abstractions for concrete realities.

No picture, however generalised, of the achievements of scientific thought in this century can omit the advance in mathematics. Here as elsewhere the genius of the epoch made itself evident. Three great Frenchmen, Descartes, Desargues, Pascal, initiated the modern period in geometry. Another Frenchman, Fermat, laid the foundations of modern analysis, and all but perfected the methods of the differential calculus. Newton and Leibniz, between them, actually did create the differential calculus as a practical method of mathematical reasoning. When the century ended, mathematics as an instrument for application to physical problems was well established in something of its modern proficiency. Modern pure mathematics, if we except geometry, was in its infancy, and had given no signs of the astonishing growth it was to make in the nineteenth century. But the mathematical physicist had appeared, bringing with him the type of mind which was to rule the scientific world in the next century. It was to be the age of 'Victorious Analysis.'

The seventeenth century had finally produced a scheme of scientific thought framed by mathematicians, for the use of mathematicians. The great characteristic of the mathematical mind is its capacity for dealing with abstractions; and for eliciting from them clear-cut demonstrative trains of reasoning, entirely satisfactory so long as it is those abstractions which you want to think about. The enormous success of the scientific abstractions, yielding on the one hand *matter* with its *simple location* in space and time, and on the other hand *mind*, perceiving, suffering, reasoning, but not interfering, has foisted onto philosophy the task of accepting them as the most concrete rendering of fact.

Thereby, modern philosophy has been ruined. It has oscillated in a complex manner between three extremes. There are the dualists, who accept matter and mind as on equal basis, and the two varieties of monists, those who put mind inside matter, and those who put matter inside mind. But this juggling with abstractions can never overcome the inherent confusion introduced by the ascription of *misplaced concreteness* to the scientific scheme of the seventeenth century.

CHAPTER IV

THE EIGHTEENTH CENTURY

IN SO FAR AS the intellectual climates of different epochs can be contrasted, the eighteenth century in Europe was the complete antithesis to the Middle Ages. The contrast is symbolised by the difference between the cathedral of Chartres and the Parisian salons, where D'Alembert conversed with Voltaire. The Middle Ages were haunted with the desire to rationalise the infinite: the men of the eighteenth century rationalized the social life of modern communities, and based their sociological theories on an appeal to the facts of nature. The earlier period was the age of faith, based upon reason. In the later period, they let sleeping dogs lie: it was the age of reason, based upon faith. To illustrate my meaning:—St. Anselm would have been distressed if he had failed to find a convincing argument for the existence of God, and on this argument he based his edifice of faith, whereas Hume based his *Dissertation on the Natural History of Religion* upon his faith in the order of nature. In comparing these epochs it is well to remember that reason can err, and that faith may be misplaced.

In my previous lecture I traced the evolution, during the seventeenth century, of the scheme of scientific ideas which has dominated thought ever since. It involves a fundamental duality, with *material* on the one hand, and on the other hand *mind*. In between there lie the concepts of life, organism, function, instantaneous reality, interaction, order of nature, which collectively form the Achilles heel of the whole system.

I also expressed my conviction that if we desired to obtain a more fundamental expression of the concrete character of natural fact, the element in this scheme which we should first criticise is the concept of *simple location*. In view therefore of the importance which this idea will assume in these lectures, I will repeat the meaning which I have attached to this phrase. To say that a bit of matter has *simple location* means that, in expressing its spatio-temporal relations, it is adequate to state that it is where it is, in a definite finite region of space, and throughout a definite finite duration of time, apart from any essential reference of the relations of that bit of matter to other regions of space and to other durations of time. Again, this concept of simple location is independent of the controversy between the absolutist and the relativist views of space or of time. So long as any theory of space, or of time, can give a meaning, either absolute or relative, to the idea of a definite region of space, and of a definite duration of time, the idea of simple location has a perfectly definite meaning. This idea is the very foundation of the seventeenth century scheme of nature. Apart from it, the scheme is incapable of expression. I shall argue that among the primary elements of nature as apprehended in our immediate experience, there is no element whatever which possesses this character of simple location. It does not follow, however, that the science of the seventeenth century was simply wrong. I hold that by a process of constructive abstraction we can arrive at abstractions which are the simply-located bits of material, and at other abstractions which are the minds included in the scientific scheme. Accordingly, the real error is an example of what I have termed: The Fallacy of Misplaced Concreteness.

The advantage of confining attention to a definite group of abstractions, is that you confine your thoughts to clear-cut definite things, with clear-cut definite relations. Accordingly, if you have a logical head, you can deduce a variety of conclusions respecting the relationships between these abstract entities. Furthermore, if the abstractions are well-founded, that is to say, if they do not abstract from everything that is important in experience, the scientific thought which confines itself to these abstractions will arrive at a variety of important truths relating to our experience of nature. We all know those clear-cut trenchant intellects, immovably encased in a hard shell of abstractions. They hold you to their abstractions by the sheer grip of personality.

The disadvantage of exclusive attention to a group of abstractions, however well-founded, is that, by the nature of the case, you have abstracted from the remainder of things. In so far as the excluded things are important in your experience, your modes of thought are not fitted to deal with them. You cannot think without abstractions; accordingly, it is of the utmost importance to be vigilant in critically revising your *modes* of abstraction. It is here that philosophy finds its niche as essential to the healthy progress of society. It is the critic of abstractions. A civilisation which cannot burst through its current abstractions is doomed to sterility after a very limited period of progress. An active school of philosophy is quite as important for the locomotion of ideas, as is an active school of railway engineers for the locomotion of fuel.

Sometimes it happens that the service rendered by philosophy is entirely obscured by the astonishing success of a scheme of abstractions in expressing the dominant interests of an epoch. This is exactly what happened during the eighteenth century. *Les philosophes* were not philosophers. They were men of genius, clear-headed and acute, who applied the seventeenth century group of scientific abstractions to the analysis of the unbounded universe. Their triumph, in respect to the circle of ideas mainly interesting to their contemporaries, was overwhelming. Whatever did not fit into their scheme was ignored, derided, disbelieved. Their hatred of Gothic architecture symbolizes their lack of sympathy with dim perspectives. It was the age of reason, healthy, manly, upstanding reason; but, of one-eyed reason, deficient in its vision of depth. We cannot overrate the debt of gratitude which we owe to these men. For a thousand years Europe had been a prey to intolerant, intolerable visionaries. The common sense of the eighteenth century, its grasp of the obvious facts of human suffering, and of the obvious demands of human nature, acted on the world like a bath of moral cleansing. Voltaire must have the credit, that he hated injustice, he hated cruelty, he hated senseless repression, and he hated hocus-pocus. Furthermore, when he saw them, he knew them. In these supreme virtues, he was typical of his century, on its better side. But if men cannot live on bread alone, still less can they do so on disinfectants. The age had its limitations; yet we cannot understand the passion with which some of its main positions are still defended, especially in the schools of science, unless we do full justice to its positive achievements. The seventeenth century scheme of concepts was proving a perfect instrument for research.

This triumph of materialism was chiefly in the sciences of rational dynamics, physics, and chemistry. So far as dynamics and physics were concerned, progress was in the form of direct developments of the main ideas of the previous epoch. Nothing fundamentally new was introduced, but there was an immense detailed development. Special case after special case was unravelled. It was as though the very Heavens were being opened, on a set plan. In the second half of the century, Lavoisier practically founded chemistry on its present basis. He introduced into it the principle that no material is lost or gained in any chemical transformations. This was the last success of materialistic thought, which has not ultimately proved to be double-edged. Chemical science now only waited for the atomic theory, in the next century.

In this century the notion of the mechanical explanation of all the processes of nature finally hardened into a dogma of science. The notion won through on its merits by reason of an almost miraculous series of triumphs achieved by the mathematical physicists, culminating in the *Méchanique Analytique* of Lagrange, which was published in 1787. Newton's *Principia* was published in 1687, so that exactly one hundred years separates the two great books. This century contains the first period of mathematical physics of the modern type. The publication of Clerk Maxwell's *Electricity and Magnetism* in 1873 marks the close of the second period. Each of these three books introduces new horizons of thought affecting everything which comes after them.

In considering the various topics to which mankind has bent its systematic thought, it is impossible not to be struck with the unequal distribution of ability among the different fields. In almost all subjects there are a few outstanding names. For it requires genius to create a subject as a distinct topic for thought. But in the case of many topics, after a good beginning very relevant to its immediate occasion, the subsequent development appears as a weak series of flounderings, so that the whole subject gradually loses its grip on the evolution of thought. It was far otherwise with mathematical physics. The more you study this subject, the more you will find yourself astonished by the almost incredible triumphs of intellect which it exhibits. The great mathematical physicists of the eighteenth and first few years of the nineteenth century, most of them French, are a case in point: Maupertuis, Clairaut, D'Alembert, Lagrange, Laplace, Fourier, form a series of names, such that each recalls to mind some achievement of the first rank. When Carlyle, as the mouthpiece of the subsequent Romantic Age, scoffingly terms the period the Age of Victorious Analysis, and mocks at Maupertuis as a 'sublimish gentleman in a white periwig,' he only exhibits the narrow side of the Romanticists whom he is then voicing.

It is impossible to explain intelligently, in a short time and without technicalities, the details of the progress made by this school. I will, however, endeavour to explain the main point of a joint achievement of Maupertuis and Lagrange. Their results, in conjunction with some subsequent mathematical methods due to two great German mathematicians of the first half of the nineteenth century, Gauss and Riemann, have recently proved themselves to be the preparatory work necessary for the new ideas which Herz and Einstein have introduced into mathematical physics. Also they inspired some of the best ideas in Clerk Maxwell's treatise, already mentioned in this lecture.

They aimed at discovering something more fundamental and more general than Newton's laws of motion which were discussed in the previous lecture. They wanted to find some wider ideas, and in the case of Lagrange some more general means of mathematical exposition. It was an ambitious enterprise, and they were completely successful. Maupertuis lived in the first half of the eighteenth century, and Lagrange's active life lay in its second half. We find in Maupertuis a tinge of the theologic age which preceded his birth. He started with the idea that the whole path of a material particle between any limits of time must achieve some perfection worthy of the providence of God. There are two points of interest in this motive principle. In the first place, it illustrates the thesis which I was urging in my first lecture that the way in which the medieval church had impressed on Europe the notion of the detailed providence of a rational personal God was one of the factors by which the trust in the order of nature had been generated. In the second place, though we are now all convinced that such modes of thought are of no direct use in detailed scientific enquiry, Maupertuis' success in this particular case shows that almost any idea which jogs you out of your current abstractions may be better than nothing. In the present case what the idea in question did for Maupertuis was to lead him to enquire what general property of the path as a whole could be deduced from Newton's laws of motion. Undoubtedly this was a very sensible procedure whatever one's theological notions. Also his general idea led him to conceive that the property found would be a quantitative sum, such that any slight deviation from the path would increase it. In this supposition he was generalising Newton's first law of motion. For an isolated particle takes the shortest route with uniform velocity. So Maupertuis conjectured that a particle travelling through a field of force would realise the least possible amount of some quantity. He discovered such a quantity and called it the integral action between the time limits considered. In modern phraseology it is the sum through successive small lapses of time of the difference between the kinetic and potential energies of the particle at each successive instant. This action, therefore, has to do with the interchange between the energy arising from motion and the energy arising from position. Maupertuis had discovered the famous theorem of least action. Maupertuis was not quite of the first rank in comparison with such a man as Lagrange. In his hands and in those of his immediate successors, his principle did not assume any dominating importance. Lagrange put the same question on a wider basis so as to make its answer relevant to actual procedure in the development of dynamics. His Principle of Virtual Work as applied to systems in motion is in effect Maupertuis' principle conceived as applying at each instant of the path of the system. But Lagrange saw further than Maupertuis. He grasped that he had gained a method of stating dynamical truths in a way which is perfectly indifferent to the particular methods of measurement employed in fixing the positions of the various parts of the system. Accordingly, he went on to deduce equations of motion which are equally applicable whatever quantitative measurements have been made, provided that they are adequate to fix positions. The beauty and almost divine simplicity of these equations is such that these formulae are worthy to rank with those mysterious symbols which in ancient times were held directly to indicate the Supreme Reason at the base of all things. Later Herz—inventor of electromagnetic waves—based mechanics on the idea of every particle traversing the shortest path open to it under the circumstances constraining its motion; and finally Einstein, by the use of the geometrical theories of Gauss and Riemann, showed that these circumstances could be construed as being inherent in the character of space-time itself. Such, in barest outline, is the story of dynamics from Galileo to Einstein.

Meanwhile Galvani and Volta lived and made their electric discoveries; and the biological sciences slowly gathered their material, but still waited for dominating ideas. Psychology, also, was beginning to disengage itself from its dependence on general philosophy. This independent growth of psychology was the ultimate result of its invocation by John Locke as a critic of metaphysical licence. All the sciences dealing with life were still in an elementary observational stage, in which classification and direct description were dominant. So far the scheme of abstractions was adequate to the occasion.

In the realm of practice, the age which produced enlightened rulers, such as the Emperor Joseph of the House of Hapsburg, Frederick the Great, Walpole, the great Lord Chatham, George Washington, cannot be said to have failed. Especially when to these rulers, it adds the invention of parliamentary cabinet government in England, of federal presidential government in the United States, and of the humanitarian principles of the French Revolution. Also in technology it produced the steam-engine, and thereby ushered in a new era of civilisation. Undoubtedly, as a practical age the eighteenth century was a success. If you had asked one of the wisest and most typical of its ancestors, who just saw its commencement, I mean John Locke, what he expected from it, he would hardly have pitched his hopes higher than its actual achievements.

In developing a criticism of the scientific scheme of the eighteenth century, I must first give my main reason for ignoring nineteenth century idealism—I am speaking of the philosophic idealism which finds the ultimate meaning of reality in mentality that is fully cognitive. This idealistic school, as hitherto developed, has been too much divorced from the scientific outlook. It has swallowed the scientific scheme in its entirety as being the only rendering of the facts of nature, and has then explained it as being an idea in the ultimate mentality. In the case of absolute idealism, the world of nature is just one of the ideas, somehow differentiating the unity of the Absolute: in the case of pluralistic idealism involving monadic mentalities, this world is the greatest common measure of the various ideas which differentiate the various mental unities of the various monads. But, however you take it, these idealistic schools have conspicuously failed to connect, in any organic fashion, the fact of nature with their idealistic philosophies. So far as concerns what will be said in these lectures, your ultimate outlook may be realistic or idealistic. My point is that a further stage of provisional realism is required in which the scientific scheme is recast, and founded upon the ultimate concept of *organism*.

In outline, my procedure is to start from the analysis of the status of space and of time, or in modern phraseology, the status of space-time. There are two characters of either. Things are separated by space, and are separated by time: but they are also together in space, and together in time, even if they be not contemporaneous. I will call these characters the *'separative'* and the *'prehensive'* characters of space-time. There is yet a third character of space-time. Everything which is in space receives a definite limitation of some sort, so that in a sense it has just that shape which it does have and no other, also in some sense it is just in this place and in no other. Analogously for time, a thing endures during a certain period, and through no other period. I will call this the *'modal'* character of space-time. It is evident that the modal character taken by itself gives rise to the idea of simple location. But it must be conjoined with the separative and prehensive characters.

For simplicity of thought, I will first speak of space only, and will afterwards extend the same treatment to time.

The volume is the most concrete element of space. But the separative character of space, analyses a volume into sub-volumes, and so on indefinitely. Accordingly, taking the separative character in isolation, we should infer that a volume is a mere multiplicity of non-voluminous elements, of points in fact. But it is the unity of volume which is the ultimate fact of experience, for example, the voluminous space of this hall. This hall as a mere multiplicity of points is a construction of the logical imagination.

Accordingly, the prime fact is the prehensive unity of volume, and this unity is mitigated or limited by the separated unities of the innumerable contained parts. We have a prehensive unity, which is yet held apart as an aggregate of contained parts. But the prehensive unity of the volume is not the unity of a mere logical aggregate of parts. The parts form an ordered aggregate, in the sense that each part is something from the standpoint of every other part, and also from the same standpoint every other part is something in relation to it. Thus if *A* and *B* and *C* are volumes of space, *B* has an aspect from the standpoint of *A*, and so has *C*, and so has the relationship of *B* and *C*. This aspect of *B* from *A* is of the essence of *A*. The volumes of space have no independent existence. They are only entities as within the totality; you cannot extract them from their environment without destruction of their very essence. Accordingly, I will say that the aspect of *B* from *A* is the *mode* in which *B* enters into the composition of *A*. This is the modal character of space, that the prehensive unity of *A* is the prehension into unity of the aspects of all other volumes from the standpoint of *A*. The shape of a volume is the formula from which the totality of its aspects can be derived. Thus the shape of a volume is more abstract than its aspects. It is evident that I can use Leibniz's language, and say that every volume mirrors in itself every other volume in space.

Exactly analogous considerations hold with respect to durations in time. An instant of time, without duration, is an imaginative logical construction. Also each duration of time mirrors in itself all temporal durations.

But in two ways I have introduced a false simplicity. In the first place, I should have conjoined space and time, and conducted my explanation in respect to four-dimensional regions of space-time. I have nothing to add in the way of explanation. In your minds, substitute such four-dimensional regions for the spatial volumes of the previous explanations.

Secondly, my explanation has involved itself in a vicious circle. For I have made the prehensive unity of the region *A* to consist of the prehensive unification of the modal presences in *A* of other regions. This difficulty arises because space-time cannot in reality be considered as a self-subsistent entity. It is an abstraction, and its explanation requires reference to that from which it has been extracted. Space-time is the specification of certain general characters of events and of their mutual ordering. This recurrence to concrete fact brings me back to the eighteenth century, and indeed to Francis Bacon in the seventeenth century. We have to consider the development in those epochs, of the criticism of the reigning scientific scheme.

No epoch is homogeneous; whatever you may have assigned as the dominant note of a considerable period, it will always be possible to produce men, and great men, belonging to the same time, who exhibit themselves as antagonistic to the tone of their age. This is certainly the case with the eighteenth century. For example, the names of John Wesley and of Rousseau must have occurred to you while I was drawing the character of that time. But I do not want to speak of them, or of others. The man, whose ideas I must consider at some length, is Bishop Berkeley. Quite at the commencement of the epoch, he made all the right criticisms, at least in principle. It would be untrue to say that he produced no effect. He was a famous man. The wife of George II was one of the few queens who, in any country, have been clever enough, and wise enough, to patronise learning judiciously; accordingly, Berkeley was made a bishop, in days when bishops in Great Britain were relatively far greater men than they are now. Also, what was more important than his bishopric, Hume studied him, and developed one side of his philosophy in a way which might have disturbed the ghost of the great ecclesiastic. Then Kant studied Hume. So, to say that Berkeley was uninfluential during the century, would certainly be absurd. But all the same, he failed to affect the main stream of scientific thought. It flowed on as if he had never written. Its general success made it impervious to criticism, then and since. The world of science has always remained perfectly satisfied with its peculiar abstractions. They work, and that is sufficient for it.

The point before us is that this scientific field of thought is now, in the twentieth century, too narrow for the concrete facts which are before it for analysis. This is true even in physics, and is more especially urgent in the biological sciences. Thus, in order to understand the difficulties of modern scientific thought and also its reactions on the modern world, we should have in our minds some conception of a wider field of abstraction, a more concrete analysis, which shall stand nearer to the complete concreteness of our intuitive experience. Such an analysis should find in itself a niche for the concepts of matter and spirit, as abstractions in terms of which much of our physical experience can be interpreted. It is in the search for this wider basis for scientific thought that Berkeley is so important. He launched his criticism shortly after the schools of Newton and Locke had completed their work, and laid his finger exactly on the weak spots which they had left. I do not propose to consider either the subjective idealism which has been derived from him, or the schools of development which trace their descent from Hume and Kant respectively. My point will be that—whatever the final metaphysics you may adopt—there is another line of development embedded in Berkeley, pointing to the analysis which we are in search of. Berkeley overlooked it, partly by reason of the over-intellectualism of philosophers, and partly by his haste to have recourse to an idealism with its objectivity grounded in the mind of God. You will remember that I have already stated that the key of the problem lies in the notion of simple location. Berkeley, in effect, criticises this notion. He also raises the question, What do we mean by things being realised in the world of nature?

In Sections 23 and 24 of his *Principles of Human Knowledge*, Berkeley gives his answer to this latter question. I will quote some detached sentences from those Sections:

> 23. But, say you, surely there is nothing easier than for me to imagine trees, for instance, in a park, or books existing in a closet, and nobody by to perceive them. I answer, you may so, there is no difficulty in it; but what is all this, I beseech you, more than framing in your mind certain ideas which you call books and trees, and at the same time omitting to frame the idea of any one that may perceive them?...
>
> When we do our utmost to conceive the existence of external bodies, we are all the while only contemplating our own ideas. But the mind taking no notice of itself, is deluded to think it can and does conceive bodies existing unthought of or without the mind, though at the same time they are apprehended by or exist in itself....
>
> 24. It is very obvious, upon the least inquiry into our thoughts, to know whether it be possible for us to understand what is meant by the absolute existence of sensible objects in themselves, or without the mind. To me it is evident those words mark out either a direct contradiction, or else nothing at all....

Again there is a very remarkable passage in Section 10, of the fourth Dialogue of Berkeley's *Alciphron*. I have already quoted it, at greater length, in my *Principles of Natural Knowledge*:

> *Euphranor*. Tell me, Alciphron, can you discern the doors, window and battlements of that same castle?
>
> *Alciphron*. I cannot. At this distance it seems only a small round tower.

> *Euph.* But I, who have been at it, know that it is no small round tower, but a large square building with battlements and turrets, which it seems you do not see.
>
> *Alc.* What will you infer from thence?
>
> *Euph.* I would infer that the very object which you strictly and properly perceive by sight is not that thing which is several miles distant.
>
> *Alc.* Why so?
>
> *Euph.* Because a little round object is one thing, and a great square object is another. Is it not so?...

Some analogous examples concerning a planet and a cloud are then cited in the dialogue, and this passage finally concludes with:

> *Euphranor.* Is it not plain, therefore, that neither the castle, the planet, nor the cloud, *which you see here*, are those real ones which you suppose exist at a distance?

It is made explicit in the first passage, already quoted, that Berkeley himself adopts an extreme idealistic interpretation. For him mind is the only absolute reality, and the unity of nature is the unity of ideas in the mind of God. Personally, I think that Berkeley's solution of the metaphysical problem raises difficulties not less than those which he points out as arising from a realistic interpretation of the scientific scheme. There is, however, another possible line of thought, which enables us to adopt anyhow an attitude of provisional realism, and to widen the scientific scheme in a way which is useful for science itself.

I recur to the passage from Francis Bacon's *Natural History*, already quoted in the previous lecture:

> It is certain that all bodies whatsoever, though they have no sense, yet they have perception: ... and whether the body be alterant or altered, evermore a perception precedeth operation; for else all bodies would be alike one to another....

Also in the previous lecture I construed *perception* (as used by Bacon) as meaning *taking account of* the essential character of the thing perceived, and I construed *sense* as meaning *cognition*. We certainly do take account of things of which at the time we have no explicit cognition. We can even have a cognitive memory of the taking account, without having had a contemporaneous cognition. Also, as Bacon points out by his statement, "… for else all bodies would be alike one to another," it is evidently some element of the essential character which we take account of, namely something on which diversity is founded and not mere bare logical diversity.

The word '*perceive*' is, in our common usage, shot through and through with the notion of cognitive apprehension. So is the word '*apprehension*', even with the adjective *cognitive* omitted. I will use the word '*prehension*' for *uncognitive apprehension*: by this I mean *apprehension* which may or or may not be cognitive. Now take Euphranor's last remark:

"Is it not plain, therefore, that neither the castle, the planet, nor the cloud, *which you see here*, are those real ones which you suppose exist at distance?" Accordingly, there is a prehension, *here* in this place, of things which have a reference to *other* places.

Now go back to Berkeley's sentences, quoted from his *Principles of Human Knowledge*. He contends that what constitutes the realisation of natural entities is the being perceived within the unity of mind.

We can substitute the concept, that the realisation is a gathering of things into the unity of a prehension; and that what is thereby realized is the prehension, and not the things. This unity of a prehension defines itself as a *here* and a *now*, and the things so gathered into the grasped unity have essential reference to other places and other times. For Berkeley's *mind*, I substitute a process of prehensive unification. In order to make intelligible this concept of the progressive realisation of natural occurrences, considerable expansion is required, and confrontation with its actual implications in terms of concrete experience. This will be the task of the subsequent lectures. In the first place, note that the idea of simple location has gone. The things which are grasped into a realised unity, here and now, are not the castle, the cloud, and the planet simply in themselves; but they are the castle, the cloud, and the planet from the standpoint, in space and time, of the prehensive unification. In other words, it is the perspective of the castle over there from the standpoint of the unification here. It is, therefore, aspects of the castle, the cloud, and the planet which are grasped into unity here. You will remember that the idea of perspectives is quite familiar in philosophy. It was introduced by Leibniz, in the notion of his monads mirroring perspectives of the universe. I am using the same notion, only I am toning down his monads into the unified events in space and time. In some ways, there is a greater analogy with Spinoza's modes; that is why I use the terms '*mode*' and '*modal.*' In the analogy with Spinoza, his one substance is for me the one underlying activity of realization individualising itself in an interlocked plurality of modes. Thus, concrete fact is process. Its primary analysis is into underlying activity of prehension, and into realised prehensive events. Each event is an individual matter of fact issuing from an individualisation of the substrate activity. But individualisation does not mean substantial independence.

An entity of which we become aware in sense perception is the terminus of our act of perception. I will call such an entity, a '*sense-object*'. For example, green of a definite shade is a sense-object; so is a sound of definite quality and pitch; and so is a definite scent; and a definite quality of touch. The way in which such an entity is related to space during a definite lapse of time is complex. I will say that a sense-object has '*ingression*' into space-time. The cognitive perception of a sense-object is the awareness of the prehensive unification (into a standpoint *A*) of various modes of various sense-objects, including the sense-object in question.

The standpoint *A* is, of course, a region of space-time; that is to say, it is a volume of space through a duration of time. But as one entity, this standpoint is a unit of realised experience. *A* mode of a sense-object at *A* (as abstracted from the sense-object whose relationship to *A* the mode is conditioning) is the aspect from *A* of some other region *B*. Thus the sense-object is present in *A* with the mode of location in *B*. Thus if green be the sense-object in question, green is not simply at *A* where it is being perceived, nor is it simply at *B* where it is perceived as located; but it is present at *A* with the mode of location in *B*. There is no particular mystery about this. You have only got to look into a mirror and to see the image in it of some green leaves behind your back. For you at *A* there will be green; but not green simply at *A* where you are. The green at *A* will be green with the mode of having location at the image of the leaf behind the mirror. Then turn round and look at the leaf. You are now perceiving the green in the same way as you did before, except that now the green has the mode of being located in the actual leaf. I am merely describing what we do perceive: we are aware of green as being one element in a prehensive unification of sense-objects; each sense-object, and among them green, having its particular mode, which is expressible as location elsewhere. There are various types of modal location. For example, sound is voluminous: it fills a hall, and so sometimes does diffused colour. But the modal location of a colour may be that of being the remote boundary of a volume, as for example the colours on the walls of a room. Thus primarily space-time is the locus of the modal ingression of sense-objects. This is the reason why space and time (if for simplicity we disjoin them) are given in their entireties. For each volume of space, or each lapse of time, includes in its essence aspects of all volumes of space, or of all lapses of time. The difficulties of philosophy in respect to space and time are founded on the error of considering them as primarily the loci of simple locations. Perception is simply the cognition of prehensive unification; or more shortly, perception is cognition of prehension. The actual world is a manifold of prehensions; and a 'prehension' is a 'prehensive occasion'; and a prehensive occasion is the most concrete finite entity, conceived as what it is in itself and for itself, and not as from its aspect in the essence of another such occasion. Prehensive unification might be said to have simple location in its volume *A*. But this would be a mere tautology. For space and time are simply abstractions from the totality of prehensive unifications as mutually patterned in each other. Thus a prehension has simple location at the volume *A* in the same way as that in which a man's face fits on to the smile which spreads over it. There is, so far as we have gone, more sense in saying that an act of perception has simple location; for it may be conceived as being simply at the cognised prehension.

There are more entities involved in nature than the mere sense-objects, so far considered. But, allowing for the necessity of revision consequent on a more complete point of view, we can frame our answer to Berkeley's question as to the character of the reality to be assigned to nature. He states it to be the reality of ideas in mind. A complete metaphysic which has attained to some notion of mind, and to some notion of ideas, may perhaps ultimately adopt that view. It is unnecessary for the purpose of these lectures to ask such a fundamental question. We can be content with a provisional realism in which nature is conceived as a complex of prehensive unifications. Space and time exhibit the general scheme of interlocked relations of these prehensions. You cannot tear any one of them out of its context. Yet each one of them within its context has all the reality that attaches to the whole complex. Conversely, the totality has the same reality as each prehension; for each prehension unifies the modalities to be ascribed, from its standpoint, to every part of the whole. A prehension is a process of unifying. Accordingly, nature is a process of expansive development, necessarily transitional from prehension to prehension. What is achieved is thereby passed beyond, but it is also retained as having aspects of itself present to prehensions which lie beyond it.

Thus nature is a structure of evolving processes. The reality is the process. It is nonsense to ask if the colour red is real. The colour red is ingredient in the process of realisation. The realities of nature are the prehensions in nature, that is to say, the events in nature.

Now that we have cleared space and time from the taint of simple location, we may partially abandon the awkward term prehension. This term was introduced to signify the essential unity of an event, namely, the event as one entity, and not as a mere assemblage of parts or of ingredients. It is necessary to understand that space-time is nothing else than a system of pulling together of assemblages into unities. But the word *event* just means one of these spatio-temporal unities. Accordingly, it may be used instead of the term 'prehension' as meaning the thing prehended.

An event has contemporaries. This means that an event mirrors within itself the modes of its contemporaries as a display of immediate achievement. An event has a past. This means that an event mirrors within itself the modes of its predecessors, as memories which are fused into its own content. An event has a future. This means that an event mirrors within itself such aspects as the future throws back onto the present, or, in other words, as the present has determined concerning the future. Thus an event has anticipation:

> The prophetic soul
> Of the wide world dreaming on things to come. [cvii]

These conclusions are essential for any form of realism. For there is in the world for our cognisance, memory of the past, immediacy of realisation, and indication of things to come.

In this sketch of an analysis more concrete than that of the scientific scheme of thought, I have started from our own psychological field, as it stands for our cognition. I take it for what it claims to be: the self-knowledge of our bodily event. I mean the total event, and not the inspection of the details of the body. This self-knowledge discloses a prehensive unification of modal presences of entities beyond itself. I generalise by the use of the principle that this total bodily event is on the same level as all other events, except for an unusual complexity and stability of inherent pattern. The strength of the theory of materialistic mechanism has been the demand, that no arbitrary breaks be introduced into nature, to eke out the collapse of an explanation. I accept this principle. But if you start from the immediate facts of our psychological experience, as surely an empiricist should begin, you are at once led to the organic conception of nature of which the description has been commenced in this lecture.

It is the defect of the eighteenth century scientific scheme that it provides none of the elements which compose the immediate psychological experiences of mankind. Nor does it provide any elementary trace of the organic unity of a whole, from which the organic unities of electrons, protons, molecules, and living bodies can emerge. According to that scheme, there is no reason in the nature of things why portions of material should have any physical relations to each other. Let us grant that we cannot hope to be able to discern the laws of nature to be necessary. But we can hope to see that it is necessary that there should be an order of nature. The concept of the order of nature is bound up with the concept of nature as the locus of organisms in process of development.

NOTE. In connection with the latter portion of this chapter a sentence from Descartes' "Reply to Objections … against the Meditations" is interesting:—"Hence the idea of the sun will be the sun itself existing in the mind, not indeed formally, as it exists in the sky, but objectively, *i.e.*, in the way in which objects are wont to exist in the mind; and this mode of being is truly much less perfect than that in which things exist outside the mind, but it is not on that account mere nothing, as I have already said." [Reply to Objections I, Translation by Haldane and Ross, vol. ii, p. 10.] I find difficulty in reconciling this theory of ideas (with which I agree) with other parts of the Cartesian philosophy.

CHAPTER V

THE ROMANTIC REACTION

My last lecture described the influence upon the eighteenth century of the narrow and efficient scheme of scientific concepts which it had inherited from its predecessor. That scheme was the product of a mentality which found the Augustinian theology extremely congenial. The Protestant Calvinism and the Catholic Jansenism exhibited man as helpless to co-operate with Irresistible Grace: the contemporary scheme of science exhibited man as helpless to co-operate with the irresistible mechanism of nature. The mechanism of God and the mechanism of matter were the monstrous issues of limited metaphysics and clear logical intellect. Also the seventeenth century had genius, and cleared the world of muddled thought. The eighteenth century continued the work of clearance, with ruthless efficiency. The scientific scheme has lasted longer than the theological scheme. Mankind soon lost interest in Irresistible Grace; but it quickly appreciated the competent engineering which was due to science. Also in the first quarter of the eighteenth century, George Berkeley launched his philosophical criticism against the whole basis of the system. He failed to disturb the dominant current of thought. In my last lecture I developed a parallel line of argument, which would lead to a system of thought basing nature upon the concept of organism, and not upon the concept of matter. In the present lecture, I propose in the first place to consider how the concrete educated thought of men has viewed this opposition of mechanism and organism. It is in literature that the concrete outlook of humanity receives its expression. Accordingly it is to literature that we must look, particularly in its more concrete forms, namely in poetry and in drama, if we hope to discover the inward thoughts of a generation.

We quickly find that the Western peoples exhibit on a colossal scale a peculiarity which is popularly supposed to be more especially characteristic of the Chinese. Surprise is often expressed that a Chinaman can be of two religions, a Confucian for some occasions and a Buddhist for other occasions. Whether this is true of China I do not know; nor do I know whether, if true, these two attitudes are really inconsistent. But there can be no doubt that an analogous fact is true of the West, and that the two attitudes involved are inconsistent. A scientific realism, based on mechanism, is conjoined with an unwavering belief in the world of men and of the higher animals as being composed of self-determining organisms. This radical inconsistency at the basis of modern thought accounts for much that is half-hearted and wavering in our civilisation. It would be going too far to say that it distracts thought. It enfeebles it, by reason of the inconsistency lurking in the background. After all, the men of the Middle Ages were in pursuit of an excellency of which we have nearly forgotten the existence. They set before themselves the ideal of the attainment of a harmony of the understanding. We are content with superficial orderings from diverse arbitrary starting points. For instance, the enterprises produced by the individualistic energy of the European peoples presupposes physical actions directed to final causes. But the science which is employed in their development is based on a philosophy which asserts that physical causation is supreme, and which disjoins the physical cause from the final end. It is not popular to dwell on the absolute contradiction here involved. It is the fact, however you gloze it over with phrases. Of course, we find in the eighteenth century Paley's famous argument, that mechanism presupposes a God who is the author of nature. But even before Paley put the argument into its final form, Hume had written the retort, that the God whom you will find will be the sort of God who makes that mechanism. In other words, that mechanism can, at most, presuppose a mechanic, and not merely *a* mechanic but *its* mechanic. The only way of mitigating mechanism is by the discovery that it is not mechanism.

When we leave apologetic theology, and come to ordinary literature, we find, as we might expect, that the scientific outlook is in general simply ignored. So far as the mass of literature is concerned, science might never have been heard of. Until recently nearly all writers have been soaked in classical and renaissance literature. For the most part, neither philosophy nor science interested them, and their minds were trained to ignore it.

There are exceptions to this sweeping statement; and, even if we confine ourselves to English literature, they concern some of the greatest names; also the indirect influence of science has been considerable.

A side light on this distracting inconsistency in modern thought is obtained by examining some of those great serious poems in English literature, whose general scale gives them a didactic character. The relevant poems are Milton's *Paradise Lost*, Pope's *Essay on Man*, Wordsworth's *Excursion*, Tennyson's *In Memoriam*. Milton, though he is writing after the Restoration, voices the theological aspect of the earlier portion of his century, untouched by the influence of the scientific materialism. Pope's poem represents the effect on popular thought of the intervening sixty years which includes the first period of assured triumph for the scientific movement. Wordsworth in his whole being expresses a conscious reaction against the mentality of the eighteenth century. This mentality means nothing else than the acceptance of the scientific ideas at their full face value. Wordsworth was not bothered by any intellectual antagonism. What moved him was a moral repulsion. He felt that something had been left out, and that what had been left out comprised everything that was most important. Tennyson is the mouthpiece of the attempts of the waning romantic movement in the second quarter of the nineteenth century to come to terms with science. By this time the two elements in modern thought had disclosed their fundamental divergence by their jarring interpretations of the course of nature and the life of man. Tennyson stands in this poem as the perfect example of the distraction which I have already mentioned. There are opposing visions of the world, and both of them command his assent by appeals to ultimate intuitions from which there seems no escape. Tennyson goes to the heart of the difficulty. It is the problem of mechanism which appalls him,

> 'The stars,' she whispers, 'blindly run.'

This line states starkly the whole philosophic problem implicit in the poem. Each molecule blindly runs. The human body is a collection of molecules. Therefore, the human body blindly runs, and therefore there can be no individual responsibility for the actions of the body. If you once accept that the molecule is definitely determined to be what it is, independently of any determination by reason of the total organism of the body, and if you further admit that the blind run is settled by the general mechanical laws, there can be no escape from this conclusion. But mental experiences are derivative from the actions of the body, including of course its internal behaviour. Accordingly, the sole function of the mind is to have at least some of its experiences settled for it, and to add such others as may be open to it independently of the body's motions, internal and external.

There are then two possible theories as to the mind. You can either deny that it can supply for itself any experiences other than those provided for it by the body, or you can admit them.

If you refuse to admit the additional experiences, then all individual moral responsibility is swept away. If you do admit them, then a human being may be responsible for the state of his mind though he has no responsibility for the actions of his body. The enfeeblement of thought in the modern world is illustrated by the way in which this plain issue is avoided in Tennyson's poem. There is something kept in the background, a skeleton in the cupboard. He touches on almost every religious and scientific problem, but carefully avoids more than a passing allusion to this one.

This very problem was in full debate at the date of the poem. John Stuart Mill was maintaining his doctrine of determinism. In this doctrine volitions are determined by motives, and motives are expressible in terms of antecedent conditions including states of mind as well as states of the body.

It is obvious that this doctrine affords no escape from the dilemma presented by a thoroughgoing mechanism. For if the volition affects the state of the body, then the molecules in the body do not blindly run. If the volition does not affect the state of the body, the mind is still left in its uncomfortable position.

Mill's doctrine is generally accepted, especially among scientists, as though in some way it allowed you to accept the extreme doctrine of materialistic mechanism, and yet mitigated its unbelievable consequences. It does nothing of the sort. Either the bodily molecules blindly run, or they do not. If they do blindly run, the mental states are irrelevant in discussing the bodily actions.

I have stated the arguments concisely, because in truth the issue is a very simple one. Prolonged discussion is merely a source of confusion. The question as to the metaphysical status of molecules does not come in. The statement that they are mere formulae has no bearing on the argument. For presumably the formulae mean something. If they mean nothing, the whole mechanical doctrine is likewise without meaning, and the question drops. But if the formulae mean anything, the argument applies to exactly what they do mean. The traditional way of evading the difficulty—other than the simple way of ignoring it—is to have recourse to some form of what is now termed 'vitalism.' This doctrine is really a compromise. It allows a free run to mechanism throughout the whole of inanimate nature, and holds that the mechanism is partially mitigated within living bodies. I feel that this theory is an unsatisfactory compromise. The gap between living and dead matter is too vague and problematical to bear the weight of such an arbitrary assumption, which involves an essential dualism somewhere.

The doctrine which I am maintaining is that the whole concept of materialism only applies to very abstract entities, the products of logical discernment. The concrete enduring entities are organisms, so that the plan of the *whole* influences the very characters of the various subordinate organisms which enter into it. In the case of an animal, the mental states enter into the plan of the total organism and thus modify the plans of the successive subordinate organisms until the ultimate smallest organisms, such as electrons, are reached. Thus an electron within a living body is different from an electron outside it, by reason of the plan of the body. The electron blindly runs either within or without the body; but it runs within the body in accordance with its character within the body; that is to say, in accordance with the general plan of the body, and this plan includes the mental state. But this principle of modification is perfectly general throughout nature, and represents no property peculiar to living bodies. In subsequent lectures it will be explained that this doctrine involves the abandonment of the traditional scientific materialism, and the substitution of an alternative doctrine of organism.

I shall not discuss Mill's determinism, as it lies outside the scheme of these lectures. The foregoing discussion has been directed to secure that either determinism or free will shall have some relevance, unhampered by the difficulties introduced by materialistic mechanism, or by the compromise of vitalism. I would term the doctrine of these lectures, the theory of *organic mechanism*. In this theory, the molecules may blindly run in accordance with the general laws, but the molecules differ in their intrinsic characters according to the general organic plans of the situations in which they find themselves.

The discrepancy between the materialistic mechanism of science and the moral intuitions, which are presupposed in the concrete affairs of life, only gradually assumed its true importance as the centuries advanced. The different tones of the successive epochs to which the poems, already mentioned, belong are curiously reflected in their opening passages. Milton ends his introduction with the prayer,

That to the height of this great argument

I may assert eternal Providence,

And justify the ways of God to men.

7-2

To judge from many modern writers on Milton, we might imagine that the *Paradise Lost* and the *Paradise Regained* were written as a series of experiments in blank verse. This was certainly not Milton's view of his work. To 'justify the ways of God to men' was very much his main object. He recurs to the same idea in the *Samson Agonistes*,

Just are the ways of God

And justifiable to men;

We note the assured volume of confidence, untroubled by the coming scientific avalanche. The actual date of the publication of the *Paradise Lost* lies just beyond the epoch to which it belongs. It is the swansong of a passing world of untroubled certitude.

A comparison between Pope's *Essay on Man* and the *Paradise Lost* exhibits the change of tone in English thought in the fifty or sixty years which separate the age of Milton from the age of Pope.

Milton addresses his poem to God, Pope's poem is addressed to Lord Bolingbroke,

> Awake, my St. John! leave all meaner things
> To low ambition and the pride of kings.
> Let us (since life can little more supply
> Than just to look about us and to die)
> Expatiate free o'er all this scene of man;
> A mighty maze! but not without a plan;

Compare the jaunty assurance of Pope,

> A mighty maze! but not without a plan.

with Milton's

> Just are the ways of God
> And justifiable to men;

But the real point to notice is that Pope as well as Milton was untroubled by the great perplexity which haunts the modern world. The clue which Milton followed was to dwell on the ways of God in dealings with man. Two generations later we find Pope equally confident that the enlightened methods of modern science provided a plan adequate as a map of the 'mighty maze.'

Wordsworth's *Excursion* is the next English poem on the same subject. A prose preface tells us that it is a fragment of a larger projected work, described as 'A philosophical poem containing views of Man, Nature, and Society.'

> Very characteristically the poem begins with the line,
> 'Twas summer, and the sun had mounted high:

Thus the romantic reaction started neither with God nor with Lord Bolingbroke, but with nature. We are here witnessing a conscious reaction against the whole tone of the eighteenth century. That century approached nature with the abstract analysis of science, whereas Wordsworth opposes to the scientific abstractions his full concrete experience.

A generation of religious revival and of scientific advance lies between the *Excursion* and Tennyson's *In Memoriam*. The earlier poets had solved the perplexity by ignoring it. That course was not open to Tennyson. Accordingly his poem begins thus:

Strong Son of God, immortal Love,
Whom we, that have not seen Thy face,
By faith, and faith alone, embrace,
Believing where we cannot prove;

The note of perplexity is struck at once. The nineteenth century has been a perplexed century, in a sense which is not true of any of its predecessors of the modern period. In the earlier times there were opposing camps, bitterly at variance on questions which they deemed fundamental. But, except for a few stragglers, either camp was whole-hearted. The importance of Tennyson's poem lies in the fact that it exactly expressed the character of its period. Each individual was divided against himself. In the earlier times, the deep thinkers were the clear thinkers,—Descartes, Spinoza, Locke, Leibniz. They knew exactly what they meant and said it. In the nineteenth century, some of the deeper thinkers among theologians and philosophers were muddled thinkers. Their assent was claimed by incompatible doctrines; and their efforts at reconciliation produced inevitable confusion.

Matthew Arnold, even more than Tennyson, was the poet who expressed this mood of individual distraction which was so characteristic of this century. Compare with *In Memoriam* the closing lines of Arnold's *Dover Beach*:

And we are here as on a darkling plain
Swept with confused alarms of struggle and flight,
Where ignorant armies clash by night.

Cardinal Newman in his *Apologia pro Vitâ Suâ* mentions it as a peculiarity of Pusey, the great Anglican ecclesiastic, "He was haunted by no intellectual perplexities." In this respect Pusey recalls Milton, Pope, Wordsworth, as in contrast with Tennyson, Clough, Matthew Arnold, and Newman himself.

So far as concerns English literature we find, as might be anticipated, the most interesting criticism of the thoughts of science among the leaders of the romantic reaction which accompanied and succeeded the epoch of the French Revolution. In English literature, the deepest thinkers of this school were Coleridge, Wordsworth, and Shelley. Keats is an example of literature untouched by science. We may neglect Coleridge's attempt at an explicit philosophical formulation. It was influential in his own generation; but in these lectures it is my object only to mention those elements of the thought of the past which stand for all time. Even with this limitation, only a selection is possible. For our purposes Coleridge is only important by his influence on Wordsworth. Thus Wordsworth and Shelley remain.

Wordsworth was passionately absorbed in nature. It has been said of Spinoza, that he was drunk with God. It is equally true that Wordsworth was drunk with nature. But he was a thoughtful, well-read man, with philosophical interests, and sane even to the point of prosiness. In addition, he was a genius. He weakens his evidence by his dislike of science. We all remember his scorn of the poor man whom he somewhat hastily accuses of peeping and botanising on his mother's grave. Passage after passage could be quoted from him, expressing this repulsion. In this respect, his characteristic thought can be summed up in his phrase, "We murder to dissect."

In this latter passage, he discloses the intellectual basis of his criticism of science. He alleges against science its absorption in abstractions. His consistent theme is that the important facts of nature elude the scientific method. It is important therefore to ask, what Wordsworth found in nature that failed to receive expression in science. I ask this question in the interest of science itself; for one main position in these lectures is a protest against the idea that the abstractions of science are irreformable and unalterable. Now it is emphatically not the case that Wordsworth hands over inorganic matter to the mercy of science, and concentrates on the faith that in the living organism there is some element that science cannot analyse. Of course he recognizes, what no one doubts, that in some sense living things are different from lifeless things. But that is not his main point. It is the brooding presence of the hills which haunts him. His theme is nature *in solido*, that is to say, he dwells on that mysterious presence of surrounding things, which imposes itself on any separate element that we set up as an individual for its own sake. He always grasps the whole of nature as involved in the tonality of the particular instance. That is why he laughs with the daffodils, and finds in the primrose "thoughts too deep for terms."

Wordsworth's greatest poem is, by far, the first book of *The Prelude*. It is pervaded by this sense of the haunting presences of nature. A series of magnificent passages, too long for quotation, express this idea. Of course, Wordsworth is a poet writing a poem, and is not concerned with dry philosophical statements. But it would hardly be possible to express more clearly a feeling for nature, as exhibiting entwined prehensive unities, each suffused with modal presences of others:

> Ye Presences of Nature in the sky
> And on the earth! Ye Visions of the hills!
> And Souls of lonely places! can I think
> A vulgar hope was yours when ye employed
> Such ministry, when ye through many a year
> Haunting me thus among my boyish sports,
> On caves and trees, upon the woods and hills,
> Impressed upon all forms the characters

> Of danger or desire; and thus did make
> The surface of the universal earth
> With triumph and delight, with hope and fear,
> Work like a sea?...

In thus citing Wordsworth, the point which I wish to make is that we forget how strained and paradoxical is the view of nature which modern science imposes on our thoughts. Wordsworth, to the height of genius, expresses the concrete facts of our apprehension, facts which are distorted in the scientific analysis. Is it not possible that the standardised concepts of science are only valid within narrow limitations, perhaps too narrow for science itself?

Shelley's attitude to science was at the opposite pole to that of Wordsworth. He loved it, and is never tired of expressing in poetry the thoughts which it suggests. It symbolises to him joy, and peace, and illumination. What the hills were to the youth of Wordsworth, a chemical laboratory was to Shelley. It is unfortunate that Shelley's literary critics have, in this respect, so little of Shelley in their own mentality. They tend to treat as a casual oddity of Shelley's nature what was, in fact, part of the main structure of his mind, permeating his poetry through and through. If Shelley had been born a hundred years later, the twentieth century would have seen a Newton among chemists.

For the sake of estimating the value of Shelley's evidence it is important to realise this absorption of his mind in scientific ideas. It can be illustrated by lyric after lyric. I will choose one poem only, the fourth act of his *Prometheus Unbound*. The Earth and the Moon converse together in the language of accurate science. Physical experiments guide his imagery. For example, the Earth's exclamation,

> The vaporous exultation not to be confined!

is the poetic transcript of "the expansive force of gases," as it is termed in books on science. Again, take the Earth's stanza,

I spin beneath my pyramid of night,
Which points into the heavens,—dreaming delight,
Murmuring victorious joy in my enchanted sleep;
As a youth lulled in love-dreams faintly sighing,
Under the shadow of his beauty lying,
Which round his rest a watch of light and warmth doth keep.

This stanza could only have been written by someone with a definite geometrical diagram before his inward eye—a diagram which it has often been my business to demonstrate to mathematical classes. As evidence, note especially the last line which gives poetical imagery to the light surrounding night's pyramid. This idea could not occur to anyone without the diagram. But the whole poem and other poems are permeated with touches of this kind.

Now the poet, so sympathetic with science, so absorbed in its ideas, can simply make nothing of the doctrine of secondary qualities which is fundamental to its concepts. For Shelley nature retains its beauty and its colour. Shelley's nature is in its essence a nature of organisms, functioning with the full content of our perceptual experience. We are so used to ignoring the implications of orthodox scientific doctrine, that it is difficult to make evident the criticism upon it which is thereby implied. If anybody could have treated it seriously, Shelley would have done so.

Furthermore Shelley is entirely at one with Wordsworth as to the interfusing of the Presence in nature. Here is the opening stanza of his poem entitled *Mont Blanc*:

The everlasting universe of Things
Flows through the Mind, and rolls its rapid waves,
Now dark—now glittering—now reflecting gloom—
Now lending splendour, where from secret springs
The source of human thought its tribute brings

Of waters,—with a sound but half its own,
Such as a feeble brook will oft assume
In the wild woods, among the Mountains lone,
Where waterfalls around it leap for ever,
Where woods and winds contend, and a vast river
Over its rocks ceaselessly bursts and raves.

Shelley has written these lines with explicit reference to some form of idealism, Kantian or Berkeleyan or Platonic. But however you construe him, he is here an emphatic witness to a prehensive unification as constituting the very being of nature.

Berkeley, Wordsworth, Shelley are representative of the intuitive refusal seriously to accept the abstract materialism of science.

There is an interesting difference in the treatment of nature by Wordsworth and by Shelley, which brings forward the exact questions we have got to think about. Shelley thinks of nature as changing, dissolving, transforming as it were at a fairy's touch. The leaves fly before the West Wind

Like ghosts from an enchanter fleeing.

In his poem *The Cloud* it is the transformations of water which excite his imagination. The subject of the poem is the endless, eternal, elusive change of things:

I change but I cannot die.

This is one aspect of nature, its elusive change: a change not merely to be expressed by locomotion, but a change of inward character. This is where Shelley places his emphasis, on the change of what cannot die.

Wordsworth was born among hills; hills mostly barren of trees, and thus showing the minimum of change with the seasons. He was haunted by the enormous permanences of nature. For him change is an incident which shoots across a background of endurance,

> Breaking the silence of the seas
> Among the farthest Hebrides.

Every scheme for the analysis of nature has to face these two facts, *change* and *endurance*. There is yet a third fact to be placed by it, *eternality*, I will call it. The mountain endures. But when after ages it has been worn away, it has gone. If a replica arises, it is yet a new mountain. A colour is eternal. It haunts time like a spirit. It comes and it goes. But where it comes, it is the same colour. It neither survives nor does it live. It appears when it is wanted. The mountain has to time and space a different relation from that which colour has. In the previous lecture, I was chiefly considering the relation to space-time of things which, in my sense of the term, are eternal. It was necessary to do so before we can pass to the consideration of the things which endure.

Also we must recollect the basis of our procedure. I hold that philosophy is the critic of abstractions. Its function is the double one, first of harmonising them by assigning to them their right relative status as abstractions, and secondly of completing them by direct comparison with more concrete intuitions of the universe, and thereby promoting the formation of more complete schemes of thought. It is in respect to this comparison that the testimony of great poets is of such importance. Their survival is evidence that they express deep intuitions of mankind penetrating into what is universal in concrete fact. Philosophy is not one among the sciences with its own little scheme of abstractions which it works away at perfecting and improving. It is the survey of sciences, with the special objects of their harmony, and of their completion. It brings to this task, not only the evidence of the separate sciences, but also its own appeal to concrete experience. It confronts the sciences with concrete fact.

The literature of the nineteenth century, especially its English poetic literature, is a witness to the discord between the aesthetic intuitions of mankind and the mechanism of science. Shelley brings vividly before us the elusiveness of the eternal objects of sense as they haunt the change which infects underlying organisms. Wordsworth is the poet of nature as being the field of enduring permanences carrying within themselves a message of tremendous significance. The eternal objects are also there for him,

> The light that never was, on sea or land.

Both Shelley and Wordsworth emphatically bear witness that nature cannot be divorced from its aesthetic values; and that these values arise from the cumulation, in some sense, of the brooding presence of the whole onto its various parts. Thus we gain from the poets the doctrine that a philosophy of nature must concern itself at least with these five notions: change, value, eternal objects, endurance, organism, interfusion.

We see that the literary romantic movement at the beginning of the nineteenth century, just as much as Berkeley's philosophical idealistic movement a hundred years earlier, refused to be confined within the materialistic concepts of the orthodox scientific theory. We know also that when in these lectures we come to the twentieth century, we shall find a movement in science itself to reorganise its concepts, driven thereto by its own intrinsic development.

It is, however, impossible to proceed until we have settled whether this refashioning of ideas is to be carried out on an objectivist basis or on a subjectivist basis. By a subjectivist basis I mean the belief that the nature of our immediate experience is the outcome of the perceptive peculiarities of the subject enjoying the experience. In other words, I mean that for this theory what is perceived is not a partial vision of a complex of things generally independent of that act of cognition; but that it merely is the expression of the individual peculiarities of the cognitive act. Accordingly what is common to the multiplicity of cognitive acts is the ratiocination connected with them. Thus, though there is a common world of thought associated with our sense-perceptions, there is no common world to think about. What we do think about is a common conceptual world applying indifferently to our individual experiences which are strictly personal to ourselves. Such a conceptual world will ultimately find its complete expression in the equations of applied mathematics. This is the extreme subjectivist position. There is of course the half-way house of those who believe that our perceptual experience does tell us of a common objective world; but that the things perceived are merely the outcome for us of this world, and are not *in themselves* elements in the common world itself.

Also there is the objectivist position. This creed is that the actual elements perceived by our senses are *in themselves* the elements of a common world; and that this world is a complex of things, including indeed our acts of cognition, but transcending them. According to this point of view the things experienced are to be distinguished from our knowledge of them. So far as there is dependence, the *things* pave the way for the *cognition*, rather than *vice versa*. But the point is that the actual things experienced enter into a common world which transcends knowledge, though it includes knowledge. The intermediate subjectivists would hold that the things experienced only indirectly enter into the common world by reason of their dependence on the subject who is cognising. The objectivist holds that the things experienced and the cognisant subject enter into the common world on equal terms. In these lectures I am giving the outline of what I consider to be the essentials of an objectivist philosophy adapted to the requirement of science and to the concrete experience of mankind. Apart from the detailed criticism of the difficulties raised by subjectivism in any form, my broad reasons for distrusting it are three in number. One reason arises from the direct interrogation of our perceptive experience. It appears from this interrogation that we are *within* a world of colours, sounds, and other sense-objects, related in space and time to enduring objects such as stones, trees, and human bodies. We seem to be ourselves elements of this world in the same sense as are the other things which we perceive. But the subjectivist, even the moderate intermediate subjectivist, makes this world, as thus described, depend on us, in a way which directly traverses our naïve experience. I hold that the ultimate appeal is to naïve experience and that is why I lay such stress on the evidence of poetry. My point is, that in our sense-experience we know away from and beyond our own personality; whereas the subjectivist holds that in such experience we merely know about our own personality. Even the intermediate subjectivist places our personality between the world we know of and the common world which he admits. The world we know of is for him the internal strain of our personality under the stress of the common world which lies behind.

My second reason for distrusting subjectivism is based on the particular content of experience. Our historical knowledge tells us of ages in the past when, so far as we can see, no living being existed on earth. Again it also tells us of countless star-systems, whose detailed history remains beyond our ken. Consider even the moon and the earth. What is going on within the interior of the earth, and on the far side of the moon! Our perceptions lead us to infer that there is something happening in the stars, something happening within the earth, and something happening on the far side of the moon. Also they tell us that in remote ages there were things happening. But all these things which it appears certainly happened, are either unknown in detail, or else are reconstructed by inferential evidence. In the face of this content of our personal experience, it is difficult to believe that the experienced world is an attribute of our own personality. My third reason is based upon the instinct for action. Just as sense-perception seems to give knowledge of what lies beyond individuality, so action seems to issue in an instinct for self-transcendence. The activity passes beyond self into the known transcendent world. It is here that final ends are of importance. For it is not activity urged from behind, which passes out into the veiled world of the intermediate subjectivist. It is activity directed to determinate ends in the known world; and yet it is activity transcending self and it is activity within the known world. It follows therefore that the world, as known, transcends the subject which is cognisant of it.

The subjectivist position has been popular among those who have been engaged in giving a philosophical interpretation to the recent theories of relativity in physical science. The dependence of the world of sense on the individual percipient seems an easy mode of expressing the meanings involved. Of course, with the exception of those who are content with themselves as forming the entire universe, solitary amid nothing, everyone wants to struggle back to some sort of objectivist position. I do not understand how a common world of thought can be established in the absence of a common world of sense. I will not argue this point in detail; but in the absence of a transcendence of thought, or a transcendence of the world of sense, it is difficult to see how the subjectivist is to divest himself of his solitariness. Nor does the intermediate subjectivist appear to get any help from his unknown world in the background.

The distinction between realism and idealism does not coincide with that between objectivism and subjectivism. Both realists and idealists can start from an objective standpoint. They may both agree that the world disclosed in sense-perception is a common world, transcending the individual percipient. But the objective idealist, when he comes to analyse what the reality of this world involves, finds that cognitive mentality is in some way inextricably concerned in every detail. This position the realist denies. Accordingly these two classes of objectivists do not part company till they have arrived at the ultimate problem of metaphysics. There is a great deal which they share in common. This is why, in my last lecture, I said that I adopted a position of provisional realism.

In the past, the objectivist position has been distorted by the supposed necessity of accepting the classical scientific materialism, with its doctrine of simple location. This has necessitated the doctrine of secondary and primary qualities. Thus the secondary qualities, such as the sense-objects, are dealt with on subjectivist principles. This is a half-hearted position which falls an easy prey to subjectivist criticism.

If we are to include the secondary qualities in the common world, a very drastic reorganisation of our fundamental concepts is necessary. It is an evident fact of experience that our apprehensions of the external world depend absolutely on the occurrences within the human body. By playing appropriate tricks on the body a man can be got to perceive, or not to perceive, almost anything. Some people express themselves as though bodies, brains, and nerves were the only real things in an entirely imaginary world. In other words, they treat bodies on objectivist principles, and the rest of the world on subjectivist principles. This will not do; especially, when we remember that it is the experimenter's perception of another person's body which is in question as evidence.

But we have to admit that the body is the organism whose states regulate our cognisance of the world. The unity of the perceptual field therefore must be a unity of bodily experience. In being aware of the bodily experience, we must thereby be aware of aspects of the whole spatio-temporal world as mirrored within the bodily life. This is the solution of the problem which I gave in my last lecture. I will not repeat myself now, except to remind you that my theory involves the entire abandonment of the notion that simple location is the primary way in which things are involved in space-time. In a certain sense, everything is everywhere at all times. For every location involves an aspect of itself in every other location. Thus every spatio-temporal standpoint mirrors the world.

If you try to imagine this doctrine in terms of our conventional views of space and time, which presuppose simple location, it is a great paradox. But if you think of it in terms of our naïve experience, it is a mere transcript of the obvious facts. You are in a certain place perceiving things. Your perception takes place where you are, and is entirely dependent on how your body is functioning. But this functioning of the body in one place, exhibits for your cognisance an aspect of the distant environment, fading away into the general knowledge that there are things beyond. If this cognisance conveys knowledge of a transcendent world, it must be because the event which is the bodily life unifies in itself aspects of the universe.

This is a doctrine extremely consonant with the vivid expression of personal experience which we find in the nature-poetry of imaginative writers such as Wordsworth or Shelley. The brooding, immediate presences of things are an obsession to Wordsworth. What the theory does do is to edge cognitive mentality away from being the necessary substratum of the unity of experience. That unity is now placed in the unity of an event. Accompanying this unity, there may or there may not be cognition.

At this point we come back to the great question which was posed before us by our examination of the evidence afforded by the poetic insight of Wordsworth and Shelley. This single question has expanded into a group of questions. What are enduring things, as distinguished from the eternal objects, such as colour and shape? How are they possible? What is their status and meaning in the universe? It comes to this: What is the status of the enduring stability of the order of nature? There is the summary answer, which refers nature to some greater reality standing behind it. This reality occurs in the history of thought under many names, The Absolute, Brahma, The Order of Heaven, God. The delineation of final metaphysical truth is no part of this lecture. My point is that any summary conclusion jumping from our conviction of the existence of such an order of nature to the easy assumption that there is an ultimate reality which, in some unexplained way, is to be appealed to for the removal of perplexity, constitutes the great refusal of rationality to assert its rights. We have to search whether nature does not in its very being show itself as self-explanatory.

By this I mean, that the sheer statement, of what things are, may contain elements explanatory of why things are. Such elements may be expected to refer to depths beyond anything which we can grasp with a clear apprehension. In a sense, all explanation must end in an ultimate arbitrariness. My demand is, that the ultimate arbitrariness of matter of fact from which our formulation starts should disclose the same general principles of reality, which we dimly discern as stretching away into regions beyond our explicit powers of discernment. Nature exhibits itself as exemplifying a philosophy of the evolution of organisms subject to determinate conditions. Examples of such conditions are the dimensions of space, the laws of nature, the determinate enduring entities, such as atoms and electrons, which exemplify these laws. But the very nature of these entities, the very nature of their spatiality and temporality, should exhibit the arbitrariness of these conditions as the outcome of a wider evolution beyond nature itself, and within which nature is but a limited mode.

One all-pervasive fact, inherent in the very character of what is real is the transition of things, the passage one to another. This passage is not a mere linear procession of discrete entities. However we fix a determinate entity, there is always a narrower determination of something which is presupposed in our first choice. Also there is always a wider determination into which our first choice fades by transition beyond itself. The general aspect of nature is that of evolutionary expansiveness. These unities, which I call events, are the emergence into actuality of something. How are we to characterise the something which thus emerges? The name '*event*' given to such a unity, draws attention to the inherent transitoriness, combined with the actual unity. But this abstract word cannot be sufficient to characterise what the fact of the reality of an event is in itself. A moment's thought shows us that no one idea can in itself be sufficient. For every idea which finds its significance in each event must represent something which contributes to what realisation is in itself. Thus no one word can be adequate. But conversely, nothing must be left out. Remembering the poetic rendering of our concrete experience, we see at once that the element of value, of being valuable, of having value, of being an end in itself, of being something which is for its own sake, must not be omitted in any account of an event as the most concrete actual something. 'Value' is the word I use for the intrinsic reality of an event. Value is an element which permeates through and through the poetic view of nature. We have only to transfer to the very texture of realisation in itself that value which we recognize so readily in terms of human life. This is the secret of Wordsworth's worship of nature. Realization therefore is in itself the attainment of value. But there is no such thing as mere value. Value is the outcome of limitation. The definite finite entity is the selected mode which is the shaping of attainment; apart from such shaping into individual matter of fact there is no attainment. The mere fusion of all that there is would be the nonentity of indefiniteness. The salvation of reality is its obstinate, irreducible, matter-of-fact entities, which are limited to be no other than themselves. Neither science, nor art, nor creative action can tear itself away from obstinate, irreducible, limited facts. The endurance of things has its significance in the self-retention of that which imposes itself as a definite attainment for its own sake. That which endures is limited, obstructive, intolerant, infecting its environment with its own aspects. But it is not self-sufficient. The aspects of all things enter into its very nature. It is only itself as drawing together into its own limitation the larger whole in which it finds itself. Conversely it is only itself by lending its aspects to this same environment in which it finds itself. The problem of evolution is the development of enduring harmonies of enduring shapes of value, which merge into higher attainments of things beyond themselves. Aesthetic attainment is interwoven in the texture of realisation. The endurance of an entity represents the attainment of a limited aesthetic success, though if we look beyond it to its external effects, it may represent an aesthetic failure. Even within itself, it may represent the conflict between a lower success and a higher failure. The conflict is the presage of disruption.

The further discussion of the nature of enduring objects and of the conditions they require will be relevant to the consideration of the doctrine of evolution which dominated the latter half of the nineteenth century. The point which in this lecture I have endeavoured to make clear is that the nature-poetry of the romantic revival was a protest on behalf of the organic view of nature, and also a protest against the exclusion of value from the essence of matter of fact. In this aspect of it, the romantic movement may be conceived as a revival of Berkeley's protest which had been launched a hundred years earlier. The romantic reaction was a protest on behalf of value.

CHAPTER VI

THE NINETEENTH CENTURY

My previous lecture was occupied with the comparison of the nature-poetry of the romantic movement in England with the materialistic scientific philosophy inherited from the eighteenth century. It noted the entire disagreement of the two movements of thought. The lecture also continued the endeavour to outline an objectivist philosophy, capable of bridging the gap between science and that fundamental intuition of mankind which finds its expression in poetry and its practical exemplification in the presuppositions of daily life. As the nineteenth century passed on, the romantic movement died down. It did not die away, but it lost its clear unity of tidal stream, and dispersed itself into many estuaries as it coalesced with other human interests. The faith of the century was derived from three sources: one source was the romantic movement, showing itself in religious revival, in art, and in political aspiration: another source was the gathering advance of science which opened avenues of thought: the third source was the advance in technology which completely changed the conditions of human life.

Each of these springs of faith had its origin in the previous period. The French Revolution itself was the first child of romanticism in the form in which it tinged Rousseau. James Watt obtained his patent for his steam-engine in 1769. The scientific advance was the glory of France and of French influence, throughout the same century.

Also even during this earlier period, the streams interacted, coalesced, and antagonised each other. But it was not until the nineteenth century that the threefold movement came to that full development and peculiar balance characteristic of the sixty years following the battle of Waterloo.

What is peculiar and new to the century, differentiating it from all its predecessors, is its technology. It was not merely the introduction of some great isolated inventions. It is impossible not to feel that something more than that was involved. For example, writing was a greater invention than the steam-engine. But in tracing the continuous history of the growth of writing we find an immense difference from that of the steam-engine. We must, of course, put aside minor and sporadic anticipations of both; and confine attention to the periods of their effective elaboration. The scale of time is so absolutely disparate. For the steam-engine, we may give about a hundred years; for writing, the time period is of the order of a thousand years. Further, when writing was finally popularised, the world was not then expecting the next step in technology. The process of change was slow, unconscious, and unexpected.

In the nineteenth century, the process became quick, conscious, and expected. The earlier half of the century was the period in which this new attitude to change was first established and enjoyed. It was a peculiar period of hope, in the sense in which, sixty or seventy years later, we can now detect a note of disillusionment, or at least of anxiety.

The greatest invention of the nineteenth century was the invention of the method of invention. A new method entered into life. In order to understand our epoch, we can neglect all the details of change, such as railways, telegraphs, radios, spinning machines, synthetic dyes. We must concentrate on the method in itself; that is the real novelty, which has broken up the foundations of the old civilisation. The prophecy of Francis Bacon has now been fulfilled; and man, who at times dreamt of himself as a little lower than the angels, has submitted to become the servant and the minister of nature. It still remains to be seen whether the same actor can play both parts.

The whole change has arisen from the new scientific information. Science, conceived not so much in its principles as in its results, is an obvious storehouse of ideas for utilisation. But, if we are to understand what happened during the century, the analogy of a mine is better than that of a storehouse. Also, it is a great mistake to think that the bare scientific idea is the required invention, so that it has only to be picked up and used. An intense period of imaginative design lies between. One element in the new method is just the discovery of how to set about bridging the gap between the scientific ideas, and the ultimate product. It is a process of disciplined attack upon one difficulty after another.

The possibilities of modern technology were first in practice realised in England, by the energy of a prosperous middle class. Accordingly, the industrial revolution started there. But the Germans explicitly realised the methods by which the deeper veins in the mine of science could be reached. They abolished haphazard methods of scholarship. In their technological schools and universities progress did not have to wait for the occasional genius, or the occasional lucky thought. Their feats of scholarship during the nineteenth century were the admiration of the world. This discipline of knowledge applies beyond technology to pure science, and beyond science to general scholarship. It represents the change from amateurs to professionals.

There have always been people who devoted their lives to definite regions of thought. In particular, lawyers and the clergy of the Christian churches form obvious examples of such specialism. But the full self-conscious realisation of the power of professionalism in knowledge in all its departments, and of the way to produce the professionals, and of the importance of knowledge to the advance of technology, and of the methods by which abstract knowledge can be connected with technology, and of the boundless possibilities of technological advance,—the realisation of all these things was first completely attained in the nineteenth century; and among the various countries, chiefly in Germany.

In the past human life was lived in a bullock cart; in the future it will be lived in an aeroplane; and the change of speed amounts to a difference in quality.

The transformation of the field of knowledge, which has been thus effected, has not been wholly a gain. At least, there are dangers implicit in it, although the increase of efficiency is undeniable. The discussion of various effects on social life arising from the new situation is reserved for my last lecture. For the present it is sufficient to note that this novel situation of disciplined progress is the setting within which the thought of the century developed.

In the period considered four great novel ideas were introduced into theoretical science. Of course, it is possible to show good cause for increasing my list far beyond the number *four*. But I am keeping to ideas which, if taken in their broadest signification, are vital to modern attempts at reconstructing the foundations of physical science.

Two of these ideas are antithetical, and I will consider them together. We are not concerned with details, but with ultimate influences on thought. One of the ideas is that of a field of physical activity pervading all space, even where there is an apparent vacuum. This notion had occurred to many people, under many forms. We remember the medieval axiom, nature abhors a vacuum. Also, Descartes' vortices at one time, in the seventeenth century, seemed as if established among scientific assumptions. Newton believed that gravitation was caused by something happening in a medium. But, on the whole, in the eighteenth century nothing was made of any of these ideas. The passage of light was explained in Newton's fashion by the flight of minute corpuscles, which of course left room for a vacuum. Mathematical physicists were far too busy deducing the consequences of the theory of gravitation to bother much about the causes; nor did they know where to look, if they had troubled themselves over the question. There were speculations, but their importance was not great. Accordingly, when the nineteenth century opened, the notion of physical occurrences pervading all space held no effective place in science. It was revived from two sources. The undulatory theory of light triumphed, thanks to Thomas Young and Fresnel. This demands that there shall be something throughout space which can undulate. Accordingly, the ether was produced, as a sort of all pervading subtle material. Again the theory of electromagnetism finally, in Clerk Maxwell's hands, assumed a shape in which it demanded that there should be electromagnetic occurrences throughout all space. Maxwell's complete theory was not shaped until the eighteen-seventies. But it had been prepared for by many great men, Ampère, Oersted, Faraday. In accordance with the current materialistic outlook, these electromagnetic occurrences also required a material in which to happen. So again the ether was requisitioned. Then Maxwell, as the immediate first-fruits of his theory, demonstrated that the waves of light were merely waves of his electromagnetic occurrences. Accordingly, the theory of electromagnetism swallowed up the theory of light. It was a great simplification, and no one doubts its truth. But it had one unfortunate effect so far as materialism was concerned. For, whereas quite a simple sort of elastic ether sufficed for light when taken by itself, the electromagnetic ether has to be endowed with just those properties necessary for the production of the electromagnetic occurrences. In fact, it becomes a mere name for the material which is postulated to underlie these occurrences. If you do not happen to hold the metaphysical theory which makes you postulate such an ether, you can discard it. For it has no independent vitality.

Thus in the seventies of the last century, some main physical sciences were established on a basis which presupposed the idea of *continuity*. On the other hand, the idea of *atomicity* had been introduced by John Dalton, to complete Lavoisier's work on the foundation of chemistry. This is the second great notion. Ordinary matter was conceived as atomic: electromagnetic effects were conceived as arising from a continuous field.

There was no contradiction. In the first place, the notions are antithetical; but, apart from special embodiments, are not logically contradictory. Secondly, they were applied to different regions of science, one to chemistry, and the other to electromagnetism. And, as yet, there were but faint signs of coalescence between the two.

The notion of matter as atomic has a long history. Democritus and Lucretius will at once occur to your minds. In speaking of these ideas as novel, I merely mean *relatively novel*, having regard to the settlement of ideas which formed the efficient basis of science throughout the eighteenth century. In considering the history of thought, it is necessary to distinguish the real stream, determining a period, from ineffectual thoughts casually entertained. In the eighteenth century every well-educated man read Lucretius, and entertained ideas about atoms. But John Dalton made them efficient in the stream of science; and in this function of efficiency atomicity was a new idea.

The influence of atomicity was not limited to chemistry. The living cell is to biology what the electron and the proton are to physics. Apart from cells and from aggregates of cells there are no biological phenomena. The cell theory was introduced into biology contemporaneously with, and independently of, Dalton's atomic theory. The two theories are independent exemplifications of the same idea of 'atomism.' The biological cell theory was a gradual growth, and a mere list of dates and names illustrates the fact that the biological sciences, as effective schemes of thought, are barely one hundred years old. Bichât in 1801 elaborated a tissue theory: Johannes Müller in 1835 described 'cells' and demonstrated facts concerning their nature and relations: Schleiden in 1838 and Schwann in 1839 finally established their fundamental character. Thus by 1840 both biology and chemistry were established on an atomic basis. The final triumph of atomism had to wait for the arrival of electrons at the end of the century. The importance of the imaginative background is illustrated by the fact that nearly half a century after Dalton had done his work, another chemist, Louis Pasteur, carried over these same ideas of atomicity still further into the region of biology. The cell theory and Pasteur's work were in some respects more revolutionary than that of Dalton. For they introduced the notion of *organism* into the world of minute beings. There had been a tendency to treat the atom as an ultimate entity, capable only of external relations. This attitude of mind was breaking down under the influence of Mendeleef's periodic law. But Pasteur showed the decisive importance of the idea of organism at the stage of infinitesimal magnitude. The astronomers had shown us how big is the universe. The chemists and biologists teach us how small it is. There is in modern scientific practice a famous standard of length. It is rather small: to obtain it, you must divide a centimetre into one hundred million parts, and take one of them. Pasteur's organisms are a good deal bigger than this length. In connection with atoms, we now know that there are organisms for which such distances are uncomfortably great.

The remaining pair of new ideas to be ascribed to this epoch are both of them connected with the notion of transition or change. They are the doctrine of the conservation of energy, and the doctrine of evolution.

The doctrine of energy has to do with the notion of quantitative permanence underlying change. The doctrine of evolution has to do with the emergence of novel organisms as the outcome of change. The theory of energy lies in the province of physics. The theory of evolution lies mainly in the province of biology, although it had previously been touched upon by Kant and Laplace in connection with the formation of suns and planets.

The convergent effect of the new power for scientific advance, which resulted from these four ideas, transformed the middle period of the century into an orgy of scientific triumph.

Clear-sighted men, of the sort who are so clearly wrong, now proclaimed that the secrets of the physical universe were finally disclosed. If only you ignored everything which refused to come into line, your powers of explanation were unlimited. On the other side, muddle-headed men muddled themselves into the most indefensible positions. Learned dogmatism, conjoined with ignorance of the crucial facts, suffered a heavy defeat from the scientific advocates of new ways. Thus to the excitement derived from technological revolution, there was now added the excitement arising from the vistas disclosed by scientific theory. Both the material and the spiritual bases of social life were in process of transformation. When the century entered upon its last quarter, its three sources of inspiration, the romantic, the technological, and the scientific had done their work.

Then, almost suddenly, a pause occurred; and in its last twenty years the century closed with one of the dullest stages of thought since the time of the First Crusade. It was an echo of the eighteenth century, lacking Voltaire and the reckless grace of the French aristocrats. The period was efficient, dull, and half-hearted. It celebrated the triumph of the professional man.

But looking backwards upon this time of pause, we can now discern signs of change. In the first place, the modern conditions of systematic research prevent absolute stagnation. In every branch of science, there was effective progress, indeed rapid progress, although it was confined somewhat strictly within the accepted ideas of each branch. It was an age of successful scientific orthodoxy, undisturbed by much thought beyond the conventions.

In the second place, we can now see that the adequacy of scientific materialism as a scheme of thought for the use of science was endangered. The conservation of energy provided a new type of quantitative permanence. It is true that energy could be construed as something subsidiary to matter. But, anyhow, the notion of *mass* was losing its unique preeminence as being the one final permanent quantity. Later on, we find the relations of mass and energy inverted; so that mass now becomes the name for a quantity of energy considered in relation to some of its dynamical effects. This train of thought leads to the notion of energy being fundamental, thus displacing matter from that position. But energy is merely the name for the quantitative aspect of a structure of happenings; in short, it depends on the notion of the functioning of an organism. The question is, can we define an organism without recurrence to the concept of matter in simple location? We must, later on, consider this point in more detail.

The same relegation of matter to the background occurs in connection with the electromagnetic fields. The modern theory presupposes happenings in that field which are divorced from immediate dependence upon matter. It is usual to provide an ether as a substratum. But the ether does not really enter into the theory. Thus again the notion of material loses its fundamental position. Also, the atom is transforming itself into an organism; and finally the evolution theory is nothing else than the analysis of the conditions for the formation and survival of various types of organisms. In truth, one most significant fact of this later period is the advance in biological sciences. These sciences are essentially sciences concerning organisms. During the epoch in question, and indeed also at the present moment, the prestige of the more perfect scientific form belongs to the physical sciences. Accordingly, biology apes the manners of physics. It is orthodox to hold, that there is nothing in biology but what is physical mechanism under somewhat complex circumstances.

One difficulty in this position is the present confusion as to the foundational concepts of physical science. This same difficulty also attaches to the opposed doctrine of vitalism. For, in this later theory, the fact of mechanism is accepted—I mean, mechanism based upon materialism—and an additional vital control is introduced to explain the actions of living bodies. It cannot be too clearly understood that the various physical laws which appear to apply to the behaviour of atoms are not mutually consistent as at present formulated. The appeal to mechanism on behalf of biology was in its origin an appeal to the well-attested self-consistent physical concepts as expressing the basis of all natural phenomena. But at present there is no such system of concepts.

Science is taking on a new aspect which is neither purely physical, nor purely biological. It is becoming the study of organisms. Biology is the study of the larger organisms; whereas physics is the study of the smaller organisms. There is another difference between the two divisions of science. The organisms of biology include as ingredients the smaller organisms of physics; but there is at present no evidence that the smaller of the physical organisms can be analysed into component organisms. It may be so. But anyhow we are faced with the question as to whether there are not primary organisms which are incapable of further analysis. It seems very unlikely that there should be any infinite regress in nature. Accordingly, a theory of science which discards materialism must answer the question as to the character of these primary entities. There can be only one answer on this basis. We must start with the event as the ultimate unit of natural occurrence. An event has to do with all that there is, and in particular with all other events. This interfusion of events is effected by the aspects of those eternal objects, such as colours, sounds, scents, geometrical characters, which are required for nature and are not emergent from it. Such an eternal object will be an ingredient of one event under the guise, or aspect, of qualifying another event. There is a reciprocity of aspects, and there are patterns of aspects. Each event corresponds to two such patterns; namely, the pattern of aspects of other events which it grasps into its own unity, and the pattern of its aspects which other events severally grasp into their unities. Accordingly, a non-materialistic philosophy of nature will identify a primary organism as being the emergence of some particular pattern as grasped in the unity of a real event. Such a pattern will also include the aspects of the event in question as grasped in other events, whereby those other events receive a modification, or partial determination. There is thus an intrinsic and an extrinsic reality of an event, namely, the event as in its own prehension, and the event as in the prehension of other events. The concept of an organism includes, therefore, the concept of the interaction of organisms. The ordinary scientific ideas of transmission and continuity are, relatively speaking, details concerning the empirically observed characters of these patterns throughout space and time. The position here maintained is that the relationships of an event are internal, so far as concerns the event itself; that is to say, that they are constitutive of what the event is in itself.

Also in the previous lecture, we arrived at the notion that an actual event is an achievement for its own sake, a grasping of diverse entities into a value by reason of their real togetherness in that pattern, to the exclusion of other entities. It is not the mere logical togetherness of merely diverse things. For in that case, to modify Bacon's words, "all eternal objects would be alike one to another." This reality means that each intrinsic essence, that is to say, what each eternal object is in itself, becomes relevant to the one limited value emergent in the guise of the event. But values differ in importance. Thus though each event is necessary for the community of events, the weight of its contribution is determined by something intrinsic in itself. We have now to discuss what that property is. Empirical observation shows that it is the property which we may call indifferently *retention*, *endurance* or *reiteration*. This property amounts to the recovery, on behalf of value amid the transitoriness of reality, of the self-identity which is also enjoyed by the primary eternal objects. The reiteration of a particular shape (or formation) of value within an event occurs when the event as a whole repeats some shape which is also exhibited by each one of a succession of its parts. Thus however you analyse the event according to the flux of its parts through time, there is the same thing-for-its-own-sake standing before you. Thus the event, in its own intrinsic reality, mirrors in itself, as derived from its own parts, aspects of the same patterned value as it realises in its complete self. It thus realises itself under the guise of an enduring individual entity, with a life history contained within itself. Furthermore, the extrinsic reality of such an event, as mirrored in other events, takes this same form of an enduring individuality; only in this case, the individuality is implanted as a reiteration of aspects of itself in the alien events composing the environment.

The total temporal duration of such an event bearing an enduring pattern, constitutes its specious present. Within this specious present the event realises itself as a totality, and also in so doing realises itself as grouping together a number of aspects of its own temporal parts. One and the same pattern is realised in the total event, and is exhibited by each of these various parts through an aspect of each part grasped into the togetherness of the total event. Also, the earlier life-history of the same pattern is exhibited by its aspects in this total event. There is, thus, in this event a memory of the antecedent life-history of its own dominant pattern, as having formed an element of value in its own antecedent environment. This concrete prehension, from within, of the life-history of an enduring fact is analysable into two abstractions, of which one is the enduring entity which has emerged as a real matter of fact to be taken account of by other things, and the other is the individualised embodiment of the underlying energy of realisation.

The consideration of the general flux of events leads to this analysis into an underlying eternal energy in whose nature there stands an envisagement of the realm of all eternal objects. Such an envisagement is the ground of the individualised thoughts which emerge as thought-aspects grasped within the life-history of the subtler and more complex enduring patterns. Also in the nature of the eternal activity there must stand an envisagement of all values to be obtained by a real togetherness of eternal objects, as envisaged in ideal situations. Such ideal situations, apart from any reality, are devoid of intrinsic value, but are valuable as elements in purpose. The individualised prehension into individual events of aspects of these ideal situations takes the form of individualised thoughts, and as such has intrinsic value. Thus value arises because there is now a real togetherness of the ideal aspects, as in thought, with the actual aspects, as in process of occurrence. Accordingly no value is to be ascribed to the underlying activity as divorced from the matter-of-fact events of the real world.

Finally, to sum up this train of thought, the underlying activity, as conceived apart from the fact of realisation, has three types of envisagement. These are: first, the envisagement of eternal objects; secondly, the envisagement of possibilities of value in respect to the synthesis of eternal objects; and lastly, the envisagement of the actual matter of fact which must enter into the total situation which is achievable by the addition of the future. But in abstraction from actuality, the eternal activity is divorced from value. For the actuality is the value. The individual perception arising from enduring objects will vary in its individual depth and width according to the way in which the pattern dominates its own route. It may represent the faintest ripple differentiating the general substrate energy; or, in the other extreme, it may rise to conscious thought, which includes poising before self-conscious judgment the abstract possibilities of value inherent in various situations of ideal togetherness. The intermediate cases will group round the individual perception as envisaging (without self-consciousness) that one immediate possibility of attainment which represents the closest analogy to its own immediate past, having regard to the actual aspects which are there for prehension. The laws of physics represent the harmonised adjustment of development which results from this unique principle of determination. Thus dynamics is dominated by a principle of least action, whose detailed character has to be learnt from observation.

The atomic material entities which are considered in physical science are merely these individual enduring entities, conceived in abstraction from everything except what concerns their mutual interplay in determining each other's historical routes of life-history. Such entities are partially formed by the inheritance of aspects from their own past. But they are also partially formed by the aspects of other events forming their environments. The laws of physics are the laws declaring how the entities mutually react among themselves. For physics these laws are arbitrary, because that science has abstracted from what the entities are in themselves. We have seen that this fact of what the entities are in themselves is liable to modification by their environments. Accordingly, the assumption that no modification of these laws is to be looked for in environments, which have any striking difference from the environments for which the laws have been observed to hold, is very unsafe. The physical entities may be modified in very essential ways, so far as these laws are concerned. It is even possible that they may be developed into individualities of more fundamental types, with wider embodiment of envisagement. Such envisagement might reach to the attainment of the poising of alternative values with exercise of choice lying outside the physical laws, and expressible only in terms of purpose. Apart from such remote possibilities, it remains an immediate deduction that an individual entity, whose own life-history is a part within the life-history of some larger, deeper, more complete pattern, is liable to have aspects of that larger pattern dominating its own being, and to experience modifications of that larger pattern reflected in itself as modifications of its own being. This is the theory of organic mechanism.

According to this theory the evolution of laws of nature is concurrent with the evolution of enduring pattern. For the general state of the universe, as it now is, partly determines the very essences of the entities whose modes of functioning these laws express. The general principle is that in a new environment there is an evolution of the old entities into new forms.

This rapid outline of a thoroughgoing organic theory of nature enables us to understand the chief requisites of the doctrine of evolution. The main work, proceeding during this pause at the end of the nineteenth century, was the absorption of this doctrine as guiding the methodology of all branches of science. By a blindness which is almost judicial as being a penalty affixed to hasty, superficial thinking, many religious thinkers opposed the new doctrine; although, in truth, a thoroughgoing evolutionary philosophy is inconsistent with materialism. The aboriginal stuff, or material, from which a materialistic philosophy starts is incapable of evolution. This material is in itself the ultimate substance. Evolution, on the materialistic theory, is reduced to the rôle of being another word for the description of the changes of the external relations between portions of matter. There is nothing to evolve, because one set of external relations is as good as any other set of external relations. There can merely be change, purposeless and unprogressive. But the whole point of the modern doctrine is the evolution of the complex organisms from antecedent states of less complex organisms. The doctrine thus cries aloud for a conception of organism as fundamental for nature. It also requires an underlying activity—a substantial activity—expressing itself in individual embodiments, and evolving in achievements of organism. The organism is a unit of emergent value, a real fusion of the characters of eternal objects, emerging for its own sake.

Thus in the process of analysing the character of nature in itself, we find that the emergence of organisms depends on a selective activity which is akin to purpose. The point is that the enduring organisms are now the outcome of evolution; and that, beyond these organisms, there is nothing else that endures. On the materialistic theory, there is material—such as matter or electricity—which endures. On the organic theory, the only endurances are structures of activity, and the structures are evolved.

Enduring things are thus the outcome of a temporal process; whereas eternal things are the elements required for the very being of the process. We can give a precise definition of endurance in this way: Let an event *A* be pervaded by an enduring structural pattern. Then *A* can be exhaustively subdivided into a temporal succession of events. Let *B* be any part of *A*, which is obtained by picking out any one of the events belonging to a series which thus subdivides *A*. Then the enduring pattern is a pattern of aspects within the complete pattern prehended into the unity of *A*, and it is also a pattern within the complete pattern prehended into the unity of any temporal slice of *A*, such as *B*. For example, a molecule is a pattern exhibited in an event of one minute, and of any second of that minute. It is obvious that such an enduring pattern may be of more, or of less, importance. It may express some slight fact connecting the underlying activities thus individualised; or it may express some very close connection. If the pattern which endures is merely derived from the direct aspects of the external environment, mirrored in the standpoints of the various parts, then the endurance is an extrinsic fact of slight importance. But if the enduring pattern is wholly derived from the direct aspects of the various temporal sections of the event in question, then the endurance is an important intrinsic fact. It expresses a certain unity of character uniting the underlying individualised activities. There is then an enduring object with a certain unity for itself and for the rest of nature. Let us use the term physical endurance to express endurance of this type. Then physical endurance is the process of continuously inheriting a certain identity of character transmitted throughout a historical route of events. This character belongs to the whole route, and to every event of the route. This is the exact property of material. If it has existed for ten minutes, it has existed during every minute of the ten minutes, and during every second of every minute. Only if you take *material* to be fundamental, this property of endurance is an arbitrary fact at the base of the order of nature; but if you take *organism* to be fundamental, this property is the result of evolution.

It looks at first sight, as if a physical object, with its process of inheritance from itself, were independent of the environment. But such a conclusion is not justified. For let *B* and *C* be two successive slices in the life of such an object, such that *C* succeeds *B*. Then the enduring pattern in *C* is inherited from *B*, and from other analogous antecedent parts of its life. It is transmitted through *B* to *C*. But what is transmitted to *C* is the complete pattern of aspects derived from such events as *B*. These complete patterns include the influence of the environment on *B*, and on the other antecedent parts of the life of the object. Thus the complete aspects of the antecedent life are inherited as the partial pattern which endures throughout all the various periods of the life. Thus a favourable environment is essential to the maintenance of a physical object.

Nature, as we know it, comprises enormous permanences. There are the permanences of ordinary matter. The molecules within the oldest rocks known to geologists may have existed unchanged for over a thousand million years, not only unchanged in themselves, but unchanged in their relative dispositions to each other. In that length of time the number of pulsations of a molecule vibrating with the frequency of yellow sodium light would be about 16.3 × 1022 = 163,000 × $(106)^3$. Until recently, an atom was apparently indestructible. We know better now. But the indestructible atom has been succeeded by the apparently indestructible electron and the indestructible proton.

Another fact to be explained is the great similarity of these practically indestructible objects. All electrons are very similar to each other. We need not outrun the evidence, and say that they are identical; but our powers of observation cannot detect any differences. Analogously, all hydrogen nuclei are alike. Also we note the great numbers of these analogous objects. There are throngs of them. It seems as though a certain similarity were a favourable condition for endurance. Common sense also suggests this conclusion. If organisms are to survive, they must work together.

Accordingly, the key to the mechanism of evolution is the necessity for the evolution of a favourable environment, conjointly with the evolution of any specific type of enduring organisms of great permanence. Any physical object which by its influence deteriorates its environment, commits suicide.

One of the simplest ways of evolving a favourable environment concurrently with the development of the individual organism, is that the influence of each organism on the environment should be favourable to the *endurance* of other organisms of the same type. Further, if the organism also favours the *development* of other organisms of the same type, you have then obtained a mechanism of evolution adapted to produce the observed state of large multitudes of analogous entities, with high powers of endurance. For the environment automatically develops with the species, and the species with the environment.

The first question to ask is, whether there is any direct evidence for such a mechanism for the evolution of enduring organisms. In surveying nature, we must remember that there are not only basic organisms whose ingredients are merely aspects of eternal objects. There are also organisms of organisms. Suppose for the moment and for the sake of simplicity, we assume, without any evidence, that electrons and hydrogen nuclei are such basic organisms. Then the atoms, and the molecules, are organisms of a higher type, which also represent a compact definite organic unity. But when we come to the larger aggregations of matter, the organic unity fades into the background. It appears to be but faint and elementary. It is there; but the pattern is vague and indecisive. It is a mere aggregation of effects. When we come to living beings, the definiteness of pattern is recovered, and the organic character again rises into prominence. Accordingly, the characteristic laws of inorganic matter are mainly the statistical averages resulting from confused aggregates. So far are they from throwing light on the ultimate nature of things, that they blur and obliterate the individual characters of the individual organisms. If we wish to throw light upon the facts relating to organisms, we must study either the individual molecules and electrons, or the individual living beings. In between we find comparative confusion. Now the difficulty of studying the individual molecule is that we know so little about its life history. We cannot keep an individual under continuous observation. In general, we deal with them in large aggregates. So far as individuals are concerned, sometimes with difficulty a great experimenter throws, so to speak, a flash light on one of them, and just observes one type of instantaneous effect. Accordingly, the history of the functioning of individual molecules, or electrons, is largely hidden from us.

But in the case of living beings, we can trace the history of individuals. We now find exactly the mechanism which is here demanded. In the first place, there is the propagation of the species from members of the same species. There is also the careful provision of the favourable environment for the endurance of the family, the race, or the seed in the fruit.

It is evident, however, that I have explained the evolutionary mechanism in terms which are far too simple. We find associated species of living things, providing for each other a favourable environment. Thus just as the members of the same species mutually favour each other, so do members of associated species. We find the rudimentary fact of association in the existence of the two species, electrons and hydrogen nuclei. The simplicity of the dual association, and the apparent absence of competition from other antagonistic species accounts for the massive endurance which we find among them.

There are thus two sides to the machinery involved in the development of nature. On one side, there is a given environment with organisms adapting themselves to it. The scientific materialism of the epoch in question emphasised this aspect. From this point of view, there is a given amount of material, and only a limited number of organisms can take advantage of it. The givenness of the environment dominates everything. Accordingly, the last words of science appeared to be the Struggle for Existence, and Natural Selection. Darwin's own writings are for all time a model of refusal to go beyond the direct evidence, and of careful retention of every possible hypothesis. But those virtues were not so conspicuous in his followers, and still less in his camp-followers. The imagination of European sociologists and publicists was stained by exclusive attention to this aspect of conflicting interests. The idea prevailed that there was a peculiar strong-minded realism in discarding ethical considerations in the determination of the conduct of commercial and national interests.

The other side of the evolutionary machinery, the neglected side, is expressed by the word *creativeness*. The organisms can create their own environment. For this purpose, the single organism is almost helpless. The adequate forces require societies of co-operating organisms. But with such cooperation and in proportion to the effort put forward, the environment has a plasticity which alters the whole ethical aspect of evolution.

In the immediate past, and at present, a muddled state of mind is prevalent. The increased plasticity of the environment for mankind, resulting from the advances in scientific technology, is being construed in terms of habits of thought which find their justification in the theory of a fixed environment.

The riddle of the universe is not so simple. There is the aspect of permanence in which a given type of attainment is endlessly repeated for its own sake; and there is the aspect of transition to other things,—it may be of higher worth, and it may be of lower worth. Also there are its aspects of struggle and of friendly help. But romantic ruthlessness is no nearer to real politics, than is romantic self-abnegation.

Chapter VII

RELATIVITY

IN THE PREVIOUS LECTURES of this course we have considered the antecedent conditions which led up to the scientific movement, and have traced the progress of thought from the seventeenth to the nineteenth century. In the nineteenth century this history falls into three parts, so far as it is to be grouped around science. These divisions are, the contact between the romantic movement and science, the development of technology and physics in the earlier part of the century, and lastly the theory of evolution combined with the general advance of the biological sciences.

The dominating note of the whole period of three centuries is that the doctrine of materialism afforded an adequate basis for the concepts of science. It was practically unquestioned. When undulations were wanted, an ether was supplied, in order to perform the duties of an undulatory material. To show the full assumption thus involved, I have sketched in outline an alternative doctrine of an organic theory of nature. In the last lecture it was pointed out that the biological developments, the doctrine of evolution, the doctrine of energy, and the molecular theories were rapidly undermining the adequacy of the orthodox materialism. But until the close of the century no one drew that conclusion. Materialism reigned supreme.

The note of the present epoch is that so many complexities have developed regarding material, space, time, and energy, that the simple security of the old orthodox assumptions has vanished. It is obvious that they will not do as Newton left them, or even as

Clerk Maxwell left them. There must be a reorganization. The new situation in the thought of to-day arises from the fact that scientific theory is outrunning common sense. The settlement as inherited by the eighteenth century was a triumph of organised common sense. It had got rid of medieval phantasies, and of Cartesian vortices. As a result it gave full reign to its anti-rationalistic tendencies derived from the historical revolt of the Reformation period. It grounded itself upon what every plain man could see with his own eyes, or with a microscope of moderate power. It measured the obvious things to be measured, and it generalised the obvious things to be generalised. For example, it generalised the ordinary notions of weight and massiveness. The eighteenth century opened with the quiet confidence that at last nonsense had been got rid of. To-day we are at the opposite pole of thought. Heaven knows what seeming nonsense may not to-morrow be demonstrated truth. We have recaptured some of the tone of the early nineteenth century, only on a higher imaginative level.

The reason why we are on a higher imaginative level is not because we have finer imagination, but because we have better instruments. In science, the most important thing that has happened during the last forty years is the advance in instrumental design. This advance is partly due to a few men of genius such as Michelson and the German opticians. It is also due to the progress of technological processes of manufacture, particularly in the region of metallurgy. The designer has now at his disposal a variety of material of differing physical properties. He can thus depend upon obtaining the material he desires; and it can be ground to the shapes he desires, within very narrow limits of tolerance. These instruments have put thought onto a new level. A fresh instrument serves the same purpose as foreign travel; it shows things in unusual combinations. The gain is more than a mere addition; it is a transformation. The advance in experimental ingenuity is, perhaps, also due to the larger proportion of national ability which now flows into scientific pursuits. Anyhow, whatever be the cause, subtle and ingenious experiments have abounded within the last generation. The result is, that a great deal of information has been accumulated in regions of nature very far removed from the ordinary experience of mankind.

Two famous experiments, one devised by Galileo at the outset of the scientific movement, and the other by Michelson with the aid of his famous interferometer, first carried out in 1881, and repeated in 1887 and 1905, illustrate the assertions I have made. Galileo dropped heavy bodies from the top of the leaning tower of Pisa, and demonstrated that bodies of different weights, if released simultaneously, would reach the earth together. So far as experimental skill, and delicacy of apparatus were concerned, this experiment could have been made at any time within the preceding five thousand years. The ideas involved merely concerned weight and speed of travel, ideas which are familiar in ordinary life. The whole set of ideas might have been familiar to the family of King Minos of Crete, as they dropped pebbles into the sea from high battlements rising from the shore. We cannot too carefully realise that science started with the organisation of ordinary experiences. It was in this way that it coalesced so readily with the anti-rationalistic bias of the historical revolt. It was not asking for ultimate meanings. It confined itself to investigating the connections regulating the succession of obvious occurrences.

Michelson's experiment could not have been made earlier than it was. It required the general advance in technology, and Michelson's experimental genius. It concerns the determination of the earth's motion through the ether, and it assumes that light consists of waves of vibration advancing at a fixed rate through the ether in any direction. Also, of course, the earth is moving through the ether, and Michelson's apparatus is moving with the earth. In the centre of the apparatus a ray of light is divided so that one half-ray goes in one direction *along* the apparatus through a given distance, and is reflected back to the centre by a mirror in the apparatus. The other half-ray goes the same distance *across* the apparatus in a direction at right angles to the former ray, and it also is reflected back to the centre. These reunited rays are then reflected onto a screen in the apparatus. If precautions are taken, you will see interference bands; namely bands of blackness where the crests of the waves of one ray have filled up the troughs of the other rays, owing to a minute difference in the lengths of paths of the two half-rays, up to certain parts of the screens. These differences in length will be affected by the motion of the earth. For it is the lengths of the paths in the ether which count. Thus, since the apparatus is moving with the earth, the path of one half-ray will be disturbed by the motion in a different manner from the path of the other half-ray. Think of yourself as moving in a railway carriage, first along the train and then across the train; and mark out your paths on the railway track which in this analogy corresponds to the ether. Now the motion of the earth is very slow compared to that of light. Thus in the analogy you must think of the train almost at a standstill, and of yourself as moving very quickly.

In the experiment this effect of the earth's motion would affect the positions on the screen of the interference bands. Also if you turn the apparatus round, through a right-angle, the effect of the earth's motion on the two half-rays will be interchanged, and the positions of the interference bands would be shifted. We can calculate the small shift which should result owing to the earth's motion round the sun. Also to this effect, we have to add that due to the sun's motion through the ether. The delicacy of the instrument can be tested, and it can be proved that these effects of shifting are large enough to be observed by it. Now the point is, that nothing was observed. There was no shifting as you turned the instrument round.

The conclusion is either that the earth is always stationary in the ether, or that there is something wrong with the fundamental principles on which the interpretation of the experiment relies. It is obvious that, in this experiment, we are very far away from the thoughts and the games of the children of King Minos. The ideas of an ether, of waves in it, of interference, of the motion of the earth through the ether, and of Michelson's interferometer, are remote from ordinary experience. But remote as they are, they are simple and obvious compared to the accepted explanation of the nugatory result of the experiment.

The ground of the explanation is that the ideas of space and of time employed in science are too simple-minded, and must be modified. This conclusion is a direct challenge to common sense, because the earlier science had only refined upon the ordinary notions of ordinary people. Such a radical reorganization of ideas would not have been adopted, unless it had also been supported by many other observations which we need not enter upon. Some form of the relativity theory seems to be the simplest way of explaining a large number of facts which otherwise would each require some *ad hoc* explanation. The theory, therefore, does not merely depend upon the experiments which led to its origination.

The central point of the explanation is that every instrument, such as Michelson's apparatus as used in the experiment, necessarily records the velocity of light as having one and the same definite speed relatively to it. I mean that an interferometer in a comet and an interferometer on the earth would necessarily bring out the velocity of light, relatively to themselves, as at the same value. This is an obvious paradox, since the light moves with a definite velocity through the ether. Accordingly two bodies, the earth and the comet, moving with unequal velocities through the ether, might be expected to have different velocities relatively to rays of light. For example, consider two cars on a road, moving at ten and twenty miles an hour respectively, and being passed by another car at fifty miles an hour. The rapid car will pass one of the two cars at the relative velocity of forty miles per hour, and the other at the rate of thirty miles per hour. The allegation as to light is that, if we substituted a ray of light for the rapid car, the velocity of the light along the roadway would be exactly the same as its velocity relatively to either of the two cars which it overtakes. The velocity of light is immensely large, being about three hundred thousand kilometres per second. We must have notions as to space and time such that just this velocity has this peculiar character. It follows that all our notions of relative velocity must be recast. But these notions are the immediate outcome of our habitual notions as to space and time. So we come back to the position, that there has been something overlooked in the current expositions of what we mean by space and of what we mean by time.

Now our habitual fundamental assumption is that there is a unique meaning to be given to space and a unique meaning to be given to time, so that whatever meaning is given to spatial relations in respect to the instrument on the earth, the same meaning must be given to them in respect to the instrument on the comet, and the same meaning for an instrument at rest in the ether. In the theory of relativity, this is denied. As far as concerns space, there is no difficulty in agreeing, if you think of the obvious facts of relative motion. But even here the change in meaning has to go further than would be sanctioned by common sense. Also the same demand is made for time; so that the relative dating of events and the lapses of time between them are to be reckoned as different for the instrument on the earth, for the instrument in the comet, and for the instrument at rest in the ether. This is a greater strain on our credulity. We need not probe the question further than the conclusion that for the earth and for the comet spatiality and temporality are each to have different meanings amid different conditions, such as those presented by the earth and the comet. Accordingly velocity has different meanings for the two bodies. Thus the modern scientific assumption is that if anything has the speed of light by reference to any one meaning of space and time, then it has the same speed according to any other meaning of space and time.

This is a heavy blow at the classical scientific materialism, which presupposes a definite present instant at which all matter is simultaneously real. In the modern theory there is no such unique present instant. You can find a meaning for the notion of the simultaneous instant throughout all nature, but it will be a different meaning for different notions of temporality.

There has been a tendency to give an extreme subjectivist interpretation to this new doctrine. I mean that the relativity of space and time has been construed as though it were dependent on the choice of the observer. It is perfectly legitimate to bring in the observer, if he facilitates explanations. But it is the observer's body that we want, and not his mind. Even this body is only useful as an example of a very familiar form of apparatus. On the whole, it is better to concentrate attention on Michelson's interferometer, and to leave Michelson's body and Michelson's mind out of the picture. The question is, why did the interferometer have black bands on its screen, and why did not these bands slightly shift as the instrument turned. The new relativity associates space and time with an intimacy not hitherto contemplated; and presupposes that their separation in concrete fact can be achieved by alternative modes of abstraction, yielding alternative meanings. But each mode of abstraction is directing attention to something which is in nature; and thereby is isolating it for the purpose of contemplation. The fact relevant to experiment, is the relevance of the interferometer to just one among the many alternative systems of these spatio-temporal relations which hold between natural entities.

What we must now ask of philosophy is to give us an interpretation of the status in nature of space and time, so that the possibility of alternative meanings is preserved. These lectures are not suited for the elaboration of details; but there is no difficulty in pointing out where to look for the origin of the discrimination between space and time. I am presupposing the organic theory of nature, which I have outlined as a basis for a thoroughgoing objectivism.

An event is the grasping into unity of a pattern of aspects. The effectiveness of an event beyond itself arises from the aspects of itself which go to form the prehended unities of other events.

Except for the systematic aspects of geometrical shape, this effectiveness is trivial, if the mirrored pattern attaches merely to the event as one whole. If the pattern endures throughout the successive parts of the event, and also exhibits itself in the whole, so that the event is the life history of the pattern, then in virtue of that enduring pattern the event gains in external effectiveness. For its own effectiveness is reënforced by the analogous aspects of all its successive parts. The event constitutes a patterned value with a permanence inherent throughout its own parts; and by reason of this inherent endurance the event is important for the modification of its environment.

It is in this endurance of pattern that time differentiates itself from space. The pattern is spatially *now*; and this temporal determination constitutes its relation to each partial event. For it is reproduced in this temporal succession of these spatial parts of its own life. I mean that this particular rule of temporal order allows the pattern to be reproduced in each temporal slice of its history. So to speak, each enduring object discovers in nature and requires from nature a principle discriminating space from time. Apart from the fact of an enduring pattern this principle might be there, but it would be latent and trivial. Thus the importance of space as against time, and of time as against space, has developed with the development of enduring organisms. Enduring objects are significant of a differentiation of space from time in respect to the patterns ingredient within events; and conversely the differentiation of space from time in the patterns ingredient within events expresses the patience of the community of events for enduring objects. There might be the community without objects, but there could not be the enduring objects without the community with its peculiar patience for them.

It is very necessary that this point should not be misunderstood. Endurance means that a pattern which is exhibited in the prehension of one event is also exhibited in the prehension of those of its parts which are discriminated by a certain rule. It is not true that any part of the whole event will yield the same pattern as does the whole. For example, consider the total bodily pattern exhibited in the life of a human body during one minute. One of the thumbs during the same minute is part of the whole bodily event. But the pattern of this part is the pattern of the thumb, and is not the pattern of the whole body. Thus endurance requires a definite rule for obtaining the parts. In the above example, we know at once what the rule is: You must take the life of the whole body during any portion of that same minute; for example, during a second or a tenth of a second. In other words, the meaning of endurance presupposes a meaning for the lapse of time within the spatio-temporal continuum.

The question now arises whether all enduring objects discover the same principle of differentiation of space from time; or even whether at different stages of its own life-history one object may not vary in its spatio-temporal discrimination. Up till a few years ago, everyone unhesitatingly assumed that there was only one such principle to be discovered. Accordingly, in dealing with one object, time would have exactly the same meaning in reference to endurance as in dealing with the endurance of another object. It would also follow then that spatial relations would have one unique meaning. But now it seems that the observed effectiveness of objects can only be explained by assuming that objects in a state of motion relatively to each other are utilising, for their endurance, meanings of space and of time which are not identical from one object to another. Every enduring object is to be conceived as at rest in its own proper space, and in motion throughout any space defined in a way which is not that inherent in its peculiar endurance. If two objects are mutually at rest, they are utilising the same meanings of space and of time for the purposes of expressing their endurance; if in relative motion, the spaces and times differ. It follows that, if we can conceive a body at one stage of its life history as in motion relatively to itself at another stage, then the body at these two stages is utilising diverse meanings of space, and correlatively diverse meanings of time.

In an organic philosophy of nature there is nothing to decide between the old hypothesis of the uniqueness of the time discrimination and the new hypothesis of its multiplicity. It is purely a matter for evidence drawn from observations[1].

In an earlier lecture, I said that an event had contemporaries. It is an interesting question whether, on the new hypothesis, such a statement can be made without the qualification of a reference to a definite space-time system. It is possible to do so, in the sense that in *some* time-system or other the two events are simultaneous. In other time-systems the two contemporary events will not be simultaneous, though they may overlap. Analogously one event will precede another without qualification, if in *every* time-system this precedence occurs. It is evident that if we start from a given event *A*, other events in general are divided into two sets, namely, those which without qualification are contemporaneous with *A* and those which either precede or succeed *A*. But there will be a set left over, namely, those events which bound the two sets. There we have a critical case. You will remember that we have a critical velocity to account for, namely the theoretical velocity of light *in vacuo*[2]. Also you will remember that the utilisation of different spatio-temporal systems means the relative motion of objects. When we analyse this critical relation of a special set of events to any given event *A*, we find the explanation of the critical velocity which we require. I am suppressing all details. It is evident that exactness of statement must be introduced by the introduction of points, and lines, and instants. Also that the origin of geometry requires discussion; for example, the measurement

1. *Cf.* my *Principles of Natural Knowledge*, Sec. 52:3.
2. This is not the velocity of light in a gravitational field or in a medium of molecules and electrons.

of lengths, the straightness of lines, and the flatness of planes, and perpendicularity. I have endeavoured to carry out these investigations in some earlier books, under the heading of the theory of extensive abstraction; but they are too technical for the present occasion.

If there be no one definite meaning to the geometrical relations of distance, it is evident that the law of gravitation needs restatement. For the formula expressing that law is that two particles attract each other in proportion to the product of their masses and the inverse square of their distances. This enunciation tacitly assumes that there is one definite meaning to be ascribed to the instant at which the attraction is considered, and also one definite meaning to be ascribed to *distance*. But distance is a purely spatial notion, so that in the new doctrine, there are an indefinite number of such meanings according to the space-time system which you adopt. If the two particles are relatively at rest, then we might be content with the space-time systems which they are both utilising. Unfortunately this suggestion gives no hint as to procedure when they are not mutually at rest. It is, therefore, necessary to reformulate the law in a way which does not presuppose any particular space-time system. Einstein has done this. Naturally the result is more complicated. He introduced into mathematical physics certain methods of pure mathematics which render the formulae independent of the particular systems of measurement adopted. The new formula introduces various small effects which are absent in Newton's law. But for the major effects Newton's law and Einstein's law agree. Now these extra effects of Einstein's law serve to explain irregularities of the planet Mercury's orbit which by Newton's law were inexplicable. This is a strong confirmation of the new theory. Curiously enough, there is more than one alternative formula, based on the new theory of multiple space-time systems, having the property of embodying Newton's law and in addition of explaining the peculiarities of Mercury's motion. The only method of selection between them is to wait for experimental evidence respecting those effects on which the formulae differ. Nature is probably quite indifferent to the aesthetic preferences of mathematicians.

It only remains to add that Einstein would probably reject the theory of multiple space-time systems which I have been expounding to you. He would interpret his formula in terms of contortions in space-time which alter the invariance theory for measure properties, and of the proper times of each historical route. His mode of statement has the greater mathematical simplicity, and only allows of one law of gravitation, excluding the alternatives. But, for myself, I cannot reconcile it with the given facts of our experience as to simultaneity, and spatial arrangement. There are also other difficulties of a more abstract character.

The theory of the relationship between events at which we have now arrived is based first upon the doctrine that the relatednesses of an event are all internal relations, so far as concerns that event, though not necessarily so far as concerns the other *relata*. For example, the eternal objects, thus involved, are externally related to events. This internal relatedness is the reason why an event can be found only just where it is and how it is,—that is to say, in just one definite set of relationships. For each relationship enters into the essence of the event; so that, apart from that relationship, the event would not be itself. This is what is meant by the very notion of internal relations. It has been usual, indeed universal, to hold that spatio-temporal relationships are external. This doctrine is what is here denied.

The conception of internal relatedness involves the analysis of the event into two factors, one the underlying substantial activity of individualisation, and the other the complex of aspects—that is to say, the complex of relatednesses as entering into the essence of the given event—which are unified by this individualised activity. In other words, the concept of internal relations requires the concept of substance as the activity synthesising the relationships into its emergent character. The event is what it is, by reason of the unification in itself of a multiplicity of relationships. The general scheme of these mutual relationships is an abstraction which presupposes each event as an independent entity, which it is not, and asks what remnant of these formative relationships is then left in the guise of external relationships. The scheme of relationships as thus impartially expressed becomes the scheme of a complex of events variously related as wholes to parts and as joint parts within some one whole. Even here, the internal relationship forces itself on our attention; for the part evidently is constitutive of the whole. Also an isolated event which has lost its status in any complex of events is equally excluded by the very nature of an event. So the whole is evidently constitutive of the part. Thus the internal character of the relationship really shows through this impartial scheme of abstract external relations.

But this exhibition of the actual universe as extensive and divisible has left out the distinction between space and time. It has in fact left out the process of realisation, which is the adjustment of the synthetic activities by virtue of which the various events become their realised selves. This adjustment is thus the adjustment of the underlying active substances whereby these substances exhibit themselves as the individualisations or modes of Spinoza's one substance. This adjustment is what introduces temporal process.

Thus, in some sense, time, in its character of the adjustment of the process of synthetic realisation, extends beyond the spatio-temporal continuum of nature[3]. There is no necessity that temporal process, in this sense, should be constituted by one single series of linear succession. Accordingly, in order to satisfy the present demands of scientific hypothesis, we introduce the metaphysical hypothesis that this is not the case. We do assume (basing ourselves upon direct observation), however, that temporal process of realisation can be analysed into a group of linear serial processes. Each of these linear series is a space-time system. In support of

3. *Cf.* my *Concept of Nature*, Ch. III.

this assumption of definite serial processes, we appeal: (1) to the immediate presentation through the senses of an extended universe beyond ourselves and *simultaneous* with ourselves, (2) to the intellectual apprehension of a meaning to the question which asks what is *now immediately happening* in regions beyond the cognisance of our senses, (3) to the analysis of what is involved in the *endurance* of emergent objects. This endurance of objects involves the display of a pattern as now realised. This display is the display of a pattern as inherent in an event, but also as exhibiting a temporal slice of nature as lending aspects to eternal objects (or, equally, of eternal objects as lending aspects to events). The pattern is spatialised in a whole duration for the benefit of the event into whose essence the pattern enters. The event is part of the duration, *i.e.*, is part of what is exhibited in the aspects inherent in itself; and conversely the duration is the whole of nature simultaneous with the event, in that sense of simultaneity. Thus an event in realising itself displays a pattern, and this pattern requires a definite duration determined by a definite meaning of simultaneity. Each such meaning of simultaneity relates the pattern as thus displayed to one definite space-time system. The actuality of the space-time systems is constituted by the realisation of pattern; but it is inherent in the general scheme of events as constituting its patience for the temporal process of realisation.

Notice that the pattern requires a duration involving a definite lapse of time, and not merely an instantaneous moment. Such a moment is more abstract, in that it merely denotes a certain relation of contiguity between the concrete events. Thus a duration is spatialised; and by 'spatialised' is meant that the duration is the field for the realised pattern constituting the character of the event. A duration, as the field of the pattern realised in the actualisation of one of its contained events, is an epoch, *i.e.*, an arrest. Endurance is the repetition of the pattern in successive events. Thus endurance requires a succession of durations, each exhibiting the pattern. In this account 'time' has been separated from 'extension' and from the 'divisibility' which arises from the character of spatio-temporal extension'. Accordingly we must not proceed to conceive time as another form of extensiveness. Time is sheer succession of epochal durations. But the entities which succeed each other in this account are durations. The duration is that which is required for the realisation of a pattern in the given event. Thus the divisibility and extensiveness is within the given duration. The epochal duration is not realised *via* its *successive* divisible parts, but is given *with* its parts. In this way, the objection which Zeno might make to the joint validity of two passages from Kant's *Critique of Pure Reason* is met by abandoning the earlier of the two passages. I refer to passages from the section 'Of the Axioms of Intuition'; the earlier from the subsection on *Extensive Quantity*, and the latter from the subsection on *Intensive Quantity* where considerations respecting quantity in general, extensive and intensive, are summed up. The earlier passage runs thus[4]:

> I call an extensive quantity that in which the representation of the whole is rendered possible by the representation of its parts, *and therefore necessarily preceded by it*[5]. I cannot represent to myself any line, however small it may be, without drawing it in thought, that is, without producing all its parts one after the other, starting from a given point, and thus, first of all, drawing its intuition. The same applies to every, even the smallest portion of time. I can only think in it the successive progress from one moment to another, thus producing in the end, by all the portions of time, and their addition, a definite quantity of time.

The second passage runs thus:

> This peculiar property of quantities that no part of them is the smallest possible part (no part indivisible) is called continuity. Time and space are quanta continua, because there is no part of them that is not enclosed between limits (points and moments),

4. Max Müller's translation.
5. Italics mine, and also in the second passage.

> *no part that is not itself again a space or a time. Space consists of spaces only, time of times. Points and moments are only limits,* mere places of limitation, and as places *presupposing always* those intuitions which they are meant to limit or to determine. Mere places or parts that might be given before space or time, could never be compounded into space or time.

I am in complete agreement with the second extract if 'time and space' is the extensive continuum; but it is inconsistent with its predecessor. For Zeno would object that a vicious infinite regress is involved. Every part of time involves some smaller part of itself, and so on. Also this series regresses backwards ultimately to nothing; since the initial moment is without duration and merely marks the relation of contiguity to an earlier time. Thus time is impossible, if the two extracts are both adhered to. I accept the later, and reject the earlier, passage. Realisation is the becoming of time in the field of extension. Extension is the complex of events, *quâ* their potentialities. In realisation the potentiality becomes actuality. But the potential pattern requires a duration; and the duration must be exhibited as an epochal whole, by the realisation of the pattern. Thus time is the succession of elements in themselves divisible and contiguous. A duration, in becoming temporal, thereby incurs realisation in respect to some enduring object. Temporalisation is realisation. Temporalisation is not another continuous process. It is an atomic succession. Thus time is atomic (*i.e.*, epochal), though what is temporalised is divisible. This doctrine follows from the doctrine of events, and of the nature of enduring objects. In the next chapter we must consider its relevance to the quantum theory of recent science.

It is to be noted that this doctrine of the epochal character of time does not depend on the modern doctrine of relativity, and holds equally—and indeed, more simply—if this doctrine be abandoned. It does depend on the analysis of the intrinsic character of an event, considered as the most concrete finite entity.

In reviewing this argument, note first that the second quotation from Kant, on which it is based, does not depend on any peculiar Kantian doctrine. The latter of the two is in agreement with Plato as against Aristotle[6]. In the second place, the argument assumes that Zeno understated his argument. He should have urged it against the current notion of time in itself, and not against motion, which involves relations between time and space. For, what becomes has duration. But no duration can become until a smaller duration (part of the former) has antecedently come into being [Kant's earlier statement]. The same argument applies to this smaller duration, and so on. Also the infinite regress of these durations converges to nothing—and even on the Aristotelian view there is no first moment. Accordingly time would be an irrational notion. Thirdly, in the epochal theory Zeno's difficulty is met by conceiving temporalisation as the realisation of a complete organism. This organism is an event holding in its essence its spatio-temporal relationships (both within itself, and beyond itself) throughout the spatio-temporal continuum.

---

6. *Cf.* 'Euclid in Greek,' by Sir T. L. Heath, Camb. Univ. Press, in a note on Points.

Chapter VIII

THE QUANTUM THEORY

THE THEORY OF RELATIVITY has justly excited a great amount of public attention. But, for all its importance, it has not been the topic which has chiefly absorbed the recent interest of physicists. Without question that position is held by the quantum theory. The point of interest in this theory is that, according to it, some effects which appear essentially capable of gradual increase or gradual diminution are in reality to be increased or decreased only by certain definite jumps. It is as though you could walk at three miles per hour or at four miles per hour, but not at three and a half miles per hour.

The effects in question are concerned with the radiation of light from a molecule which has been excited by some collision. Light consists of waves of vibration in the electromagnetic field. After a complete wave has passed a given point everything at that point is restored to its original state and is ready for the next wave which follows on. Picture to yourselves the waves on the ocean, and reckon from crest to crest of successive waves. The number of waves which pass a given point in one second is called the frequency of that system of waves. A system of light-waves of definite frequency corresponds to a definite colour in the spectrum. Now a molecule, when excited, vibrates with a certain number of definite frequencies. In other words, there are a definite set of modes of vibration of the molecule, and each mode of vibration has one definite frequency. Each mode of vibration can stir up in the electromagnetic field waves of its own frequency. These waves carry away the energy of the vibration; so that finally (when such waves are in being) the molecule loses the energy of its excitement and the waves cease. Thus a molecule can radiate light of certain definite colours, that is to say, of certain definite frequencies.

You would think that each mode of vibration could be excited to any intensity, so that the energy carried away by light of that frequency could be of any amount. But this is not the case. There appear to be certain minimum amounts of energy which cannot be subdivided. The case is analogous to that of a citizen of the United States who, in paying his debts in the currency of his country, cannot subdivide a cent so as to correspond to some minute subdivision of the goods obtained. The cent corresponds to the minimum quantity of the light energy, and the goods obtained correspond to the energy of the exciting cause. This exciting cause is either strong enough to procure the emission of one cent of energy, or fails to procure the emission of any energy whatsoever. In any case the molecule will only emit an integral number of cents of energy. There is a further peculiarity which we can illustrate by bringing an Englishman onto the scene. He pays his debts in English currency, and his smallest unit is a farthing which differs in value from the cent. The farthing is in fact about half a cent, to a very rough approximation. In the molecule, different modes of vibration have different frequencies. Compare each mode to a nation. One mode corresponds to the United States, and another mode corresponds to England. One mode can only radiate its energy in an integral number of cents, so that a cent of energy is the least it can pay out; whereas the other mode can only radiate its energy in an integral number of farthings, so that a farthing of energy is the least that it can pay out. Also a rule can be found to tell us the relative value of the cent of energy of one mode to the farthing of energy of another mode. The rule is childishly simple: Each smallest coin of energy has a value in strict proportion to the frequency belonging to that mode. By this rule, and comparing farthings with cents, the frequency of an American would be about twice that of an Englishman. In other words, the American would do about twice as many things in a second as an Englishman. I must leave you to judge whether this corresponds to the reputed characters of the two nations. Also I suggest that there are merits attaching to both ends of the solar spectrum. Sometimes you want red light and sometimes violet light.

There has been, I hope, no great difficulty in comprehending what the quantum theory asserts about molecules. The perplexity arises from the effort to fit the theory into the current scientific picture of what is going on in the molecule or atom.

It has been the basis of the materialistic theory, that the happenings of nature are to be explained in terms of the locomotion of material. In accordance with this principle, the waves of light were explained in terms of the locomotion of a material ether, and the internal happenings of a molecule are now explained in terms of the locomotion of separate material parts. In respect to waves of light, the material ether has retreated to an indeterminate position in the background, and is rarely talked about. But the principle is unquestioned as regards its application to the atom. For example a neutral hydrogen atom is assumed to consist of at least two lumps of material; one lump is the nucleus consisting of a material called positive electricity, and the other is a single electron which is negative electricity. The nucleus shows signs of being complex, and of being subdivisible into smaller lumps, some of positive electricity and others electronic. The assumption is, that whatever vibration takes place in the atom is to be attributed to the vibratory locomotion of some bit of material, detachable from the remainder. The difficulty with the quantum theory is that, on this hypothesis, we have to picture the atom as providing a limited number of definite grooves, which are the sole tracks along which vibration can take place, whereas the classical scientific picture provides none of these grooves. The quantum theory wants trolley-cars with a limited number of routes, and the scientific picture provides horses galloping over prairies. The result is that the physical doctrine of the atom has got into a state which is strongly suggestive of the epicycles of astronomy before Copernicus.

On the organic theory of nature there are two sorts of vibrations which radically differ from each other. There is vibratory locomotion, and there is vibratory organic deformation; and the conditions for the two types of change are of a different character. In other words, there is vibratory locomotion of a given pattern as one whole, and there is vibratory change of pattern.

A complete organism in the organic theory is what corresponds to a bit of material on the materialistic theory. There will be a primary genus, comprising a number of species of organisms, such that each primary organism, belonging to a species of the primary genus, is not decomposable into subordinate organisms. I will call any organism of the primary genus a primate. There may be different species of primates.

It must be kept in mind that we are dealing with the abstractions of physics. Accordingly, we are not thinking of what a primate is in itself, as a pattern arising from the prehension of the concrete aspects; nor are we thinking of what a primate is for its environment, in respect to its concrete aspects prehended therein. We are thinking of these various aspects merely in so far as their effects on patterns and on locomotion are expressible in spatio-temporal terms. Accordingly, in the language of physics, the aspects of a primate are merely its contributions to the electromagnetic field. This is in fact exactly what we know of electrons and protons. An electron for us is merely the pattern of its aspects in its environment, so far as those aspects are relevant to the electromagnetic field.

Now in discussing the theory of relativity, we saw that the relative motion of two primates means simply that their organic patterns are utilising diverse space-time systems. If two primates do not continue either mutually at rest, or mutually in uniform relative motion, at least one of them is changing its intrinsic space-time system. The laws of motion express the conditions under which these changes of space-time systems are effected.

The conditions for vibratory *locomotion* are founded upon these general laws of motion.

But it is possible that certain species of primates are apt to go to pieces under conditions which lead them to effect changes of space-time systems. Such species would only experience a long range of endurance, if they had succeeded in forming a favourable association among primates of different species, such that in this association the tendency to collapse is neutralised by the environment of the association. We can imagine the atomic nucleus as composed of a large number of primates of differing species, and perhaps with many primates of the same species, the whole association being such as to favour stability. An example of such an association is afforded by the association of a positive nucleus with negative electrons to obtain a neutral atom. The neutral atom is thereby shielded from any electric field which would otherwise produce changes in the space-time system of the atom.

The requirements of physics now suggest an idea which is very consonant with the organic philosophical theory. I put it in the form of a question: Has our organic theory of endurance been tainted by the materialistic theory in so far as it assumes without question that endurance must mean undifferentiated sameness throughout the life-history concerned? Perhaps you noticed that (in a previous chapter) I used the word 'reiteration' as a synonym of 'endurance.' It obviously is not quite synonymous in its meaning; and now I want to suggest that *reiteration* where it differs from *endurance* is more nearly what the organic theory requires. The difference is very analogous to that between the Galileans and the Aristotelians: Aristotle said 'rest' where Galileo added 'or uniform motion in a straight line.' Thus in the organic theory, a pattern need not endure in undifferentiated sameness through time. The pattern may be essentially one of aesthetic contrasts requiring a lapse of time for its unfolding. A tune is an example of such a pattern. Thus the endurance of the pattern now means the reiteration of its succession of contrasts. This is obviously the most general notion of endurance on the organic theory, and 'reiteration' is perhaps the word which expresses it with most directness. But when we translate this notion into the abstractions of physics, it at once becomes the technical notion of 'vibration.' This vibration is not the vibratory locomotion: it is the vibration of organic deformation. There are certain indications in modern physics that for the role of corpuscular organisms at the base of the physical field, we require vibratory entities. Such corpuscles would be the corpuscles detected as expelled from the nuclei of atoms, which then dissolve into waves of light. We may conjecture that such a corpuscular body has no great stability of endurance, when in isolation. Accordingly, an unfavourable environment leading to rapid changes in its proper space-time system, that is to say, an environment jolting it into violent accelerations, causes the corpuscles to go to pieces and dissolve into light-waves of the same period of vibration.

A proton, and perhaps an electron, would be an association of such primates, superposed on each other, with their frequencies and spatial dimensions so arranged as to promote the stability of the complex organism, when jolted into accelerations of locomotion. The conditions for stability would give the associations of periods possible for protons. The expulsion of a primate would come from a jolt which leads the proton either to settle down into an alternative association, or to generate a new primate by the aid of the energy received.

A primate must be associated with a definite frequency of vibratory organic deformation so that when it goes to pieces it dissolves into light waves of the same frequency, which then carry off all its average energy. It is quite easy (as a particular hypothesis) to imagine stationary vibrations of the electromagnetic field of definite frequency, and directed radially to and from a centre, which, in accordance with the accepted electromagnetic laws, would consist of a vibratory spherical nucleus satisfying one set of conditions and a vibratory external field satisfying another set of conditions. This is an example of vibratory organic deformation.

Further [on this particular hypothesis], there are two ways of determining the subsidiary conditions so as to satisfy the ordinary requirements of mathematical physics. The total energy, according to one of these ways, would satisfy the quantum condition; so that it consists of an integral number of units or cents, which are such that the cent of energy of any primate is proportional to its frequency. I have not worked out the conditions for stability or for a stable association. I have mentioned the particular hypothesis by way of showing by example that the organic theory of nature affords possibilities for the reconsideration of ultimate physical laws, which are not open to the opposed materialistic theory.

In this particular hypothesis of vibratory primates, the Maxwellian equations are supposed to hold throughout all space, including the interior of a proton. They express the laws governing the vibratory production and absorption of energy. The whole process for each primate issues in a certain average energy characteristic of the primate, and proportional to its mass. In fact the energy is the mass. There are vibratory radial streams of energy, both without and within a primate. Within the primate, there are vibratory distributions of electric density. On the materialistic theory such density marks the presence of material: on the organic theory of vibration, it marks the vibratory production of energy. Such production is restricted to the interior of the primate.

All science must start with some assumptions as to the ultimate analysis of the facts with which it deals. These assumptions are justified partly by their adherence to the types of occurrence of which we are directly conscious, and partly by their success in representing the observed facts with a certain generality, devoid of *ad hoc* suppositions. The general theory of the vibration of primates, which I have outlined, is merely given as an example of the sort of possibilities which the organic theory leaves open for physical science. The point is that it adds the possibility of organic deformation to that of mere locomotion. Light waves form one great example of organic deformation.

At any epoch the assumptions of a science are giving way, when they exhibit symptoms of the epicyclic state from which astronomy was rescued in the sixteenth century. Physical science is now exhibiting such symptoms. In order to reconsider its foundations, it must recur to a more concrete view of the character of real things, and must conceive its fundamental notions as abstractions derived from this direct intuition. It is in this way that it surveys the general possibilities of revision which are open to it.

The discontinuities introduced by the quantum theory require revision of physical concepts in order to meet them. In particular, it has been pointed out that some theory of discontinuous existence is required. What is asked from such a theory, is that an orbit of an electron can be regarded as a series of detached positions, and not as a continuous line.

The theory of a primate or a vibrating pattern, given above, together with the distinction between temporality and extensiveness in the previous chapter, yields exactly this result. It will be remembered that the continuity of the complex of events arises from the relationships of extensiveness; whereas the temporality arises from the realisation in a subject-event of a pattern which requires for its display that the whole of a duration be spatialised (*i.e.*, arrested), as given by its aspects in the event. Thus realization proceeds viâ a succession of epochal durations; and the continuous transition, *i.e.*, the organic deformation, is within the duration which is already given. The vibratory organic deformation is in fact the reiteration of the pattern. One complete period defines the duration required for the complete pattern. Thus the primate is realised atomically in a succession of durations, each duration to be measured from one maximum to another. Accordingly, so far as the primate as one enduring whole entity is to be taken account of, it is to be assigned to these durations successively. If it is considered as one thing, its orbit is to be diagrammatically exhibited by a series of detached dots. Thus the locomotion of the primate is discontinuous in space and time. If we go below the quanta of time which are the successive vibratory periods of the primate, we find a succession of vibratory electromagnetic fields, each stationary in the space-time of its own duration. Each of these fields exhibits a single complete period of the electromagnetic vibration which constitutes the primate. This vibration is not to be thought of as the becoming of reality; it is what the primate is in one of its discontinuous realisations. Also the successive durations in which the primate is realised are contiguous; it follows that the life history of the primate can be exhibited as being the continuous development of occurrences in the electromagnetic field. But these occurrences enter into realization as whole atomic blocks, occupying definite periods of time.

There is no need to conceive that time is atomic in the sense that all patterns must be realised in the same successive durations. In the first place, even if the periods were the same in the case of two primates, the durations of realisation may not be the same. In other words, the two primates may be out of phase. Also if the periods are different, the atomism of any one duration of one primate is necessarily subdivided by the boundary moments of durations of the other primate.

The laws of the locomotion of primates express under what conditions any primate will change its space-time system.

It is unnecessary to pursue this conception further. The justification of the concept of vibratory existence must be purely experimental. The point illustrated by this example is that the cosmological outlook, which is here adopted, is perfectly consistent with the demands for discontinuity which have been urged from the side of physics. Also if this concept of temporalisation as a successive realisation of epochal durations be adopted, the difficulty of Zeno is evaded. The particular form, which has been given here to this concept, is purely for that purpose of illustration and must necessarily require recasting before it can be adapted to the results of experimental physics.

Chapter IX

SCIENCE AND PHILOSOPHY

In the present lecture, it is my object to consider some reactions of science upon the stream of philosophic thought during the modern centuries with which we are concerned. I shall make no attempt to compress a history of modern philosophy within the limits of one lecture. We shall merely consider some contacts between science and philosophy, in so far as they lie within the scheme of thought which it is the purpose of these lectures to develop. For this reason the whole of the great German idealistic movement will be ignored, as being out of effective touch with its contemporary science so far as reciprocal modification of concepts is concerned. Kant, from whom this movement took its rise, was saturated with Newtonian physics, and with the ideas of the great French physicists—such as Clairaut[1], for instance—who developed the Newtonian ideas. But the philosophers who developed the Kantian school of thought, or who transformed it into Hegelianism, either lacked Kant's background of scientific knowledge, or lacked his potentiality of becoming a great physicist if philosophy had not absorbed his main energies.

1. *Cf.* the curious evidence of Kant's scientific reading in the *Critique of Pure Reason, Transcendental Analytic, Second Analogy of Experience*, where he refers to the phenomenon of capillary action. This is an unnecessarily complex illustration; a book resting on a table would have equally well sufficed. But the subject had just been adequately treated for the first time by Clairaut in an appendix to his *Figure of the Earth*. Kant evidently had read this appendix, and his mind was full of it.

The origin of modern philosophy is analogous to that of science, and is contemporaneous. The general trend of its development was settled in the seventeenth century, partly at the hands of the same men who established the scientific principles. This settlement of purpose followed upon a transitional period dating from the fifteenth century. There was in fact a general movement of European mentality, which carried along with its stream, religion, science and philosophy. It may shortly be characterised as being the direct recurrence to the original sources of Greek inspiration on the part of men whose spiritual shape had been derived from inheritance from the Middle Ages. There was therefore no revival of Greek mentality. Epochs do not rise from the dead. The principles of aesthetics and of reason, which animated the Greek civilisation, were reclothed in a modern mentality. Between the two there lay other religions, other systems of law, other anarchies, and other racial inheritances, dividing the living from the dead.

Philosophy is peculiarly sensitive to such differences. For, whereas you can make a replica of an ancient statue, there is no possible replica of an ancient state of mind. There can be no nearer approximation than that which a masquerade bears to real life. There may be understanding of the past, but there is a difference between the modern and the ancient reactions to the same stimuli.

In the particular case of philosophy, the distinction in tonality lies on the surface. Modern philosophy is tinged with subjectivism, as against the objective attitude of the ancients. The same change is to be seen in religion. In the early history of the Christian Church, the theological interest centred in discussions on the nature of God, the meaning of the Incarnation, and apocalyptic forecasts of the ultimate fate of the world. At the Reformation, the Church was torn asunder by dissension as to the individual experiences of believers in respect to justification. The individual subject of experience had been substituted for the total drama of all reality. Luther asked, 'How am I justified?'; modern philosophers have asked, 'How do I have knowledge?' The emphasis lies upon the subject of experience. This change of standpoint is the work of Christianity in its pastoral aspect of shepherding the company of believers. For century after century it insisted upon the infinite worth of the individual human soul. Accordingly, to the instinctive egotism of physical desires, it has superadded an instinctive feeling of justification for an egotism of intellectual outlook. Every human being is the natural guardian of his own importance. Without a doubt, this modern direction of attention emphasises truths of the highest value. For example, in the field of practical life, it has abolished slavery, and has impressed upon the popular imagination the primary rights of mankind.

Descartes, in his *Discourse on Method*, and in his *Meditations*, discloses with great clearness the general conceptions which have since influenced modern philosophy. There is a subject receiving experience: in the *Discourse* this subject is always mentioned in the first person, that is to say, as being Descartes himself. Descartes starts with himself as being a mentality, which in virtue of its consciousness of its own inherent presentations of sense and of thought, is thereby conscious of its own existence as a unit entity. The subsequent history of philosophy revolves round the Cartesian formulation of the primary datum. The ancient world takes its stand upon the drama of the Universe, the modern world upon the inward drama of the Soul. Descartes, in his *Meditations*, expressly grounds the existence of this inward drama upon the possibility of error. There may be no correspondence with objective fact, and thus there must be a soul with activities whose reality is purely derivative from itself. For example, here is a quotation[2] from *Meditation II*:

> But it will be said that these presentations are false, and that I am dreaming. Let it be so. At all events it is certain that I seem to see light, hear a noise, and feel heat; this cannot be false, and this is what in me is properly called perceiving (sentire), which is

2. Quoted from Veitch's translation.

> nothing else than thinking. From this I begin to know what I am with somewhat greater clearness and distinctness than heretofore.

Again in *Meditation III:*

> ...; for, as I before remarked, although the things which I perceive or imagine are perhaps nothing at all apart from me, I am nevertheless assured that those modes of consciousness which I call perceptions and imaginations, in as far only as they are modes of consciousness, exist in me.

The objectivism of the medieval and the ancient worlds passed over into science. Nature is there conceived as for itself, with its own mutual reactions. Under the recent influence of relativity, there has been a tendency towards subjectivist formulations. But, apart from this recent exception, nature, in scientific thought, has had its laws formulated without any reference to dependence on individual observers. There is, however, this difference between the older and the later attitudes towards science. The anti-rationalism of the moderns has checked any attempt to harmonise the ultimate concepts of science with ideas drawn from a more concrete survey of the whole of reality. The material, the space, the time, the various laws concerning the transition of material configurations, are taken as ultimate stubborn facts, not to be tampered with.

The effect of this antagonism to philosophy has been equally unfortunate both for philosophy and for science. In this lecture we are concerned with philosophy. Philosophers are rationalists. They are seeking to go behind stubborn and irreducible facts: they wish to explain in the light of universal principles the mutual reference between the various details entering into the flux of things. Also, they seek such principles as will eliminate mere arbitrariness; so that, whatever portion of fact is assumed or given, the existence of the remainder of things shall satisfy some demand of rationality. They demand meaning. In the words of Henry Sidgwick[3]—

3. *Cf. Henry Sidgwick: A Memoir*, Appendix I.

> It is the primary aim of philosophy to unify completely, bring into clear coherence, all departments of rational thought, and this aim cannot be realised by any philosophy that leaves out of its view the important body of judgments and reasonings which form the subject matter of ethics.

Accordingly, the bias towards history on the part of the physical and social sciences with their refusal to rationalise below some ultimate mechanism, has pushed philosophy out of the effective currents of modern life. It has lost its proper rôle as a constant critic of partial formulations. It has retreated into the subjectivist sphere of mind, by reason of its expulsion by science from the objectivist sphere of matter. Thus the evolution of thought in the seventeenth century co-operated with the enhanced sense of individual personality derived from the Middle Ages. We see Descartes taking his stand upon his own ultimate mind, which his philosophy assures him of; and asking about its relations to the ultimate matter—exemplified, in the second *Meditation*, by the human body and a lump of wax—which his science assumes. There is Aaron's rod, and the magicians' serpents; and the only question for philosophy is, which swallows which; or whether, as Descartes thought, they all lived happily together. In this stream of thought are to be found Locke, Berkeley, Hume, Kant. Two great names lie outside this list, Spinoza and Leibniz. But there is a certain isolation of both of them in respect to their philosophical influence so far as science is concerned; as though they had strayed to extremes which lie outside the boundaries of safe philosophy, Spinoza by retaining older ways of thought, and Leibniz by the novelty of his monads.

The history of philosophy runs curiously parallel to that of science. In the case of both, the seventeenth century set the stage for its two successors. But with the twentieth century a new act commences. It is an exaggeration to attribute a general change in a climate of thought to any one piece of writing, or to any one author. No doubt Descartes only expressed definitely and in decisive form what was already in the air of his period. Analogously, in attributing to William James the inauguration of a new stage in philosophy, we should be neglecting other influences of his time. But, admitting this, there still remains a certain fitness in contrasting his essay, *Does Consciousness Exist*, published in 1904, with Descartes' *Discourse on Method*, published in 1637. James clears the stage of the old paraphernalia; or rather he entirely alters its lighting. Take for example these two sentences from his essay:

> To deny plumply that 'consciousness' exists seems so absurd on the face of it—for undeniably 'thoughts' do exist—that I fear some readers will follow me no farther. Let me then immediately explain that I mean only to deny that the word stands for an entity, but to insist most emphatically that it does stand for a function.

The scientific materialism and the Cartesian Ego were both challenged at the same moment, one by science and the other by philosophy, as represented by William James with his psychological antecedents; and the double challenge marks the end of a period which lasted for about two hundred and fifty years. Of course, 'matter' and 'consciousness' both express something so evident in ordinary experience that any philosophy must provide some things which answer to their respective meanings. But the point is that, in respect to both of them, the seventeenth century settlement was infected with a presupposition which is now challenged. James denies that consciousness is an entity, but admits that it is a function. The discrimination between an entity and a function is therefore vital to the understanding of the challenge which James is advancing against the older modes of thought. In the essay in question, the character which James assigns to consciousness is fully discussed. But he does not unambiguously explain what he means by the notion of an entity, which he refuses to apply to consciousness. In the sentence which immediately follows the one which I have already quoted, he says:

> There is, I mean, no aboriginal stuff or quality of being, contrasted with that of which material objects are made, out of which our thoughts of them are made; but there is a function in experience which thoughts perform, and for the performance of which this quality of being is invoked. That function is *knowing*. 'Consciousness' is supposed necessary to explain the fact that things not only are, but get reported, are known.

Thus James is denying that consciousness is a 'stuff.'

The term 'entity,' or even that of 'stuff,' does not fully tell its own tale. The notion of 'entity' is so general that it may be taken to mean anything that can be thought about. You cannot think of mere nothing; and the something which is an object of thought may be called an entity. In this sense, a function is an entity. Obviously, this is not what James had in his mind.

In agreement with the organic theory of nature which I have been tentatively putting forward in these lectures, I shall for my own purposes construe James as denying exactly what Descartes asserts in his *Discourse* and his *Meditations*. Descartes discriminates two species of entities, *matter* and *soul*. The essence of matter is spatial extension; the essence of soul is its cogitation, in the full sense which Descartes assigns to the word '*cogitare*.' For example, in Section Fifty-three of Part I of his *Principles of Philosophy*, he enunciates:

> That of every substance there is one principal attribute, as thinking of the mind, extension of the body.

In the earlier, Fifty-first Section, Descartes states:

> By substance we can conceive nothing else than a thing which exists in such a way as to stand in need of nothing beyond itself in order to its existence.

Furthermore, later on, Descartes says:

> For example, because any substance which ceases to endure ceases also to exist, duration is not distinct from substance except in thought;....

Thus we conclude that, for Descartes, minds and bodies exist in such a way as to stand in need of nothing beyond themselves individually (God only excepted, as being the foundation of all things); that both minds and bodies endure, because without endurance they would cease to exist; that spatial extension is the essential attribute of bodies; and that cogitation is the essential attribute of minds.

It is difficult to praise too highly the genius exhibited by Descartes in the complete sections of his *Principles* which deal with these questions. It is worthy of the century in which he writes, and of the clearness of the French intellect. Descartes in his distinction between time and duration, and in his way of grounding time upon motion, and in his close relation between matter and extension, anticipates, as far as it was possible at his epoch, modern notions suggested by the doctrine of relativity, or by some aspects of Bergson's doctrine of the generation of things. But the fundamental principles are so set out as to presuppose independently existing substances with simple location in a community of temporal durations, and, in the case of bodies, with simple location in the community of spatial extensions. Those principles lead straight to the theory of a materialistic, mechanistic nature, surveyed by cogitating minds. After the close of the seventeenth century, science took charge of the materialistic nature, and philosophy took charge of the cogitating minds. Some schools of philosophy admitted an ultimate dualism; and the various idealistic schools claimed that nature was merely the chief example of the cogitations of minds. But all schools admitted the Cartesian analysis of the ultimate elements of nature. I am excluding Spinoza and Leibniz from these statements as to the main stream of modern philosophy, as derivative from Descartes; though of course they were influenced by him, and in their turn influenced philosophers. I am thinking mainly of the effective contacts between science and philosophy.

This division of territory between science and philosophy was not a simple business; and in fact it illustrated the weakness of the whole cut-and-dried presupposition upon which it rested. We are aware of nature as an interplay of bodies, colours, sounds, scents, tastes, touches and other various bodily feelings, displayed as in space, in patterns of mutual separation by intervening volumes, and of individual shape. Also the whole is a flux, changing with the lapse of time. This systematic totality is disclosed to us as one complex of things. But the seventeenth century dualism cuts straight across it. The objective world of science was confined to mere spatial material with simple location in space and time, and subjected to definite rules as to its locomotion. The subjective world of philosophy annexed the colours, sounds, scents, tastes, touches, bodily feelings, as forming the subjective content of the cogitations of the individual minds. Both worlds shared in the general flux; but time, as measured, is assigned by Descartes to the cogitations of the observer's mind. There is obviously one fatal weakness to this scheme. The cogitations of mind exhibit themselves as holding up entities, such as colours for instance, before the mind as the termini of contemplation. But in this theory these colours are, after all, merely the furniture of the mind. Accordingly, the mind seems to be confined to its own private world of cogitations. The subject-object conformation of experience in its entirety lies within the mind as one of its private passions. This conclusion from the Cartesian data is the starting point from which Berkeley, Hume, and Kant developed their respective systems. And, antecedently to them, it was the point upon which Locke concentrated as being the vital question. Thus the question as to how any knowledge is obtained of the truly objective world of science becomes a problem of the first magnitude. Descartes states that the objective body is perceived by the intellect. He says (*Meditation II*):

> I must, therefore, admit that I cannot even comprehend by imagination what the piece of wax is, and that it is the mind alone which perceives it. I speak of one piece in particular; for, as to wax in general, this is still more evident. But what is the piece of wax that can be perceived only by the mind?... The perception of it is neither an act of sight, of touch, nor of imagination, and never was either of these, though it might formerly seem so, but is simply an *intuition* (*inspectio*) of the mind,...

It must be noted that the Latin word 'inspectio' is associated in its classical use with the notion of theory as opposed to practice.

The two great preoccupations of modern philosophy now lie clearly before us. The study of mind divides into psychology, or the study of mental functionings as considered in themselves and in their mutual relations, and into epistemology, or the theory of the knowledge of a common objective world. In other words, there is the study of the cogitations, *quâ* passions of the mind, and their study *quâ* leading to an inspection (*intuition*) of an objective world. This is a very uneasy division, giving rise to a host of perplexities whose consideration has occupied the intervening centuries.

As long as men thought in terms of physical notions for the objective world and of mentality for the subjective world, the setting out of the problem, as achieved by Descartes, sufficed as a starting point. But the balance has been upset by the rise of physiology. In the seventeenth century men passed from the study of physics to the study of philosophy. Towards the end of the nineteenth century, notably in Germany, men passed from the study of physiology to the study of psychology. The change in tone has been decisive. Of course, in the earlier period the intervention of the human body was fully considered, for example, by Descartes in Part V of the *Discourse on Method*. But the physiological instinct had not been developed. In considering the human body,

Descartes thought with the outfit of a physicist; whereas the modern psychologists are clothed with the mentalities of medical physiologists. The career of William James is an example of this change in standpoint. He also possessed the clear, incisive genius which could state in a flash the exact point at issue.

The reason why I have put Descartes and James in close juxtaposition is now evident. Neither philosopher finished an epoch by a final solution of a problem. Their great merit is of the opposite sort. They each of them open an epoch by their clear formulation of terms in which thought could profitably express itself at particular stages of knowledge, one for the seventeenth century, the other for the twentieth century. In this respect, they are both to be contrasted with St. Thomas Aquinas, who expressed the culmination of Aristotelian scholasticism.

In many ways neither Descartes nor James were the most characteristic philosophers of their respective epochs. I should be disposed to ascribe these positions to Locke and to Bergson respectively, at least so far as concerns their relations to the science of their times. Locke developed the lines of thought which kept philosophy on the move; for example he emphasized the appeal to psychology. He initiated the age of epoch-making enquiries into urgent problems of limited scope. Undoubtedly, in so doing, he infected philosophy with something of the anti-rationalism of science. But the very groundwork of a fruitful methodology is to start from those clear postulates which must be held to be ultimate so far as concerns the occasion in question. The criticism of such methodological postulates is thus reserved for another opportunity. Locke discovered that the philosophical situation bequeathed by Descartes involved the problems of epistemology and psychology.

Bergson introduced into philosophy the organic conceptions of physiological science. He has most completely moved away from the static materialism of the seventeenth century. His protest against spatialisation is a protest against taking the Newtonian conception of nature as being anything except a high abstraction. His so-called anti-intellectualism should be construed in this sense. In some respects he recurs to Descartes; but the recurrence is accompanied with an instinctive grasp of modern biology.

There is another reason for associating Locke and Bergson. The germ of an organic theory of nature is to be found in Locke. His most recent expositor, Professor Gibson[4], states that Locke's way of conceiving the identity of self-consciousness 'like that of a living organism, involves a genuine transcending of the mechanical view of nature and of mind, embodied in the composition theory.' But it is to be noticed that in the first place Locke wavers in his grasp of this position; and in the second place, what is more important still, he only applies his idea to self-consciousness. The physiological attitude has not yet established itself. The effect of physiology was to put mind back into nature. The neurologist traces first the effect of stimuli along the bodily nerves, then integration at nerve centres, and finally the rise of a projective reference beyond the body with a resulting motor efficacy in renewed nervous excitement. In biochemistry, the delicate adjustment of the chemical composition of the parts to the preservation of the whole organism is detected. Thus the mental cognition is seen as the reflective experience of a totality, reporting for itself what it is in itself as one unit occurrence. This unit is the integration of the sum of its partial happenings, but it is not their numerical aggregate. It has its own unity as an event. This total unity, considered as an entity for its own sake, is the prehension into unity of the patterned aspects of the universe of events. Its knowledge of itself arises from its own relevance to the things of which it prehends the aspects. It knows the world as a system of mutual relevance, and thus sees itself as mirrored in other things. These other things include more especially the various parts of its own body.

---

4. *Cf.* his book, *Locke's Theory of Knowledge and its Historical Relations*, Camb. Univ. Press, 1917.

It is important to discriminate the bodily pattern, which endures, from the bodily event, which is pervaded by the enduring pattern, and from the parts of the bodily event. The parts of the bodily event are themselves pervaded by their own enduring patterns, which form elements in the bodily pattern. The parts of the body are really portions of the environment of the total bodily event, but so related that their mutual aspects, each in the other, are peculiarly effective in modifying the pattern of either. This arises from the intimate character of the relation of whole to part. Thus the body is a portion of the environment for the part, and the part is a portion of the environment for the body; only they are peculiarly sensitive, each to modifications of the other. This sensitiveness is so arranged that the part adjusts itself to preserve the stability of the pattern of the body. It is a particular example of the favourable environment shielding the organism. The relation of part to whole has the special reciprocity associated with the notion of organism, in which the part is for the whole; but this relation reigns throughout nature and does not start with the special case of the higher organisms.

Further, viewing the question as a matter of chemistry, there is no need to construe the actions of each molecule in a living body by its exclusive particular reference to the pattern of the complete living organism. It is true that each molecule is affected by the aspect of this pattern as mirrored in it, so as to be otherwise than what it would have been if placed elsewhere. In the same way, under some circumstances an electron may be a sphere, and under other circumstances an egg-shaped volume. The mode of approach to the problem, so far as science is concerned, is merely to ask if molecules exhibit in living bodies properties which are not to be observed amid inorganic surroundings. In the same way, in a magnetic field soft iron exhibits magnetic properties which are in abeyance elsewhere. The prompt self-preservative actions of living bodies, and our experience of the physical actions of our bodies following the determinations of will, suggest the modification of molecules in the body as the result of the total pattern. It seems possible that there may be physical laws expressing the modification of the ultimate basic organisms when they form part of higher organisms with adequate compactness of pattern. It would, however, be entirely in consonance with the empirically observed action of environments, if the direct effects of aspects as between the whole body and its parts were negligible. We should expect transmission. In this way the modification of total pattern would transmit itself by means of a series of modifications of a descending series of parts, so that finally the modification of the cell changes its aspect in the molecule, thus effecting a corresponding alteration in the molecule,—or in some subtler entity. Thus the question for physiology is the question of the physics of molecules in cells of different characters.

We can now see the relation of psychology to physiology and to physics. The private psychological field is merely the event considered from its own standpoint. The unity of this field is the unity of the event. But it is the event as one entity, and not the event as a sum of parts. The relations of the parts, to each other and to the whole, are their aspects, each in the other. A body for an external observer is the aggregate of the aspects for him of the body as a whole, and also of the body as a sum of parts. For the external observer the aspects of shape and of sense-objects are dominant, at least for cognition. But we must also allow for the possibility that we can detect in ourselves direct aspects of the mentalities of higher organisms. The claim that the cognition of alien mentalities must necessarily be by means of indirect inferences from aspects of shape and of sense-objects is wholly unwarranted by this philosophy of organism. The fundamental principle is that whatever merges into actuality, implants its aspects in every individual event.

Further, even for self-cognition, the aspects of the parts of our own bodies partly take the form of aspects of shape, and of sense-objects. But that part of the bodily event, in respect to which the cognitive mentality is associated, is for itself the unit psychological field. Its ingredients are not referent to the event itself; they are aspects of what lies beyond that event. Thus the self-knowledge inherent in the bodily event is the knowledge of itself as a complex unity, whose ingredients involve all reality beyond itself, restricted under the limitation of its pattern of aspects. Thus we know ourselves as a function of unification of a plurality of things which are other than ourselves. Cognition discloses an event as being an activity, organising a real togetherness of alien things. But this psychological field does not depend on its cognition; so that this field is still a unit event as abstracted from its self-cognition.

Accordingly, consciousness will be the function of knowing. But what is known is already a prehension of aspects of the one real universe. These aspects are aspects of other events as mutually modifying, each the others. In the pattern of aspects they stand in their pattern of mutual relatedness.

The aboriginal data in terms of which the pattern weaves itself are the aspects of shapes, of sense-objects, and of other eternal objects whose self-identity is not dependent on the flux of things. Wherever such objects have ingression into the general flux, they interpret events, each to the other. They are here in the perceiver; but, as perceived by him, they convey for him something of the total flux which is beyond himself. The subject-object relation takes its origin in the double rôle of these eternal objects. They are modifications of the subject, but only in their character of conveying aspects of other subjects in the community of the universe. Thus no individual subject can have independent reality, since it is a prehension of limited aspects of subjects other than itself.

The technical phrase 'subject-object' is a bad term for the fundamental situation disclosed in experience. It is really reminiscent of the Aristotelian 'subject-predicate.' It already presupposes the metaphysical doctrine of diverse subjects qualified by their private predicates. This is the doctrine of subjects with private worlds of experience. If this be granted, there is no escape from solipsism. The point is that the phrase 'subject-object' indicates a fundamental entity underlying the objects. Thus the 'objects,' as thus conceived, are merely the ghosts of Aristotelian predicates. The primary situation disclosed in cognitive experience is 'ego-object amid objects.' By this I mean that the primary fact is an impartial world transcending the 'here-now' which marks the ego-object, and transcending the 'now' which is the spatial world of simultaneous realisation. It is a world also including the actuality of the past, and the limited potentiality of the future, together with the complete world of abstract potentiality, the realm of eternal objects, which transcends, and finds exemplification in and comparison with, the actual course of realisation. The ego-object, as consciousness here-now, is conscious of its experient essence as constituted by its internal relatedness to the world of realities, and to the world of ideas. But the ego-object, in being thus constituted, is within the world of realities, and exhibits itself as an organism requiring the ingression of ideas for the purpose of this status among realities. This question of consciousness must be reserved for treatment on another occasion.

The point to be made for the purposes of the present discussion is that a philosophy of nature as organic must start at the opposite end to that requisite for a materialistic philosophy. The materialistic starting point is from independently existing substances, matter and mind. The matter suffers modifications of its external relations of locomotion, and the mind suffers modifications of its contemplated objects. There are, in this materialistic theory, two sorts of independent substances, each qualified by their appropriate passions. The organic starting point is from the analysis of process as the realisation of events disposed in an interlocked community. The event is the unit of things real. The emergent enduring pattern is the stabilisation of the emergent achievement so as to become a fact which retains its identity throughout the process. It will be noted that endurance is not primarily the property of enduring beyond itself, but of enduring within itself. I mean that endurance is the property of finding its pattern reproduced in the temporal parts of the total event. It is in this sense that a total event carries an enduring pattern. There is an intrinsic value identical for the whole and for its succession of parts. Cognition is the emergence, into some measure of individualised reality, of the general substratum of activity, poising before itself possibility, actuality, and purpose.

It is equally possible to arrive at this organic conception of the world if we start from the fundamental notions of modern physics, instead of, as above, from psychology and physiology. In fact by reason of my own studies in mathematics and mathematical physics, I did in fact arrive at my convictions in this way. Mathematical physics presumes in the first place an electromagnetic field of activity pervading space and time. The laws which condition this field are nothing else than the conditions observed by the general activity of the flux of the world, as it individualises itself in the events. In physics, there is an abstraction. The science ignores what anything is in itself. Its entities are merely considered in respect to their extrinsic reality, that is to say, in respect to their aspects in other things. But the abstraction reaches even further than that; for it is only the aspects in other things, as modifying the spatio-temporal specifications of the life histories of those other things, which count. The intrinsic reality of the observer comes in: I mean what the observer is for himself is appealed to. For example, the fact that he will see red or blue enters into scientific statements. But the red which the observer sees does not in truth enter into science. What is relevant is merely the bare diversity of the observer's red experiences from all of his other experiences. Accordingly, the intrinsic character of the observer is merely relevant in order to fix the self-identical individuality of the physical entities. These entities are only considered as agencies in fixing the routes in space and in time of the life histories of enduring entities.

The phraseology of physics is derived from the materialistic ideas of the seventeenth century. But we find that, even in its extreme abstraction, what it is really presupposing is the organic theory of aspects as explained above. First, consider any event in empty space where the word 'empty' means devoid of electrons, or protons, or of any other form of electric charge. Such an event has three rôles in physics. In the first place, it is the actual scene of an adventure of energy, either as its *habitat* or as the locus of a particular stream of energy: anyhow, in this rôle the energy is there, either as located in space during the time considered, or as streaming through space.

In its second rôle, the event is a necessary link in the pattern of transmission, by which the character of every event receives some modification from the character of every other event.

In its third rôle, the event is the repository of a possibility, as to what would happen to an electric charge, either by way of deformation or of locomotion, if it should have happened to be there.

If we modify our assumption by considering an event which includes in itself a portion of the life-history of an electric charge, then the analysis of its three rôles still remains; except that the possibility embodied in the third rôle is now transformed into an actuality. In this replacement of possibility by actuality, we obtain the distinction between empty and occupied events.

Recurring to the empty events, we note the deficiency in them of individuality of intrinsic content. Considering the first rôle of an empty event, as being a *habitat* of energy, we note that there is no individual discrimination of an individual bit of energy, either as statically located, or as an element in the stream. There is simply a quantitative determination of activity, without individualisation of the activity in itself. This lack of individualisation is still more evident in the second and third rôles. An empty event is something in itself, but it fails to realise a stable individuality of content. So far as its content is concerned, the empty event is one realised element in a general scheme of organised activity.

Some qualification is required when the empty event is the scene of the transmission of a definite train of recurrent wave-forms. There is now a definite pattern which remains permanent in the event. We find here the first faint trace of enduring individuality. But it is individuality without the faintest capture of originality: for it is merely a permanence arising solely from the implication of the event in a larger scheme of patterning.

Turning now to the examination of an occupied event, the electron has a determinate individuality. It can be traced throughout its life-history through a variety of events. A collection of electrons, together with the analogous atomic charges of positive electricity, forms a body such as we ordinarily perceive. The simplest body of this kind is a molecule, and a set of molecules forms a lump of ordinary matter, such as a chair, or a stone. Thus a charge of electricity is the mark of individuality of content, as additional to the individuality of an event in itself. This individuality of content is the strong point of the materialistic doctrine.

It can, however, be equally well explained on the theory of organism. When we look into the function of the electric charge, we note that its rôle is to mark the origination of a pattern which is transmitted through space and time. It is the key of some particular pattern. For example, the field of force in any event is to be constructed by attention to the adventures of electrons and protons, and so also are the streams and distributions of energy. Further, the electric waves find their origin in the vibratory adventures of these charges. Thus the transmitted pattern is to be conceived as the flux of aspects throughout space and time derived from the life history of the atomic charge. The individualisation of the charge arises by a conjunction of two characters, in the first place by the continued identity of its mode of functioning as a key for the determination of a diffusion of pattern; and, in the second place, by the unity and continuity of its life history.

We may conclude, therefore, that the organic theory represents directly what physics actually does assume respecting its ultimate entities. We also notice the complete futility of these entities, if they are conceived as fully concrete individuals. So far as physics is concerned, they are wholly occupied in moving each other about, and they have no reality outside this function. In particular for physics, there is no intrinsic reality.

It is obvious that the basing of philosophy upon the presupposition of organism must be traced back to Leibniz[5]. His monads are for him the ultimately real entities. But he retained the Cartesian substances with their qualifying passions, as also equally expressing for him the final characterisation of real things. Accordingly for him there was no concrete reality of internal relations. He had therefore on his hands two distinct points of view. One was that the final real entity is an organising activity, fusing ingredients into a unity, so that this unity is the reality. The other point of view is that the final real entities are substances supporting qualities. The first point of view depends upon the acceptance of internal relations binding together all reality. The latter is inconsistent with the reality of such relations. To combine these two points of view, his monads were therefore windowless; and their passions merely mirrored the universe by the divine arrangement of a preëstablished harmony. This system thus presupposed an aggregate of independent entities. He did not discriminate the event, as the unit of experience, from the enduring organism as its stabilization into importance, and from the cognitive organism as expressing an increased completeness of individualisation. Nor did he admit the many-termed relations, relating sense-data to various events in diverse ways. These many-termed relations are in fact the perspectives which Leibniz does admit, but only on the condition that they are purely qualities

5. *Cf.* Bertrand Russell, *The Philosophy of Leibniz*, for the suggestion of this line of thought.

of the organising monads. The difficulty really arises from the unquestioned acceptance of the notion of simple location as fundamental for space and time, and from the acceptance of the notion of independent individual substance as fundamental for a real entity. The only road open to Leibniz was thus the same as that later taken by Berkeley [in a prevalent interpretation of his meaning], namely an appeal to a *Deux ex machinâ* who was capable of rising superior to the difficulties of metaphysics.

In the same way as Descartes introduced the tradition of thought which kept subsequent philosophy in some measure of contact with the scientific movement, so Leibniz introduced the alternative tradition that the entities, which are the ultimate actual things, are in some sense procedures of organisation. This tradition has been the foundation of the great achievements of German philosophy. Kant reflected the two traditions, one upon the other. Kant was a scientist, but the schools derivative from Kant have had but slight effect on the mentality of the scientific world. It should be the task of the philosophical schools of this century to bring together the two streams into an expression of the world-picture derived from science, and thereby end the divorce of science from the affirmations of our aesthetic and ethical experiences.

Chapter X

ABSTRACTION

IN THE PREVIOUS CHAPTERS I have been examining the reactions of the scientific movement upon the deeper issues which have occupied modern thinkers. No one man, no limited society of men, and no one epoch can think of everything at once. Accordingly for the sake of eliciting the various impacts of science upon thought, the topic has been treated historically. In this retrospect I have kept in mind that the ultimate issue of the whole story is the patent dissolution of the comfortable scheme of scientific materialism which has dominated the three centuries under review. Accordingly various schools of criticism of the dominant opinions have been stressed; and I have endeavoured to outline an alternative cosmological doctrine, which shall be wide enough to include what is fundamental both for science and for its critics. In this alternative scheme, the notion of material, as fundamental, has been replaced by that of organic synthesis. But the approach has always been from the consideration of the actual intricacies of scientific thought, and of the peculiar perplexities which it suggests.

In the present chapter, and in the immediately succeeding chapter, we will forget the peculiar problems of modern science, and will put ourselves at the standpoint of a dispassionate consideration of the nature of things, antecedently to any special investigation into their details. Such a standpoint is termed 'metaphysical.' Accordingly those readers who find metaphysics, even in two slight chapters, irksome, will do well to proceed at once to the Chapter on 'Religion and Science,' which resumes the topic of the impact of science on modern thought.

These metaphysical chapters are purely descriptive. Their justification is to be sought, (i) in our direct knowledge of the actual occasions which compose our immediate experience, and (ii) in their success as forming a basis for harmonising our systematised accounts of various types of experience, and (iii) in their success as providing the concepts in terms of which an epistemology can be framed. By (iii) I mean that an account of the general character of what we know must enable us to frame an account of how knowledge is possible as an adjunct within things known.

In any occasion of cognition, that which is known is an actual occasion of experience, as diversified[1] by reference to a realm of entities which transcend that immediate occasion in that they have analogous or different connections with other occasions of experience. For example a definite shade of red may, in the immediate occasion, be implicated with the shape of sphericity in some definite way. But that shade of red, and that spherical shape, exhibit themselves as transcending that occasion, in that either of them has other relationships to other occasions. Also, apart from the actual occurrence of the same things in other occasions, every actual occasion is set within a realm of alternative interconnected entities. This realm is disclosed by all the untrue propositions which can be predicated significantly of that occasion. It is the realm of alternative suggestions, whose foothold in actuality transcends each actual occasion. The real relevance of untrue propositions for each actual occasion is disclosed by art, romance, and by criticism in reference to ideals. It is the foundation of the metaphysical position which I am maintaining that the understanding of actuality requires a reference to ideality. The two realms are intrinsically inherent in the total metaphysical situation. The truth that some proposition respecting an actual occasion is

1. *Cf.* my *Principles of Natural Knowledge*, Ch. V, Sec. 13.

untrue may express the vital truth as to the aesthetic achievement. It expresses the 'great refusal' which is its primary characteristic. An event is decisive in proportion to the importance (for it) of its untrue propositions: their relevance to the event cannot be dissociated from what the event is in itself by way of achievement. These transcendent entities have been termed 'universals.' I prefer to use the term 'eternal objects,' in order to disengage myself from presuppositions which cling to the former term owing to its prolonged philosophical history. Eternal objects are thus, in their nature, abstract. By 'abstract' I mean that what an eternal object is in itself—that is to say, its essence—is comprehensible without reference to some one particular occasion of experience. To be abstract is to transcend particular concrete occasions of actual happening. But to transcend an actual occasion does not mean being disconnected from it. On the contrary, I hold that each eternal object has its own proper connection with each such occasion, which I term its mode of ingression into that occasion. Thus an eternal object is to be comprehended by acquaintance with (i) its particular individuality, (ii) its general relationships to other eternal objects as apt for realisation in actual occasions, and (iii) the general principle which expresses its ingression in particular actual occasions.

These three headings express two principles. The first principle is that each eternal object is an individual which, in its own peculiar fashion, is what it is. This particular individuality is the individual essence of the object, and cannot be described otherwise than as being itself. Thus the individual essence is merely the essence considered in respect to its uniqueness. Further, the essence of an eternal object is merely the eternal object considered as adding its own unique contribution to each actual occasion. This unique contribution is identical for all such occasions in respect to the fact that the object in all modes of ingression is just its identical self. But it varies from one occasion to another in respect to the differences of its modes of ingression. Thus the metaphysical status of an eternal object is that of a possibility for an actuality. Every actual occasion is defined as to its character by how these possibilities are actualised for that occasion. Thus actualisation is a selection among possibilities. More accurately, it is a selection issuing in a gradation of possibilities in respect to their realisation in that occasion. This conclusion brings us to the second metaphysical principle: An eternal object, considered as an abstract entity, cannot be divorced from its reference to other eternal objects, and from its reference to actuality generally; though it is disconnected from its actual modes of ingression into definitive actual occasions. This principle is expressed by the statement that each eternal object has a 'relational essence.' This relational essence determines how it is possible for the object to have ingression into actual occasions.

In other words: If *A* be an eternal object, then what *A* is in itself involves *A*'s status in the universe, and *A* cannot be divorced from this status. In the essence of *A* there stands a determinateness as to the relationships of *A* to other eternal objects, and an indeterminateness as to the relationships of *A* to actual occasions. Since the relationships of *A* to other eternal objects stand determinately in the essence of *A*, it follows that they are internal relations. I mean by this that these relationships are constitutive of *A*; for an entity which stands in internal relations has no being as an entity not in these relations. In other words, once with internal relations, always with internal relations. The internal relationships of *A* conjointly form its significance.

Again an entity cannot stand in external relations unless in its essence there stands an indeterminateness which is its patience for such external relations. The meaning of the term 'possibility' as applied to *A* is simply that there stands in the essence of *A* a patience for relationships to actual occasions. The relationships of *A* to an actual occasion are simply how the eternal relationships of *A* to other eternal objects are graded as to their realisation in that occasion.

Thus the general principle which expresses A's ingression in the particular actual occasion α is the indeterminateness which stands in the essence of A as to its ingression into α, and is the determinateness which stands in the essence of α as to the ingression of *A* into α. Thus the synthetic prehension, which is α, is the solution of the indeterminateness of *A* into the determinateness of α. Accordingly the relationship between *A* and α is external as regards *A*, and is internal as regards α. Every actual occasion α is the solution of all modalities into actual categorical ingressions: truth and falsehood take the place of possibility. The complete ingression of *A* into α is expressed by all the true propositions which are about both *A* and α, and also—it may be—about other things.

The determinate relatedness of the eternal object *A* to every other eternal object is how *A* is systematically and by the necessity of its nature related to every other eternal object. Such relatedness represents a possibility for realisation. But a relationship is a fact which concerns all the implicated *relata*, and cannot be isolated as if involving only one of the *relata*. Accordingly there is a general fact of systematic mutual relatedness which is inherent in the character of possibility. The realm of eternal objects is properly described as a 'realm,' because each eternal object has its status in this general systematic complex of mutual relatedness.

In respect to the ingression of *A* into an actual occasion α, the mutual relationships of *A* to other eternal objects, as thus graded in realisation, require for their expression a reference to the status of *A* and of the other eternal objects in the spatio-temporal relationship. Also this status is not expressible (for this purpose) without a reference to the status of α and of other actual occasions in the same spatio-temporal relationship. Accordingly the spatio-temporal relationship, in terms of which the actual course of events is to be expressed, is nothing else than a selective limitation within the general systematic relationships among eternal objects. By 'limitation,' as applied to the spatio-temporal continuum, I mean those matter-of-fact determinations—such as the three dimensions of space, and the four dimensions of the spatio-temporal continuum—which are inherent in the actual course of events, but which present themselves as arbitrary in respect to a more abstract possibility. The consideration of these general limitations at the base of actual things, as distinct from the limitations peculiar to each actual occasion, will be more fully resumed in the chapter on 'God.'

Further, the status of all possibility in reference to actuality requires a reference to this spatio-temporal continuum. In any particular consideration of a possibility we may conceive this continuum to be transcended. But in so far as there is any definite reference to actuality, the definite *how* of transcendence of that spatio-temporal continuum is required. Thus primarily the spatio-temporal continuum is a locus of relational possibility, selected from the more general realm of systematic relationship. This limited locus of relational possibility expresses one limitation of possibility inherent in the general system of the process of realisation. Whatever possibility is generally coherent with that system falls within this limitation. Also whatever is abstractedly possible in relation to the general course of events—as distinct from the particular limitations introduced by particular occasions—pervades the spatio-temporal continuum in every alternative spatial situation and at all alternative times.

Fundamentally, the spatio-temporal continuum is the general system of relatedness of all possibilities, in so far as that system is limited by its relevance to the general fact of actuality. Also it is inherent in the nature of possibility that it should include this relevance to actuality. For possibility is that in which there stands achievability, abstracted from achievement.

It has already been emphasised that an actual occasion is to be conceived as a limitation; and that this process of limitation can be still further characterised as a gradation. This characteristic of an actual occasion (α, say) requires further elucidation: An indeterminateness stands in the essence of any eternal object

(*A*, say). The actual occasion α synthesises in itself every eternal object; and, in so doing, it includes the *complete* determinate relatedness of *A* to every other eternal object, or set of eternal objects. This synthesis is a limitation of realisation but *not* of content. Each relationship preserves its inherent self-identity. But grades of entry into this synthesis are inherent in each actual occasion, such as α. These grades can be expressed only as relevance of value. This relevance of value varies—as comparing different occasions—in grade from the inclusion of the individual essence of *A* as an element in the aesthetic synthesis (in some grade of inclusion) to the lowest grade which is the exclusion of the individual essence of *A* as an element in the aesthetic synthesis. In so far as it stands in this lowest grade, every determinate relationship of *A* is merely ingredient in the occasion in respect to the determinate *how* this relationship is an unfulfilled alternative, not contributing any aesthetic value, except as forming an element in the systematic substratum of unfulfilled content. In a higher grade, it may remain unfulfilled, but be aesthetically relevant.

Thus *A*, conceived merely in respect to its relationships to other eternal objects, is '*A* conceived as *not-being*'; where 'not-being' means 'abstracted from the determinate fact of inclusions in, and exclusions from, actual events.' Also '*A* as *not-being* in respect to a definite occasion α' means that *A* in all its determinate relationships is excluded from α. Again '*A* as *being* in respect to α' means that *A* in some of its determinate relationships is included in α. But there can be no occasion which includes *A* in all its determinate relationships; for some of these relationships are contraries. Thus, in regard to excluded relationships, *A* will be *not-being* in α, even when in regard to other relationships A will be *being* in α. In this sense, every occasion is a synthesis of *being* and *not-being*. Furthermore, though some eternal objects are synthesised in an occasion α merely *quâ not-being*, each eternal object which is synthesised *quâ being* is also synthesised *quâ not-being*. '*Being*' here means 'individually effective in the aesthetic synthesis.' Also the 'aesthetic synthesis' is the 'experient synthesis' viewed as self-creative, under the limitations laid upon it by its internal relatedness to all other actual occasions. We thus conclude—what has already been stated above—that the general fact of the synthetic prehension of all eternal objects into every occasion wears the double aspect of the indeterminate relatedness of each eternal object to occasions generally, and of its determinate relatedness to each particular occasion. This statement summarises the account of how external relations are possible. But the account depends upon disengaging the spatio-temporal continuum from its mere implication in actual occasions—according to the usual explanation—and upon exhibiting it in its origin from the general nature of abstract possibility, as limited by the general character of the actual course of events.

The difficulty which arises in respect to internal relations is to explain how any particular truth is possible. In so far as there are internal relations, everything must depend upon everything else. But if this be the case, we cannot know about anything till we equally know everything else. Apparently, therefore, we are under the necessity of saying everything at once. This supposed necessity is palpably untrue. Accordingly it is incumbent on us to explain how there can be internal relations, seeing that we admit finite truths.

Since actual occasions are selections from the realm of possibilities, the ultimate explanation of how actual occasions have the general character which they do have, must lie in an analysis of the general character of the realm of possibility.

The *analytical character* of the realm of eternal objects is the primary metaphysical truth concerning it. By this character it is meant that the status of any eternal object *A* in this realm is capable of analysis into an indefinite number of subordinate relationships of limited scope. For example if *B* and *C* are two other eternal objects, then there is some perfectly definite relationship *R*(*A*, *B*, *C*) which involves *A*, *B*, *C* only, as to require the mention of no other definite eternal objects in the capacity of *relata*. Of course, the relationship *R*(*A*, *B*, *C*) may involve subordinate relationships which are themselves eternal objects, and *R*(*A*, *B*, *C*) is also itself an eternal object. Also there will be other relationships which in the same sense involve only *A*, *B*, *C*. We have now to examine how, having regard to the internal relatedness of eternal objects, this limited relationship *R*(*A*, *B*, *C*) is possible.

The reason for the existence of finite relationships in the realm of eternal objects is that relationships of these objects among themselves are entirely unselective, and are systematically complete. We are discussing possibility; so that every relationship which is possible is thereby in the realm of possibility. Every such relationship of each eternal object is founded upon the perfectly definite status of that object as a *relatum* in the general scheme of relationships. This definite status is what I have termed the 'relational essence' of the object. This relational essence is determinable by reference to that object alone, and does not require reference to any other objects, except those which are specifically involved in its individual essence when that essence is complex (as will be explained immediately). The meaning of the words 'any' and 'some' springs from this principle—that is to say, the meaning of the 'variable' in logic. The whole principle is that a particular determination can be made of the *how* of some definite relationship of a definite eternal object *A* to a definite finite number *n* of other eternal objects, *without* any determination of the other *n* objects, X_1, X_2, … X_n, except that they have, each of them, the requisite status to play their respective parts in that multiple relationship. This principle depends on the fact that the relational essence of an eternal object is not unique to that object. The mere relational essence of each eternal object determines the complete uniform scheme of relational essences, since each object stands internally in all its possible relationships. Thus the realm of possibility provides a uniform scheme of relationships among finite sets of eternal objects; and all eternal objects stand in all such relationships, so far as the status of each permits.

Accordingly the relationships (as in possibility) do not involve the individual essences of the eternal objects; they involve *any* eternal objects as *relata*, subject to the proviso that these *relata* have the requisite relational essences. [It is this proviso which, automatically and by the nature of the case, limits the 'any' of the phrase 'any eternal objects.'] This principle is the principle of the *Isolation of Eternal Objects* in the realm of possibility. The eternal objects are isolated, because their relationships as possibilities are expressible without reference to their respective individual essences. In contrast to the realm of possibility, the inclusion of eternal objects within an actual occasion means that in respect to some of their possible relationships there is a togetherness of their individual essences. This realised togetherness is the achievement of an emergent value defined—or, shaped—by the definite eternal relatedness in respect to which the real togetherness is achieved. Thus the eternal relatedness is the form—the εἶδος—; the emergent actual occasion is the *superject* of informed value; value, as abstracted from any particular superject, is the abstract matter—the ὕλη—which is common to all actual occasions; and the synthetic activity which prehends valueless possibility into superjicient informed value is the substantial activity. This substantial activity is that which is omitted in any analysis of the static factors in the metaphysical situation. The analysed elements of the situation are the attributes of the substantial activity.

The difficulty inherent in the concept of finite internal relations among eternal objects is thus evaded by two metaphysical principles, (i) that the relationships of any eternal object *A*, considered as constitutive of *A*, merely involve other eternal objects as bare *relata* without reference to their individual essences, and (ii) that the divisibility of the general relationship of *A* into a multiplicity of finite relationships of *A* stands therefore in the essence of that eternal object. The second principle obviously depends upon the first. To understand *A* is to understand the *how* of a general scheme of relationship. This scheme of relationship does not require the individual uniqueness of the other *relata* for its comprehension. This scheme also discloses itself as being analysable into a multiplicity of limited relationships which have their own individuality and yet at the same time presupposes the total relationship within possibility. In respect to actuality there is first the general limitation of relationships, which reduces this general unlimited scheme to the four dimensional spatio-temporal scheme. This spatio-temporal scheme is, so to speak, the greatest common measure of the schemes of relationship (as limited by actuality) inherent in all the eternal objects. By this it is meant that, *how* select relationships of an eternal object (*A*) are realised in any actual occasion, is always explicable by expressing the status of *A* in respect to this spatio-temporal scheme, and by expressing in this scheme the relationship of the actual occasion to other actual occasions. A definite finite relationship involving the definite eternal objects of a limited set of such objects is itself an eternal object: it is those eternal objects as in that relationship. I will call such an eternal object 'complex.' The eternal objects which are the *relata* in a complex eternal object will be called the 'components' of that eternal object. Also if any of these *relata* are themselves complex, their components will be called 'derivative components' of the original complex object. Also the components of derivative components will also be called derivative components of the original object. Thus the complexity of an eternal object means its analysability into a relationship of component eternal objects. Also the analysis of the general scheme of relatedness of eternal objects means its exhibition as a multiplicity of complex eternal objects. An eternal object, such as a definite shade of green, which cannot be analysed into a relationship of components, will be called 'simple.'

We can now explain how the analytical character of the realm of eternal objects allows of an analysis of that realm into grades.

In the lowest grade of eternal objects are to be placed those objects whose individual essences are simple. This is the grade of zero complexity. Next consider any set of such objects, finite or infinite as to the number of its members. For example, consider the set of three eternal objects *A, B, C*, of which none is complex. Let us write *R*(*A, B, C*) for some definite possible relatedness of *A, B, C*. To take a simple example, *A, B, C* may be three definite colours with the spatio-temporal relatedness to each other of three faces of a regular tetrahedron, anywhere at any time. Then *R*(*A, B, C*) is another eternal object of the lowest complex grade. Analogously there are eternal objects of successively higher grades. In respect to any complex eternal object, $S(D_1, D_2, \ldots D_n)$, the eternal objects $D_1, \ldots D_n$, whose individual essences are constitutive of the individual essence of $S(D_1, \ldots D_n)$, are called the components of $S(D_1, \ldots D_n)$. It is obvious that the grade of complexity to be ascribed to $S(D_1, \ldots D_n)$ is to be taken as one above the highest grade of complexity to be found among its components.

There is thus an analysis of the realm of possibility into simple eternal objects, and into various grades of complex eternal objects. A complex eternal object is an abstract situation. There is a double sense of 'abstraction,' in regard to the abstraction of *definite* eternal objects, *i.e.*, non-mathematical abstraction. There is abstraction from actuality, and abstraction from possibility. For example, *A* and *R*(*A, B, C*) are both abstractions from the realm of possibility. Note that *A* must mean *A* in all its possible relationships, and among them *R*(*A, B, C*). Also *R*(*A, B, C*) means *R*(*A, B, C*) in all its relationships. But this meaning of *R*(*A, B, C*) excludes other relationships into which *A* can enter. Hence A as in *R*(*A, B, C*) is more abstract than *A simpliciter*. Thus as we pass from the grade of simple eternal objects to higher and higher grades of complexity, we are indulging in higher grades of abstraction from the realm of possibility.

We can now conceive the successive stages of a definite progress towards some assigned mode of abstraction from the realm of possibility, involving a progress (in thought) through successive grades of increasing complexity. I will call any such route of progress 'an abstractive hierarchy.' Any abstractive hierarchy, finite or infinite, is based upon some definite group of simple eternal objects. This group will be called the 'base' of the hierarchy. Thus the base of an abstractive hierarchy is a set of objects of zero complexity. The formal definition of an abstractive hierarchy is as follows:

An "abstractive hierarchy based upon *g*," where *g* is a group of simple eternal objects, is a set of eternal objects which satisfy the following conditions,

(i) the members of *g* belong to it, and are the only simple eternal objects in the hierarchy,

(ii) the components of any complex eternal object in the hierarchy are also members of the hierarchy, and

(iii) any set of eternal objects belonging to the hierarchy, whether all of the same grade or whether differing among themselves as to grade, are jointly among the components or derivative components of at least one eternal object which also belongs to the hierarchy.

It is to be noticed that the components of an eternal object are necessarily of a lower grade of complexity than itself. Accordingly any member of such a hierarchy, which is of the first grade of complexity, can have as components only members of the group *g*; and any member of the second grade can have as components only members of the first grade, and members of *g*; and so on for the higher grades.

The third condition to be satisfied by an abstractive hierarchy will be called the condition of connexity. Thus an abstractive hierarchy springs from its base; it includes every successive grade from its base either indefinitely onwards, or to its maximum grade; and it is 'connected' by the reappearance (in a higher grade) of any set of its members belonging to lower grades, in the function of a set of components or derivative components of at least one member of the hierarchy.

An abstractive hierarchy is called 'finite' if it stops at a finite grade of complexity. It is called 'infinite' if it includes members belonging respectively to all degrees of complexity.

It is to be noted that the base of an abstractive hierarchy may contain any number of members, finite or infinite. Further, the infinity of the number of the members of the base has nothing to do with the question as to whether the hierarchy be finite or infinite.

A finite abstractive hierarchy will, by definition, possess a grade of maximum complexity. It is characteristic of this grade that a member of it is a component of no other eternal object belonging to any grade of the hierarchy. Also it is evident that this grade of maximum complexity must possess only one member; for otherwise the condition of connexity would not be satisfied. Conversely any complex eternal object defines a finite abstractive hierarchy to be discovered by a process of analysis. This complex eternal object from which we start will be called the 'vertex' of the abstractive hierarchy: it is the sole member of the grade of maximum complexity. In the first stage of the analysis we obtain the components of the vertex. These components may be of varying complexity; but there must be among them at least one member whose complexity is of a grade one lower than that of the vertex. A grade which is one lower than that of a given eternal object will be called the 'proximate grade' for that object. We take then those components of the vertex which belong to its proximate grade; and as the second stage we analyse them into their components. Among these components there must be some belonging to the proximate grade for the objects thus analysed. Add to them the components of the vertex which also belong to this grade of 'second proximation' from the vertex; and, at the third stage analyse as before. We thus find objects belonging to the grade of third proximation from the vertex; and we add to them the components belonging to this grade, which have been left over from the preceding stages of the analysis. We proceed in this way through successive stages, till we reach the grade of simple objects. This grade forms the base of the hierarchy.

It is to be noted that in dealing with hierarchies we are entirely within the realm of possibility. Accordingly the eternal objects are devoid of real togetherness: they remain within their 'isolation.'

The logical instrument which Aristotle used for the analysis of actual fact into more abstract elements was that of classification into species and genera. This instrument has its overwhelmingly important application for science in its preparatory stages. But its use in metaphysical description distorts the true vision of the metaphysical situation. The use of the term 'universal' is intimately connected with this Aristotelian analysis: the term has been broadened of late; but still it suggests that classificatory analysis. For this reason I have avoided it.

In any actual occasion α, there will be a group g of simple eternal objects which are ingredient in that group in the most concrete mode. This complete ingredience in an occasion, so as to yield the most complete fusion of individual essence with other eternal objects in the formation of the individual emergent occasion, is evidently of its own kind and cannot be defined in terms of anything else. But it has a peculiar characteristic which necessarily attaches to it. This characteristic is that there is an *infinite* abstractive hierarchy based upon g which is such that all its members are equally involved in this complete inclusion in α.

The existence of such an infinite abstractive hierarchy is what is meant by the statement that it is impossible to complete the description of an actual occasion by means of concepts. I will call this infinite abstractive hierarchy which is associated with α 'the associated hierarchy of α.' It is also what is meant by the notion of the connectedness of an actual occasion. This connectedness of an occasion is necessary for its synthetic unity and for its intelligibility. There is a connected hierarchy of concepts applicable to the occasion, including concepts of all degrees of complexity. Also in the actual occasion, the individual essences of the eternal objects involved in these complex concepts achieve an aesthetic synthesis, productive of the occasion as an experience for its own sake. This associated hierarchy is the shape, or pattern, or form, of the occasion in so far as the occasion is constituted of what enters into its full realisation.

Some confusion of thought has been caused by the fact that abstraction from possibility runs in the opposite direction to an abstraction from actuality, so far as degree of abstractness is concerned. For evidently in describing an actual occasion α, we are nearer to the total concrete fact when we describe α by predicating of it some member of its associated hierarchy, which is of a high grade of complexity. We have then said more about α. Thus, with a high grade of complexity we gain in approach to the full concreteness of α, and with a low grade we lose in this approach. Accordingly the simple eternal objects represent the extreme of abstraction from an actual occasion; whereas simple eternal objects represent the minimum of abstraction from the realm of possibility. It will, I think, be found that, when a high degree of abstraction is spoken of, abstraction from the realm of possibility is what is usually meant—in other words, an elaborate logical construction.

So far I have merely been considering an actual occasion on the side of its full concreteness. It is this side of the occasion in virtue of which it is an event in nature. But a natural event, in this sense of the term, is only an abstraction from a complete actual occasion. A complete occasion includes that which in cognitive experience takes the form of memory, anticipation, imagination, and thought. These elements in an experient occasion are also modes of inclusion of complex eternal objects in the synthetic prehension, as elements in the emergent value. They differ from the concreteness of full inclusion. In a sense this difference is inexplicable; for each mode of inclusion is of its own kind, not to be explained in terms of anything else. But there is a common difference which discriminates these modes of inclusion from the full concrete ingression which has been discussed. This *differentia* is *abruptness*. By 'abruptness' I mean that what is remembered, or anticipated, or imagined, or thought, is exhausted by a finite complex concept. In each case there is one finite eternal object prehended within the occasion as the vertex of a finite hierarchy. This breaking off from an actual illimitability is what in any occasion marks off that which is termed mental from that which belongs to the physical event to which the mental functioning is referred.

In general there seems to be some loss of vividness in the apprehension of the eternal objects concerned: for example, Hume speaks of 'faint copies.' But this faintness seems to be a very unsafe ground for differentiation. Often things realised in thought are more vivid than the same things in inattentive physical experience. But the things apprehended as mental are always subject to the condition that we come to a stop when we attempt to explore ever higher grades of complexity in their realised relationships. We always find that we have thought of just this—whatever it may be—and of no more. There is a limitation which breaks off the finite concept from the higher grades of illimitable complexity.

Thus an actual occasion is a prehension of one infinite hierarchy (its associated hierarchy) together with various finite hierarchies. The synthesis into the occasion of the infinite hierarchy is according to its specific mode of realisation, and that of the finite hierarchies is according to various other specific modes of realisation. There is one metaphysical principle which is essential for the rational coherence of this account of the general character of an experient occasion. I call this principle, 'The Translucency of Realisation.' By this I mean that any eternal object is just itself in whatever mode of realisation it is involved. There can be no distortion of the individual essence without thereby producing a different eternal object. In the essence of each eternal object there stands an indeterminateness which expresses its indifferent patience for any mode of ingression into any actual occasion. Thus in cognitive experience, there can be the cognition of the same eternal object as in the same occasion having ingression with implication in more than one grade of realisation. Thus the translucency of realisation, and the possible multiplicity of modes of ingression into the same occasion, together form the foundation for the correspondence theory of truth.

In this account of an actual occasion in terms of its connection with the realm of eternal objects, we have gone back to the train of thought in our second chapter, where the nature of mathematics was discussed. The idea, ascribed to Pythagoras, has been amplified, and put forward as the first chapter in metaphysics. The next chapter is concerned with the puzzling fact that there is an actual course of events which is in itself a limited fact, in that metaphysically speaking it might have been otherwise. But other metaphysical investigations are omitted; for example, epistemology, and the classification of some elements in the unfathomable wealth of the field of possibility. This last topic brings metaphysics in sight of the special topics of the various sciences.

CHAPTER XI

GOD

Aristotle found it necessary to complete his metaphysics by the introduction of a Prime Mover—God. This, for two reasons, is an important fact in the history of metaphysics. In the first place if we are to accord to anyone the position of the greatest metaphysician, having regard to genius of insight, to general equipment in knowledge, and to the stimulus of his metaphysical ancestry, we must choose Aristotle. Secondly, in his consideration of this metaphysical question he was entirely dispassionate; and he is the last European metaphysician of first rate importance for whom this claim can be made. After Aristotle, ethical and religious interests began to influence metaphysical conclusions. The Jews dispersed, first willingly and then forcibly, and the Judaic-Alexandrian school arose. Then Christianity closely followed by Mahometanism, intervened. The Greek gods who surrounded Aristotle were subordinate metaphysical entities, well within nature. Accordingly on the subject of his Prime Mover, he would have no motive, except to follow his metaphysical train of thought whithersoever it led him. It did not lead him very far towards the production of a God available for religious purposes. It may be doubted whether any properly general metaphysics can ever, without the illicit introduction of other considerations, get much further than Aristotle. But his conclusion does represent a first step without which no evidence on a narrower experiential basis can be of much avail in shaping the conception. For nothing, within any limited type of experience, can give intelligence to shape our ideas of any entity at the base of all actual things, unless the general character of things requires that there be such an entity.

The phrase, Prime Mover, warns us that Aristotle's thought was enmeshed in the details of an erroneous physics and an erroneous cosmology. In Aristotle's physics special causes were required to sustain the motions of material things. These could easily be fitted into his system, provided that the general cosmic motions could be sustained. For then in relation to the general working system, each thing could be provided with its true end. Hence the necessity for a Prime Mover who sustains the motions of the spheres on which depend the adjustment of things. To-day we repudiate the Aristotelian physics and the Aristotelian cosmology, so that the exact form of the above argument manifestly fails. But if our general metaphysics is in any way similar to that outlined in the previous chapter, an analogous metaphysical problem arises which can be solved only in an analogous fashion. In the place of Aristotle's God as Prime Mover, we require God as the Principle of Concretion. This position can be substantiated only by the discussion of the general implication of the course of actual occasions,—that is to say, of the process of realisation.

We conceive actuality as in essential relation to an unfathomable possibility. Eternal objects inform actual occasions with hierarchic patterns, included and excluded in every variety of discrimination. Another view of the same truth is that every actual occasion is a limitation imposed on possibility, and that by virtue of this limitation the particular value of that shaped togetherness of things emerges. In this way we express how a single occasion is to be viewed in terms of possibility, and how possibility is to be viewed in terms of a single actual occasion. But there are no single occasions, in the sense of isolated occasions. Actuality is through and through togetherness—togetherness of otherwise isolated eternal objects, and togetherness of all actual occasions. It is my task in this chapter to describe the unity of actual occasions. The previous chapter centered its interest in the abstract: the present chapter deals with the concrete, *i.e.*, that which has grown together.

Consider an occasion α:—we have to enumerate how other actual occasions are in α, in the sense that their relationships with α are constitutive of the essence of α. What α is in itself, is that it is a unit of realised experience; accordingly we ask how other occasions are in the experience which is α. Also for the present I am excluding cognitive experience. The complete answer to this question is, that the relationships among actual occasions are as unfathomable in their variety of type as are those among eternal objects in the realm of abstraction. But there are fundamental types of such relationships in terms of which the whole complex variety can find its description.

A preliminary for the understanding of these types of entry (of one occasion into the essence of another) is to note that they are involved in the modes of realisation of abstractive hierarchies, discussed in the previous chapter. The spatio-temporal relationships, involved in those hierarchies as realised in α, have all a definition in terms of α and of the occasions entrant in α. Thus the entrant occasions lend their aspects to the hierarchies, and thereby convert spatio-temporal modalities into categorical determinations; and the hierarchies lend their forms to the occasions and thereby limit the entrant occasions to being entrant only under those forms. Thus in the same way (as seen in the previous chapter) that every occasion is a synthesis of all eternal objects under the limitation of gradations of actuality, so every occasion is a synthesis of all occasions under the limitation of gradations of types of entry. Each occasion synthesises the totality of content under its own limitations of mode.

In respect to these types of internal relationship between α and other occasions, these other occasions (as constitutive of α) can be classified in many alternative ways. These are all concerned with different definitions of past, present, and future. It has been usual in philosophy to assume that these various definitions must necessarily be equivalent. The present state of opinion in physical science conclusively shows that this assumption is without metaphysical justification, even though any such discrimination may be found to be unnecessary for physical science. This question has already been dealt with in the chapter on Relativity. But the physical theory of relativity touches only the fringe of the various theories which are metaphysically tenable. It is important for my argument to insist upon the unbounded freedom within which the actual is a unique categorical determination.

Every actual occasion exhibits itself as a process: it is a becomingness. In so disclosing itself, it places itself as one among a multiplicity of other occasions, without which it could not be itself. It also defines itself as a particular individual achievement, focusing in its limited way an unbounded realm of eternal objects.

Any one occasion α issues from other occasions which collectively form its *past*. It displays for itself other occasions which collectively form its *present*. It is in respect to its associated hierarchy, as displayed in this immediate present, that an occasion finds its own originality. It is that display which is its own contribution to the output of actuality. It may be conditioned, and even completely determined by the past from which it issues. But its display in the present under those conditions is what directly emerges from its prehensive activity. The occasion α also holds within itself an indetermination in the form of a future, which has partial determination by reason of its inclusion in α and also has determinate spatio-temporal relatedness to α and to actual occasions of the past from α and of the present for α.

This future is a synthesis in α of eternal objects as not-being and as requiring the passage from α to other individualisations (with determinate spatio-temporal relations to α) in which not-being becomes being.

There is also in α what, in the previous chapter, I have termed the 'abrupt' realisation of finite eternal objects. This abrupt realisation requires *either* a reference of the basic objects of the finite hierarchy to determinate occasions other than α (as their situations), in past, present, future; *or* requires a realisation of these eternal objects in determinate relationships, but under the aspect of exemption from inclusion in the spatio-temporal scheme of relatedness between actual occasions. This abrupt synthesis of eternal objects in each occasion is the inclusion in actuality of the analytical character of the realm of eternality. This inclusion has those limited gradations of actuality which characterise every occasion by reason of its essential limitation. It is this realised extension of eternal relatedness beyond the mutual relatedness of the actual occasions, which prehends into each occasion the full sweep of eternal relatedness. I term this abrupt realisation the 'graded envisagement' which each occasion prehends into its synthesis. This graded envisagement is how the actual includes what (in one sense) is not-being as a positive factor in its own achievement. It is the source of error, of truth, of art, of ethics, and of religion. By it, fact is confronted with alternatives.

This general concept, of an event as a process whose outcome is a unit of experience, points to the analysis of an event into (i) substantial activity, (ii) conditioned potentialities which are there for synthesis, and (iii) the achieved outcome of the synthesis. The unity of all actual occasions forbids the analysis of substantial activities into independent entities. Each individual activity is nothing but the mode in which the general activity is individualised by the imposed conditions. The envisagement which enters into the synthesis is also a character which conditions the synthesising activity. The general activity is not an entity in the sense in which occasions or eternal objects are entities. It is a general metaphysical character which underlies all occasions, in a particular mode for each occasion. There is nothing with which to compare it: it is Spinoza's one infinite substance. Its attributes are its character of individualisation into a multiplicity of modes, and the realm of eternal objects which are variously synthesised in these modes. Thus eternal possibility and modal differentiation into individual multiplicity are the attributes of the one substance. In fact each general element of the metaphysical situation is an attribute of the substantial activity.

Yet another element in the metaphysical situation is disclosed by the consideration that the general attribute of modality is limited. This element must rank as an attribute of the substantial activity. In its nature each mode is limited, so as not to be other modes. But, beyond these limitations of particulars, the general modal individualisation is limited in two ways: In the first place it is an actual course of events, which might be otherwise so far as concerns eternal possibility, but *is* that course. This limitation takes three forms, (i) the special logical relations which all events must conform to, (ii) the selection of relationships to which the events do conform, and (iii) the particularity which infects the course even within those general relationships of logic and causation. Thus this first limitation is a limitation of antecedent selection. So far as the general metaphysical situation is concerned, there might have been an indiscriminate modal pluralism apart from logical or other limitation. But there could not then have been these modes, for each mode represents a synthesis of actualities which are limited to conform to a standard. We here come to the second way of limitation. Restriction is the price of value. There cannot be value without antecedent standards of value, to discriminate the acceptance or rejection of what is before the envisaging mode of activity. Thus there is an antecedent limitation among values, introducing contraries, grades, and oppositions.

According to this argument the fact that there is a process of actual occasions, and the fact that the occasions are the emergence of values which require such limitation, both require that the course of events should have developed amid an antecedent limitation composed of conditions, particularisation, and standards of value.

Thus as a further element in the metaphysical situation, there is required a principle of limitation. Some particular *how* is necessary, and some particularisation in the *what* of matter of fact is necessary. The only alternative to this admission, is to deny the reality of actual occasions. Their apparent irrational limitation must be taken as a proof of illusion and we must look for reality behind the scene. If we reject this alternative behind the scene, we must provide a ground for limitation which stands among the attributes of the substantial activity. This attribute provides the limitation for which no reason can be given: for all reason flows from it. God is the ultimate limitation, and His existence is the ultimate irrationality. For no reason can be given for just that limitation which it stands in His nature to impose. God is not concrete, but He is the ground for concrete actuality. No reason can be given for the nature of God, because that nature is the ground of rationality.

In this argument the point to notice is, that what is metaphysically indeterminate has nevertheless to be categorically determinate. We have come to the limit of rationality. For there is a categorical limitation which does not spring from any metaphysical reason. There is a metaphysical need for a principle of determination, but there can be no metaphysical reason for what is determined. If there were such a reason, there would be no need for any further principle: for metaphysics would already have provided the determination. The general principle of empiricism depends upon the doctrine that there is a principle of concretion which is not discoverable by abstract reason. What further can be known about God must be sought in the region of particular experiences, and therefore rests on an empirical basis. In respect to the interpretation of these experiences, mankind have differed profoundly. He has been named respectively, Jehovah, Allah, Brahma, Father in Heaven, Order of Heaven, First Cause, Supreme Being, Chance. Each name corresponds to a system of thought derived from the experiences of those who have used it.

Among medieval and modern philosophers, anxious to establish the religious significance of God, an unfortunate habit has prevailed of paying to Him metaphysical compliments. He has been conceived as the foundation of the metaphysical situation with its ultimate activity. If this conception be adhered to, there can be no alternative except to discern in Him the origin of all evil as well as of all good. He is then the supreme author of the play, and to Him must therefore be ascribed its shortcomings as well as its success. If He be conceived as the supreme ground for limitation, it stands in His very nature to divide the Good from the Evil, and to establish Reason 'within her dominions supreme.'

Chapter XII

RELIGION AND SCIENCE

The difficulty in approaching the question of the relations between Religion and Science is, that its elucidation requires that we have in our minds some clear idea of what we mean by either of the terms, 'religion' and 'science.' Also I wish to speak in the most general way possible, and to keep in the background any comparison of particular creeds, scientific or religious. We have got to understand the type of connection which exists between the two spheres, and then to draw some definite conclusions respecting the existing situation which at present confronts the world.

The *conflict* between religion and science is what naturally occurs to our minds when we think of this subject. It seems as though, during the last half-century, the results of science and the beliefs of religion had come into a position of frank disagreement, from which there can be no escape, except by abandoning either the clear teaching of science, or the clear teaching of religion. This conclusion has been urged by controversialists on either side. Not by all controversialists, of course, but by those trenchant intellects which every controversy calls out into the open.

The distress of sensitive minds, and the zeal for truth, and the sense of the importance of the issues, must command our sincerest sympathy. When we consider what religion is for mankind, and what science is, it is no exaggeration to say that the future course of history depends upon the decision of this generation as to the relations between them. We have here the two strongest general forces (apart from the mere impulse of the various senses) which influence men, and they seem to be set one against the other—the force of our religious intuitions, and the force of our impulse to accurate observation and logical deduction.

A great English statesman once advised his countrymen to use large-scale maps, as a preservative against alarms, panics, and general misunderstanding of the true relations between nations. In the same way in dealing with the clash between permanent elements of human nature, it is well to map our history on a large scale, and to disengage ourselves from our immediate absorption in the present conflicts. When we do this, we immediately discover two great facts. In the first place, there has always been a conflict between religion and science; and in the second place, both religion and science have always been in a state of continual development. In the early days of Christianity, there was a general belief among Christians that the world was coming to an end in the lifetime of people then living. We can make only indirect inferences as to how far this belief was authoritatively proclaimed; but it is certain that it was widely held, and that it formed an impressive part of the popular religious doctrine. The belief proved itself to be mistaken, and Christian doctrine adjusted itself to the change. Again in the early Church individual theologians very confidently deduced from the Bible opinions concerning the nature of the physical universe. In the year A. D. 535, a monk named Cosmas[1] wrote a book which he entitled, *Christian Topography*. He was a travelled man who had visited India and Ethiopia; and finally he lived in a monastery at Alexandria, which was then a great centre of culture. In this book, basing himself upon the direct meaning of Biblical texts as construed by him in a literal fashion, he denied the existence of the antipodes, and asserted that the world is a flat parallelogram whose length is double its breadth.

In the seventeenth century the doctrine of the motion of the earth was condemned by a Catholic tribunal. A hundred years ago

1. *Cf.* Lecky's *The Rise and Influence of Rationalism in Europe*, Ch. III.

the extension of time demanded by geological science distressed religious people, Protestant and Catholic. And to-day the doctrine of evolution is an equal stumbling-block. These are only a few instances illustrating a general fact.

But all our ideas will be in a wrong perspective if we think that this recurring perplexity was confined to contradictions between religion and science; and that in these controversies religion was always wrong, and that science was always right. The true facts of the case are very much more complex, and refuse to be summarised in these simple terms.

Theology itself exhibits exactly the same character of gradual development, arising from an aspect of conflict between its own proper ideas. This fact is a commonplace to theologians, but is often obscured in the stress of controversy. I do not wish to overstate my case; so I will confine myself to Roman Catholic writers. In the seventeenth century a learned Jesuit, Father Petavius, showed that the theologians of the first three centuries of Christianity made use of phrases and statements which since the fifth century would be condemned as heretical. Also Cardinal Newman devoted a treatise to the discussion of the development of doctrine. He wrote it before he became a great Roman Catholic ecclesiastic; but throughout his life, it was never retracted and continually reissued.

Science is even more changeable than theology. No man of science could subscribe without qualification to Galileo's beliefs, or to Newton's beliefs, or to all his own scientific beliefs of ten years ago.

In both regions of thought, additions, distinctions, and modifications have been introduced. So that now, even when the same assertion is made to-day as was made a thousand, or fifteen hundred years ago, it is made subject to limitations or expansions of meaning, which were not contemplated at the earlier epoch. We are told by logicians that a proposition must be either true or false, and that there is no middle term. But in practice, we may know that a proposition expresses an important truth, but that it is subject to limitations and qualifications which at present remain undiscovered. It is a general feature of our knowledge, that we are insistently aware of important truths; and yet that the only formulations of these truths which we are able to make presuppose a general standpoint of conceptions which may have to be modified. I will give you two illustrations, both from science: Galileo said that the earth moves and that the sun is fixed; the Inquisition said that the earth is fixed and the sun moves; and Newtonian astronomers, adopting an absolute theory of space, said that both the sun and the earth move. But now we say that any one of these three statements is equally true, provided that you have fixed your sense of 'rest' and 'motion' in the way required by the statement adopted. At the date of Galileo's controversy with the Inquisition, Galileo's way of stating the facts was, beyond question, the fruitful procedure for the sake of scientific research. But in itself it was not more true than the formulation of the Inquisition. But at that time the modern concepts of relative motion were in nobody's mind; so that the statements were made in ignorance of the qualifications required for their more perfect truth. Yet this question of the motions of the earth and the sun expresses a real fact in the universe; and all sides had got hold of important truths concerning it. But with the knowledge of those times, the truths appeared to be inconsistent.

Again I will give you another example taken from the state of modern physical science. Since the time of Newton and Huyghens in the seventeenth century there have been two theories as to the physical nature of light. Newton's theory was that a beam of light consists of a stream of very minute particles, or corpuscles, and that we have the sensation of light when these corpuscles strike the retinas of our eyes. Huyghens' theory was that light consists of very minute waves of trembling in an all-pervading ether, and that these waves are travelling along a beam of light. The two theories are contradictory. In the eighteenth century Newton's theory was believed, in the nineteenth century Huyghens' theory was believed. To-day there is one large group of phenomena which can be explained only on the wave theory, and another large group which can be explained only on the corpuscular theory. Scientists have to leave it at that, and wait for the future, in the hope of attaining some wider vision which reconciles both.

We should apply these same principles to the questions in which there is a variance between science and religion. We would believe nothing in either sphere of thought which does not appear to us to be certified by solid reasons based upon the critical research either of ourselves or of competent authorities. But granting that we have honestly taken this precaution, a clash between the two on points of detail where they overlap should not lead us hastily to abandon doctrines for which we have solid evidence. It may be that we are more interested in one set of doctrines than in the other. But, if we have any sense of perspective and of the history of thought, we shall wait and refrain from mutual anathemas.

We should wait: but we should not wait passively, or in despair. The clash is a sign that there are wider truths and finer perspectives within which a reconciliation of a deeper religion and a more subtle science will be found.

In one sense, therefore, the conflict between science and religion is a slight matter which has been unduly emphasised. A mere logical contradiction cannot in itself point to more than the necessity of some readjustments, possibly of a very minor character on both sides. Remember the widely different aspects of events which are dealt with in science and in religion respectively. Science is concerned with the general conditions which are observed to regulate physical phenomena; whereas religion is wholly wrapped up in the contemplation of moral and aesthetic values. On the one side there is the law of gravitation, and on the other the contemplation of the beauty of holiness. What one side sees, the other misses; and vice versa.

Consider, for example, the lives of John Wesley and of Saint Francis of Assisi. For physical science you have in these lives merely ordinary examples of the operation of the principles of physiological chemistry, and of the dynamics of nervous reactions: for religion you have lives of the most profound significance in the history of the world. Can you be surprised that, in the absence of a perfect and complete phrasing of the principles of science and of the principles of religion which apply to these specific cases, the accounts of these lives from these divergent standpoints should involve discrepancies? It would be a miracle if it were not so.

It would, however, be missing the point to think that we need not trouble ourselves about the conflict between science and religion. In an intellectual age there can be no active interest which puts aside all hope of a vision of the harmony of truth. To acquiesce in discrepancy is destructive of candour, and of moral cleanliness. It belongs to the self-respect of intellect to pursue every tangle of thought to its final unravelment. If you check that impulse, you will get no religion and no science from an awakened thoughtfulness. The important question is, In what spirit are we going to face the issue? There we come to something absolutely vital.

A clash of doctrines is not a disaster—it is an opportunity. I will explain my meaning by some illustrations from science. The weight of an atom of nitrogen was well known. Also it was an established scientific doctrine that the average weight of such atoms in any considerable mass will be always the same. Two experimenters, the late Lord Rayleigh and the late Sir William Ramsay, found that if they obtained nitrogen by two different methods, each equally effective for that purpose, they always observed a persistent slight difference between the average weights of the atoms in the two cases. Now I ask you, would it have been rational of these men to have despaired because of this conflict between chemical theory and scientific observation? Suppose that for some reason the chemical doctrine had been highly prized throughout some district as the foundation of its social order:—would it have been wise, would it have been candid, would it have been moral, to forbid the disclosure of the fact that the experiments produced discordant results? Or, on the other hand, should Sir William Ramsay and Lord Rayleigh have proclaimed that chemical theory was now a detected delusion? We see at once that either of these ways would have been a method of facing the issue in an entirely wrong spirit. What Rayleigh and Ramsay did do was this: They at once perceived that they had hit upon a line of investigation which would disclose some subtlety of chemical theory that had hitherto eluded observation. The discrepancy was not a disaster: it was an opportunity to increase the sweep of chemical knowledge. You all know the end of the story: finally argon was discovered, a new chemical element which had lurked undetected, mixed with the nitrogen. But the story has a sequel which forms my second illustration. This discovery drew attention to the importance of observing accurately minute differences in chemical substances as obtained by different methods. Further researches of the most careful accuracy were undertaken. Finally another physicist, F. W. Aston, working in the Cavendish Laboratory at Cambridge in England, discovered that even the same element might assume two or more distinct forms, termed *isotopes*, and that the law of the constancy of average atomic weight holds for each of these forms, but as between the different isotopes differs slightly. The research has effected a great stride in the power of chemical theory, far transcending in importance the discovery of argon from which it originated. The moral of these stories lies on the surface, and I will leave to you their application to the case of religion and science.

In formal logic, a contradiction is the signal of a defeat: but in the evolution of real knowledge it marks the first step in progress towards a victory. This is one great reason for the utmost toleration of variety of opinion. Once and forever, this duty of toleration has been summed up in the words, 'Let both grow together until the harvest.' The failure of Christians to act up to this precept, of the highest authority, is one of the curiosities of religious history. But we have not yet exhausted the discussion of the moral temper required for the pursuit of truth. There are short cuts leading merely to an illusory success. It is easy enough to find a theory, logically harmonious and with important applications in the region of fact, provided that you are content to disregard half your evidence. Every age produces people with clear logical intellects, and with the most praiseworthy grasp of the importance of some sphere of human experience, who have elaborated, or inherited, a scheme of thought which exactly fits those experiences which claim their interest. Such people are apt resolutely to ignore, or to explain away, all evidence which confuses their scheme with contradictory instances. What they cannot fit in is for them nonsense. An unflinching determination to take the whole evidence into account is the only method of preservation against the fluctuating extremes of fashionable opinion. This advice seems so easy, and is in fact so difficult to follow.

One reason for this difficulty is that we cannot think first and act afterwards. From the moment of birth we are immersed in action, and can only fitfully guide it by taking thought. We have, therefore, in various spheres of experience to adopt those ideas which seem to work within those spheres. It is absolutely necessary to trust to ideas which are generally adequate, even though we know that there are subtleties and distinctions beyond our ken. Also apart from the necessities of action, we cannot even keep before our minds the whole evidence except under the guise of doctrines which are incompletely harmonised. We cannot think in terms of an indefinite multiplicity of detail; our evidence can acquire its proper importance only if it comes before us marshalled by general ideas. These ideas we inherit—they form the tradition of our civilisation. Such traditional ideas are never static. They are either fading into meaningless formulae, or are gaining power by the new lights thrown by a more delicate apprehension. They are transformed by the urge of critical reason, by the vivid evidence of emotional experience, and by the cold certainties of scientific perception. One fact is certain, you cannot keep them still. No generation can merely reproduce its ancestors. You may preserve the life in a flux of form, or preserve the form amid an ebb of life. But you cannot permanently enclose the same life in the same mould.

The present state of religion among the European races illustrates the statements which I have been making. The phenomena are mixed. There have been reactions and revivals. But on the whole, during many generations, there has been a gradual decay of religious influence in European civilisation. Each revival touches a lower peak than its predecessor, and each period of slackness a lower depth. The average curve marks a steady fall in religious tone. In some countries the interest in religion is higher than in others. But in those countries where the interest is relatively high, it still falls as the generations pass. Religion is tending to degenerate into a decent formula wherewith to embellish a comfortable life. A great historical movement on this scale results from the convergence of many causes. I wish to suggest two of them which lie within the scope of this chapter for consideration.

In the first place for over two centuries religion has been on the defensive, and on a weak defensive. The period has been one of unprecedented intellectual progress. In this way a series of novel situations have been produced for thought. Each such occasion has found the religious thinkers unprepared. Something, which has been proclaimed to be vital, has finally, after struggle, distress, and anathema, been modified and otherwise interpreted. The next generation of religious apologists then congratulates the religious world on the deeper insight which has been gained. The result of the continued repetition of this undignified retreat, during many generations, has at last almost entirely destroyed the intellectual authority of religious thinkers. Consider this contrast: when Darwin or Einstein proclaim theories which modify our ideas, it is a triumph for science. We do not go about saying that there is another defeat for science, because its old ideas have been abandoned. We know that another step of scientific insight has been gained.

Religion will not regain its old power until it can face change in the same spirit as does science. Its principles may be eternal, but the expression of those principles requires continual development. This evolution of religion is in the main a disengagement of its own proper ideas from the adventitious notions which have crept into it by reason of the expression of its own ideas in terms of the imaginative picture of the world entertained in previous ages. Such a release of religion from the bonds of imperfect science is all to the good. It stresses its own genuine message. The great point to be kept in mind is that normally an advance in science will show that statements of various religious beliefs require some sort of modification. It may be that they have to be expanded or explained, or indeed entirely restated. If the religion is a sound expression of truth, this modification will only exhibit more adequately the exact point which is of importance. This process is a gain. In so far, therefore, as any religion has any contact with physical facts, it is to be expected that the point of view of those facts must be continually modified as scientific knowledge advances. In this way, the exact relevance of these facts for religious thought will grow more and more clear. The progress of science must result in the unceasing modification of religious thought, to the great advantage of religion.

The religious controversies of the sixteenth and seventeenth centuries put theologians into a most unfortunate state of mind. They were always attacking and defending. They pictured themselves as the garrison of a fort surrounded by hostile forces. All such pictures express half-truths. That is why they are so popular. But they are dangerous. This particular picture fostered a pugnacious party spirit which really expresses an ultimate lack of faith. They dared not modify, because they shirked the task of disengaging their spiritual message from the associations of a particular imagery.

Let me explain myself by an example. In the early medieval times, Heaven was in the sky, and Hell was underground; volcanoes were the jaws of Hell. I do not assert that these beliefs entered into the official formulations: but they did enter into the popular understanding of the general doctrines of Heaven and Hell. These notions were what everyone thought to be implied by the doctrine of the future state. They entered into the explanations of the most influential exponents of Christian belief. For example, they occur in the *Dialogues* of Pope Gregory[2], the Great, a man whose high official position is surpassed only by the magnitude of his services to humanity. I am not saying what we ought to believe about the future state. But whatever be the right doctrine, in this instance the clash between religion and science, which has relegated the earth to the position of a second-rate planet attached to a second-rate sun, has been greatly to the benefit of the spirituality of religion by dispersing these medieval fancies.

Another way of looking at this question of the evolution of religious thought is to note that any verbal form of statement which has been before the world for some time discloses ambiguities; and that often such ambiguities strike at the very heart of the meaning. The effective sense in which a doctrine has been held in the past cannot be determined by the mere logical analysis of verbal statements, made in ignorance of the logical trap. You have to take into account the whole reaction of human nature to the scheme of thought. This reaction is of a mixed character, including elements of emotion derived from our lower natures. It is here that the impersonal criticism of science and of philosophy comes to the aid of religious evolution. Example after example can be given of this motive force in development. For example, the logical difficulties inherent in the doctrine of the moral cleansing of human nature by the power of religion rent Christianity in the days of Pelagius and Augustine—that is to say, at the beginning of the fifth century. Echoes of that controversy still linger in theology.

2. *Cf.* Gregorovius' *History of Rome in the Middle Ages*, Book III, Ch. III, Vol. II, English Trans.

So far, my point has been this: that religion is the expression of one type of fundamental experiences of mankind: that religious thought develops into an increasing accuracy of expression, disengaged from adventitious imagery: that the interaction between religion and science is one great factor in promoting this development.

I now come to my second reason for the modern fading of interest in religion. This involves the ultimate question which I stated in my opening sentences. We have to know what we mean by religion. The churches, in their presentation of their answers to this query, have put forward aspects of religion which are expressed in terms either suited to the emotional reactions of bygone times or directed to excite modern emotional interests of a nonreligious character. What I mean under the first heading is that religious appeal is directed partly to excite that instinctive fear of the wrath of a tyrant which was inbred in the unhappy populations of the arbitrary empires of the ancient world, and in particular to excite that fear of an all-powerful arbitrary tyrant behind the unknown forces of nature. This appeal to the ready instinct of brute fear is losing its force. It lacks any directness of response, because modern science and modern conditions of life have taught us to meet occasions of apprehension by a critical analysis of their causes and conditions. Religion is the reaction of human nature to its search for God. The presentation of God under the aspect of power awakens every modern instinct of critical reaction. This is fatal; for religion collapses unless its main positions command immediacy of assent. In this respect the old phraseology is at variance with the psychology of modern civilisations. This change in psychology is largely due to science, and is one of the chief ways in which the advance of science has weakened the hold of the old religious forms of expression. The nonreligious motive which has entered into modern religious thought is the desire for a comfortable organisation of modern society. Religion has been presented as valuable for the ordering of life. Its claims have been rested upon its function as a sanction to right conduct. Also the purpose of right conduct quickly degenerates into the formation of pleasing social relations. We have here a subtle degradation of religious ideas, following upon their gradual purification under the influence of keener ethical intuitions. Conduct is a by-product of religion—an inevitable by-product, but not the main point. Every great religious teacher has revolted against the presentation of religion as a mere sanction of rules of conduct. Saint Paul denounced the Law, and Puritan divines spoke of the filthy rags of righteousness. The insistence upon rules of conduct marks the ebb of religious fervour. Above and beyond all things, the religious life is not a research after comfort. I must now state, in all diffidence, what I conceive to be the essential character of the religious spirit.

Religion is the vision of something which stands beyond, behind, and within, the passing flux of immediate things; something which is real, and yet waiting to be realised; something which is a remote possibility, and yet the greatest of present facts; something that gives meaning to all that passes, and yet eludes apprehension; something whose possession is the final good, and yet is beyond all reach; something which is the ultimate ideal, and the hopeless quest.

The immediate reaction of human nature to the religious vision is worship. Religion has emerged into human experience mixed with the crudest fancies of barbaric imagination. Gradually, slowly, steadily the vision recurs in history under nobler form and with clearer expression. It is the one element in human experience which persistently shows an upward trend. It fades and then recurs. But when it renews its force, it recurs with an added richness and purity of content. The fact of the religious vision, and its history of persistent expansion, is our one ground for optimism. Apart from it, human life is a flash of occasional enjoyments lighting up a mass of pain and misery, a bagatelle of transient experience.

The vision claims nothing but worship; and worship is a surrender to the claim for assimilation, urged with the motive force of mutual love. The vision never overrules. It is always there, and it has the power of love presenting the one purpose whose fulfilment is eternal harmony. Such order as we find in nature is never force—it presents itself as the one harmonious adjustment of complex detail. Evil is the brute motive force of fragmentary purpose, disregarding the eternal vision. Evil is overruling, retarding, hurting. The power of God is the worship He inspires. That religion is strong which in its ritual and its modes of thought evokes an apprehension of the commanding vision. The worship of God is not a rule of safety—it is an adventure of the spirit, a flight after the unattainable. The death of religion comes with the repression of the high hope of adventure.

Chapter XIII

REQUISITES FOR SOCIAL PROGRESS

It has been the purpose of these lectures to analyse the reactions of science in forming that background of instinctive ideas which control the activities of successive generations. Such a background takes the form of a certain vague philosophy as to the last word about things, when all is said. The three centuries, which form the epoch of modern science, have revolved round the ideas of *God*, *mind*, *matter*, and also of *space* and *time* in their characters of expressing *simple location* for matter. Philosophy has on the whole emphasised *mind*, and has thus been out of touch with science during the two latter centuries. But it is creeping back into its old importance owing to the rise of psychology and its alliance with physiology. Also, this rehabilitation of philosophy has been facilitated by the recent breakdown of the seventeenth century settlement of the principles of physical science. But, until that collapse, science seated itself securely upon the concepts of matter, space, time, and latterly, of energy. Also there were arbitrary laws of nature determining locomotion. They were empirically observed, but for some obscure reason were known to be universal. Anyone who in practice or theory disregarded them was denounced with unsparing vigour. This position on the part of scientists was pure bluff, if one may credit them with believing their own statements. For their current philosophy completely failed to justify the assumption that the immediate knowledge inherent in any present occasion throws any light either on its past, or its future.

I have also sketched an alternative philosophy of science in which *organism* takes the place of *matter*. For this purpose, the mind involved in the materialist theory dissolves into a function of organism. The psychological field then exhibits what an event is in itself. Our bodily event is an unusually complex type of organism and consequently includes cognition. Further, space and time, in their most concrete signification, become the locus of events. An organism is the realisation of a definite shape of value. The emergence of some actual value depends on limitation which excludes neutralising cross-lights. Thus an event is a matter of fact which by reason of its limitation is a value for itself; but by reason of its very nature it also requires the whole universe in order to be itself.

Importance depends on endurance. Endurance is the retention through time of an achievement of value. What endures is identity of pattern, self-inherited. Endurance requires the favourable environment. The whole of science revolves round this question of enduring organisms.

The general influence of science at the present moment can be analysed under the headings: General Conceptions Respecting the Universe, Technological Applications, Professionalism in Knowledge, Influence of Biological Doctrines on the Motives of Conduct. I have endeavoured in the preceding lectures to give a glimpse of these points. It lies within the scope of this concluding lecture to consider the reaction of science upon some problems confronting civilised societies.

The general conceptions introduced by science into modern thought cannot be separated from the philosophical situation as expressed by Descartes. I mean the assumption of bodies and minds as independent individual substances, each existing in its own right apart from any necessary reference to each other.

Such a conception was very concordant with the individualism which had issued from the moral discipline of the Middle Ages. But, though the easy reception of the idea is thus explained, the derivation in itself rests upon a confusion, very natural but none the less unfortunate. The moral discipline had emphasized the intrinsic value of the individual entity. This emphasis had put the notions of the individual and of its experiences into the foreground of thought. At this point the confusion commences. The emergent individual value of each entity is transformed into the independent substantial existence of each entity, which is a very different notion.

I do not mean to say that Descartes made this logical, or rather illogical, transition, in the form of explicit reasoning. Far from it. What he did, was first to concentrate upon his own conscious experiences, as being facts within the independent world of his own mentality. He was led to speculate in this way by the current emphasis upon the individual value of his total self. He implicitly transformed this emergent individual value, inherent in the very fact of his own reality, into a private world of passions, or modes, of independent substance.

Also the independence ascribed to bodily substances carried them away from the realm of values altogether. They degenerated into a mechanism entirely valueless, except as suggestive of an external ingenuity. The heavens had lost the glory of God. This state of mind is illustrated in the recoil of Protestantism from aesthetic effects dependent upon a material medium. It was taken to lead to an ascription of value to what is in itself valueless. This recoil was already in full strength antecedently to Descartes. Accordingly, the Cartesian scientific doctrine of bits of matter, bare of intrinsic value, was merely a formulation, in explicit terms, of a doctrine which was current before its entrance into scientific thought or Cartesian philosophy. Probably this doctrine was latent in the scholastic philosophy, but it did not lead to its consequences till it met with the mentality of northern Europe in the sixteenth century. But science, as equipped by Descartes, gave stability and intellectual status to a point of view which has had very mixed effects upon the moral presuppositions of modern communities. Its good effects arose from its efficiency as a method for scientific researches within those limited regions which were then best suited for exploration. The result was a general clearing of the European mind away from the stains left upon it by the hysteria of remote barbaric ages. This was all to the good, and was most completely exemplified in the eighteenth century.

But in the nineteenth century, when society was undergoing transformation into the manufacturing system, the bad effects of these doctrines have been very fatal. The doctrine of minds, as independent substances, leads directly not merely to private worlds of experience, but also to private worlds of morals. The moral intuitions can be held to apply only to the strictly private world of psychological experience. Accordingly, self-respect, and the making the most of your own individual opportunities, together constituted the efficient morality of the leaders among the industrialists of that period. The western world is now suffering from the limited moral outlook of the three previous generations.

Also the assumption of the bare valuelessness of mere matter led to a lack of reverence in the treatment of natural or artistic beauty. Just when the urbanisation of the western world was entering upon its state of rapid development, and when the most delicate, anxious consideration of the aesthetic qualities of the new material environment was requisite, the doctrine of the irrelevance of such ideas was at its height. In the most advanced industrial countries, art was treated as a frivolity. A striking example of this state of mind in the middle of the nineteenth century is to be seen in London where the marvellous beauty of the estuary of the Thames, as it curves through the city, is wantonly defaced by the Charing Cross railway bridge, constructed apart from any reference to aesthetic values.

The two evils are: one, the ignoration of the true relation of each organism to its environment; and the other, the habit of ignoring the intrinsic worth of the environment which must be allowed its weight in any consideration of final ends.

Another great fact confronting the modern world is the discovery of the method of training professionals, who specialise in particular regions of thought and thereby progressively add to the sum of knowledge within their respective limitations of subject. In consequence of the success of this professionalising of knowledge, there are two points to be kept in mind, which differentiate our present age from the past. In the first place, the rate of progress is such that an individual human being, of ordinary length of life, will be called upon to face novel situations which find no parallel in his past. The fixed person for the fixed duties, who in older societies was such a godsend, in the future will be a public danger. In the second place, the modern professionalism in knowledge works in the opposite direction so far as the intellectual sphere is concerned. The modern chemist is likely to be weak in zoology, weaker still in his general knowledge of the Elizabethan drama, and completely ignorant of the principles of rhythm in English versification. It is probably safe to ignore his knowledge of ancient history. Of course I am speaking of general tendencies; for chemists are no worse than engineers, or mathematicians, or classical scholars. Effective knowledge is professionalised knowledge, supported by a restricted acquaintance with useful subjects subservient to it.

This situation has its dangers. It produces minds in a groove. Each profession makes progress, but it is progress in its own groove. Now to be mentally in a groove is to live in contemplating a given set of abstractions. The groove prevents straying across country, and the abstraction abstracts from something to which no further attention is paid. But there is no groove of abstractions which is adequate for the comprehension of human life. Thus in the modern world, the celibacy of the medieval learned class has been replaced by a celibacy of the intellect which is divorced from the concrete contemplation of the complete facts. Of course, no one is merely a mathematician, or merely a lawyer. People have lives outside their professions or their businesses. But the point is the restraint of serious thought within a groove. The remainder of life is treated superficially, with the imperfect categories of thought derived from one profession.

The dangers arising from this aspect of professionalism are great, particularly in our democratic societies. The directive force of reason is weakened. The leading intellects lack balance. They see this set of circumstances, or that set; but not both sets together. The task of cordination is left to those who lack either the force or the character to succeed in some definite career. In short, the specialised functions of the community are performed better and more progressively, but the generalised direction lacks vision. The progressiveness in detail only adds to the danger produced by the feebleness of coordination.

This criticism of modern life applies throughout, in whatever sense you construe the meaning of a community. It holds if you apply it to a nation, a city, a district, an institution, a family, or even to an individual. There is a development of particular abstractions, and a contraction of concrete appreciation. The whole is lost in one of its aspects. It is not necessary for my point that I should maintain that our directive wisdom, either as individuals or as communities, is less now than in the past. Perhaps it has slightly improved. But the novel pace of progress requires a greater force of direction if disasters are to be avoided. The point is that the discoveries of the nineteenth century were in the direction of professionalism, so that we are left with no expansion of wisdom and with greater need of it.

Wisdom is the fruit of a balanced development. It is this balanced growth of individuality which it should be the aim of education to secure. The most useful discoveries for the immediate future would concern the furtherance of this aim without detriment to the necessary intellectual professionalism.

My own criticism of our traditional educational methods is that they are far too much occupied with intellectual analysis, and with the acquirement of formularised information. What I mean is, that we neglect to strengthen habits of concrete appreciation of the individual facts in their full interplay of emergent values, and that we merely emphasise abstract formulations which ignore this aspect of the interplay of diverse values.

In every country the problem of the balance of the general and specialist education is under consideration. I cannot speak with first-hand knowledge of any country but my own. I know that there, among practical educationalists, there is considerable dissatisfaction with the existing practice. Also, the adaptation of the whole system to the needs of a democratic community is very far from being solved. I do not think that the secret of the solution lies in terms of the antithesis between thoroughness in special knowledge and general knowledge of a slighter character. The make-weight which balances the thoroughness of the specialist intellectual training should be of a radically different kind from purely intellectual analytical knowledge. At present our education combines a thorough study of a few abstractions, with a slighter study of a larger number of abstractions. We are too exclusively bookish in our scholastic routine. The general training should aim at eliciting our concrete apprehensions, and should satisfy the itch of youth to be doing something. There should be some analysis even here, but only just enough to illustrate the ways of thinking in diverse spheres. In the Garden of Eden Adam saw the animals before he named them: in the traditional system, children named the animals before they saw them.

There is no easy single solution of the practical difficulties of education. We can, however, guide ourselves by a certain simplicity in its general theory. The student should concentrate within a limited field. Such concentration should include all practical and intellectual acquirements requisite for that concentration. This is the ordinary procedure; and, in respect to it, I should be inclined even to increase the facilities for concentration rather than to diminish them. With the concentration there are associated certain subsidiary studies, such as languages for science. Such a scheme of professional training should be directed to a clear end congenial to the student. It is not necessary to elaborate the qualifications of these statements. Such a training must, of course, have the width requisite for its end. But its design should not be complicated by the consideration of other ends. This professional training can only touch one side of education. Its centre of gravity lies in the intellect, and its chief tool is the printed book. The centre of gravity of the other side of training should lie in intuition without an analytical divorce from the total environment. Its object is immediate apprehension with the minimum of eviscerating analysis. The type of generality, which above all is wanted, is the appreciation of variety of value. I mean an aesthetic growth. There is something between the gross specialised values of the mere practical man, and the thin specialised values of the mere scholar. Both types have missed something; and if you add together the two sets of values, you do not obtain the missing elements. What is wanted is an appreciation of the infinite variety of vivid values achieved by an organism in its proper environment. When you understand all about the sun and all about the atmosphere and all about the rotation of the earth, you may still miss the radiance of the sunset. There is no substitute for the direct perception of the concrete achievement of a thing in its actuality. We want concrete fact with a high light thrown on what is relevant to its preciousness.

What I mean is art and aesthetic education. It is, however, art in such a general sense of the term that I hardly like to call it by that name. Art is a special example. What we want is to draw out habits of aesthetic apprehension. According to the metaphysical doctrine which I have been developing, to do so is to increase the depth of individuality. The analysis of reality indicates the two factors, activity emerging into individualised aesthetic value. Also the emergent value is the measure of the individualisation of the activity. We must foster the creative initiative towards the maintenance of objective values. You will not obtain the apprehension without the initiative, or the initiative without the apprehension. As soon as you get towards the concrete, you cannot exclude action. Sensitiveness without impulse spells decadence, and impulse without sensitiveness spells brutality. I am using the word 'sensitiveness' in its most general signification, so as to include apprehension of what lies beyond oneself; that is to say, sensitiveness to all the facts of the case. Thus 'art' in the general sense which I require is any selection by which the concrete facts are so arranged as to elicit attention to particular values which are realisable by them. For example, the mere disposing of the human body and the eyesight so as to get a good view of a sunset is a simple form of artistic selection. The habit of art is the habit of enjoying vivid values.

But, in this sense, art concerns more than sunsets. A factory, with its machinery, its community of operatives, its social service to the general population, its dependence upon organising and designing genius, its potentialities as a source of wealth to the holders of its stock is an organism exhibiting a variety of vivid values. What we want to train is the habit of apprehending such an organism in its completeness. It is very arguable that the science of political economy, as studied in its first period after the death of Adam Smith (1790), did more harm than good. It destroyed many economic fallacies, and taught how to think about the economic revolution then in progress. But it riveted on men a certain set of abstractions which were disastrous in their influence on modern mentality. It de-humanised industry. This is only one example of a general danger inherent in modern science. Its methodological procedure is exclusive and intolerant, and rightly so. It fixes attention on a definite group of abstractions, neglects everything else, and elicits every scrap of information and theory which is relevant to what it has retained. This method is triumphant, provided that the abstractions are judicious. But, however triumphant, the triumph is within limits. The neglect of these limits leads to disastrous oversights. The anti-rationalism of science is partly justified, as a preservation of its useful methodology; it is partly mere irrational prejudice. Modern professionalism is the training of minds to conform to the methodology. The historical revolt of the seventeenth century, and the earlier reaction towards naturalism, were examples of transcending the abstractions which fascinated educated society in the Middle Ages. These early ages had an ideal of rationalism, but they failed in its pursuit. For they neglected to note that the methodology of reasoning requires the limitations involved in the abstract. Accordingly, the true rationalism must always transcend itself by recurrence to the concrete in search of inspiration. A self-satisfied rationalism is in effect a form of anti-rationalism. It means an arbitrary halt at a particular set of abstractions. This was the case with science.

There are two principles inherent in the very nature of things, recurring in some particular embodiments whatever field we explore—the spirit of change, and the spirit of conservation. There can be nothing real without both. Mere change without conservation is a passage from nothing to nothing. Its final integration yields mere transient non-entity. Mere conservation without change cannot conserve. For after all, there is a flux of circumstance, and the freshness of being evaporates under mere repetition. The character of existent reality is composed of organisms enduring through the flux of things. The low type of organisms have achieved a self-identity dominating their whole physical life. Electrons, molecules, crystals, belong to this type. They exhibit a massive and complete sameness. In the higher types, where life appears, there is greater complexity. Thus, though there is a complex, enduring pattern, it has retreated into deeper recesses of the total fact. In a sense, the self-identity of a human being is more abstract than that of a crystal. It is the life of the spirit. It relates rather to the individualisation of the creative activity; so that the changing circumstances received from the environment, are differentiated from the living personality, and are thought of as forming its perceived field. In truth, the field of perception and the perceiving mind are abstractions which, in the concrete, combine into the successive bodily events. The psychological field, as restricted to sense-objects and passing emotions, is the minor permanence, barely rescued from the nonentity of mere change; and the mind is the major permanence, permeating that complete field, whose endurance is the living soul. But the soul would wither without fertilisation from its transient experiences. The secret of the higher organisms lies in their two grades of permanences. By this means the freshness of the environment is absorbed into the permanence of the soul. The changing environment is no longer, by reason of its variety, an enemy to the endurance of the organism. The pattern of the higher organism has retreated into the recesses of the individualised activity. It has become a uniform way of dealing with circumstances; and this way is only strengthened by having a proper variety of circumstances to deal with.

This fertilisation of the soul is the reason for the necessity of art. A static value, however serious and important, becomes unendurable by its appalling monotony of endurance. The soul cries aloud for release into change. It suffers the agonies of claustrophobia. The transitions of humour, wit, irreverence, play, sleep, and—above all—of art are necessary for it. Great art is the arrangement of the environment so as to provide for the soul vivid, but transient, values. Human beings require something which absorbs them for a time, something out of the routine which they can stare at. But you cannot subdivide life, except in the abstract analysis of thought. Accordingly, the great art is more than a transient refreshment. It is something which adds to the permanent richness of the soul's self-attainment. It justifies itself both by its immediate enjoyment, and also by its discipline of the inmost being. Its discipline is not distinct from enjoyment, but by reason of it. It transforms the soul into the permanent realisation of values extending beyond its former self. This element of transition in art is shown by the restlessness exhibited in its history. An epoch gets saturated by the masterpieces of any one style. Something new must be discovered. The human being wanders on. Yet there is a balance in things. Mere change before the attainment of adequacy of achievement, either in quality or output, is destructive of greatness. But the importance of a living art, which moves on and yet leaves its permanent mark, can hardly be exaggerated.

In regard to the aesthetic needs of civilised society the reactions of science have so far been unfortunate. Its materialistic basis has directed attention to *things* as opposed to *values*. The antithesis is a false one, if taken in a concrete sense. But it is valid at the abstract level of ordinary thought. This misplaced emphasis coalesced with the abstractions of political economy, which are in fact the abstractions in terms of which commercial affairs are carried on. Thus all thought concerned with social organisation expressed itself in terms of material things and of capital. Ultimate values were excluded. They were politely bowed to, and then handed over to the clergy to be kept for Sundays. A creed of competitive business morality was evolved, in some respects curiously high; but entirely devoid of consideration for the value of human life. The workmen were conceived as mere hands, drawn from the pool of labour. To God's question, men gave the answer of Cain—"Am I my brother's keeper?"; and they incurred Cain's guilt. This was the atmosphere in which the industrial revolution was accomplished in England, and to a large extent elsewhere. The internal history of England during the last half century has been an endeavour slowly and painfully to undo the evils wrought in the first stage of the new epoch. It may be that civilisation will never recover from the bad climate which enveloped the introduction of machinery. This climate pervaded the whole commercial system of the progressive northern European races. It was partly the result of the aesthetic errors of Protestantism and partly the result of scientific materialism, and partly the result of the natural greed of mankind, and partly the result of the abstractions of political economy. An illustration of my point is to be found in Macaulay's Essay criticising Southey's *Colloquies on Society*. It was written in 1830. Now Macaulay was a very favourable example of men living at that date, or at any date. He had genius; he was kind-hearted, honourable, and a reformer. This is the extract:

> We are told, that our age has invented atrocities beyond the imagination of our fathers; that society has been brought into a state compared with which extermination would be a blessing; and all because the dwellings of cotton-spinners are naked and rectangular. Mr. Southey has found out a way he tells us, in which the effects of manufactures and agriculture may be compared. And what is this way? To stand on a hill, to look at a cottage and a factory, and to see which is the prettier.

Southey seems to have said many silly things in his book; but, so far as this extract is concerned, he could make a good case for himself if he returned to earth after the lapse of nearly a century. The evils of the early industrial system are now a commonplace of knowledge. The point which I am insisting on is the stone-blind eye with which even the best men of that time regarded the importance of aesthetics in a nation's life. I do not believe that we have as yet nearly achieved the right estimate. A contributory cause, of substantial efficacy to produce this disastrous error, was the scientific creed that matter in motion is the one concrete reality in nature; so that aesthetic values form an adventitious, irrelevant addition.

There is another side to this picture of the possibilities of decadence. At the present moment a discussion is raging as to the future of civilisation in the novel circumstances of rapid scientific and technological advance. The evils of the future have been diagnosed in various ways, the loss of religious faith, the malignant use of material power, the degradation attending a differential birth rate favouring the lower types of humanity, the suppression of aesthetic creativeness. Without doubt, these are all evils, dangerous and threatening. But they are not new. From the dawn of history, mankind has always been losing its religious faith, has always suffered from the malignant use of material power, has always suffered from the infertility of its best intellectual types, has always witnessed the periodical decadence of art. In the reign of the Egyptian king, Tutankhamen, there was raging a desperate religious struggle between Modernists and Fundamentalists; the cave pictures exhibit a phase of delicate aesthetic achievement as superseded by a period of comparative vulgarity; the religious leaders, the great thinkers, the great poets and authors, the whole clerical caste in the Middle Ages, have been notably infertile; finally, if we attend to what actually has happened in the past, and disregard romantic visions of democracies, aristocracies, kings, generals, armies, and merchants, material power has generally been wielded with blindness, obstinacy and selfishness, often with brutal malignancy. And yet, mankind has progressed. Even if you take a tiny oasis of peculiar excellence, the type of modern man who would have most chance of happiness in ancient Greece at its best period is probably (as now) an average professional heavy-weight boxer, and not an average Greek scholar from Oxford or Germany. Indeed, the main use of the Oxford scholar would have been his capability of writing an ode in glorification of the boxer. Nothing does more harm in unnerving men for their duties in the present, than the attention devoted to the points of excellence in the past as compared with the average failure of the present day.

But, after all, there have been real periods of decadence; and at the present time, as at other epochs, society is decaying, and there is need for preservative action. Professionals are not new to the world. But in the past, professionals have formed unprogressive castes. The point is that professionalism has now been mated with progress. The world is now faced with a self-evolving system, which it cannot stop. There are dangers and advantages in this situation. It is obvious that the gain in material power affords opportunity for social betterment. If mankind can rise to the occasion, there lies in front a golden age of beneficent creativeness. But material power in itself is ethically neutral. It can equally well work in the wrong direction. The problem is not how to produce great men, but how to produce great societies. The great society will put up the men for the occasions. The materialistic philosophy emphasised the given quantity of material, and thence derivatively the given nature of the environment. It thus operated most unfortunately upon the social conscience of mankind. For it directed almost exclusive attention to the aspect of struggle for existence in a fixed environment. To a large extent the environment is fixed, and to this extent there is a struggle for existence. It is folly to look at the universe through rose-tinted spectacles. We must admit the struggle. The question is, who is to be eliminated. In so far as we are educators, we have to have clear ideas upon that point; for it settles the type to be produced and the practical ethics to be inculcated.

But during the last three generations, the exclusive direction of attention to this aspect of things has been a disaster of the first magnitude. The watchwords of the nineteenth century have been, struggle for existence, competition, class warfare, commercial antagonism between nations, military warfare. The struggle for existence has been construed into the gospel of hate. The full conclusion to be drawn from a philosophy of evolution is fortunately of a more balanced character. Successful organisms modify their environment. Those organisms are successful which modify their environments so as to assist each other. This law is exemplified in nature on a vast scale. For example, the North American Indians accepted their environment, with the result that a scanty population barely succeeded in maintaining themselves over the whole continent. The European races when they arrived in the same continent pursued an opposite policy. They at once co-operated in modifying their environment. The result is that a population more than twenty times that of the Indian population now occupies the same territory, and the continent is not yet full. Again, there are associations of different species which mutually co-operate. This differentiation of species is exhibited in the simplest physical entities, such as the association between electrons and positive nuclei, and in the whole realm of animate nature. The trees in a Brazilian forest depend upon the association of various species of organisms, each of which is mutually dependent on the other species. A single tree by itself is dependent upon all the adverse chances of shifting circumstances. The wind stunts it: the variations in temperature check its foliage: the rains denude its soil: its leaves are blown away and are lost for the purpose of fertilisation. You may obtain individual specimens of fine trees either in exceptional circumstances, or where human cultivation has intervened. But in nature the normal way in which trees flourish is by their association in a forest. Each tree may lose something of its individual perfection of growth, but they mutually assist each other in preserving the conditions for survival. The soil is preserved and shaded; and the microbes necessary for its fertility are neither scorched, nor frozen, nor washed away. A forest is the triumph of the organisation of mutually dependent species. Further a species of microbes which kills the forest, also exterminates itself. Again the two sexes exhibit the same advantage of differentiation. In the history of the world, the prize has not gone to those species which specialised in methods of violence, or even in defensive armour. In fact, nature began with producing animals encased in hard shells for defence against the ills of life. It also experimented in size. But smaller animals, without external armour, warm-blooded, sensitive, and alert, have cleared these monsters off the face of the earth. Also, the lions and tigers are not the successful species. There is something in the ready use of force which defeats its own object. Its main defect is that it bars cooperation. Every organism requires an environment of friends, partly to shield it from violent changes, and partly to supply it with its wants. The Gospel of Force is incompatible with a social life. By *force*, I mean *antagonism* in its most general sense.

Almost equally dangerous is the Gospel of Uniformity. The differences between the nations and races of mankind are required to preserve the conditions under which higher development is possible. One main factor in the upward trend of animal life has been the power of wandering. Perhaps this is why the armour-plated monsters fared badly. They could not wander. Animals wander into new conditions. They have to adapt themselves or die. Mankind has wandered from the trees to the plains, from the plains to the seacoast, from climate to climate, from continent to continent, and from habit of life to habit of life. When man ceases to wander, he will cease to ascend in the scale of being. Physical wandering is still important, but greater still is the power of man's spiritual adventures—adventures of thought, adventures of passionate feeling, adventures of aesthetic experience. A diversification among human communities is essential for the provision of the incentive and material for the Odyssey of the human spirit. Other nations of different habits are not enemies: they are godsends. Men require of their neighbours something sufficiently akin to be understood, something sufficiently different to provoke attention, and something great enough to command admiration. We must not expect, however, all the virtues. We should even be satisfied if there is something odd enough to be interesting.

Modern science has imposed on humanity the necessity for wandering. Its progressive thought and its progressive technology make the transition through time, from generation to generation, a true migration into uncharted seas of adventure. The very benefit of wandering is that it is dangerous and needs skill to avert evils. We must expect, therefore, that the future will disclose dangers. It is the business of the future to be dangerous; and it is among the merits of science that it equips the future for its duties. The prosperous middle classes, who ruled the nineteenth century, placed an excessive value upon placidity of existence. They refused to face the necessities for social reform imposed by the new industrial system, and they are now refusing to face the necessities for intellectual reform imposed by the new knowledge. The middle class pessimism over the future of the world comes from a confusion between civilisation and security. In the immediate future there will be less security than in the immediate past, less stability. It must be admitted that there is a degree of instability which is inconsistent with civilisation. But, on the whole, the great ages have been unstable ages.

I have endeavoured in these lectures to give a record of a great adventure in the region of thought. It was shared in by all the races of western Europe. It developed with the slowness of a mass movement. Half a century is its unit of time. The tale is the epic of an episode in the manifestation of reason. It tells how a particular direction of reason emerges in a race by the long preparation of antecedent epochs, how after its birth its subject-matter gradually unfolds itself, how it attains its triumphs, how its influence moulds the very springs of action of mankind, and finally how at its moment of supreme success its limitations disclose themselves and call for a renewed exercise of the creative imagination. The moral of the tale is the power of reason, its decisive influence on the life of humanity. The great conquerors, from Alexander to Caesar, and from Caesar to Napoleon, influenced profoundly the lives of subsequent generations. But the total effect of this influence shrinks to insignificance, if compared to the entire transformation of human habits and human mentality produced by the long line of men of thought from Thales to the present day, men individually powerless, but ultimately the rulers of the world.

Adventures of Ideas

PREFACE

THE TITLE OF THIS book, *Adventures of Ideas,* bears two meanings, both applicable to the subject-matter. One meaning is the effect of certain ideas in promoting the slow drift of mankind towards civilization. This is the Adventure of Ideas in the history of mankind. The other meaning is the author's adventure in framing a speculative scheme of ideas which shall be explanatory of the historical adventure.

The book is in fact a study of the concept of civilization, and an endeavour to understand how it is that civilized beings arise. One point, emphasized throughout, is the importance of Adventure for the promotion and preservation of civilization.

The three books—*Science and The Modern World, Process and Reality, Adventures of Ideas*—are an endeavour to express a way of understanding the nature of things. and to point out how that way of understanding is illustrated by a survey of the mutations of human experience. Each book can be read separately; but they supplement each other's omissions or compressions.

The books that have chiefly influenced my *general way* of looking at this historical topic are Gibbon's *Decline and Fall,* Cardinal Newman's *Essay on the Development of Christian Doctrine,* Paul Sarpi's *History of the Council of Trent,* Henry Osborn Taylor's *The Mediæval Mind,* Leslie Stephen's *English Thought in the Eighteenth Century,* and various well-known collections of letters. While on the subject of literature, I venture to commend to the notice of those interested in an earlier development of English Thought, and also in good literature, the sermons of the Elizabethan and Jacobean divines. Also H. O. Taylor's *Thought and Expression in the Sixteenth Century* presents the currents and cross-currents of thought in those times. The twentieth century, so far as it has yet advanced, bears some analogy to that predecessor in European history, both in clash of thought and in clash of political interest.

In Part II, dealing with Cosmology, I have made constant use of two books published by the Oxford University Press in 1928, namely, *A Commentary on Plato's Timæus,* by Professor A. E. Taylor of the University of Edinburgh, and *The Greek Atomists and Epicurus,* by Dr. Cyril Bailey, Tutor of Balliol College, Oxford.

Use has already been made of some parts of the book in response to invitations which I had the honour to receive. The main substance of Chapters I, II, III, VII, VIII was delivered as the four Mary Flexner Lectures at Bryn Mawr College, during the session 1929-30: they have not been hitherto published. Also Chapter IX, *Science and Philosophy—not* previously published—was delivered as the Davies Lecture in Philosophy, at the Institute of Arts and Sciences, Columbia University, March, 1932. Chapter VI, *Foresight,* was delivered as a lecture at the Harvard Business School, and by the request of Dean W. B. Donham was published as a preface to his book, *Business Adrift,* McGraw-Hill Book Company, Inc., New York, 1931. Also Chapter XVI, *Objects and Subjects,* was delivered as the presidential address to the eastern division of the American Philosophical Association, at New Haven, December, 1931; and has since been published in *The Philosophical Review,* Vol. XLI, 1932, Longmans, Green, and Company, New York.

Some unpublished lectures, delivered at Dartmouth College, New Hampshire, in 1926, embodied a preliminary sketch of the topic of this book. They were concerned with the two levels of ideas which are required for successful civilization, namely, particularized ideas of low generality, and philosophic ideas of high generality. The former set are required to reap the fruit of the type of civilization immediately attained; the latter set are required to guide the adventure toward novelty, and to secure the immediate realization of the worth of such ideal aim.

I am indebted to my wife for many ideas fundamental to the discussion; and also for the great labour of revision of the successive drafts of the various chapters.

ALFRED NORTH WHITEHEAD

Harvard University
September, 1932

PART I

SOCIOLOGICAL

Chapter I

INTRODUCTION

SECTION I. IN ITS widest possible extension the title of this book—Adventures of Ideas—might be taken as a synonym for The History of The Human Race, in respect to its wide variety of mental experiences. In this sense of the title, the Human Race must experience its own history. It cannot be written in its total variety.

Throughout this book I propose to consider critically the *sort* of history which ideas can have in the life of humanity, and to illustrate my thesis by an appeal to some well-known examples. The particular topics chosen for illustration will be dictated by the arbitrary limitations of my own knowledge, and by the consideration of their general interest and importance in our modern life. Also for our purpose in the book the notion of History includes the present and the future together with the past, affording a mutual elucidation and wrapped in common interest. For the facts in detail we shall be dependent upon that great band of critical scholars whose labours today, and for the past three centuries, lay upon mankind the obligation to deepest reverence.

Theories are built upon facts; and conversely the reports upon facts are shot through and through with theoretical interpretation. Direct visual observation is concerned with the vision of coloured shapes in motion—'questionable shapes'. Direct aural observation is concerned with auditions of sounds. But some contemporary observer of such shapes and noises, for example, some envoy resident at a foreign Court, interpreting the so-called 'bare' facts, states that 'he interviewed the minister of state, who manifested considerable emotion and explained with great clearness the measures with which he would meet the impending crisis'. In such ways contemporary evidence is contemporary interpretation, including the assumption of data other than these bare sensa.

In some subsequent age the critical scholar in accordance with his own theoretical judgments selects from bygone contemporary observations: he criticizes the contemporary observers, and gives his own interpretations of the contemporary evidence. We thus arrive at 'pure history', according to the faith of the school of history prevalent in the latter part of the nineteenth century. This notion of historians, of history devoid of æsthetic prejudice, of history devoid of any reliance on metaphysical principles and cosmological generalizations, is a figment of the imagination. The belief in it can only occur to minds steeped in provinciality,—the provinciality of an epoch, of a race, of a school of learning, of a trend of interest—, minds unable to divine their own unspoken limitations.

The historian in his description of the past depends on his own judgment as to what constitutes the importance of human life. Even when he has rigorously confined himself to one selected aspect, political or cultural, he still depends on some decision as to what constitutes the culmination of that phase of human experience and as to what constitutes its degradation. For example, considering the political history of mankind, Hegel saw in the Prussian State of his date its culmination: a generation later Macaulay saw that culmination in the English constitutional system of his date. The whole judgment on thoughts and actions depend upon such implicit presuppositions. You cannot consider wisdom or folly, progress or decadence, except in relation to some standard of judgment, some end in view. Such standards, such ends, when widely diffused, constitute the driving force of ideas in the history of mankind. They also guide the composition of historical narrative.

In considering the history of ideas, I maintain that the notion of 'mere knowledge' is a high abstraction which we should dismiss from our minds. Knowledge is always accompanied with accessories of emotion and purpose. Also we must remember that there are grades in the generality of ideas. Thus a general idea occurs *in* history in special forms determined by peculiar circumstances of race and of stage of civilization. The higher generalities rarely receive any accurate verbal expression. They are hinted at through their special forms appropriate to the age in question. Also the emotional accompaniments are partly due to the vague feeling of importance derived from the superior generality, and partly due to the special interest of special forms in which generalities make their appearance. Some people are stirred by a flag, a national anthem; others by the vague feeling of the form of civilization which their country stands for. In most people the two origins of emotion are fused together.

Gibbon's history demonstrates a twofold tale. It tells of the Decline and Fall of the Roman Empire through a thousand years. We see the greatness of that Empire at its height, its military organization, its provincial administration, its welter of races, the rise and clash of two religions, the passage of Greek philosophy into Christian theology. Gibbon displays before us the greatness and the littleness of soldiers and of statesmen, of philosophers and of priests, the pathos, the heroism, the grossness of the general multitude of humanity. He shows us the happiness of mankind and the horrors which it has endured.

But throughout this history, it is Gibbon who speaks. He was the incarnation of the dominant spirit of his own times. In this way his volumes also tell another tale. They are a record of the mentality of the eighteenth century. They are at once a detailed history of the Roman Empire, and a demonstration of the general ideas of the silver age of the modern European Renaissance. This silver age, like its Roman counterpart seventeen hundred years earlier, was oblivious of its own imminent destruction by the impact of the Age of Steam and of Democracy, the counterparts of the Barbarians and of the Christians. Thus Gibbon narrates the Decline and Fall of the Roman Empire and exemplifies the prelude to the Decline and Fall of his own type of culture.

SECTION II. The history of ideas is dominated by a dichotomy which is illustrated by this comparison of Steam and Democracy in recent times to Barbarians and Christians in the classical civilization. Steam and Barbarians, each in their own age, were the senseless agencies driving their respective civilizations away from inherited modes of order. These senseless agencies are what Greek writers sometimes [*e.g.* in the *Timæus* of Plato, and *passim* throughout general literature] call 'compulsion' [ἀνάγχη], and sometimes 'violence' [βία]. They are apt to speak of 'compulsion' when these agencies appear with a general coordination among themselves, and of 'violence· when they appear as a welter of sporadic outbursts. It is one task of history to display the types of compulsion and of violence characteristic of each age. On the other hand, Democracy in modern times, and Christianity in the Roman Empire, exemplify articulated beliefs issuing from aspirations, and issuing into aspirations. Their force was that of consciously formulated ideals at odds with the ancestral pieties which had preserved and modulated existing social institutions. For example, we find the Christian theologian, Clement of Alexandria, exhorting his contemporaries to shun custom [συνήθεία]. These Christian ideals were among the persuasive agencies re-fashioning their respective ages.

The well-marked transition from one age into another can always be traced to some analogues to Steam and Democracy, or—if you prefer it—to some analogues to Barbarians and Christians. Senseless agencies and formulated aspirations cooperate in the work of driving mankind from its old anchorage. Sometimes the period of change is an age of hope, sometimes it is an age of despair. When mankind has slipped its cables, sometimes it is bent on the discovery of a New World, and sometimes it is haunted by the dim sound of the breakers dashing on the rocks ahead. The Fall of the Roman Empire occurred in a prolonged age of despair: Steam and Democracy belong to an age of hope.

It is easy to exaggerate the contrast between these two kinds of ages of transition. It all depends upon the surviving records. Whose feelings do they express? After all, even during the worst period of the decline of Rome the barbarians were enjoying themselves. To Attila and his hordes their incursion into Europe was an enjoyable episode diversifying the monotonous round of a pastoral life. But we have preserved for us hymns and ejaculations of sentinels in North Italian towns as they paced the walls amid the gathering gloom of a winter's night: —'From the fury of the Huns, Good Lord deliver us.' In this instance it seems easy to discriminate; barbarism and civilization were at odds with each other, and we stand for civilization. I waive the point that we now know something about the social state of central Asia at that epoch, and that the imagination of a sentinel on the walls of Padua or Aquileia was not quite adequate in its presentation of the Huns.

In every age of well-marked transition there is the pattern of habitual dumb practice and emotion which is passing, and there is oncoming of a new complex of habit. Between the two lies a zone of anarchy, either a passing danger or a prolonged welter involving misery of decay and zest of young life. In our estimate of these· agencies everything depends upon our standpoint of criticism. In other words, our history of ideas is derivative from our ideas of history, that is to say, upon our own intellectual standpoint.

Mankind is not wholly dumb, and in this respect it differs from other races of animals. Yet in the history of the world of animals even among the ancestors of men, there have been transitions of patterns of habit which exemplify a history of forms of behaviour devoid of any contemporary intellectual expression, either in the form of antecedently expressed purpose or in the form of subsequently expressed reflection. For example, at a remote period urged by the growth of forests some mammals ascended trees and became apes; and then later, after the lapse of some vast period, urged by the decay of forests, the same race descended from trees and became men.

We have here history on its senseless side, with its transitions pushed forward either by rainfall and trees, or by brute barbarians, or by coal, steam, electricity and oil. Yet even the senseless side of history refuses to accept its own proper category of sheer senselessness. The rainfall and the trees are items in a majestic order of nature: Attila's Huns had their own intellectual point of view in some respects surprisingly preferable to that of the degenerate Romans: the age of coal and steam was pierced through and through by the intellectual abilities of particular men who urged forward the transition. But finally, with all this qualification, rainfall and Huns and steam-engines represent brute necessity, as conceived in Greek thought, urging forward mankind apart from any human conception of an end intellectually expressed. Fragmentary intellectual agencies cooperated blindly to turn apes into men, to turn the classic civilization into mediaeval Europe, to overwhelm the Renaissance by the Industrial Revolution. Men knew not what they did.

SECTION III. The fragment of human history, upon which this book is concentrated, is concerned with the transmission of civilization from the Near East to Western Europe. The topic is limited to the story of the energizing of two or three main ideas, whose effective entertainment constitutes civilization. These ideas are traced in outline from their status in the ancient world of the Near East up to the present time. The boundaries of a civilization are indefinite, whether we are speaking of geography or of time, or of essential character. This vagueness more especially characterizes the eastern boundaries of Western Europe, and the boundaries of the Near East. Also these boundaries fluctuate as the centuries pass. In its latest phase of brilliance the Near East touched the Atlantic Ocean. But during its earlier period of greatness, before the age of the Greeks, it stretched from the Nile Valley to Mesopotamia, and from the Indian Ocean to the Euxine and the Caspian Seas. It also penetrated into the Ægean Basin, and later into the Western Mediterranean. But the Near East is only important for this discussion in its function of the origin and the background of modern Europe.

The whole point of the present enquiry is to demonstrate those factors in Western civilization which jointly constitute a new element in the history of culture. Of course no novelty is wholly novel. Factors which were present sporadically and as the dreams of individuals, or as a faint tinge upon other modes of mentality, received a new importance in the later civilization of Europe. The question is to understand how the shift of emphasis happened, and to recognize the effects of this shift upon the sociology of the Western World. In this way we obtain some presuppositions of thought which the detailed criticism of modern sociological development requires. We can then discern the status of the impulses which are driving forward the World of mankind.

In the story of this transmission of civilization from East to West, the Hebrew, the Hellenic, and the Hellenistic epochs can, with equal reason, be considered together, *either* as outposts of the Near East in the process of differentiating itself into the first phase of European mentality, *or* as the earliest groups of Europeans to receive the torch and successfully to assert their spiritual independence. Between them, the Hebrews and the Greeks introduced into Europe, and into the latest phase of the Near East, notions concerning the status of mankind in general, and of individual men in particular, and a discipline and direction in the general exercise of mentality, which in their combination have started the modern phase of progress within the European races. The first part of this book is occupied with the most general aspect of the sociological functions arising from, and issuing into, ideas concerning the human race; and the second part is concerned with modern cosmological principles which also are the outcome of ancient Greek and Hebrew thought. A simple-minded interest in ideas with one or other of these two types of generality is the main source from which mankind acquires novelty of outlook.

Chapter II

THE HUMAN SOUL

SECTION I. IN ANY human society, one fundamental idea tingeing every detail of activity is the general conception of the status of the individual members of that group, considered apart from any special preeminence. In such societies as they emerge into civilization, the members recognize each other as individuals exercising the enjoyment of emotions, passions, comforts and discomforts, perceptions, hopes, fears, and purposes. Also there are powers of intellectual understanding involving discrimination of details of characters, judgments of 'true or false', and of 'beautiful or ugly', and of 'good or bad'. We pass our lives vaguely and flittingly entertaining groups of such experiences, and we attribute like ways of existence to others.

But in the early stages of civilization such experiences and beliefs are mere matters of course. They provoke no abrupt reflective reaction isolating them for thoughtful inspection. Accordingly there is no modification of habit arising from the valuation of human beings as such. Thus the various members of a society find themselves cherishing each other, destroying, obeying or commanding, as the case may be. There is a communal organization, and there are beliefs about it slowly forming themselves into explanations.

We are to discuss the later phases when civilization has reached its modern height, a period of three thousand years at the most. Thinkers have now arisen. The notion of duty has dawned and received some definition. Above all the notion of a psyche,—

that is, of a mind—has dawned. In its first phase of gradual emergence, this great notion was instinctively used as a master-key to make intelligible the baffling occurrences of nature. The two most obvious characteristics of Nature, writes Lytton Strachey[1], are loveliness and power. The beauty dawned later upon human intelligences than did its power. Also in early phases of thought the powers of nature became the minds of Nature—minds bestial, ruthless, and yet placable. In all stages of civilization the popular gods represent the more primitive brutalities of the tribal life. The progress of religion is defined by the denunciation of gods. The keynote of idolatry is contentment with the prevalent gods.

The factor in human life provocative of a noble discontent is the gradual emergence into prominence of a sense of criticism, founded upon appreciations of beauty, and of intellectual distinction, and of duty. The moral element is derivative from the other factors in experience. For otherwise there is no content for duty to operate upon. There can be no mere morality in a vacuum. Thus the primary factors in experience are first the animal passions such as love, sympathy, ferocity, together with analogous appetitions and satisfactions; and secondly, the more distinctly human experiences of beauty, and of intellectual fineness, consciously enjoyed. Here the notion of intellectual distinction, or of fineness, is somewhat broader than that of 'truth', which is ordinarily cited in this conection. There is a grandeur of achievement in the delicate adjustment of thought to thought, which is independent of the mere blunt question of truth. We may term it 'beauty'. But intellectual beauty, however capable of being hymned in terms relevant to sensible beauty, is yet beautiful by stretch of metaphor. The same consideration applies to moral beauty. All three types of character partake in the highest ideal of satisfaction possible for actual realization, and in this sense can be termed that beauty which provides the final contentment for the Eros of the Universe.

1. Cf. *Books and Characters*, Chapter on 'The Poetry of Blake'.

For European thought, the effective expression of this critical discontent, which is the gadfly of civilization, has been provided by Hebrew and Greek thought. Its most adequate expression, so far as concerns literary delicacy and definition of the issues involved, is to be found in Plato's dialogues. We there find him criticizing the customary gods of the poets—indeed he would banish all poets—, and analyzing the capacities latent in the human soul. The religion of Plato is founded on his conception of what a God can be, with gaze fixed upon forms of eternal beauty; and his sociology is derived from his conception of what man can be, in virtue of a nature, which for its full description requires terms applicable to the nature of gods. Between them, the Hebrews and the Greeks provided a program for discontent. But the value of their discontent lies in the hope which never deserted their glimpses of perfection.

SECTION II. The intellectual agencies involved in the modification of epochs are the proper subject of this book. When we examine them we find a rough division into two types, one of general ideas, the other of highly specialized notions. Among the former, there are the ideas of high generality expressing conceptions of the nature of things, of the possibilities of human society, of the final aim which should guide the conduct of individual men. In each age of the world distinguished by high activity there will be found at its culmination, and among the agencies leading to that culmination, some profound cosmological outlook, implicitly accepted, impressing its own type upon the current springs of action. This ultimate cosmology is only partly expressed. and the details of such expression issue into derivative specialized questions of violent controversy. The intellectual strife of an age is mainly concerned with these latter questions of secondary generality which conceal a general agreement upon first principles almost too obvious to need expression, and almost too general to be capable of expression. In each period there is a general form of the forms of thought; and, like the air we breathe, such a form is so translucent, and so pervading, and so seemingly necessary, that only by extreme effort can we become aware of it.

In order to find an example capable of ready expression, we must descend below the utmost generality. In the region of political theory, consider the divergence of outlook in the classical Mediterranean civilization. Think of the differences between Pericles and Cleon, Plato and Alexander the Great, Marius and Sulla, Cicero and Cæsar. Yet they all agreed in one fundamental notion which lies at the base of all political theory. Throughout the Hellenic and Hellenistic Roman civilizations—those civilizations which we term 'classical'—it was universally assumed that a large slave population was required to perform services which were unworthy to engage the activities of a fully civilized man. In other words in that epoch a civilized community could not be self-sustaining. A comparatively barbarous substratum had to be interwoven in the social structure, so as to sustain the civilized apex. This assumption that a complex urban civilization requires a base of slavery was so universal, both in practice and in implicit presuppositions, that we may assume it to be derived from some well-founded reason in the conditions permitting the formation of the earlier phases of civilized life. The Egyptians wanted bricks, so they captured the Hebrews. The confusion of tongues associated with the tower of Babel may be historically doubtful in the form of the surviving legend: it is at least well-found as a reference to the confusion of races amid the slave populations supplying the mechanized man-power for the building of cities.

Now in respect to the political factions of the ancient world nothing has yet been settled. Every problem which Plato discusses is still alive today. Yet there is a vast difference between ancient and modern political theories. For we differ from the ancients on the one premise on which they were all agreed. Slavery was the presupposition of political theorists then; Freedom is the presupposition of political theorists now. In those days the penetrating minds found a difficulty in reconciling their doctrine of slavery to certain plain facts of moral feeling and of sociological practice; and in these days our sociological speculations find a difficulty in reconciling our doctrine of freedom to another group of plain facts, perplexing, irreconcilable, only to be conceived as a hateful brute necessity. Yet, when all such qualifications have been made, Freedom and Equality constitute an inevitable presupposition for modern political thought, with an admixture of subsequent lame qualification; while Slavery was a corresponding presupposition for the ancients, with their admixture of lame qualification. For both sets of thinkers God has been a great resource: a lot of things, which won't work on Earth, can be conceived as true in his sight. Ancients and Moderns in respect to this question face in directly opposite directions.

SECTION III. This growth of the idea of the essential rights of human beings, arising from their sheer humanity, affords a striking example in the history of ideas. Its formation and its effective diffusion can be reckoned as a triumph—a chequered triumph—of the later phase of civilization. We shall find out how general ideas arise and are diffused, if we examine the sort of history which belongs to this particular instance.

The great classical civilization is remarkable for two facts. First, it constituted a culmination of slavery, especially at the height of the Roman Empire. At that moment slavery reached its height, in necessity, in quantity, in horror, and in danger. In earlier, simpler communities slavery may have been conceived as an accidental mercy, a favour granted to a few fortunate communities or to a few fortunate individuals within any community. But for a thousand years of the classical civilization, to be civilized was to be a slave-owner. Some slave-owners were kind, some were brutal: probably, they were mostly mediocre. In Plato's Symposium Agathon, the host, is represented with a uniform well-bred kindliness both towards his slaves and his guests. Cicero and the younger Pliny exhibit themselves in their Letters as kindly masters. But on the whole the Roman capitalists with their vast estates exemplify the necessity for ancient civilization that it be built upon iniquity. Efficiency spelt Brutality. When such evils culminate, either they are corrected by the introduction of some new principle, or they destroy society. In the case of the classical civilizations, these alternatives were not exclusive: they both happened.

We now come to the second fact for which the classical period was remarkable. It was the first period which introduced moral principles forming an effective criticism of the whole system. The Athenians were slave-owners: but they seem to have humanized the institution. Plato was an aristocrat by birth and by conviction, also he must have owned slaves. But it is difficult to read some of his Dialogues without an uneasy feeling about the compulsory degradation of mankind. Also the Stoic lawyers of the Roman Empire introduced a legal reformation largely motived by the principle that human nature has essential rights. But neither the humane slave-owners, nor the inspired Plato, nor the clear-headed lawyers, initiated any campaign against slavery. They accepted it as a matter of course. It was presuposed in the very structure of society; and such necessity limits the scope of all generalities. Distinctions were introduced, the sort of distinctions which are conclusive so long as you know that in practice you have got to accept them.

We see here the first stage of the introduction of great ideas. They start as speculative suggestions in the minds of a small, gifted group. They acquire a limited application to human life at the hands of various sets of leaders with special functions in the social structure. A whole literature arises which explains how inspiring is the general idea, and how slight need be its effect in disturbing a comfortable society. Some transition has been produced by the agency of the new idea. But on the whole the social system has been inoculated against the full infection of the new principle. It takes its place among the interesting notions which have a restricted application.

But a general idea is always a danger to the existing order. The whole bundle of its conceivable special embodiments in various usages of society constitutes a program of reform. At any moment the smouldering unhappiness of mankind may seize on some such program and initiate a period of rapid change guided by the light of its doctrines. In this way, the conception of the dignity of human nature was quietly energizing in the minds of Roman officials, producing somewhat better government and nerving men like Marcus Aurelius to rise to the height of their appointed task. It was a worthy moral force, but society had been inoculated against its revolutionary application. For six hundred years, the ideal of the intellectual and moral grandeur of the human soul had haunted the ancient Mediterranean world. It had in a way, transformed the moral ideas of mankind: it had readjusted religions: and yet it had failed to close with the basic weakness of the civilization in which it flourished. It was the faint light of the dawn of a new order of life.

SECTION IV. In the midst of this period of progress and decadence, Christianity arose. Jn its early form it was a religion of fierce enthusiasm and of impracticable moral ideals. Luckily these ideals have been preserved for us in a literature which is almost contemporary with the origin of the religion. They have constituted an unrivalled program for reform, which has been one element in the evolution of Western civilization. The progress of humanity can be defined as the process of transforming society so as to make the original Christian ideals increasingly practicable for its individual members. As society is now constituted a literal adherence to the moral precepts scattered throughout the Gospels would mean sudden death.

Christianity rapidly assimilated the Platonic doctrine of the human soul. The philosophy and the religion were very congenial to each other in their respective teachings; although, as was natural, the religious version was much more specialized than the philosophic version. We have here an example of the principle that dominates the history of ideas. There will be a general idea in the background flittingly, waveringly, realized by the few in its full generality—or perhaps never expressed in any adequate universal form with persuasive force. Such persuasive expression depends on the accidents of genius; for example, it depends on the chance that a man like Plato appears. But this general idea, whether expressed or implicitly just below the surface of consciousness, embodies itself in special expression after special expression. It condescends so as to lose the magnificence of its generality, but it gains in the force of its peculiar adaptation to the concrete circumstances of a particular age. It is a hidden driving force, haunting humanity, and ever appearing in specialized guise as compulsory on action by reason of its appeal to the uneasy conscience of the age. The force of the appeal lies in the fact that the specialized principle of immediate conduct exemplifies the grandeur of the _wider truth arising from the very nature of the order of things, a truth which mankind has grown to the stature of being able to feel though perhaps as yet unable to frame in fortunate expression.

The greatness of Christianity—the greatness of any valuable religion—consists in its 'interim ethics'. The founders of Christianity and their earlier followers firmly believed that the end of the world was at hand. The result was that with passionate earnestness they gave free reign to their absolute ethical intuitions respecting ideal possibilities without a thought of the preservation of society. The crash of society was certain and imminent. 'Impracticability' was a word which had lost its meaning; or rather, practical good sense dictated concentration on ultimate ideas. The last things had arrived: intermediate stages were of no account.

This consideration was of more influence in framing the mentality of the earlier followers than in the initial foundation of the religion. It enabled these followers to transmit in their full purity the primitive notions. But the religion arose in a more tranquil atmosphere although highly sensitive in regard to religious emotion, and with some admixture of apocalyptic belief. The Galilean peasantry, having regard to their climate and simplicity of life, were neither rich nor poor: they were unusually intellectual for a peasantry, by reason of their habits of study of historical and religious records: they were protected from disturbance, from within or from without, by the guardian structure of the Roman Empire. They had no responsibility for the maintenance of this complex system. Their own society was of the simplest; and they were ignorant of the conditions by which the Empire arose, of the conditions requisite for its efficiency, and of the conditions necessary for its preservation. They were ignorant even of the services which the Empire was rendering them. The alternation of procurators was like that of the seasons, some were better and some were worse; but all alike, seasons and procurators of Judaea, issued from an inscrutable order of things.

The tone of life of this peasantry provided an ideal environment in which concepts of ideal relations between rational beings could be formulated—concepts devoid of ferocity, concepts gracious, kindly, and shrewd, concepts in which mercy prevailed over judicial classification. In this ideal world forgiveness could be stretched to seventy times seven, whereas in the real world of the Herods and the Roman Empire a sevenfold forgiveness touched upon the impracticable. But the Galilean people were unconcerned with the discipline of the Roman legions, with the imperial inspection of the doings of proconsuls, and with the complexities of a legal system which was to impose an order upon multitudinous transactions, stretching from the hills of Scotland to the marshes of Mesopotamia. A gracious, simple mode of life, combined with a fortunate ignorance, endowed mankind with its most precious instrument of progress—the impracticable ethics of Christianity.

A standard had now been created, expressed in concrete illustrations foolproof against perversions. This standard is a gauge by which to test the defects of human society. So long as the Galilean images are but the dreams of an unrealized world, so long they must spread the infection of an uneasy spirit.

SECTION V. In ethical ideals we find the supreme example of consciously formulated ideas acting as a driving force effecting transitions from social state to social state. Such ideas are at once gadflies irritating, and beacons luring, the victims among whom they dwell. The conscious agency of such ideas should be contrasted with senseless forces, floods, barbarians, and mechanical devices. The great transitions are due to a coincidence of forces derived from both sides of the world, its physical and its spiritual natures. Mere physical nature lets loose a flood, but it requires intelligence to provide a system of irrigation.

The ethical ideas, embodied in the great religions, Christianity for instance, though representing a high approach to final generality, are yet specializations of the Platonic generality. Partly these ethical intuitions are a direct application of metaphysical doctrine for the determination of practice. The ethical principle is then a parable illuminating the superior generality on which it depends. Thus the codes of all religions also embody the particular temperaments and stages of civilization of their adherents. No religion can be considered in abstraction from its followers, or even from its various types of followers. Religious ideas represent highly specialized forms of general notions. Sometimes these specializations are concrete embodiments with peculiar beauty and aptness: sometimes they are the result of a throw back to barbaric brutality. Neither religions nor individual men demonstrate their sanctity by their ejaculations. We find however this whole bundle of more special notions, legal, political, ethical, religious, driving forward human life, and deriving a force of grandeur from their various exemplifications of the mystery of the human soul in its journey toward the source of all harmony. It is a story of crime, misunderstanding, profanation. Great ideas enter into reality with evil associates and with disgusting alliances. But the greatness remains, nerving the race in its slow ascent.

In the Middle Ages institutional Christianity was honourably distinguished as a driving force toward the grander intuitions.

Unfortunately, in accordance with the habits of all institutions, it adapted itself to its environment. It became an instrument of conservation instead of an instrument of progress. After a short period of progressive energy, the Reformation Churches again accepted the same idolatrous role. On the whole, well-established religious institutions are to be reckoned among the conservative forces of society. They soon become the grand support of what Clement had termed 'communal custom'. But the ultimate ideals, of which they profess themselves the guardians, are a standing criticism of current practices.

Accordingly the next resurgence of the notion of· the essential greatness of the human soul is associated with the sceptical humanitarianism of the eighteenth century. We have arrived at the Age of Reason and the Rights of Man. This great French age of thought has remade the presuppositions of the civilized world, in speculation, in science, and in sociological premises. It was derived from the English thought of the seventeenth century, Francis Bacon, Isaac Newton, and John Locke. Also it gained inspiration from the English revolutions of the same epoch. But the English modes always retained the note of insularity. The French broadened, clarified, and universalized. They thus made world-wide, ideas which such a man as Edmund Burke could only grasp in their application to one race, and even at times to one island.

But the thought of John Locke survived also in England. Its influence was reinforced by the general pride in the doctrines of freedom embodied in the English Common Law. There was thus a Whiggish tinge even to Tory Parliaments in those days. In this way the British Government was the first government to make effective two decisive steps in the abolition of slavery. Two parliaments determined the new policies. They were composed of aristocratic landowners and evangelical bankers and merchants, one parliament Tory and the other Whig. The first step was the abolition of the British slave-trade in 1808, and the second step was the purchase and freeing of all slaves in the British Dominions in the year 1833. This latter operation cost twenty million pounds at a time of grave financial difficulty.

But the problem was comparatively simple for the English people. None the less this action constituted a foretaste of the final triumph of that same wavering alliance of philosophy, law, and religion which had its first success in the reforms of the Roman Imperial system. We notice that a great idea in the background of dim consciousness is like a phantom ocean beating upon the shores of human life in successive waves of specialization. A whole succession of such waves are as dreams slowly doing their work of sapping the base of some cliff of habit: but the seventh wave is a revolution—'And the nations echo round'. In the last quarter of the eighteenth century, Democracy was born, with its earliest incarnations in America and in France; and finally it was Democracy that freed the slaves. In the modern world, Democracy has a deeper import than among the ancients. At last, in the nineteenth century, the fundamental question of slavery has been explicitly faced. In Europe, it was already a decaying institution, slowly withdrawing from slavery to serfdom, from serfdom to feudalism, from feudalism to aristocracy, from aristocracy to legal equality, from legal equality to careers effectively open to talent. But the question was assuming a new and menacing form by reason of the impact of the European and Arabian races upon the African tribes.

So modern Democrats, in the nineteenth century, nerved themselves to face the question of Slavery, explicitly and with thoroughness. The slow working of ideas is thereby illustrated. Two thousand years had elapsed since the foundation of Plato's Academy, since the reforms of the Stoic lawyers, since the composition of the Gospels. The great program of reform bequeathed by the classical civilization was achieving another triumph.

SECTION VI. The slow issue of general ideas into practical consequences is not wholly due to inefficiency of human character. There is a problem to be solved, and its complexity is habitually ignored by impetuous seekers. The difficulty is just this: —It may be impossible to conceive a reorganization of society adequate for the removal of some admitted evil without destroying the social organization and the civilization which depends on it. An allied plea is that there is no known way of removing the evil without the introduction of worse evils of some other type.

Such arguments are usually implicit. Even the wisest are unable to conceive the possibility of untried forms of social relations. Human nature is so complex that paper plans for society are to the statesman not worth even the price of the defaced paper. Successful progress creeps from point to point, testing each step. It is not difficult to frame the sort of defence that Cicero would have advanced, if challenged on the question of slavery. The Roman Government, he would have said, is the one hope for the human race. Destroy Rome; and Where will you find the firmness of the Roman Senate, the discipline of its legions, the wisdom of its lawyers, the restraints upon misgovernment, the appreciative protection of Greek learning? But he would not have said this. His genius would have risen to prophecy, and he would have foreseen and quoted the lines of Virgil on the mission of the Eternal City.

In fact, we do know exactly the stand taken upon this very question by the lawyers, Pagan and Christian, and by the bishops and popes, of the five centuries succeeding Cicero. Among them were statesmen with more than Cicero's practical sagacity, and his equals in moral sensibility. They introduced careful legal restraints upon the powers of the masters; they protected some of the essential rights of slaves. But they preserved the institution. Civilization, Hellenic and Roman, was preserved intact for more than seven centuries after the death of Plato. The slaves were the martyrs whose toil made progress possible. There is a famous statue of a Scythian slave sharpening a knife. His body is bent, but his glance is upward. That figure has survived the ages, a message to us of what we owe to the suffering millions in the dim past.

We may ask, Would Rome have been destroyed by a crusade for the abolition of slavery in the time of Cicero or in the time of Augustus? Throughout the whole period of classical civilization the foundations of social order could scarcely sustain the weight upon them—the wars between states, the surrounding barbarians, the political convulsions, the evils of the slave system. In the age from the birth of Cicero to the accession of Augustus to undisputed power, the whole structure almost collapsed before it had finished its appointed task. Even earlier, it had nearly met its fate, and later by a few centuries came the final collapse. It is impossible to doubt the effect of any vigorous effort for the immediate abolition of the only social system that men knew. It may be better that the heavens should fall, but it is folly to ignore the fact that they will fall.

Suppose that, in the middle of the nineteenth century, the shock that overwhelmed the Confederate States in the American Civil War had equally overwhelmed the whole of North America and the whole of Europe. The sole hope of progressive civilization would have been lost. We may speculate about a recovery, but of that we know nothing. In the ancient world, the dangers were immeasurably greater.

SECTION VII. The argument of the previous section can be generalized. It amounts to this: —that the final introduction of a reform does not necessarily prove the moral superiority of the reforming generation. It certainly does require that that generation exhibits reforming energy. But conditions may have changed, so that what is possible now may not have been possible then. A great idea is not to be conceived as merely waiting for enough good men to carry it into practical effect. That is a childish view of the history of ideas. The ideal in the background is promoting the gradual growth of the requisite communal customs, adequate to sustain the load of its exemplification.

Many factors contributed to the final inversion of sociological theory, from the presupposition of slavery to the presupposition of freedom. The chief factor has already been mentioned, namely, the sceptical, humanitarian movement of the eighteenth century, of which Voltaire and Rousseau were among the chief exponents, and the French Revolution the culmination.

Thus in a sense, and more especially when we consider the whole world-wide movement, religion was in the background. But in one section of this stirring of mankind the religious motive was among the chief agencies. Throughout the Anglo-Saxon world, English and American, the Wesleyan protestant revival was in full activity. It had been reserved for a great French historian, Elie Halevy, to point out the full sociological significance of this episode. The Methodist preachers aimed at saving men's souls in the next world, but incidentally they gave a new direction to emotions energizing in this world. The movement was singularly devoid of new ideas, and singularly rich in vivid feelings. It is the first decisive landmark indicating the widening chasm between the theological tradition and the modern intellectual world. From the earliest Greek theologians to Jerome and Augustine: from Augustine to Aquinas: from Aquinas to Luther, Calvin, and Suarez: from Suarez to Leibniz and John Locke: every great religious movement was accompanied by a noble rationalistic justification. You may disagree with the theologians—indeed it is impossible to agree with all of them—but you cannot complain that they have been unwilling to indulge in rational argument. The Middle Ages argued, Luther defended ninety-seven theses, Calvin produced his Institute, the Council of Trent argued on and off for eighteen years, the judicious Hooker argued, at the Synod of Dort Arminians and Calvinists argued.

The great Methodist movement more than deserves the eulogies bestowed on it. But it can appeal to no great intellectual construction explanatory of its modes of understanding. It may have chosen the better way. Its instinct may be sound. However that may be, it was a notable event in the history of ideas when the clergy of the western races began to waver in their appeal to constructive reason. More recently scientists and critical philosophers have followed the Methodist example.

In an age of aristocracy in England, the Methodists appealed to the direct intuitions of working men and of retail traders concerned with working men. In America they appealed to the toiling, isolated groups of pioneers. They brought hope, fear, emotional release, spiritual insight. They stemmed the inroads of revolutionary ideas. Also, allowing for many qualifications, they must be credited with one supreme achievement. They made the conception of the brotherhood of man and of the importance of men, a vivid reality. They had produced the final effective force which hereafter made slavery impossible among progressive races.

In the history of ideas the great danger is over-simplification. It is true that the Methodists produced the final wave of popular feeling which drove the anti-slavery movement to success. But the Methodist movement succeeded because it came at the right time. In this section we are discussing the religious influences. During the sixteenth, seventeenth, and eighteenth centuries the Church of Rome—to use a Quaker phrase—had a 'concern' for the races, groaning under European exploitation, which far surpassed that of the combined Protestant churches. The priests did not consider the problem in terms of human freedom. But, not to speak of the rest of the world, in America alone the heroism of the Catholic missionaries extended their self-sacrifice from the northern to the southern icefields. It is impossible to doubt but that their example kept alive a sensitiveness of the European conscience respecting the obligations of men to men.

Neither the Catholics, nor the Methodists, gave the first modern formulation of an explicit purpose to procure the abolition of slavery. This supreme honour belongs to the Quakers, and in particular to that Apostle of Human Freedom, John Woolman. Also the American Civil War was the tremendous episode constituting the climax of this sombre journey of civilization toward the light.

Thus in the evolution of the strands of thought which constituted the final stage in the destruction of the iniquitous slave-foundation of civilization, there are interwoven the insights and the heroisms of sceptical humanitarians, of Catholics, of Methodists, of Quakers. But the intellectual origin of the movement is to be traced back for more than two thousand years to the speculations of the philosophical Greeks upon functions of the human soul, and its status in the world of flux.

SECTION VIII. In this chapter the story of the translation of the Greek metaphysical speculations into the sociological concept of human freedom has been only half told. In the next chapter I shall consider in more detail some nineteenth century criticisms of this whole movement towards Democracy and Freedom. But, so far as it has gone, the story illustrates the extreme difficulty of expressing in language the final generalities. The importance of man as the supreme example of a living organism is beyond question. Yet when we try to express the general notions thus involved, and their bearing upon conduct, at every step controversy arises. The immense history of Plato's metaphysical concept of the soul, with its influence on religion, and on social theory, carries this moral decisively.

Human life is driven forward by its dim apprehension of notions too general for its existing language. Such ideas cannot be grasped singly, one by one in isolation. They require that mankind advances in its apprehension of the general nature of things, so as to conceive systems of ideas elucidating each other. But the growth of generality of apprehension is the slowest of all evolutionary changes. It is the task of philosophy to promote this growth in mentality. In so far as there is success, the specialized applications of great ideas are purified from their gross associations with savage fancies. The Carthaginians were a great civilized trading nation.

They belonged racially to one of the great progressive sections of mankind. They traded from the shores of Syria, throughout the Mediterranean Sea, up the Atlantic Coast of Europe, to the tin mines of Cornwall in England. They circumnavigated Africa. They ruled Spain and Sicily and North Africa. Yet, when Plato was speculating, this great people could so conceive the supreme powers of the Universe that they sacrificed their children to Moloch as an act of religious propitiation. The growth in generality of understanding makes such savagery impossible in corresponding civilizations today.

Human Sacrifice, Human Slavery are instances of great intuitions of religion and of civilized purposes expressing themselves by means of inherited brutalities of instinctive behaviour. Direct religious intuitions, even those of the purest origin, are in danger of allying themselves with lower practices and emotions which in fact pervade existing society. Religion lends a driving force to philosophy. But in its turn, Speculative philosophy guards our higher intuitions from base alliances by its suggestions of ultimate meanings, disengaged from the facts of current modes of behaviour.

The history of ideas is a history of mistakes. But through all mistakes it is also the history of the gradual purification of conduct. When there is progress in the development of favourable order, we find conduct protected from relapse into brutalization by the increasing agency of ideas consciously entertained. In this way Plato is justified in his saying. The creation of the world—that is to say, the world of civilized order—is the victory of persuasion over force.

Chapter III

THE HUMANITARIAN IDEAL

SECTION I. IN THE previous chapter we considered the combined influence of philosophy, law, and religion, upon the evolution from the notion of society based upon servitude to that of society based upon individual freedom. To this transformation philosophy contributed its generality, law contributed the constructive ability, religion the moral energy. By themselves and apart from correction by the Platonic philosophy, the religions derived from Western Asia were tinged with the mentality of the older civilizations of that region. They conceived the universe in terms of despots and slaves. None of these religions have been able wholly to shake off the horrible implications latent in such a conception. But the fortunate coalescence of the initial Christian institutions with the philosophic Platonic doctrines provided the Western Races with a beautiful sociological ideal, intellectually expressed, and closely allied with intermittent bursts of emotional energy. Unfortunately, interwoven with this ideal in Christian theology and in the patterns of Christian emotion, there has survived throughout history the older concept of a Divine Despot and a slavish Universe, each with the morals of its kind.

The theme of the former chapter has been the agency of these sociological ideals in the transformation of society. They constitute the intellectual side of the transformation, combined with an explanation how such intellectual concepts acquired driving force. In the present chapter we first glance at accessory causes, and then proceed to the criticism of the humanitarian ideal, a criticism which has been gathering strength since its origin in the nineteenth century. Finally, the barest sketch of a reply to this criticism is suggested.

The growth of technology is the greatest among the accessory causes which weakened the necessity for slavery. But this agency hardly came into play before the seventeenth century. Till that time the technology of the ancients, in their prime, probably surpassed that of the moderns. From that century onward, technological advance has more than satisfied the complex demands for effective labour, without recourse to slavery. Of course, the fixed order of society in a well-managed feudal system must not be confused with slavery, even in its application to the agricultural labourers at the base of the whole structure. Each order had its rights and duties, and in the happier examples of later feudalism the villagers were quite competent to go to law with their feudal chief. The system was very liable to degenerate into practical slavery, and often did so. Indeed, there is evidence[1] that, during the early Norman period in England, there was a relatively small class of slaves whose lives were at the arbitrary will of their owners. But the slave-trade shocked the conscience of those times. William the Conqueror legislated against it, and Bishops denounced it. In those times, it must be remembered, to be attached to the land was a protection as well as a restriction. It was the basis of a recognized status in an organized society—so far as the social system was organized, and was not a welter of violence.

The modern evolution of big business involves a closer analogy to feudalism, than does feudalism to slavery. In fact, the modern social system with its variety of indispensable, interlocked avocations necessitates such organization. The only questions at issue are the freedom of individuals to circulate among the grades, and satisfactory legal conceptions of the variety of relations of the

1. Cf. *Mediæval England*, pp. 100, 101, by Mary Bateson, T. Fisher Unwin, London 1903, and G. P. Putnam's Sons, New York.

grades with each other. Individualists and socialists are merely debating over the details of the neo-feudalism which modern industry requires. The self-sufficing independent man, with his peculiar property which concerns no one else, is a concept without any validity for modern civilization. Unfortunately this notion has been embodied in ancient moral codes applicable to Syrian deserts, and has reappeared tingeing western political theory in the commercial epoch immediately succeeding the decay of mediaeval feudalism. But it is not the practicable alternative to a slave society. The problem of social life is the problem of the coordination of activities, including the limits of such coordination.

The sense of the unity of civilization fostered by the Catholic Church, the general similarities of mankind throughout Europe, and the simplicities of life in the middle ages, are probably the main reasons why mediaeval wars were dissociated from slave-raiding expeditions. We hear of Saxon slaves in the slave-market in Rome. But that was in the lifetime of Gregory the Great, and the Saxons were not Christians. Indeed, whenever the European races came into contact with non-Christian foreign races, they seem to have had no compunction about slavery. We read of Saracen slaves, of the enslavement of the indigenous American tribes, and, above all, of negro slavery. But thanks to the growth of technology concurrently with the advance of civilization, the European races have avoided slavery in temperate climates. Finally, the humanitarian movement of the eighteenth century, combined with a religious sense of the kinship of men, has issued in the settled policy of the great civilized governments to extirpate slavery from the world.

SECTION II. This success came only just in time. For before and during the nineteenth century, several strands of thought emerged whose combined effect was in direct opposition to the humanitarian ideal. At the moment when the 'brotherhood of man· triumphed, the intellectual world was meditating on political economy conceived in terms of unrestrained competition, on

Malthus· iron law that the mass of the population must always press on the limits of bare subsistence, and on the zoological law of natural selection by which an iron environment crushed out the less favoured species, and on Hume's criticism of the notion of the soul. This new trend of thought was in its immediate origin British and is to be compared and contrasted with the antecedent Wesleyan movement. In neither case did the leaders intend the sociological effects which followed from their efforts. It is often the case that the originators belong to the antecedent epoch, and stand outside the epoch of their followers. The Methodist preachers did not intend to transform society, their object was to save souls. In like manner, Adam Smith was a typical figure of the eighteenth century enlightenment.

He and Hume are two of the last great Scotchmen who mark the tradition affiliation of Scotland with France, which had survived from the earlier centuries of joint antagonism to England. At their date the intellectual life of Edinburgh and Glasgow is not to be assimilated with that of England. Throughout the greater part of the eighteenth century, during its central portion, the intellectual life of England, so far as concerns any originative energy, is negligible. Indeed, one of the reasons for the separation of America from England was that the particular circumstances of English life were not applicable to America, and that England was not fermenting with any universal ideas capable of specialization for American conditions. English influence survived, it is true, in the Common Law; but, apart from that exception, the mentality of men like Jefferson and Franklin was French. There was the homeland of their thoughts. It has required the whole of the activity of the nineteenth century, from 1790 onward, to reconstruct the intellectual influence of England on the outside world. In the eighteenth century, France looked to England; but it was to the England of the seventeenth century, Bacon, Newton, Locke and the Regicides. In order to understand the intellectual history of

Europe, it is essential to remember the collapse of Germany during and after The Thirty Years' War, to remember the collapse of Italy owing to the supersession of the Mediterranean trade route to the East, owing to the Catholic Reaction with its activity of censorship, and owing to the domination of Spaniards and Habshurgs, and to remember the collapse of England owing to absorption in the commercial expansion of the eighteenth century—in the words of the old song, 'When George and pudding-time came round'. In the eighteenth century France carried the 'White Man's Burden' of intellectual advance.

Perhaps it was owing to the loss of the habit of speculative thoroughness, that in the revival of intellectual activity in England the issue of the emerging lines of thought was not discerned. Hume's flux of impressions and of reactions to impressions, each impression a distinct, self-sufficient existence, was very different to the Platonic soul. The status of man in the universe required reconsidering. 'What is man that thou are mindful of him?' The brotherhood of man at the top of creation ceased to be the well-defined foundation for moral principles. There seems no very obvious reason why one flux of impressions should not be related to another flux of impressions in the relative status of master to slave. To put the matter at its very lowest, the point requires arguing. It is no answer to point out that Hume and Huxley were united in their dislike of slavery—certainly Huxley, probably Hume. The question is what reason could they give, apart from their own psychological inheritance from the Platonic religious tradition. For example, in Book III, of his *Treatise,* Part II, Section I, Hume writes, "In general, it may be affirm'd that there is no such passion in human minds, as the love of mankind, merely as such, independent of personal qualities, or services, or of relation to ourself." This sentence seems very remote from the Catholic missionaries in America, from the Quaker John Woolman, or from the free-thinking Thomas Paine. In some mysterious way, they all cared for 'mankind, merely as such'.

SECTION III. In the Middle Ages of Europe the keynote of sociological theory is 'coordination'. The Church coordinated religious speculations; the Feudal System coordinated the intimate structure of society; the Empire—or, Was it the Church? Here dispute crept in—coordinated the Governments of the provincial regions, Counts, Dukes, Kings, and City-Republics. In the provinces of theology and of clerical organization, the success was considerable. To a less degree the Feudal system effected its purpose. No other system can be suggested which at that time and in those circumstances could have replaced it successfully: although the towns with their commercial and artisan populations stood outside it. more particularly in Italy. The Empire was a failure mitigated by a few successes. The Church, as an agent of large-scale political organization, was more successful than the Empire. Its agents were better educated and—allowing for many exceptions—had a higher morale. Also its influence extended to regions which the Empire never reached. But, on the whole, the attempts at large-scale organization of Europe were a failure. There is a pathetic interest in Dante's *De Monarchia* with its initial premise of the desire of mankind for peace and quietness. We have only to remember the state of Europe at that time, the state of Italy, and Dante's own life. Indeed, men do long for peace and quietness but their desire is chequered by other impulses. The Middle Ages were always haunted by the ghost of the old Roman Empire, with its message of vast success in the imposition of order upon men.

The Renaissance men read the classical authors, and decisively ignored the ideals of the Roman statesmen. Plato, perhaps, would have been gratified by the attention his works then received. But he would have been horrified at the outburst of individualism. In the men of the Italian Renaissance Plato would have recognized reproductions of the character of the younger Dionysius of Syracuse. At the time the incongruity was not perceived. But the inevitable issues followed. Finally in the nineteenth century, amid the triumph of humanitarian principles, the basic positions of the social theories derived from Platonism and Christianity were questioned. Previously, they had never been fully acted on. They were impracticable. But they had not been questioned as a social ideal.

SECTION IV. The collapse of the Middle Ages was, in one of its aspects, a revolt against coordination. The new keynote is expressed in the word 'competition'—

> 'Thou shalt not murder, but tradition
>
> Approves all forms of competition.'

Private life now dominated the social life of Europe in all its special forms—The Right of Private Judgment, Private Property, The Competition of Private Traders, Private Amusement. The notion that every action is at once a private experience and a public utility had to be born again. It sickened and died with the disappearance of the 'mediaeval mind'. Wherever men looked, they saw 'competition' written across the face of things. Nations arose, and men thought of nations in terms of international competition. They examined the theory of trade, and they construed its interactions in terms of competition. mitigated by 'higgling.' They considered the bounty of nature in the provision of food, and they saw the masses of mankind competing for insufficient supplies. They saw the fecundity of nature in the provision of a myriad species of living things, and they construed the explanation in terms of the competition of species. What the notions of 'form' and 'harmony' were to Plato, that the notions of 'individuality' and 'competition' were to the nineteenth century. God had placed his bow in the skies as a symbol; and the strip of colours, rightly read, spelt 'competition.' The prize to be competed for was 'life'. Unsuccessful competitors died; and thus, by a beautiful provision of nature, ceased from constituting a social problem.

Now it is quite obvious that a much needed corrective to an unqualified, sentimental humanitarianism is here being supplied.

Strife is at least as real a fact in the world as Harmony. If you side with Francis Bacon and concentrate on the efficient causes, you can interpret large features of the growth of structure in terms of 'strife'. If, with Plato, you fix attention on the end, rationally worthy, you can interpret large features in terms of 'harmony'. But until some outline of understanding has been reached which elucidates the interfusion of strife and harmony, the intellectual driving force of successive generations will sway uneasily between the two.

There have been many interpretations of special aspects of European society in terms of strife: Machiavelli's 'Prince', the political policies of the great Renaissance Monarchs, Charles the Fifth, Philip the Second, Francis the First, Henry the Eighth, Henri Quatre, William the Silent, Queen Elizabeth. The people, thus indicated, found strife. They could not evade it. Fleets, armies, hatreds, assassin's daggers, burnings at the stake, insurrections were there as real present facts. To survive, as persons or as nations, meant force and policy suppressing competitors. Harmony crept in under the guise of the joy of the adventure, of faculties stretched to the full. But such harmony was a secondary effect, merely Romance gilding Strife.

In the hands of theologians both in the Middle Ages and in the first period of its supersession, the Platonic-Christian tradition leant heavily towards its mystical religious side. It abandoned this world to the Evil Prince thereof, and concentrated thought upon another world and a better life. Plato himself explicitly considers this solution at the end of his dialogue, the *Republic.* But he there gives it another twist to that adopted by later theologians. He conceives the perfect Republic in Heaven as an immediate present possession in the consciousness of the wise in the temporal world. Thus for Plato, at least in his mood when he concluded this dialogue, the joy of heaven is realizable on earth: the wise are happy. Theoretically, this doctrine also tinged mediaeval

Christianity. But in practice there has always been the temptation to abandon the immediate experience of this world as a lost cause. The shadows pass—says mystical Religion. But they also recur, and recur—whispers the Experience of Mankind. Be tranquil, they will end—rejoins Religion. The mystical religion which most whole-heartedly adopts this attitude is Buddhism. In it despair of this world is conjoined with a program for the world's abolition by a mystic tranquillity. Christianity has wavered between Buddhistic renunciation, and its own impracticable ideals culminating in a crude Millennium within the temporal flux. The difference between the two consists in the difference between a program for reform and a program for abolition. I hazard the prophecy that that religion will conquer which can render clear to popular understanding some eternal greatness incarnate in the passage of temporal fact.

SECTION V. The political, liberal faith of the nineteenth century was a compromise between the individualistic, competitive doctrine of strife and the optimistic doctrine of harmony. It was believed that the laws of the Universe were such that the strife of individuals issued in the progressive realization of a harmonious society. In this way, it was possible to cherish the emotional belief in the Brotherhood of Man, while engaging in relentless competition with all individual men. Theoretically, it seemed possible to conciliate the belief with the practice without the intrusion of contradiction. Unfortunately, while this liberalism was winning triumph after triumph as a political force in Europe and America, the foundations of its doctrine were receiving shock after shock.

The new industrial system which should have been a triumph for the liberal doctrines, did not work well. It had first developed in England under treatment exclusively dictated by the doctrines of economic liberalism. On this point, in their treatment of the manufacturing and mining industries, the English Tories at first were as orthodox as the English Whigs. Unfortunately after two generations of such industrial development, the widespread misery at the base of the whole organization, in the mines, in the factories, in the slums, aroused the public conscience. This foundation of social relations upon individualism and competition, with no mitigating practices, was not working well under the new industrial conditions, such as mining for raw materials and mechanized manufacturing for finished products. At least this judgment holds for the old, comparatively crowded, nations of Europe. England was the pioneer and tried the system whole-heartedly. It failed. The evidence is scattered through the records of the two decades from 1830 to 1850. For example it can be found summarized in any life of the Lord Shaftesbury of the period—a great philanthropist—, in some of Disraeli's early novels, in the joint writings of J. L. Hammond and Barbara Hammond, dealing with the state of the labourers, town and country. The mere doctrines of freedom, individualism, and competition, had produced a resurgence of something very like industrial slavery at the base of society.

The industrial politics of the nineteenth century in Europe can only be understood by remembering this fact. The pure doctrine of nineteenth-century liberalism failed. During the decade of the eighteen forties and since, in England and in every European country a series of remedial industrial measures were introduced. The great liberal leaders, Cobden, Bright, and even Gladstone, were either opposed, or were notably cold, to these measures. They infringed the purity of the liberal doctrine. The important internal division of the political liberals in England was not the prominent one between Radicals and Whigs. It was the division between the pure liberals and the modified liberals. These modified liberals were in some ways nearer to the old Tories. They repudiated the liberal doctrine of an atomistic society. Unfortunately for the liberal political party in England, its later leaders, Gladstone, Lord Hartington, Asquith belonged to the pure liberal faction. If Campbell-Bannerman had been somewhat abler and, what is still more important, if he had lived, political history in England would have been different. As it was, in the last phase, English political liberalism under Asquith's leadership was engaged in direct opposition, or apathy, in respect to every reform which it was the task of a reforming political party to undertake—the Women's movement, Education, Industrial Reorganization. During the seventy years of its greatest triumphs, from 1830 onward, English liberalism was slowly decaying by its failure to acquire a coherent system of practicable ideals. On the whole, the pure liberals retained command of the political machine in England, from Mr. Gladstone in the last third of the nineteenth century to Mr. Asquith in the opening phase of the twentieth century.

Notwithstanding this reluctance of the great representative liberals, before the middle of the century a whole new movement of social coordination arose, in the form of Governmental measures, regulative of mining, of factories, of slum areas. The Industrial System then spread to Germany, where the necessity for coordination and the failure of free competition were at once taken for granted. The early form of the industrial doctrine of liberalism was never even tried in that country. But the modification of the liberal doctrines came grudgingly; and its failure generated a new formulation of an old idea. Karl Marx proclaimed the doctrine of 'The Class War'. The learned economists are unanimous in telling us that *Das Kapital* does not express a sound scientific doctrine, which will stand comparison with the facts. The success of the book—for it is still with us as a power—can then only be accounted for by the magnitude of the evils ushered in by the first phase of the industrial revolution.

The early liberal faith that by the decree of benevolent Providence, individualistic competition and industrial activity, would necessarily work together for human happiness had broken down as soon as it was tried. Perhaps a more enlightened training of the directing classes was required. Then coordination should mainly be directed towards education and sociological training:

Perhaps, governmental agency regulating the conditions of all employments was the proper corrective: Perhaps the State, controlled by the workers, should be the sole employer. All these suggestions are still matters of fierce debate. In some country or other almost every solution has been tried. But no one now holds that, apart from some further directive agency, mere individualistic competition, of itself and by its own self-righting character, will produce a satisfactory society.

Unfortunately, the Malthusian doctrine, in its popular rendering, affirmed that as a law of nature the masses of mankind could never emerge into a high state of well-being. Still worse, biological science drew the conclusion that the destruction of individuals was the very means by which advance was made to higher types of species. This was the famous doctrine of Natural Selection, promulgated in 1859, by Charles Darwin. This exclusive reliance upon Natural Selection was not characteristic of Darwin's own theory. For him, it was one agency among many others. But, in the form in which the doctrine reigned in thought from that day to this, Natural Selection was the sole factor to be seriously considered. As applied to human society this theory is a challenge to the whole humanitarian movement. The contrast between the dominant theories of Lamarck and Darwin made all the difference. Instead of dwelling on the brotherhood of man, we are now directed to procure the extermination of the unfit. Again the modern doctrines of heredity, gained partly from the experience of breeders of stock, partly from practical horticulturists, partly from the statistical researches of Francis Galton, Karl Pearson. and their school, partly from the laws of heredity discovered by Mendel, the Austrian Abbot, who published his unnoticed researches contemporaneously with the publication of Darwin's *Origin of Species*,—these doctrines have all weakened the Stoic-Christian ideal of democratic brotherhood.

Religion by itself has always wavered between that conception and the despot-slaves conception of God and his creatures. But the democratic liberalism of the late eighteenth and early nineteenth centuries was the triumph of the Stoic-Christian strain of thought. In Hume's criticism of the doctrine of the soul, in the breakdown of pure unmitigated competitive individualism as a practical working system, in the Malthusian doctrine of the pressure of population on the means of subsistence, in the scientific doctrine of the elimination of the unfit as the engine of progress, in the Galtonian and Mendelian doctrines of heredity, in the rejection of the Lamarckian doctrine that usage can raise the standard of fitness,—in the concurrence of all these strands of thought the liberalism of the early nineteenth century lost its security of intellectual justification.

SECTION VI. There are two intellectual movements to be set on the other side of the account. One is Jeremy Bentham's legal reformation based on the Utilitarian Principle of 'The Greatest Happiness of The Greatest Number': the other is Auguste Comte's 'Religion of Humanity', that is to say, Positivism. Most of what has been practically effective, in morals, in religion, or in political theory, from their day to this has derived strength from one or other of these men. Their doctrines have been largely repudiated as theoretical foundations, but as practical working principles they dominate the world. On the whole, their influence has been democratic. They have swept away mysterious claims of privileged orders of men, based on mystical intuitions originated by religion or philosophy. They carried back to the Roman Stoic lawyers, though they repudiated the ultimate metaphysical doctrines of Stoicism. They were in effect a resurrection of this Stoic legal movement, but devoid of its intellectual grandeur. From another point of view, they recurred to the scientific revolt again metaphysics, led by Newton, in the seventeenth century. They extended this revolt to moral and political theory.

For two thousand years, Platonic philosophic theories and Christian intuitions had furnished the intellectual justification for the slow growth in Western Europe of emotions of respect and friendliness between man and man—the notion of brotherhood. These emotions are at the basis of all social groups. As relatively blind emotions they must pervade animal society, namely, the urge to cooperate, to help, to feed, to cherish, to play together, to express affection. Among mankind these fundamental feelings reign with great strength within limited societies. But the range of human intelligence,—its very foresight as to dangers and opportunities the power of the imaginative entertaining of differences between group and group, of their divergencies of habit and sentiment—this range of intelligence has produced a ferocity of inversion of this very sentiment of inter-racial benevolence. Mankind is distinguished by its strength of tribal feeling, and conversely it is also distinguished by far-reaching malign exploitation and inter-tribal warfare. Also the tribal feeling is apt to be chequered by limitations of benevolence to special sections within the boundary of the same community.

For two thousand years philosophy and religion had held up before Western Europe the ideal figure of man, as man, and had claimed for it a supreme worth. Under this urge, Jesuits had gone to Patagonia, John Woolman had denounced slavery, Tom Paine had revolted against social oppression and against the doctrine of original sin. These Jesuits, these Quakers, and these Freethinkers differed among themselves. But they owed their emotions towards men, as men, to the generalization of feeling produced by the joint influence of philosophy and religion.

Jeremy Bentham and Auguste Comte accepted these generalized emotions as ultimate moral intuitions, clear matter of fact, requiring no justification and requiring no ultimate understanding of their relations to the rest of things. They discarded metaphysics. In so doing, they effected an immense service to democratic liberalism. For they produced a practicable program of reform, and practicable modes of expression which served to unite men whose ultimate notions differed vastly.

Unfortunately, owing to the advance of scientific theory, the relations of the emotions to the rest of things refused to be ignored. In the evolution of life Nature is implacable: Nature discriminates. Whence comes this universal benevolence 'The Religion of Humanity' should be replaced by a cult of a select assortment of Humanity: 'The Greatest Happiness of the Greatest Number' should be replaced by 'The Humane Extinction of Inferior Specimens'. Hume denies that there is any 'such passion . . . as the love of mankind merely as such'. Modern science gives a plausible explanation why no such passion is required. It can only stand in the way of the scavenging process of evolution. If any people are subject to this passion, of course they will act on it. But no reason can be given why we should inculcate the passion in others, or why we should pervert legislation to subserve the ends of such an unreasonable emotion. I am certainly in greater sympathy with Bentham and Comte than with this deduction from Hume and modern Zoology. But, if it proves nothing else, the deduction does show that Bentham and Comte were mistaken in thinking that they had found a clear foundation for morals, religion, and legislation, to the exclusion of all ultimate cosmological principles. On the surface, their pet doctrines are just as liable to sceptical attack as metaphysical dogmas ever were. They have gained nothing in the way of certainty by dropping Plato and Religion.

More ultimate reasons are required either to justify discriminations in the mixture, or to provide a reconstructed justification for the doctrine of regard to man, as man. Further mere 'survival value' is not sufficient: for there are conditions which stamp out just those types which we find ourselves most willing to preserve amid happiness.

SECTION VII. Auguste Comte founded his Positivism on the assured results of science, the physical and moral science of his own day. He died in 1857, and two years later Darwin published his *Origin of Species.* We have already discussed some of the difficulties for the Religion of Humanity introduced by the subsequent phases of the Evolution Theory. Such a foundation may be adequate to shape the methodology of a group of men with limited interests at some definite date. But certainly this adequacy does not arise from any adequate clarity of the point of view. Many a worshipper obtains his purpose of spiritual consolation by bowing towards the sunrise and muttering an incantation; but he may be totally unable to render any coherent account of the grounds, metaphysical or pragmatic, which render his procedure effective.

Apart from his difficulty of conciliating the physical with the mental sciences, physical science, taken by itself, has some difficulty with its own fundamental notions. This perplexity is relevant to Platonic religious tradition whose fortunes and specializations we have been tracing. We can classify the topics of physical science under four headings: — (1) The true and real things which endure, (2) The true and real things which occur, (3) The abstract things which recur, (4) The Laws of Nature. An example of the first heading is a piece of rock, or—to pass beyond mere physical science—the individuality of a human being, his soul, as Plato would have it. An example of the second kind is any happenings. in a street, in a room, in an animal body, or—again to pass beyond mere physical science—our individual complex experience within a tenth of a second. An example of the third type is the shape of a rock. It seems doubtful whether a shade of colour, or the qualitative element in the performance of a musical symphony, are to be reckoned as concerned with nature or mentality. But certainly they recur. On the other hand a *sort* of feeling of affection is a recurrence which belongs decidedly to the mental side of things. An example of the fourth heading is the Law of Gravitation, or the geometrical Relations of Things.

I am not going to plunge into a metaphysical discussion at the close of a chapter, already sufficiently complex. But it is relevant to point out, how superficial are our controversies on sociological theory apart from some more fundamental determination of what we are talking about. The four topics above at once suggest a host of perplexing questions, which have puzzled thinkers from the time of Plato to the prevent time. In these two chapters we have been tracing the history of three very different types of thought, (a) the Platonic-Religious ideas, (b) Individualistic, Competitive ideas of Commercial Society, (c) the idea of physical science. Also each of these types involves internal complexities. Now we may hold, indeed I think we must hold, that each of these strains of theory is the outcome of valid intuitions and embodies truths about the nature of things which cannot be set aside. It seems an easy solution to hold that each type of idea is within its own sphere autonomous. In that case, the controversies arise from the illegitimate poaching of one type over the proper territory of some other type. For example, it is fashionable to state that religion and science can never clash because they deal with different topics. I believe that this solution is entirely mistaken. In this world at least, you cannot tear apart minds and bodies. But as soon as you try to adjust ideas you find the supreme importance of making perfectly clear, what you are talking about. It is fatal to oscillate uncritically from the things which endure to the things which occur, and from the things which occur to the things which recur. Discussions based on no metaphysical clarity in the discrimination of endurance, occurrence, recurrence, can be made sophistically to prove anything.

For example, in the statement of the Utilitarian Principle, we find the phrase 'The Greatest Happiness of The Greatest Number'. Evidently this phrase has a meaning, at least sufficient for us to take it as a rough guide to action. But when we use the formula as a criticism of the other points of view we are entitled to ask what it means. The 'Happiness' is evidently a recurrent, and it is differentiated into grades of intensity, so that one occurrence may be more intense than another in point of Happiness. But what is meant by the addition of the Happinesses of different occurrences. There is no occurrence with the Happiness of this addition sum. At least, if there tie such an occurrence, it ought to be indicated in the principle, and this indication will lead us in the direction of the discarded Platonism. Again, we must know the relation of the endurances to the occurrences in order to understand the principle. As usually employed, the phrase refers to the greatest number of men. It therefore refers to endurances and not to occurrences. But can we really correlate the happiness of three shortlived men with that of one longlived man? Then again there are the qualitative differences between different types of happiness. Finally we conclude that before we can profitably proceed with this discussion, it is necessary to attain some clarity in our metaphysical notions respecting endurances, occurrences, and things that recur.

SECTION VIII. We now pass to Science and ask whether it provides us with any clear notions, independently of a metaphysical discussion. Science is founded on the notion of Law,—The Laws of Nature. The notion is that there are many things in the world, whose behaviour towards each other always exemplifies fixed rules. These rules are evidently indicating recurrences which never fail to recur. Yet here a perplexity arises as to the connection of the Laws with the behaving things. Behaviours differ widely in a city—New York, for instance—, in a forest, in a subtropical desert, in an Arctic icefield. Also, to travel further, they differ widely on the Moon, on the atmosphere of the Sun, in the interior of a dense star, in inter-stellar space.

This is very superficial. We all know that if we analyse the things into molecules the laws of chemistry are the same in the city, the forest, the desert and the icefield. These laws of chemistry express the mutual behaviour of molecules, packed with sufficient closeness. But molecules are analysable. Things behave very differently amid a close pack of molecules from their behaviour amid the vibrations of so-called empty space. The chemical laws are merely relevant to the inter-relations of molecules. In empty space we are driven back to the fundamental electromagnetic laws controlling the flux of energy. At this point we have to stop our regression, merely because our penetration has come to an end.

But there is no reason to doubt, that the laws are the outcome of the environment of electromagnetic occasions. This whole process of regression suggests an inversion of ideas. The laws are the outcome of the character of the behaving things: they are the 'communal customs' of which Clement spoke. This conception should replace the older idea of given things with mutual behaviour conditioned by imposed laws. What we know of external nature is wholly in terms of how the various occasions in nature contribute to each other's natures. The whole environment participates in the nature of each of its occasions. Thus each occasion takes its initial form from the character of its environment. Also the laws which condition each environment merely express the general character of the occasions composing that environment. This is the doctrine of the definition of things in terms of their modes of functioning.

But we are now drawing close to the impracticable ethics of Christianity. The ideals cherished in the souls of men enter into the character of their actions. These interactions within society modify the social laws by modifying the occasions to which those laws apply. Impracticable ideals are a program for reform. Such a program is not to be criticized by immediate possibilities. Progress consists in modifying the laws of nature so that the Republic on Earth may conform to that Society to be discerned ideally by the divination of Wisdom.

In these two chapters, we have been considering the adventures in the history of Europe of a great idea. Plato conceived the notion of the ideal relations between men based upon a conception of the intrinsic possibilities of human character. We see this idea enter into human consciousness in every variety of specialization. It forms alliances with allied notions generated by religion. It differentiates its specializations according to the differentiations of the diverse religions and diverse scepticisms associated with it.

At times it dies down. But it ever recurs. It is criticized, and it is also a critic. Force is always against it. Its victory is the victory of persuasion over force. The force is the sheer fact of what the antecedent volume of the world in fact contains. The idea is a prophecy which procures its own fulfillment.

The power of an ideal consists in this. When we examine the general world of occurrent fact, we find that its general character, practically inescapable, is neutral in respect to the realization of intrinsic value. The electromagnetic occasions and the electromagnetic laws, the molecular occasions and the molecular laws, are all alike neutral. They condition the sort of values which are possible, but they do not determine the specialties of value. When we examine the specializations of societies which determine values with some particularity, such specializations as societies of men, forests, deserts, prairies, icefields, we find, within limits, plasticity. The story of Plato's idea is the story of its energizing within a local plastic environment. It has a creative power, making possible its own approach to realization.

Chapter IV

ASPECTS OF FREEDOM

SECTION I. THE CULTURAL history of Western Civilization for the period illuminated by written records can be considered from many aspects. It can be conceived under the guise of a steady economic progression, diversified by catastrophic collapses to lower levels. Such a point of view emphasizes technology and economic organization. Alternatively, history can be conceived as a series of oscillations between worldliness and other-worldliness, or as a theatre of contest between greed and virtue, or between truth and error. Such points of view emphasize religion, morality, and contemplative habits eliciting generalizations of thought. Each mode of consideration is a sort of searchlight elucidating some of the facts, and retreating the remainder into an omitted background. Of course in any history, even with a restricted topic, limited to politics, or to art, or to science, many points of view are in fact interwoven, each with varying grades of generality.

One of the most general philosophic notions to be used in the analysis of civilized activities is to consider the effect on social life due to the variations of emphasis between Individual Absoluteness and Individual Relativity. Here 'absoluteness' means the notion of release from essential dependence on other members of the community in respect to modes of activity, while relativity means the converse fact of essential relatedness. In one of their particularizations these ideas appear in the antagonism between notions of freedom and of social organization. In another they appear in the relative importance to be ascribed to the welfare of the state and to the welfare of its individual members. The character of each epoch as to its social institutions, its jurisprudence, its notions of ideal ends within the range of practicability, depends largely upon those various patches of activity within which one or other of these notions, individual absoluteness or individual relativity, is dominant for that epoch. No period is wholly controlled by either one of these extremes, reigning through its whole range of activities. Repression in one direction is balanced by freedom in others. Military discipline is severe. In the last resort individual soldiers are sacrificed to the army. But in many fields of human activity soldiers are left completely unfettered both by regulation and by custom. For members of university faculties the repressions and the freedoms are very different from those which obtain for soldiers.

Distribution of emphasis between absoluteness and relativity is seemingly arbitrary. Of course there is always a historical reason for the pattern. Frequently the shifting of emphasis is to be ascribed to the general tendency to revolt from the immediate past—to inter-change black and white wherever we find them. Also the transformation may be a judgment upon dogmas held responsible for inherited failures. It should be one function of history to disengage such a judgment from the irritation due to transient circumstances.

More often changes in the social pattern of intellectual emphasis arise from a shift of power from one class or group of classes, to another class, or group of classes. For example, an oligarchic aristocratic government and a democratic government may each tend to emphasize social organization, that is to say, the relativity of individuals to the state. But governments mainly satisfying the trading and professional classes, whether nominally they be aristocratic, democratic, or absolute, emphasize personal freedom, that is to say, individual absoluteness. Governments of the latter kind have been that of Imperial Rome with its middle class imperial agents, and its middle class stoic lawyers, and in its happiest period its middle class emperors; and that of England in the eighteenth and nineteenth centuries.

With the shift of dominant classes, points of view which in one epoch are submerged, only to be detected by an occasional ripple, later emerge into the foreground of action and literary expression. Thus the various activities of each age—governmental, literary, scientific, religious, purely social—express the mentalities of various classes in the community whose influence for those topics happens to be dominant. In one of his speeches on the American Revolution, Burke exclaims, "For heaven's sake, satisfy *somebody.*"

Governments are best classified by considering who are the 'somebodies' they are in fact endeavouring to satisfy. Thus the English government of the first sixty years of the eighteenth century was, as to its form and its persons, aristocratic. But in policy it was endeavouring to satisfy the great merchants of the City of London and of the City of Bristol. Their dissatisfaction was the immediate source of danger. Sir Robert Walpole and William Pitt, the Great Commoner, personify the changing moods of this class, in the earlier period sick of wars, and later imperialistic.

In a period when inherited modes of life are operating with their traditional standard of efficiency, or inefficiency, the class to be actively satisfied may be relatively restricted, for example, the merchants of eighteenth century England. The majority will then be relatively quiescent, and conservative statesmen, such as Walpole, will be anxious to do nothing to stir the depths—'*Quieta non movere.*' Walpole was an active reformer in respect to trade interests, otherwise a conservative.

The corresponding statesmen in France were actively concerned with the interests of the Court whose power was based on a bureaucracy (legal, administrative, and ecclesiastical) and an army. As in contemporary England, the personnel of the whole French organization, civil and military, was aristocratic and middle class. French politics ran more smoothly, but unfortunately for France its active political element was more divorced from the main interests of the country than the active element in England, though in each country government exhibited its periods of insight and folly. The French emphasis was towards coordination, the English towards individual freedom. In the latter portion of this century, in England the more active class politically were the rural landowners. Note for instance the way in which, at the end of his political life, Burke hugs the improbable belief that he understood agriculture. Also the municipality of the City of London was in the earlier period an element of support for the government, and—until the excesses of the French Revolution—in the later period an element of opposition.

In the later period the oncoming industrial revolution absorbed the energies of that English industrial class, whom at the earlier period the slogan, 'The Protestant Succession' had stirred to political activity because for them it spelled 'Industrial Freedom'. The mass of the people were now, towards the end of the century, stirring uneasily, as yet ignorant of the ways in which their interests were being determined, and with its better members engaged in saving their souls according to the directions of John Wesley. Finally out of this welter, after a delay caused by the wars of the French Revolution, the Victorian epoch emerged. The solution was merely temporary, and so is the planet itself.

SECTION II. In our endeavour to understand sociological change we must not concentrate too exclusively on the effect of abstract doctrine, verbally formulated and consciously assented to. Such elaborate intellectual efforts play their part in preserving, or transforming, or destroying. For example, the history of Europe is not to be understood without some reference to the Augustinian doctrines of original sin, of divine grace, and of the consequent mission of the Catholic church. The history of the United States requires in addition some knowledge of the English political doctrines of the seventeenth century, and of French thought in the eighteenth century. Men are driven by their thoughts as well as by the molecules in their bodies, by intelligence and by senseless forces. Social history, however, concentrates on modes of human experience prevalent at different periods The physical conditions are merely the background which partially controls the flux of modes and of moods. Even here we must not over-intellectualize the various types of human experience. Mankind is the animal at the head of the Primates, and cannot escape habits of mind which cling closely to habits of body.

Our consciousness does not initiate our modes of functioning. We awake to find ourselves engaged in process, immersed in satisfactions and dissatisfactions, and actively modifying, either by intensification, or by attenuation, or by the introduction of novel purposes. This primary procedure which is presupposed in consciousness, I will term Instinct. It is the mode of experience directly arising out of the urge of inheritance, individual and environmental. Also, after instinct and intellectual ferment have done their work, there is a decision which determines the mode of coalescence of instinct with intelligence. I will term this factor Wisdom. It is the function of wisdom to act as a modifying agency on the intellectual ferment so as to produce a self-determined issue from the given conditions. Thus for the purpose of understanding social institutions, this crude three-fold division of human nature is required: Instinct, Intelligence, Wisdom.

But this division must not be made too sharply. After all, intellectual activity is itself an inherited factor. We do not initiate thought by an effort of self-consciousness. We find ourselves thinking, just as we find ourselves breathing and enjoying the sunset. There is a habit of daydreaming, and a habit of thoughtful elucidation. Thus the autonomy of thought is strictly limited, often negligible, generally beyond the threshold of consciousness. The ways of thought of a nation are as much instinctive—that is to say, are subject to routine—as are its ways of emotional reaction. But most of us believe that there is a spontaneity of thought which lies beyond routine. Otherwise, the moral claim for freedom of thought is without meaning. This spontaneity of thought is, in its turn, subject to control as to its maintenance and efficiency. Such control is the judgment of the whole, attenuating or strengthening the partial flashes of self-determination. The whole determines what it wills to be, and thereby adjusts the relative importance of its own inherent flashes of spontaneity. This final determination is its Wisdom or, in other words, its subjective aim as to its own nature, with its limits set by inherited factors.

Wisdom is proportional to the width of the evidence made effective in the final self-determination. The intellectual operations consist in the coordination of notions derived from the primary facts of instinctive experience into a logically coherent system. Those facts, whose qualitative aspects are thus coordinated, gain importance in the final self-determination. This intellectual coordination is more readily achieved when the primary facts are selected so as to dismiss the baffling aspects of things into intellectual subordination. For this reason intellectual activity is apt to flourish at the expense of Wisdom. To some extent, to understand is always to exclude a background of intellectual incoherence. But Wisdom is persistent pursuit of the deeper understanding, ever confronting intellectual system with the importance of its omissions. These three elements, Instinct, Intelligence, Wisdom, cannot be torn apart. They integrate, react, and merge into hybrid factors. It is the case of the whole emerging from its parts, and the parts emerging within the whole. In judging social institutions, their rise, their culmination, and their decay, we have to estimate the types of instinct, of intelligence, and of wisdom which have cooperated with natural forces to develop the story. The folly of intelligent people, clear-headed and narrow-visioned, has precipitated many catastrophes.

However far we go back in recorded history, we are within the period of the high grade functioning of mankind, far removed from mere animal savagery. Also, within that period it would be difficult to demonstrate that mankind has improved upon its inborn mental capacity. Yet there can be no doubt that there has been an immense expansion of the outfit which the environment provides for the service of thought. This outfit can be summarized under the headings, modes of communication, physical and mental, writing, preservation of documents, variety of modes of literature, critical thought, systematic thought, constructive thought, history, comparison of diverse languages, mathematical symbolism, improved technology providing physical ease. This list is obviously composed of many partially redundant and overlapping items. But it serves to remind us of the various ways in which we have at our service facilities for thought and suggestions for thought. far beyond those at hand for our predecessors who lived anywhere from two to five thousand years ago. Indeed the last two hundred years has added to this outfit in a way which may create a new epoch unless mankind degenerates. Of course, a large share of this outfit had already accumulated between two and three thousand years ago. It is the brilliant use which the leading men of that millennium made of their opportunities which makes us doubt of any improvement in the native intelligence of mankind.

But the total result is that we now discern a certain simple-mindedness in the way our predecessors adjusted themselves to inherited institutions. To a far greater extent the adjustment was a matter of course, in short, it was instinctive. In the great period they discovered what we have inherited. But there was a naivete about the discovery, a surprise. Instinctive adaptation was so pervasive that it was unnoticed. Probably the Egyptians did not know that they were governed despotically, or that the priests limited the royal power, because they had no alternative as a contrast either in fact or in imagination. They were nearer in their thoughts to the political philosophy prevalent in an anthill.

Another aspect of this fact is that in such societies, relativity is stressed rather than individual freedom. Indeed, in the earlier stages freedom is almost a meaningless notion. Action and mood both spring from an instinct based upon ancestral coordination. In such societies, whatever is not the outcome of inherited relativity, imposing coordination of action, is sheer destructive chaos. Alien groups are then evil groups. An energetic prophet hewed Agag in pieces. Unfortunately the spiritual descendants of Samuel still survive, archaic nuisances.

SECTION III. We can watch some of the episodes in the discovery of freedom. About fourteen hundred years before Christ the Egypitan king Akhnaton evidently belonged to an advanced group who thought for themselves and made a step beyond the inherited religious notions. Such groups, with flashes of free thought, must have arisen sporadically many times before, during countless thousands of years, some successful and most of them failures. Otherwise the transition to civilization, as distinct from the mere diversity of adaptions of thoughtless customs, could never have arisen. Bees and ants have diverse social organizations; but, so far as we know, neither species is in any sense civilized. They may enjoy thoughtless adaptations of social customs. Anyhow their flashes of freedom are below the level that we can discern. But Akhnaton, having exercised his freedom, evidently had no conception of freedom as such. We have all the evidence archæology can provide, that he rigidly endeavoured to impose his notions upon the thoughts and customs of the whole Egyptian nation. Apparently he failed; for there was a reaction. But reactions never restore with minute accuracy. Thus in all probability there remained a difference which the evidence before us is unable to discriminate.

A more successful group were the Hebrew prophets about eight or nine hundred years later. Spurred by the evils of their times they exercised a freedom in the expression of moral intuition, and fitted out the character of Jehovah with the results of their thoughts. Our civilization owes to them more than we can express. They constitute one of the few groups of men who decisively altered history in any intimate sense. Most spectacular upheavals merely replace one set of individuals by another analogous set; so that history is mostly a barren change of names. But the Hebrew prophets really produced a decisive qualitative alteration, and what is still more rare, a change for the better; yet the conception of freedom never entered into the point of view of the Jehovah of the prophets. Intolerance is the besetting sin of moral fervour. The first important pronouncement in which tolerance is associated with moral fervour, is in the Parable of the Tares and the Wheat, some centuries later.

Subsequent examples of intolerance supervening upon the exercise of freedom are afforded by the Christian Church after its establishment by Constantine, and by the Protestants under the guidance of Luther and Calvin. At the period of the Reformation mankind had begun to know better and so charity of judgment upon the Reformers begins to wear thin. But then charity is a virtue allied to tolerance, so we must be careful. All advanced thinkers, sceptical or otherwise, are apt to be intolerant, in the past and also now. On the whole, tolerance is more often found in connection with a genial orthodoxy. The apostles of modern tolerance—in so far as it exists—are Erasmus, the Quakers, and John Locke. They should be commemorated in every laboratory, in every church, and in every court of law. We must however remember that many of the greatest seventeenth century statesmen and thinkers, including John Locke, owed their lives to the wide tolerance of the Dutch Republic.

Certainly these men were not the originators of their admirable ideas. To find the origins we must go behind them for two thousand years. So slow is translation of idea into custom. We must however first note that the examples cited have all been concerned with religion. There are other forms of behaviour, active and contemplative. The Athenians have given us the first surviving instance of the explicit recognition of the importance of tolerance in respect to varieties of social behaviour. No doubt antecedent civilizations must have provided many practical examples of it. For example, it is difficult to believe that in big metropolitan cities such as Babylon and Nineveh, there was much detailed supervision of social behaviour. On the other hand, the ways of life in Egypt seem to have been tightly organized. But the first explicit defence of social tolerance, as a requisite for high civilization, is found in the speech of Pericles as reported by Thucydides. It puts forth the conception of the organized society successfully preserving freedom of behaviour for its individual members. Fifty years later, in the same social group, Plato introduced deeper notions from which all claims for freedom must spring. His general concept of the psychic factors in the Universe stressed them as the source of all spontaneity, and ultimately as the ground of all life and motion. The human psychic activity thus contains the origins of precious harmonies within the transient world. The end of human society is to elicit such psychic energies. But spontaneity is of the essence of soul. Such in outline is the argument from Platonic modes of thought to the importance of social freedom.

Plato's own writings constitute one prolonged apology for freedom of contemplation, and for freedom for the communication of contemplative experiences. In the persistent exercise of this right Socrates and Plato lived, and it was on its behalf that Socrates died. There are exceptional passages, but throughout the bulk of the Dialogues Socrates and Plato are engaged in expressing manners of thought. Hardly ever is there a passage which can be directly translated into a particular action. The conclusions of the Republic will work only in heaven. The great exception is The Laws, which is a minutely practical scheme for the establishment of small city-states of the type then prevalent in the Ægean area. The Thucydidean Pericles stresses the other side. He is thinking of the activities of the individual citizens. The peculiar civilization of the speech arises from its stress upon the æsthetic end of all action. A Barbarian speaks in terms of power. He dreams of the superman with the mailed fist. He may plaster his lust with sentimental morality of Carlyle's type. But ultimately his final good is conceived as one will imposing itself upon other wills. This is intellectual barbarism. The Periclean ideal is action weaving itself into a texture of persuasive beauty analogous to the delicate splendor of nature.

The establishment of freedom requires more than its mere intellectual defence. Plato above all men introduced into the world this further essential element of civilization. For he exihibited the tone of mind which alone can maintain a free society, and he expressed the reasons justifying that tone. His Dialogues are permeated with a sense of the variousness of the Universe, not to be fathomed by our intellects, and in his Seventh Epistle he expressly disclaims the possibility of an adequate philosophic system. The moral of his writings is that all points of view, reasonably coherent and in some sense with an application, have something to contribute to our understanding of the universe, and also involve omissions whereby they fail to include the totality of evident fact. The duty of tolerance is our finite homage to the abundance of inexhaustible novelty which is awaiting the future, and to the complexity of accomplished fact which exceeds our stretch of insight.

Thus two types of character must be excluded from those effectually promoting freedom. One type belongs to those who despair of attaining any measure of truth, the Sceptics. Such temperaments can obviously have no message for those who hold that thought does count. Again the pursuit of freedom with an intolerant mentality is self-defeating. For all his equipment of imagination, learning, and literary magnificence in defence of freedom, the example of Milton's life probably does as much to retard the cause as to advance it. He promotes a frame of mind of which the issue is intolerance.

The ancient world of paganism was tolerant as to creeds. Provided that your actions conformed, your speculations were unnoticed. Indeed, one mark of progress beyond purely instinctive social relations is an uneasy feeling as to the destructive effect of speculative thought. Creeds are at once the outcome of speculation and efforts to curb speculation. But they are always relevant to it. Antecedently to speculation there can be no creeds. Wherever there is a creed, there is a heretic round the corner or in his grave. Amid the great empires, Egyptian, Mesopotamian, and Hittite, and with the discovery of navigation, the intercourse between races promoted shrewd comparisons gradually broadening into speculative thought. In its beginnings this shift in human mentality must have developed slowly. Where there is no anticipation, change has to wait upon chance, and peters out amid neglect. Fortunately the Bible preserves for us fragments of the process as it affected one gifted race at a nodal point. The record has been written up by editors with the mentality of later times. Thus the task of modern scholars is analogous to an endeavour to recover the histories of Denmark and Scotland from a study of Hamlet and Macbeth. We can see initial antagonisms broadening into speculative attempts to rationalize the welter. We can watch Samuel and Agag succeeded by Solomon and the Queen of Sheba. There are the meditations of Job and his friends, the prophetical books, and the 'wisdom' books of the Bible. And with a leap of six hundred years one version of the story ends with the creed of the Council at Nicrea.

SECTION IV. The episode of Greek civilization during its short phase of independence created a new situation. Speculation was explicitly recognized. It was ardently pursued. Its various modes and methods were discovered. The relation of the Greeks to their predecessors is analogous, as to stretch of time and intensity of effect, to that of the second phase of the modern industrial revolution during the last fifty years to the first phase which in truth sprawls over the long centuries from the fifteenth century to the close of the nineteenth.

By reason of its inheritance from the episode of Hellenic culture the Roman Empire was more self-conscious than its predecessors in its treatment of the problem of liberty and of the allied problem of social institutions. So far as concerns Western Europe, the origin of the Mediaeval civilization must be dated from the Emperor

Augustus and the Journeys of St. Paul. For the Byzantine, Semitic, Egyptian area, the date must be pushed back to the death of Alexander the Great, and the renaissance of Græco-Egyptian learning. For the first two centuries after Augustus the former area, centered in Italy, was incomparably the more important. Latin literature is the translation of Hellenic culture into the mediaeval modes of thought, extending that period to end with the French Revolution. Throughout that whole period culture was backward looking. Lucretius, Cicero, Virgil were mediaevals in their relation to Hellenic literature and speculation; though they lacked the Semitic factor. After that first Latin period, the notable contributions to thought, Pagan, Christian, and Mahometan, all derive from the eastern region, with the important exception of Augustine. Finally, the centre of culture again swings westward, as the Eastern civilization collapses under the prolonged impacts of Tartars and Turks. The notes of these three allied cultures, the Eastern, the Latin, and the later European, are scholarly learning, recurrence to Hellenic speculation restated in creedal forms, imitative literatures stressing humane aspirations, the canalization of curiosity into professional grooves, and—in the West—a new grade of intelligence exhibited in the development of a variety of social institutions. It is this last factor which has saved the progress of mankind.

The new epoch in the formation of social institutions unfolded itself very gradually. It is not yet understood in its full importance. Social philosophy has not grasped the relevant principles, so that even now each case is treated as a peculiar fact. But the problem of liberty has been transformed by it. The novelty consists in the deliberate formation of institutions, embodying purposes of special groups, and unconcerned with the general purposes of any political state, or of any embodiment of tribal unity playing the part of a state. Of course any big empire involves a coalescence of diverse tribes, customs, and modes of thought. But in the earlier examples, each subject race had its own status in the complex empire, and its ways of procedure were part of the imperial system. Also there must have been complex modes of behaviour, peculiar to the various races, inherited and tolerated as a matter of course. In the case of the smaller units such as the Greek city states, we find a condition of affairs in which all corporate action is an element in state-policy. The freedom was purely individual, never corporate. All incorporation, religious or secular, was communal, or patriarchal. The saying, "Render unto Cæsar the things that are Cæsar's and unto God the things that are God's" was uttered by Christ in the reign of Tiberius, and not by Plato four hundred years earlier. However limited may be the original intention of the saying, very quickly God was conceived as a principle of organization in complete disjunction from Cæsar.

It is interesting to speculate on the analogies and differences between the deaths of Socrates and of Paul. Both were martyrs. Socrates died because his speculative opinions were held to be subversive of the communal life. It is difficult to believe that the agents of Claudius, or Nero, or Galba, were much concerned with Paul's speculative opinions as to the ways of God to man. Later on, Lucian's opinions were as unorthodox as Paul's. But he died in his bed. Unfortunately for Paul, as he journeyed he left behind him organized groups, indulging in activities uncoordinated with any purposes of state. Thus imperial agents were alarmed, and sympathized with popular prejudice. Indeed, we know exactly what one of the best of the Roman Emperors about half a century later thought of the matter. Trajan in his letter to the younger Pliny dismisses Christian Theology as negligible. He is even unconcerned with their organization into groups, so long as no overt action emerges affronting the traditional association of the state with religion. Yet he recognizes that the Christians will fit into no current political philosophy, and that they represent corporate actions on the verge of the intolerable. Thus if circumstances unearth them, they are to be questioned, dismissed if possible, but punished when their actions become glaring. It is interesting to compare the Christians in the Roman Empire, from Nero to Trajan, with the Communists in modern America.

Trajan shews himself as a fine statesman dealing with the faint dawn of a new epoch, not understood, and indeed not yet understood. The old organization of mankind was being affected by the influence of the new width of intellectuality due to Hellenism. Organizations mainly derived from blind inheritance, and affected by the intellect only in detail and in interpretation, are to receive the shock of other types founded primarily on the intellectual appreciation of private ends, that is to say, of ends unconcerned with the State. What Henry Osborn Taylor has termed 'rational consideration' is becoming a major force in human organization. Of course, Plato and Aristotle exhibited rational consideration on a magnificent scale. But a group of thinkers do not necessarily constitute a political force. Centuries, sometimes thousands of years, have to elapse before thought can capture action. It is typical of this gap, that Aristotle's manuscripts are said to have been stowed in a cellar for two hundred years, and that even to this day Plato is mainly valued as a religious mystic and a supreme literary artist. In these latter functions, Plato represents the world he inherited and not the world he created. Perhaps these constitute his best part. But he played two roles.

The situation in the Roman Empire was in effect novel. Pericles had conceived a freedom for private actions, of a certain civilized type within narrowly restricted bounds. Plato voices the claim for contemplative freedom. But the Empire was faced with the claim for freedom of corporate action. Modern political history, from that day to this, is the confused story of the strenuous resistance of the State, and of its partial concessions. The Empire reasserted the old doctrine of the divine Emperor; but also yielded by admitting as legal principle the Stoic doctrine of the Voice of Nature. The Middle Ages compromised with the doctrine of the two swords. In recent times, the State is fighting behind its last ditch, which is the legal doctrine of sovereignty. The thought of the seventeenth and eighteenth centuries rationalized its political philosophy under the fiction of the 'Original Contract'. This concept proved itself formidable. It helped to dismiss the Stuarts into romance, to found the American Republic, and to bring about the French Revolution. Indeed, it was one of the most timely notions known to history. Its weakness is that it antedates the era of the importance of rational consideration, and overestimates the political importance which at any time reason has possessed. The antagonistic doctrine was that of the 'Divine Right of Kings', which is the ghost of the 'divine Emperor'.

SECTION V. Political philosophy can claim no exemption from the doctrine of the golden mean. Unrestricted liberty means complete absence of any compulsory coordination. Human society in the absence of any compulsion is trusting to the happy coordination of individual emotions, purposes, affections, and actions. Civilization can only exist amid a population which in the mass does exhibit this fortunate mutual adaptation. Unfortunately a minority of adverse individual instances, when unchecked, are sufficient to upset the social structure. A few men in the whole caste of their character, and most men in some of their actions, are anti-social in respect to the peculiar type of any society possible in their time. There can be no evasion of the plain fact that compulsion is necessary and that compulsion is the restriction of liberty.

It follows that a doctrine as to the social mingling of liberty and compulsion is required. A mere unqualified demand for liberty is the issue of shallow philosophy, equally noxious with the antithetical cry for mere conformation to standard pattern. Probably, there can be no one solution of this problem adapted to all the circumstances of human societies which have been and will be. We must confine ourselves to the way in which at the present day the issue is being adjusted in the western civilization, European and American.

Roughly speaking, the main effectiveness of this solution presupposes a wide distribution of institutions founded upon professional qualifications and exacting such qualifications. Obviously the canalization of a variety of occupations into professions is a prerequisite. Here the term Profession means an avocation whose activities are subjected to the theoretical analysis, and are modified by theoretical conclusions derived from that analysis. This analysis has regard to the purposes of the avocation and to the adaptation of the activities for the attainment of those purposes. Such criticism must be founded upon some understanding of the natures of the things involved in those activities, so that the results of action can be foreseen. Thus foresight based upon theory, and theory based upon understanding of the nature of things, are essential to a profession. Again the purposes of a profession are not a simple bundle of definite ends. There is a general purpose, such as the curing of sickness, which defines medicine. But in a multitude of ways every human body might be in a better state of biological fitness, and might easily be worse. There has in every case to be a selection of ends dependent partly on intrinsic importance if attained, and partly upon practicability of attainment. It is for this reason that the practice of a profession cannot be disjoined from its theoretical understanding, and *vice versa.* We do however find it necessary to specialize even further, not only within some department of that profession, such as surgery, but also either to a major consideration of its theory or to a major devotion to its current practice.

The antithesis to a profession is an avocation based upon customary activities and modified by the trial and error of individual practice. Such an avocation is a Craft, or at a lower level of individual skill it is merely a customary direction of muscular labour. The ancient civilizations were dominated by crafts. Modern life ever to a greater extent is grouping itself into professions. Thus ancient society was a coordination of crafts for the instinctive purposes of communal life, whereas modern society is a coordination of professions. Without question the distinction between crafts and professions is not clear-cut. In all stages of civilization, crafts are shot through and through with flashes of constructive understanding, and professions are based upon inherited procedures. Nor is it true that the type of men involved are to be ranked higher in proportion to the dominance of abstract mentality in their lives. On the contrary, a due proportion of craftsmanship seems to breed the finer types. The brilliant ability, in proportion to population, of Europe in the fifteenth, sixteenth, and seventeenth centuries suggests that at about that period the best harmony had been reached. Pure mentality easily becomes trivial in its grasp of fact.

The organization of professions by means of self-governing institutions places the problem of liberty at a new angle. For now it is the institution which claims liberty and also exercises control. In ancient Egypt the Pharaoh decided, acting through his agents. In the modern world a variety of institutions have the power of action without immediate reference to the state. This new form of liberty which is the autonomous institution limited to special purposes, was especially exemplified in the guilds of the middle ages; and that period was characterized by a remarkable growth of civilized genius. The meaning that—in England at least—was then assigned to the word 'liberty' illustrates the projection of the new social structure upon the older form of customary determination. For a 'liberty' did not then mean a general freedom, but a special license to a particular group to organize itself within a special field of action. For this reason 'liberties' were sometimes a general nuisance.

Of course the Catholic Church was the great 'liberty' which first confronted the Roman Empire, and then dominated mediaeval life. In its early stages it is seen in its proper theoretical relation to other autonomous societies. For example in the pagan Empire, its legal status seems to have been analogous to that of the pagan burial societies; although the status of the Church property before the age of Constantine has not yet been finally elucidated by scholars. But in the middle ages, the Church so towered above other institutions that it out-rivalled the state itself. Accordingly its analogy to secular guilds and to other professional institutions such as universities was obscured by its greatness. The Catholic Church had another characteristic of priceless value. It was, so far as concerned Europe, universal, that is to say, Catholic. Until the approach of the Renaissance there were no European nations in the modern sense. But the Church transcended all governmental boundaries, all racial divisions and all geographic divisions. It was a standing challenge to any form of communal despotism, a universal 'liberty'.

SECTION VI. From the beginning of the sixteenth century this first form of institutional civilization, with its feudalism, its guilds, its universities, its Catholic Church, was in full decay. The new middle classes, whether scholars or traders, would have none of it. They were individualists. For them the universities were secondary, the monasteries were a nuisance, the Church was a nuisance, feudalism was a nuisance, the guilds were a nuisance. They wanted good order, and to be let alone with their individual activities. The great thinkers of the sixteenth and seventeenth centuries were singularly detached from universities. Erasmus wanted printers, and Bacon, Hervey, Descartes, Galileo, Leibniz, wanted governmental patronage, or protection, more than university colleagues, mostly reactionary. When Luther, Descartes, Galileo, or Leibniz shifted his residence, it was not to find a better university, but a more suitable government—a Duke who would protect, a Prince who would pay, or a Dutch Republic which would not ask questions. Nevertheless, the universities survived the change better than other institutions. In some ways it was a great time for them, though they shrank to be national. What finally emerged was the modern national organization of Europe with the sovereign state dictating every form of institutional organization, as subordinate elements for its own purposes. This was a recurrence to that earlier form of human organization which showed its faint signs of decay during the period of the Roman

Empire. Naturally there were great differences. For nothing is ever restored. In fact the reaction was a failure, because mankind has outgrown the simplicities of the earlier form of civilization.

The political philosophy of the modern era was a retrogression, based upon a recurrence to the philosophers and lawyers of the old classical civilizations. The Middle Ages, in the simplified form of the relations of Church with State, were considering the problem of a civilization in which men owed a divided allegiance to many intersecting institutions pursuing diverse ends. This is the real problem in a world dominated by fraternity derived from the catholic diffusion of ideas, and from the international distribution of property. The solution provided by the doctrine of the sole sovereignty of the state, however grateful to protestants and to sovereigns, is both shocking and unworkable, a mere stick with which to beat Papists in the sixteenth and seventeenth centuries, a mere way to provide policemen for the counting-houses of merchants. But, amid this reactionary triumph of Periclean individualism in the political philosophies of the eighteenth and nineteenth centuries, there was an outcrop of institutions based upon the vigour of modern intellectual interests. These institutions, even when national, were concerned with interests impartial among the nations. These were the centuries in which science triumphed, and science is universal. Thus scientific institutions, though in form national, informally established a catholic league. Again the advance of scholarship, and of natural science, transformed the professions. It intellectualized them far beyond their stage of advance in earlier times. Professions first appear as customary activities largely modified by detached strains of theory. Theories are often wrong; and some of the earlier professional doctrines erred grievously and were maintained tenaciously. Doctrines emerged as plausible deductions, and survived as the wisdom of ancestors. Thus the older professional practice was rooted upon custom, though it was turning towards the intellectual sunlight. Here and there individuals stood out far in advance of their colleagues. For example, in the fourteen hundred years separating Galen from Vesalius, the standard of European medical practice was not to be compared with the attainments of either of these men. Also more than a century after Vesalius. Charles the Second, of England, on his deathbed was tortured by physicians employing futile remedies customary at that time. Again, as a designing engineer Leonardo da Vinci was unequalled until the advent of Vauban and James Watt. In the earlier centuries the professional influence, as a general sociological fact, was mainly a welter of bygone flashes of intelligence relapsing into customary procedures. It represented the continual lapse of intellect into instinct. But the culmination of science completely inverted the roles of custom and intelligence in the older professions. By this inversion professional institutions have acquired an international life. Each such institution practices within its own nation, but its sources of life are worldwide. Thus loyalties stretch beyond sovereign states.

Perhaps the most important function of these institutions is the supervision of standards of individual professional competence and of professional practice. For this purpose there is a complex interweaving of universities and more specialized institutions. The problem of freedom comes in here. For it is not opinions which are censured, but learning and ability. Thus in the more important fields of thought, opinion is free and so are large divergencies of practice. The community is provided with objective information as to the sort of weight to be attached to individuals and as to the sort of freedom of action which may safely be granted. Whatever is done can be subjected to the test of general professional opinion, acting through this network of institutions. Further, even large freedom can now be allowed to non-professional individuals. For the great professional organizations, so long as they are efficient, should be able to demonstrate the dangers of extravagant notions. In this way, where sudden action is not in question, reason has obtained an entrenchment which should be impregnable. Indeed individual freedom, standing apart from organization, has now its indispensable role. For all organizations are liable to decay, and license for outside criticism is the best safeguard for the professions.

Also the sovereign state of modern legal theory has its sphere of action and its limitation. The state represents the general wisdom of the community derived from an experience broader than the topics of the various sciences. The role of the state is a general judgment on the activity of the various organizations. It can judge whether they welcome ability, whether they stand high among the kindred institutions throughout the world. But where the state ceases to exercise any legitimate authority is when it presumes to decide upon questions within the purview of sciences or professions.

For example, in the teaching profession it is obvious that young students cannot be subjected to the vagaries of individual teachers. In this sense, the claim for the freedom of teaching is nonsense. But the general community is very incompetent to determine either the subject matter to be taught or the permissible divergences to be allowed, or the individual competence. There can be only one appeal, and this is to general professional opinion as exhibited in the practice of accredited institutions. The appeal is catholic. The State of Tennessee did not err in upholding the principle that there are limits to the freedom of teaching in schools and colleges. But it exhibited a gross ignorance of its proper functions when it defied a professional opinion which throughout the world is practically unanimous. Even here that State is hardly to be blamed. For the current political philosophy of sovereignty is very weak as to the limitations of moral authority. Of course whoever at any moment has physical power has that power of physical compulsion, whether he be a bandit, or a judge, or political ruler. But moral authority is limited by competence to attain those ends whose immediate dominance is evident to enlightened wisdom. Political loyalty ceases at the frontiers of radical incapacity.

The functions of professional institutions have been considered in some detail because they constitute a clear-cut novelty within modern societies. There were faint anticipations in the ancient world, for example the schools at Athens, in particular those founded by Plato, Aristotle, and the Stoics, and elsewhere the great foundation at Alexandria. Also later the theologians of the Christian Church formed another professional group which even stretched its claim to authority beyond all bounds of good sense. It is by reason of these anticipations, and of the legal developments of the Roman and Byzantine schools of law, that the beginnings of the modern world, in respect to the problem of freedom and of moral authority, have been placed as early as Alexander and Augustus.

SECTION VII. In the immediate present, economic organization constitutes the most massive problem of human relationships. It is passing into a new phase, and presents confused outlines. Evidently something new is developing. The individualistic liberalism of the nineteenth century has collapsed, quite unexpectedly. So long as the trading middle classes were dominant as the group to be satisfied, its; doctrines were self-evident. As soon as industrialism and education produced in large numbers the modern type of artisan, its whole basis was widely challenged. Again the necessity for large capital, with the aid of legal ingenuity produced the commercial corporation with limited liability. These fictitious persons are exempt from physiological death and can only disappear by a voluntary dissolution or by bankruptcy. The introduction into the arena of this new type of 'person' has considerably modified the effective meaning of the characteristic liberal doctrine of contractual freedom. It is one thing to claim such freedom as a natural right for human persons, and quite another to claim it for corporate persons. And again the notion of private property had a simple obviousness at the foot of Mount Sinai and even in the eighteenth century. When there were current political philosophy of sovereignty is very weak as to the limitations of moral authority. Of course whoever at any moment has physical power has that power of physical compulsion, whether he be a bandit, or a judge, or political ruler. But moral authority is limited by competence to attain those ends whose immediate dominance is evident to enlightened wisdom. Political loyalty ceases at the frontiers of radical incapacity.

The functions of professional institutions have been considered in some detail because they constitute a clear-cut novelty within modern societies. There were faint anticipations in the ancient world, for example the schools at Athens, in particular those founded by Plato, Aristotle, and the Stoics, and elsewhere the great foundation at Alexandria. Also later the theologians of the Christian Church formed another professional group which even stretched its claim to authority beyond all bounds of good sense. It is by reason of these anticipations, and of the legal developments of the Roman and Byzantine schools of law, that the beginnings of the modern world, in respect to the problem of freedom and of moral authority, have been placed as early as Alexander and Augustus.

SECTION VII. In the immediate present, economic organization constitutes the most massive problem of human relationships. It is passing into a new phase, and presents confused outlines. Evidently something new is developing. The individualistic liberalism of the nineteenth century has collapsed, quite unexpectedly. So long as the trading middle classes were dominant as the group to be satisfied, its; doctrines were self-evident. As soon as industrialism and education produced in large numbers the modern type of artisan, its whole basis was widely challenged. Again the necessity for large capital, with the aid of legal ingenuity produced the commercial corporation with limited liability. These fictitious persons are exempt from physiological death and can only disappear by a voluntary dissolution or by bankruptcy. The introduction into the arena of this new type of 'person' has considerably modified the effective meaning of the characteristic liberal doctrine of contractual freedom. It is one thing to claim such freedom as a natural right for human persons, and quite another to claim it for corporate persons. And again the notion of private property had a simple obviousness at the foot of Mount Sinai and even in the eighteenth century. When there were primitive roads, negligible drains, private wells, no elaborate system of credit, when payment meant the direct production of gold-pieces, when each industry was reasonably self-contained—in fact when the world was not as it is now—then it was fairly obvious what was meant by private property, apart from any current legal fictions. Today private property is mainly a legal fiction, and apart from such legal determination its outlines are completely indefinite. Such legal determination is probably, indeed almost certainly, the best way of arranging society. But the 'voice of nature' is a faint echo when we are dealing with it. There is a striking analogy between the hazy notions of justice in Plato's Republic, and the hazy notions of private property today. The modern artisan, like Thrasymachus of old, is apt to define it as 'the will of the stronger'.

Of course these extremes as to the nature of property—simple-minded assertion and simple-minded denial—are exaggeration. The whole concept of absolute individuals with absolute rights, and with a contractual power of forming fully defined external relations, has broken down. The human being is inseparable from its environment in each occasion of its existence. The environment which the occasion inherits is immanent in it, and conversely it is immanent in the environment which it helps to transmit. The favorite doctrine of the shift from a customary basis for society to a contractual basis, is founded on shallow sociology. There is no escape from customary status. This status is merely another name for the inheritance immanent in each occasion. Inevitably customary status is there, an inescapable condition. On the other hand, the inherited status is never a full determination. There is always the freedom for the determination of individual emphasis. In terms of high-grade human society, there is always the customary fact as an essential element in the meaning of every contractual obligation.

There can be no contract which does not presuppose custom, and no custom leaving no loophole for spontaneous contract. It is this truth that gives vitality to the Anglo-American Common Law. It is an instrument, in the hands of skilled experts, for the interpretation of explicit contract in terms of implicit status. No code of verbal statement can ever exhaust the shifting background of presupposed fact. What does alter for dominant interests within each social system is the relative importance of the contractual and customary factors in general conscious experience. This balance, fortunate or unfortunate, largely depends on the type of social inheritance provided by that society. But contract is a mode of expression for spontaneity. Otherwise it is meaningless, a futile gesture of consciousness.

In the end nothing is effective except massively coordinated inheritance. Sporadic spontaneity is composed of flashes mutually thwarting each other. Ideas have to be sustained, disentangled, diffused, and coordinated with the background. Finally they pass into exemplification in action. The distinguishing mark of modern civilization is the number of institutions whose origin can be traced to the initial entertainment of some idea. In the ancient civilizations thought was mainly explanatory. It was only creative in respect to individual actions. But the corporate actions preceded thought. The ancient Gods, either as notions or as persons, did not create the thunderstorm, they explained it. Jehovah did not create the Hebrew tribal emotions, he explained them. He never made a covenant which initiated Hebrew history; the notion of the covenant was an explanatory idea. It was influential; but the idea arose as an explanation of the tribal history. Nevertheless it intensified a preexisting fact. The Old Testament is on the verge of the dividing line between ancient and modern. This watershed is Hellenism. The difference is only one of proportion, of more or less. But a sufficient change of proportion makes all the difference. In the last phase of ancient life there is a haunting feeling that corporate actions ought to have originated from ideas. Thus their historical imagination unconsciously imported types of explanation of their past which were faintly relevant to their own present: explanations fantastic, incredible, fit only for exposure by scholars. It was the shadow of the future thrown back onto the past.

Returning to the economic side of life, in the ancient world there were economic transactions between tribes and between states, and there were also the economic activities of craftsmen, merchants, and bankers. There was communal activity and individual activity. Cicero's financial worries are preserved for us in his letters to Atticus They are very analogous to Gibbon's letters to Holroyd, which are characteristic of educated Europe in the eighteenth century. Certainly Cicero's affairs were sufficiently complex. It is not in that respect that the ancient world fell short. It would be worth sacrificing a good deal of Latin literature to know what Atticus thought of Cicero's financial position. Even after two thousand years it is difficult not to entertain a friendly anxiety on the subject. Perhaps as Cicero put his head out of the litter he had been dreaming of bankruptcy, when the sword of the soldier gave him death.

That ancient world is modern both in the physical facts which await us, and in the ripples of anxiety arising from its social intricacies. At that time the human mind was singularly powerful for the generation of ideas. To the epoch between Plato and Justinian, we can trace our philosophical ideas, our religious ideas, our legal ideas, and the model of modern governmental organization. We can recognize Pliny as he discusses whether the parents should serve on the board of governors of the Grammar School he had founded. Sidonius Apollinaris is an anticipation of many New England gentlemen, ecclesiastic and lay. But within that period the ferment of ideas had not persisted for a sufficient time to transform society by a profusion of corporations originated by explicit thought. In particular the great commercial corporations awaited modern times, The Bank of St. George at Genoa, The Bank of England. The great trading companies to

India and the East. Atticus was a banker; but he was not the president of a banking corporation. Private wealth was deposited in pagan temples; but temples were corporations devoted to the customary rites of religion. The state taxes were farmed by private corporations of Roman capitalists. Here we approach modern notions. Yet after all the *publicani* were engaged in performing one of the direct services of the state. Their actions were communal and traditional with a tinge of modern modes of incorporation. No doubt many anticipations of modern commercial institutions can be found. Those times lie within the modern world. But it was modern commerce in its infancy. Indeed, the examples quoted of modern commercial activity belong to an intermediate period, and only recently has the influence of ideas produced its full economic effect. But wherever ideas are effective, there is freedom.

Section VIII. Unfortunately the notion of freedom has been eviscerated by the literary treatment devoted to it. Men of letters, artists in symphonies of pictorial imagination, have staged the shock of novel thought against tradition. The concept of freedom has been narrowed to the picture of contemplative people shocking their generation. When we think of freedom, we are apt to confine ourselves to freedom of thought, freedom of the press, freedom for religious opinions. Then the limitations to freedom are conceived as wholly arising from the antagonisms of our fellow men. This is a thorough mistake. The massive habits of physical nature, its iron laws, determine the scene for the sufferings of men. Birth and death, heat, cold, hunger, separation, disease, the general impracticability of purpose, all bring their quota to imprison the souls of women and of men. Our experiences do not keep step with our hopes. The Platonic Eros, which is the soul stirring itself to life and motion, is maimed. The essence of freedom is the practicability of purpose. Mankind has chiefly suffered from the frustration of its prevalent purposes, even such as belong to the very definition of its species. The literary exposition of freedom deals mainly with the frills. The Greek myth was more to the point. Prometheus did not bring to mankind freedom of the press. He procured fire, which obediently to human purpose cooks and gives warmth. In fact, freedom of action is a primary human need. In modern thought, the expression of this truth has taken the form of 'the economic interpretation of history'.

The fact that the 'economic interpretation' is itself a novel thought arising within the last sixty or seventy years illustrates an important sociological fact. The literary world through all ages belonged mainly to the fortunate section of mankind whose basic human wants have been amply satisfied. A few literary men have been in want throughout their lives, many have occasionally suffered. The fact shocks us. It is remembered because it is rare. The fortunate classes are oblivious to the fact that throughout the ages the masses of mankind have lived in conscious dread of such disaster—a drought, a wet summer, a bad harvest, a cattle disease, a raid of pirates. Also the basic needs when they are habitually satisfied cease to dominate thought. Delicacies of taste displace the interest in fullness of stomach. Thus the motives which stir the fortunate directing classes to conscious activity have a long range forecaste and an æsthetic tinge: —Power, glory, safety in the distant future, forms of government, luxury, religion, excitement, dislike of strange ways, contemplative curiosity, play. Mankind survived by evolving a peculiar excitability whereby it quickly adapts itself to novel circumstance. This instability is quickly diverted to some simple form of the more abstract interests of the minority. The great convulsions happen when the economic urge on the masses has dove-tailed with some simplified ideal end. Intellect and instinct then combine, and some ancient social order passes away. But the masses of the population are always there, requiring at least a minimum of satisfaction, with their standard of life here higher and there lower, also rising or falling. Thus, even when the minority is dominant, the plain economic facts of life must be the governing force in social development. Yet in general the masses are intellectually quiescent, though the more ideal ends of the minority, good and bad, permeate the masses, directing policies according to the phantasies of the generations. And the primary demand for freedom is to be found in the general urge for the accomplishment of these general ends, which are a fusion of ideal and economic policies, making the stuff of history. In so far as a population is dominated by some general appetition, freedom presents no peculiar problem to the statesman. The tribal actions are shaped inevitably, and that group of mankind is pushed towards accomplishment or frustration.

In modern states there is a complex problem. There are many types of character. Freedom means that within each type the requisite coordination should he possible without the destruction of the general ends of the whole community. Indeed, one general end is that these variously coordinated groups should contribute to the complex pattern of community life, each in virtue of its own peculiarity. In this way individuality gains the effectiveness which issues from coordination, and freedom obtains power necessary for its perfection.

This is the hope of the statesman, the solution which the long course of history is patiently disclosing. But it is not the intuition which has nerved men to surpass the limitations of mankind. After all, societies of primates, of animals, of life on the earth's surface, are transient details. There is a freedom lying beyond circumstance, derived from the direct intuition that life can be grounded upon its absorption in what is changeless amid change. This is the freedom at which Plato was groping, the freedom which Stoics and Christians obtained as the gift of Hellenism. It is the freedom of that virtue directly derived from the source of all harmony. For it is conditioned only by its adequacy of understanding. And understanding has this quality that, however it be led up to, it issues in the soul freely conforming its nature to the supremacy of insight. It is the reconciliation of freedom with the compulsion of the truth. In this sense the captive can be free, taking as his own the supreme insight, the indwelling persuasion towards the harmony which is the height of existence.

Chapter V

FROM FORCE TO PERSUASION

SECTION I. THE GRADUAL development of Persuasive Agencies in the communal life of mankind was not wholly due to the energizing of ideas. Indeed the very habit of intellectual activity was promoted by the slow natural development of persuasive intercourse within the social life of each community, and between different communities. Evidently the existence of each family group involves a mixture of love, dependence, sympathy, persuasion, and compulsion. There can never have been any period when the gentler modes of human relations were wholly absent. Indeed the ferocity may have been the later development, due to the increase of intelligent self-interest. It may easily have arisen as a strain of character necessary for preservation, and have developed into an overgrowth checking upward evolution beyond a low level of life. We find civilized communities. struggling with two kinds of compulsion. There are the natural necessities, such as food, warmth, and shelter. There are also the necessities for a coordination of social activities. This coordination is produced partly by instinctive habit, sustained by flashes of good sense, partly by the compulsion exercised by other members of the community, and partly by reasonable persuasion. In so far as the area of reasonable persuasion widens, an environment has been provided within which the higher mental activities and the subtler feelings can find their use and their enjoyment. But with the growth of intellect the range of necessity diminishes. Some command over nature has been attained. Thus a widespread reliance on persuasion produces its reward in the shape of an upward evolution. At least, it produces conditions favourable to such an upward trend.

In this chapter, we consider the effect of some of the natural necessities, such as food and clothing, and also the effect of activities, such as commerce, which naturally promote the persuasive reactions within society, and between societies. Also we consider the transition of these agencies into various types of restlessness.

Such activities, energizing for centuries, indeed for thousands of years, lie behind the intellectual ferment which we find driving onward the Hebrew prophets and the Greek philosophers. Indeed, apart from the continuing vigour of such agencies, the intellectual life of mankind would wither, without roots, and without any material content for thought or purpose.

SECTION II. The term Commerce, as used in this chapter, will have an enlarged sense. It will include the interchange of material commodities, and their manufacture for the purpose of such interchange. It will also include the management of currency, which is a conventionalized commodity, possibly but not necessarily possessing some intrinsic value of its own apart from its use as currency. Finally we shall extend the meaning of the term even beyond these limits, passing beyond the bounds of material things. [n its most general sense, the commerce of mankind involves every species of interchange which proceeds by way of mutual persuasion.

All commercial values are psychological, that is to say, they are measured by the desire widely spread among sections of mankind to acquire the numerous articles in question. Such desire may be closely connected with some physical necessity arising out of possession or deprivation, for example, the satisfaction of hunger or starvation. When there is a complete absence of any such physical necessity or æsthetic fact, so that the sole advantages of possession depend on the possibility of renewed exchange, we are essentially concerned with currency founded on credit. In this field of human behaviour the psychological peculiarities of mankind produce their fullest effect. Very often, even in connection with currencies, there is no explicit contract, but the advantage of possession consists in the belief as to the stability of certain habits of mankind, habits which are not founded on physical necessities for the preservation of life. For example, gold currencies depend for their prestige upon the habit of highly prizing the possession of gold. This habit has a long and complex history. One comparatively late element in this history is the well-established use of coined gold pieces as a medium of exchange. Another element is the unfounded belief that the value of gold is still mainly independent of its use as currency, by reason of its æsthetic and metallurgic uses. Another element is the well-founded belief that so long as gold is generally used as currency, no Government can arbitrarily increase its stock of gold pieces. All of these characteristics of gold are alterable. A chemical discovery in the remote future may render the production of gold as easy as that of paper currency-notes. The superstitious reverence for gold may pass away. The governments of the world may prefer paper currencies, perhaps for the very reason that they can increase the number of paper notes at their arbitrary will, thus freeing society from one type of physical compulsion. But the fundamental fact is that so long as the generality of mankind deem gold to be wealth, then it is wealth; and as soon as this opinion passes, gold then becomes a metal of subsidiary importance.

Currencies represent only one particular case of this dependence on habits of mankind. All producers and retail traders are in this position. One extreme example is afforded by the commerce in religious emblems, such as the production of idols for worship in Central Africa, or the production of black gowns for the vesture of Calvinistic or Unitarian preachers in some countries. However, most commodities belong to a mixed type.

In temperate climates dress is a physical necessity, but fashions of dress depend upon taste and are in fact very alterable. Even food, though a more pressing necessity than dress, in modern times includes an abundance of alternatives. The upshot of all these considerations is that the doctrines of Commerce have to be founded upon assumptions concerning necessities, habits, technology, and prevalent knowledge. But habits, technology, and knowledge are variable from epoch to epoch, and even in any one epoch differ in different sections of humanity. Thus any theory of Commerce depends upon presuppositions as to the populations concerned, and cannot be extended beyond these limits apart from a direct investigation of the wider populations. For example, any considerable change in technology alters in effect the populations, and thus requires a corresponding shift in commercial theory. This conclusion has been well-known to the great masters of economic doctrine. But certainly it has not been adequately attended to by the majority of people engaged in the theory or the practice of commerce or in its political regulation. The classical political economy which dominated the nineteenth century was largely based upon sociological observation of the middle classes of northern Europe and northern America in the eighteenth century, also with some reference to Mediterranean commerce of earlier epochs. Everything else, discernible in other sections of the European populations or in other continents, was dismissed as irrelevant interruption to the pure practice of perfect commerce.

The development of economics was, in truth, affected by the moralizing tendency of the class mainly concerned. Their ideal of commercial activity as the main occupation of perfected civilization led to the consideration of economic laws which *should* hold, and to the neglect of economic procedures which in fact *did* hold. For example, in England in the mid-nineteenth century radical manufactures opposed the enactment of adulteration laws, basing their action on the axiom *Caveat emptor.* In this instance their individualistic doctrine of society, combined with their presupposition that respectable men and women are mainly engaged in safeguarding all details of their commercial interests, led them to neglect questions of prevalent fact. In the study of ideas, it is necessary to remember, that insistence on hard-headed clarity issues from sentimental feeling, as it were a mist, cloaking the perplexities of fact. Insistence on clarity at all costs is based on sheer superstition as to the mode in which human intelligence functions. Our reasonings grasp at straws for premises and float on gossamers for deductions.

SECTION III. Another instance of ill-judged simplification is the use made of the Malthusian Law of Population. This law, in any reasonably accurate statement, is undeniable. The increase of population apart from checks on impulse, or on childbearing, or on survival, proceeds by a law with some analogy to geometric progression. Also, apart from these checks, the numerical factor of the geometric increase is greater than unity by a difference which is not negligible. Again the means of subsistence—food, clothing, shelter—, so far as they are provided by appliances of given types, can only be increased by the production of additional appliances of these types. Such additional production, even if variable, must conform to the general type of arithmetical progression. But a geometric progression will always overtake an arithmetic progression. It was then concluded, as a consequence of this Malthusian Law, that population will always overtake the means of subsistence. The further inference was then drawn that, apart from short exceptional periods, the normal structure of society was that of a comparatively affluent minority subsisting on the labours of a teeming population checked by starvation and other discomforts.

These sociological conclusions, if true, are of enormous importance to commerce, in the enlarged sense in which we have used that term. For, in the first place, the normal structure of society is now defined. It consists of the fortunate few, and of the semi-destitute many. Thus producers must, in the long run, design their production to suit these types of customers. Again the hope of improving the social system by a humane adjustment of social conditions in factories must be abandoned. It is of course possible, here and there, as the result of isolated charity. But in the long run, there must be a pool of labour, starving and destitute, ready to work on the wages of bare subsistence. Factories taking advantage of such cheap labour will drive out of trade those managed on fanciful humanitarian lines. Hence the final improvement of the social system is mirage. In so far as medicine saves life, there will be only more to starve.

These sociological conclusions from the Malthusian Law assume first that all the restraints upon increase of mankind are secondary in their effect until they are raised to dominance by excessive population. Secondly they assume that within the span of time required for the operation of the Malthusian Law, sudden increases of productive power, due to improved technology will not be introduced. Perhaps such improved technology may even require additional population. Thirdly they assume that the geographic situation of the population concerned will not be seriously affected by migration. In truth there is a complex situation depending on the balance of many factors. By arbitrarily seizing upon one or two factors, and by relegating the remainder to the status of secondary disturbances, almost any law of population can be deduced. Thus the Malthusian Law, with its sociological consequences, is not an iron necessity. It is a possibility inherent in the facts, which may afford an interpretation of the circumstances of some human societies, perhaps of all.

A recourse to observation at once discloses the importance of the doctrine of Malthus. China and India both afford examples of societies which illustrate his law. They contain large populations whose standard of life is perilously near to the margin of subsistence. We must conclude, therefore, that for nearly half the human race, Malthus has provided an interpretation for some of the dominant facts of history occurring within the last few centuries, and perhaps stretching into a longer period. Now India and China are instances of civilized societies which for a long period in their later history maintained themselves with arrested technology and with fixed geographical location. They provided the exact conditions required for the importance of the Malthusian Law.

When we turn to the European races the evidence is more perplexing. The superficial fact is that during the eleven centuries from the age of Charlemagne to the present day a persistently increasing population has been accompanied by an equally persistent rise in the general standard of life. Thus any simple-minded Malthusian correlation of density of population with deficiency in the necessaries of life does not apply. Of course, the stock answer to this conclusion is that the checks, which the leading Malthusians have always explictly recognized, have intervened to delay the inevitable issue. But Europe, even Western Europe, is a large region, and a thousand years is a long time, about one-sixth of the whole past of civilization within the historical period. The plain truth is that during this period and over that area, the so-called checks were such that the Malthusian law represented a possibility, unrealized and of no importance. Also these checks were not even in proportion to the density of the population. For examples the plagues depended mainly on insanitary habits, and the densities of rats, insects, and microbes. At the time of the Black Death, a Malthusian discussing the excessive birth rate would have been talking irrelevant nonsense. Soap, water, and drains were the key to the situation. The Thirty Years' War halved the population of Germany. It was due to many causes, a few creditable, but most of them discreditable. An excessive population in Germany has never been mentioned among them. Of course there was plenty of misery in the Middle Ages, and during the Renaissance. For example, we read of Peasants' risings. But this misery certainly did not prevail in any proportion to density of population. Thus, in the early years of the sixteenth century, Flanders which was thickly populated was notably more prosperous than the country-districts in Germany where, at that time, there was a rising of the peasants. Of course the reasons for this contrast are too obvious to be worth mentioning. But among these reasons, the fact emerges that the Malthusian Law is largely irrelevant for the discussion of sociological conditions in Europe.

SECTION IV. Nevertheless there have been such occasions of relevance. It is a mistake to discuss the development of Western Europe in isolation. The history of Europe has been decisively influenced by its reactions with the Near East. Here the term Near East is used to denote that large region, including three metropolitan districts, on its coastal boundaries,—Constantinople, Mesopotamia, and the Delta of the Nile, and also including the Arabian Desert with its fertile fringes, and the plateaus and mountains of Asia Minor. The history of civilization in the Old World is the history of the internal development of the four continental regions fringing Asia, namely, China, India, The Near East, and Europe. These four histories cannot be understood apart from a study of the reactions of these vast regions on each other. For example, the Hellenic and Hellenistic epochs comprise the story of how the ancient civilization of the Near East brought to birth the new civilization of Europe, and how European civilization asserted its independence of the social system to which it owed its nurture. The subsequent collapse of the older civilization is the tragedy of history, foreshadowed by the decline of the Roman Empire whose imperial system had reverted to Eastern ideals.

The reactions between mediaeval Europe and the Near East can be classified under four headings, Malthus, Religion, Technology, Commerce. It must be remembered, however, that all the major crises in the story were precipitated by a concurrence of many causes. It is a great mistake in sociological theory to link impulse towards activity with abject destitution. In fact, when a population has sunk its standard of life to the marginal level for subsistence, the poverty of life weakens the impulse towards adventure. The Malthusian impulse towards conquest arises when a well-nurtured, hardy population is only beginning to feel the pressure of its numbers on its resources. There was no evidence of starvation at the Courts of Central Asia or among the Arabian tribes. Probably there was a growing hard dullness of life provoking unrest. But the active stimulants for the eruptions of the Tartar and Arabian tribes were adventure, the dream of fabulous luxury, religion. The dream of luxury is the first, and more dangerous, phase of the Malthusian pressure on a population. It arises before the inroad of enfeeblement. But the initial phase of emotional unrest can take a more intellectual form, and clothe itself in religious concepts. A new mass-religion can then arise, with the mission to subdue the Earth and destroy the infidels. In fact, it is a commonplace of history, that the pressure of population upon its resources is one main ingredient in the catastrophic reactions between large regions, and between diverse classes within the same social system. On the whole, catastrophes are disastrous to civilization. They are a plunge into the unknown; and civilization is not the average result of raw nature. It depends upon the long-time operation of selective agency.

Three reasons stand out to explain why the internal conditions in Europe, for more than a thousand years, reduced to insignificance the operation of the Malthusian Law. They are, Expansion of Commerce, Development of Technology, and Discovery of Empty Continents. All these causes are interconnected. Also the activities involved in each can be represented as due to a population seeking means of subsistence. But the point is that mankind has developed an unstable sensitivity in respect to its emotional and intellectual functions. Thus in fortunate societies faint signs of economic pressure develop disproportionate forms of adventure, physical and intellectual. Avocations are initiated as means of subsistence: they end as passions. The result in Europe has been the introduction of novelties, of Commerce, of Scientific

Technology, and of Geographic Knowledge, which have entirely masked sociological consequences of the Malthusian type.

The central activity from which the other two developed was Commerce. We are speaking of Europe from the Age of Charlemagne onwards. If we had included the six hundred years preceding that Age, the migration of Peoples within Europe was one main factor. But in the period under review these great migrations were over. The diffusion of the Scandinavian Northmen was still in progress. But this migration was hardly a mass movement. It is best conceived as the diffusion of the ablest governing class that Europe has ever seen,—Canute and his Danes, Norman Barons in France, and in England, and in Southern Italy. Also their direct activities were not such as to mask the Malthusian Laws. They introduced order, and good order is a condition for the increase of population. Order, as such, gives no reason for escape from the consequences of an increasing population. Also an enumeration of some main interests of the epoch is not to the point. For example, the various activities of the Catholic Church, the scholastic controversies, the Holy Roman Empire, architecture, the artistic and literary interests of the Renaissance, the Reformation, had no direct bearing on the evasion of Malthusian consequences arising from the increase of population. Granting the increase of population, History has only disclosed three ways of escape,—expanding Commerce, improving Technology, and utilization of Empty Regions. The most fundamental of all sociological classifications is that between civilized societies for which one or more of these conditions do obtain, and those for which they do not obtain. In the wide sense of the term, Commerce covers all three conditions. Thus Commerce is one central factor, essential for a prosperous civilization. As soon as there is an arrest, when expansion, improvement, and novel utilization cease, then slowly and imperceptibly a blight settles upon the populations concerned. China and India survived, with populations blighted by hopeless poverty, the Roman Empire fell by reason of the blight, the Near East is the store-house of buried cities recording ancient magnificence. The central factor is Commerce; and more than that, it is Commerce developed adventurously.

In the first three hundred years of the slow development of the Feudal System after Charlemagne, we see a population barely gaining a livelihood by hard toil. This state of things exemplifies the application of Malthus' Doctrine in the primitive stages of civilization. The only way of coping with an increase of population was to cut down another forest, and arithmetically to add field to field, till fertile land was fully occupied. Also fertility itself became exhausted, so that until the close of the eighteenth century fallow fields bore witness to the iron limits that nature set to agriculture. The essence of technology is to enable mankind to transcend such limitations of unguided nature. For example, the rotation of the crops, the scientific understanding of fertilizers and of genetics, have already altered the bounds set to food production.

In those early times the Malthusian Laws set their limits to life. The 'checks' were operating, and population hardly increased. The slow growth of Commerce, the foundation of centres of trade with the peculiar privileges of the burgesses and the guilds, the strange knowledge of the Jews, pilgrims, the glimpses of the Near East provided by Medi1erranean trade, and later by the Crusades, the intelligence housed in the great monasteries—all these factors gradually removed the repression of raw nature upon the possibilities of human existence. European life began to approach the standards of the Near East and of China so far as concerned technology and general commercial activities. But these older civilizations were about to face new limitations, equally inexorable, granting their stage of technology and of social organization.

SECTION V. Nature is plastic, although to every prevalent state of mind there corresponds iron nature setting its bounds to life. Modern history begins when Europeans passed into a new phase of understanding which enabled them to introduce new selective agencies, unguessed by the older civilizations. It is a false dichotomy to think of Nature *and* Man. Mankind is that factor *in* Nature which exhibits in its most intense form the plasticity of nature. Plasticity is the introduction of novel law. The doctrine of the Uniformity of Nature is to be ranked with the contrasted doctrine of magic and miracle, as an expression of partial truth, unguarded and uncoordinated with the immensities of the Universe. Our interpretations of experience determine the limits of what we can do with the world.

For the purpose of understanding how it happened that European life escaped the restrictions which finally bound China, India, and The Near East, it is important to recapture the attitude towards Commerce prevalent in various epochs. I do not mean records of trade, but records of the kinds of mentality governing commercial relations. We can only understand a society by knowing what sort of people undertook what sort of functions in that society. It must be remembered that China and Bagdad, at the height of their prosperity, exhibited forms of human life in many ways more gracious than our own. They were great civilizations. But they became arrested, and the arrest is the point of our enquiry. We have to understand the reasons for the greatness and the final barriers to advancement. Of course, such an ambitious design is absurd. It would mean the solution of the main problem of sociology. What can be done, is to note some indications of relevant tones of mind apparently widely spread in various districts at different epochs.

There is ample evidence of active Commerce in China and the Near East in ancient times, contemporary with the pre-Hellenic and Hellenic periods of the Ægean Basin. There are Codes of Law which determine commercial problems. Also among the early inscriptions recovered from Babylon and Nineveh there are a mass of records of private transactions between merchants. Three thousand years ago the importance of credit would have been no news either in Mesopotamia or in China. Also there was foreign trade beyond the boundaries of the Near East. There are evidences of ocean-borne trade between India and Egypt, perhaps even between China and Egypt, with Ceylon as an intermediary. Also Central Asia was nearing its last phase of prosperity before it faded out into desert. It seems to have provided the route for a flourishing overland trade between China and the Near East. Thus these great civilizations were supported by internal trade and by external trade with each other. Also there was the whole coast-line of semi-barbarous Europe,—the shores of the Black Sea, the shores of the Western Mediterranean, the Atlantic coasts of Europe.

Having regard to relative backwardness of the art of navigation then, compared with the same art in the fifteenth and sixteenth centuries after Christ, the boldness of the Phœnician sailors and the enterprise of their traders at least equals that in any of the later feats. It is impossible to be more than absolutely fearless: and considering the dim geographic knowledge possessed by the ancients, the Phœnicians must be allowed the fame of having displayed that extremity of courage. The Greeks were bold sailors, but the Phœnicians led the way. There is no reason to believe that in later times a Greek or a Roman vessel ever saw a coast-line not previously visited by Phœnician traders. Also, remembering Hanna's voyage in the sixth century before Christ, the whole oceanic coast-line of Africa was explored by the men of the Near East, where western Europeans did not venture till the lapse of nigh two thousand years. In the last few hundred years, European races have been apt to forget the greatness of the Near East, whose populations, with no predecessors to guide them, carried mankind from the stage of semi-barbarism only half-erect from the soil, to peaks of civilized life, in art, in religion, and in adventure, which remain unsurpassed. Their civilization in its prime was founded on Expanding Commerce, Development of Technology, and Discovery of Empty Continents. But in this list one item has been omitted, The Souls of Men.

The vigour of the Near East survived the first effort to establish a widespread European civilization. This European attempt was embodied in the Western portion of the Roman Empire. It was sustained during four hundred and fifty, or five hundred years. The limits of this period may be approximately assigned from Cæsar and Augustus at the commencement down to the taking of Rome by Alaric in the year 410 A.D. The failure did not consist in the decline and fall of its political institutions. Such state-systems are transient expedients upon the surface of civilization. The real failure consists in the fact that in the year 600 A.D., Western Europe was less civilized than in the year 100 A.D., and was far behind the Eastern Mediterranean during the third and fourth centuries before Christ. Pope Gregory, the Great, would have been poor company for Sophocles, Aristotle, Eratosthenes, or Archimedes. Gregory was the man for his time. But the delicacies of civilization—in art, or in thought, or in human behaviour—were then at a discount.

In every sense of the term, the Western Empire had lacked expansive force. Across the Rhine and the Danube the northern forests were impenetrable. On the west, the Atlantic Ocean was trackless. With the minor exception of the conquest of Britain, all attempt at physical expansion ceased after Varus lost the legions of Augustus. The Western Empire in all its ramifications was a purely defensive institution, in its sociological functionings and in its external behaviour. Its learning lacked speculative adventure. In no sense, however we stretch the metaphor, did it discover a New World. Unfortunately life is an offensive, directed against the repetitious mechanism of the Universe. It is the thesis of this discussion that a policy of sociological defence is doomed to failure. We are analysing those types of social functioning which provide that expansion and novelty which life demands. Life can only be understood as an aim at that perfection which the conditions of its environment allow. But the aim is always beyond the attained fact. The goal is some type of perfected things, however lowly and basically sensual. Inorganic nature is characterized by its acceptance of matter of fact. In nature, the soil rests, while the root of the plant pursues the sources of its refreshment. In the Western Empire there was no pursuit. Its remnants of irritability were devoid of transcendent aim.

Of course Christianity was a tremendous exception. But on the whole, in its immediate effect it was a destructive agency. Its disregard of temporal fact, based on apocalyptic prophecy, was too extreme. It was not till its first few centuries were passed that it began to acquire a fortunate worldliness. Indeed the translation of Eastern modes of thought—Semitic, Greek, and Egyptian—to Western Europe had the unfortunate effect of making the ideal side of civilization appear more abstract than it was in the lands and the epochs of its origin. It had this effect in the Near East itself when by the lapse of time circumstances altered. For the early Hebrews, their God was a personage whose aims were expressible in terms of the immediate political and social circumstances. Their religious notions had singularly slight reference to another World. The absorption of the Greek philosophers in the city life of their times is evident. But in other times and, still more, in other lands, such thoughts and ideals took on an abstract tinge. They had lost their practical application. The notion arose that the man of culture and the man of ideal aim was a stranger in the busy world. It is true that such a notion haunted Plato. But it dominated Augustine. Yet in Augustine's age, towards the close of the century after Constantine, the mission of the Church for the reformation of this World was in its first phase. The obstinate survival of the present World was upsetting the unworldly tactics of the early Christians.

But the civilization of the Near East, including its Byzantine fringe, contained other sources of vigour, preserving it from the decadence of its Western off-shoot. The true successors of Alexander, the men who realized his fabled dream of extending the Near Eastern civilization from the Tigris to the western shores of the

Mediterranean, belonged to the age of Justinian and to the age of Mahometan expansion. Justinian's success was incomplete. It was a false dawn. But the Mahometans represent the complete triumph of the Near East, after it had absorbed the novel ingredients introduced by Hellenism and Hebrewism, its two great off-shoots destined to re-create civilization. Thus there are two peaks to the Near Eastern Culture. The earlier is embodied in the first known examples of high civilization in Babylon and Egypt. The metaphor of a peak here fails; for this earlier type of life maintained itself for long ages. The advent of the Persians represents a transitional period. They almost antedated the Mahometans. But the times were not ready.

The distinction separating the Byzantines and the Mahometans from the Romans is that the Romans were themselves deriving the civilization which they spread. In their hands it assumed a frozen form. Thought halted, and literature copied. The Byzantines and the Mahometans were themselves the civilization. Thus their culture retained its intrinsic energies, sustained by physical and spiritual adventure. They traded with the far East: they expanded westward: they codified law: they developed new forms of art: they elaborated theologies: they transformed mathematics: they developed medicine. In this final period of Near Eastern greatness the Jews played the same part as did the Greeks during the Persian epoch. Finally, the Near East as a centre of civilization was destroyed by the Tartars and the Turks.

Luckily for Europe, the more northern thrust of the Tartars across Russia seems to have been checked by the forests of Poland and the more southern hills and mountains. These conquerors of the Near East were never civilized in any effective sense of the term. During the later centuries, the Turkish pressure on Europe constituted merely the threat of Europe produced by a lower civilization, an ingenious compound of primitive brutality and decadent refinement. In the eighteenth and nineteenth centuries much history was written under the impression that the Turks were the authentic representatives of the previous Near Eastern civilization. Thus the early Greeks were staged as its opponents and not as its derivatives. In fact the long pupillage of Europe to the Near East was entirely misrepresented.

SECTION VI. At the close of the Dark Ages Europe started upon its second effort after civilization with three main advantages: its Christian ethics: its instinct for legal organization transcending local boundaries, derived from the Church and the reminiscence of the Empire: and thirdly its wider inheritance of antecedent thought, gradually disclosing itself as Hebrew, Greek, and Roman literatures. The total effect was the increased sense of the dignity of man, as man. There has been a growth, slow and wavering, of respect for the preciousness of human life. This is the humanitarian spirit, gradually emerging in the slow sunrise of a thousand years.

The creation of the world—said Plato—is the victory of persuasion over force. The worth of men consists in their liability to persuasion. They can persuade and can be persuaded by the disclosure of alternatives, the better and the worse. Civilization is the maintenance of social order, by its own inherent persuasiveness as embodying the nobler alternative. The recourse to force, however, unavoidable, is a disclosure of the failure of civilization, either in the general society or in a remnant of individuals. Thus in a live civilization there is always an element of unrest. For sensitiveness to ideas means curiosity, adventure, change. Civilized order survives on its merits, and is transformed by its power of recognizing its imperfections.

Now the intercourse between individuals and between social groups takes one of two forms, force or persuasion. Commerce is the great example of intercourse in the way of persuasion. War, slavery, and governmental compulsion exemplify the reign of force. The weakness of the Near Eastern civilizations consisted in their large reliance upon force. The growth of persuasive intercourse within the texture of society became halted. These civilizations never eradicated a large reliance upon the sway of conquerors over conquered populations, and upon the rule of individual masters over slaves. This habit of dominance spread its infection beyond these limits. A rule of men over women remained an established feature of highly civilized societies. It survived as a hangover from barbarism. But its demoralizing effects increased with civilization. This inequality of men and women seems to have been based upon physical superiorities, and the absorption of women in the birth and care of children. Anyhow it issued in the degradation of women below the level of the males. Thus these eastern races entered upon the fatal experiment of maintaining themselves at two levels of culture, and of dominating subject populations at yet a third level. The enjoyment of power is fatal to the subtleties of life. Ruling classes degenerate by reason of their lazy indulgence in obvious gratifications.

Commerce followed upon the gradual acquirement of means for easy locomotion in small groups. Whole communities had wandered, gradually shifting to other environments. But travel and return, undertaken by small groups or even by individual men, is an enterprise of entirely different character. It requires either open country, free from fores1 barriers, or the navigation of rivers and seas. The strangers arrive in small groups. They are thus under no temptation to dominate, and excite no fear. Commerce may stabilize itself into a steady traditional routine. This halt in progress has happened over large areas for long periods of time. But on the whole, Commerce is unstable. It brings together groups of men with different modes of life, different technologies, and different ways of thought. Apart from Commerce, the mariners· compass, with the vast theory which it has suggested, would never have reached the shores of the Atlantic, and printing would not have spread from Peking to Cairo.

The expanding Commerce of mediaeval and modern Europe was promoted in the first place by the great roads which were the legacy from the Roman Empire, by the improving art of navigation which enabled the indented coast-line to be utilized, and by the sense of unity promoted by the Catholic Church and Christian ethics. There were pirates, and feudal wars, and rough sporadic disorder. But men from different regions, of different races, and of different occupation were meeting together on the basis of free persuasion. Even the feudal castle, though it often harboured men with the mentality of gangsters, was more apt for defence than for offence. Also feudal levies, with their short periods of service, were mostly effective as defensive forces. In later times the evils of this system outweighed its merits. But in its origin it can be compared to the modern police, quite as aptly as to the modern army. Of course it differed from both. The point is that the feudal castle was mostly a sensible mode of self-protection for a peaceful district. The merit of Commerce lies in its close relation to technology. The novelty of experience promoted by Commerce suggests alternatives in ways of production. Again European technology was fertilized from another source. The art of clear thinking. of criticism of premises, of speculative assumption, of deductive reasoning—this great art was discovered, at least in embryo, by the Greeks, and was inherited by Europe. Like other inventions it has often been disastrously misused. But its effect on intellectual capacity can only be compared with that of fire and iron and steel for the production of the blades of Damascus and Toledo. Mankind was now armed intellectually, as well as physically.

Curiosity was now progressive. The static wisdom of the proverbs of Solomon. and of the Wisdom Books of the Bible, has been supplanted by Euclid's Elements, by Newton's Physics, by the modem epoch in industry. 'All the rivers run into the sea; there is nothing new under the sun', was the final judgment of the Near East. When we have allowed for all its brilliance, and for its many modes of activity, this great civilization finally sank under the barren criticism of disillusioned sensualists. It is the nemesis of the reign of force, of the worship of power, that the ideals of the semi-divine rulers centre upon some variant of Solomon's magnificent harem of three hundred wives and seven hundred concubines. The variation may be towards decency, but it is equally decadent. Christianity has only escaped from the Near East with scars upon it.

SECTION VII. In this rapid survey of the rise and fall of civilizations, we have noted four factors which decisively govern the fate of social groups. First, there stands the inexorable law that apart from some transcendent aim the civilized life either wallows in pleasure or relapses slowly into a barren repetition with waning intensities of feeling. Secondly, there stands the iron compulsion of nature that the bodily necessities of food, clothing, and shelter be provided. The rigid limits which are thereby set to modes of social existence can only be mitigated by the growth of an understanding by which the interplay between man and the rest of nature can be adjusted. Thirdly, the compulsory dominion of men over men has a double significance. It has a benign effect so far as it secures the coordination of behaviour necessary for social welfare. But it is fatal to extend this dominion beyond the barest limits necessary for this coordination. The progressive societies are those which most decisively have trusted themselves to the fourth factor which is the way of persuasion. Amidst all the activities of mankind there are three which chiefly have promoted this last factor in human life. They are family affections aroused in sex relations and in the nurture of children, intellectual curiosity leading to enjoyment in the interchange of ideas, and—as soon as large-scale societies arose—the practice of Commerce. But beyond these special activities a greater bond of sympathy has arisen. This bond is the growth of reverence for that power in virtue of which nature harbours ideal ends, and produces individual beings capable of conscious discrimination of such ends. This reverence is the foundation of the respect for man as man. It thereby secures that liberty of thought and action, required for the upward adventure of life on this Earth.

Chapter VI

FORESIGHT

SECTION I. BY THE phrase Historical Foresight, I mean something quite different from the accurate exercise of Scientific Induction. Science is concerned with· generalities. The generalities apply, but they do not determine the course of history apart from some anchorage in fact. There might have been many alternative courses of history conditioned by the same laws. Perhaps, if we knew enough of the laws, then we should understand that the development of the future from the past is completely determined by the details of the past and by these scientific laws which condition all generation. Unfortunately our knowledge of scientific laws is woefully defective, and our knowledge of the relevant facts of the present and the past is scanty in the extreme. Thus as the result of all our science, we are ignorant of that remote epoch when there will be a second collision between the sun and a passing star, we are ignorant of the future of life on the earth, we are ignorant of the future of mankind, we are ignorant of the course of history a year hence, we are ignorant of most of the domestic details of our lives tomorrow, we are even ignorant of the term that has been set to our own existence.

This catalogue of ignorances at once reminds us that our state is not that of blank absence of knowledge. Our ignorance is suffused with Foresight. Also the basis of our defect in foresight is our scant knowledge of the relevant detailed facts in past and present which are required for the application of the scientific laws. Where the circumstances are comparatively simple, as in Astronomy, we know that the facts and the astronomical laws provide an apparatus of great accuracy in forecast. The main difficulty in Historical Foresight is the power of collecting and selecting the facts relevant to the particular type of forecast which we wish to make. Discussions on the method of science wander off onto the topic of experiment. But experiment is nothing else than a mode of cooking the facts for the sake of exemplifying the law. Unfortunately the facts of history, even those of private individual history, are on too large a scale. They surge forward beyond control.

It is thus evident that this topic of Historical Foresight is not to be exhausted by a neat description of some definite methods. It is faced with two sources of difficulty, where science has only one. Science seeks the laws only, but Foresight requires in addition due emphasis on the relevant facts from which the future is to emerge. Of the two tasks required for Foresight, this selection amid the welter is the more difficult. Probably a neat doctrine of Foresight is impossible. But what can be done is to confine attention to one field of human activity, and to describe the type of mentality which seems requisite for the attainment of Foresight within that field. The present state of the world, and the course of the discussions in this book, suggest the field of Commercial relations. This field will therefore be chosen to illustrate the function of ideas in the provision of anticipation and purpose.

To avoid misunderstanding I must disclaim the foolish notion that it is possible for anyone, devoid of personal experience of commerce, to provide useful suggestions for its detailed conduct. There is no substitute for first-hand practice. Also the word 'commerce' is here used in the largest sense of that term, in which it includes a variety of activities. Any useful theory, capable of immediate application to specific instances, must depend on a direct knowledge of the relevant reactions of men and women composing that society, or perhaps group of nations, within which the specific business in question is to flourish. In this discussion there is no pretence of such detailed knowledge.

There remains, however, the question of the general type of mentality which in the present condition of the world will promote the general success of a commercial community. Such a type is, of course, very complex. But we are considering one unquestioned element in it, namely Foresight, and will discuss the conditions for its development and its successful exercise.

Some people are born with astounding knacks of the mind. For example, there are calculating boys who can perform intricate operations of mental arithmetic in a flash, there are also other sorts of peculiar faculties of divination; in particular there are men with a knack of shrewdness in judging circumstances within the narrow range of their immediate observation. But after all, bankers prefer that their clerks should learn arithmetic. and trained geologists are preferred to men with divining rods. In the same way, there are general conditions of training which promote the development of a wider type of foresight.

It is a great mistake to divide people into sharp classes, namely. people with such-and-such a knack and people without it. These trenchant divisions are simply foolish. Most humans are born with certain aptitudes. But these aptitudes can easily remain latent unless they are elicited into activity by fortunate circumstances. If anyone has no aptitude of a certain type, no training can elicit it. But, granted the aptitude, we can discuss the ways of training it. Foresight depends upon understanding. In practical affairs it is a habit. But the habit of foreseeing is elicited by the habit of understanding. To a large extent, understanding can be acquired by a conscious effort and it can be taught. Thus the training of Foresight is by the medium of Understanding. Foresight is the product of Insight.

SECTION II. The general topic to be understood is the entire internal functioning of human society, including its technologies, the biological and physical laws on which these technologies depend, and including the sociological reactions of humans depending on fundamental psychological principles. In fact, the general topic is sociology in the broadest sense of the term, including its auxiliary sciences. Such a width of understanding is, of course, beyond the grasp of any single human. But no part of it is entirely foreign to the provision of foresight in business. Such a complete understanding is a cooperative enterprise; and a business community maintains its success for long periods so far as its average foresight is dominated by some approach to such general understanding.

We shall comprehend better the varieties of individual understanding which go to complete this general equipment of an ideal business community, if we commence by considering the contrast between understanding and routine.

Routine is the god of every social system; it is the seventh heaven of business, the essential component in the success of every factory, the ideal of every statesman. The social machine should run like clockwork. Every crime should be followed by an arrest, every arrest by a judicial trial, every trial by a conviction, every conviction by a punishment, every punishment by a reformed character. Or, you can conceive an analogous routine concerning the making of a motor car, starting with the iron in the ore, and the coal in the mine, and ending with the car driving out of the factory and with the President of the Corporation signing the dividend warrants, and renewing his contracts with the mining Corporations. In such a routine everyone from the humblest miner to the august president is exactly trained for his special job. Every action of miner or president is the product of conditioned reflexes, according to current physiological phraseology. When the routine is perfect, understanding can be eliminated, except such minor flashes of intelligence as are required to deal with familiar accidents, such as a flooded mine, a prolonged drought, or an epidemic of influenza. A system will be the product of intelligence. But when the adequate routine is established, intelligence vanishes, and the system is maintained by a coordination of conditioned reflexes.

What is then required from the humans is receptivity of special training. No one, from President to miner, need understand the system as a whole. There will be no foresight, but there will be complete success in the maintenance of the routine.

Now it is the beginning of wisdom to understand that social life is founded upon routine. Unless society is permeated, through and through, with routine, civilization vanishes. So many sociological doctrines, the products of acute intellects, are wrecked by obliviousness to this fundamental sociological truth. Society requires stability, foresight itself presupposes stability, and stability is the product of routine. But there are limits to routine, and it is for the discernment of these limits, and for the provision of the consequent action, that foresight is required.

The two extremes of complete understanding and of complete routine are never realized in human society. But of the two, routine is more fundamental than understanding, that is to say, routine modified by minor flashes of short range intelligence. Indeed the notion of complete understanding controlling action is an ideal in the clouds, grotesquely at variance with practical life. But we have under our eyes countless examples of societies entirely dominated by routine. The elaborate social organizations of insects appear to be thoroughgoing examples of routine. Such organizations achieve far-reaching, complex purposes: they involve a differentiation of classes, from cows to serfs, from serfs to workers, from workers to warriors, from warriors to janitors, and from janitors to queens. Such oganizations have regard to needs in a distant future, especially if the comparatively short space of life of the individual insects is taken into account as the unit of measurement.

These insect societies have been astoundingly successful, so far as concerns survival power. They seem to have a past extending. over tens of thousands of years, perhaps of millions of years. It is the greatest of mistakes to believe that it has required the high-grade intelligence of mankind to construct an elaborate social organization. A particular instance of this error is the prevalent assumption that any social routine whose purposes are not obvious to our analysis is thereby to be condemned as foolish. We can observe insects performing elaborate routine actions whose purposes they cannot possibly understand, which yet are essential either for their own individual survival or for race-survival.

But these insect societies have one great characteristic in common. They are not progressive. It is exactly this characteristic that discriminates communities of mankind from communities of insects. Further, this great fact of progressiveness, be it from worse to better, or from better to worse, has become of greater and greater importance in Western civilization as we come to modern times. The rate of change has increased even in my life-time. It is possible that in future ages mankind may relapse into the stage of stable societies. But such a relapse is extremely unlikely within any span of time which we need take into account.

SECTION III. The recent shortening of the time-span between notable changes in social customs is very obvious, if we examine history. Originally it depended upon some slow development of physical causes. For example, a gradual change of physical configuration such as the elevation of mountains: the time-span for such a change is of the order of a million years. Again, a gradual change of climate: the time-span for such a change is of the order of five-thousand years. Again a gradual over-population of the region occupied by some community with its consequent swarming into new territories: having regard to the huge death-rate of pre-scientific ages, the time-span for such a change was of the order of five-hundred years. Again, the sporadic inventions of new technologies, such as the chipping of flints, the invention of fire, the taming of animals, the invention of metallurgy: in the pre-scientific ages, the average time-span for such changes was, at least, of the order of five-hundred years. If we compare the technologies of civilizations west of Mesopotamia at the epochs 100 A.D., the culmination of the Roman Empire, and 1400 A.D., the close of the Middle Ages, we find practically no advance in technology. There was some gain in metallurgy, some elaboration of clockwork, the recent invention of gun powder with its influence all in the future, some advance in the art of navigation, also with its influence in the future. If we compare 1400 A.D. with 1700 A.D., there is a great advance; gunpowder, and printing, and navigation, and the technique of commerce, had produced their effect. But even then, the analogy between life in the eighteenth century and life in the great period of ancient Rome was singularly close, so that the peculiar relevance of Latin literature was felt vividly. In the fifty years between 1780 and 1830, a number of inventions came with a rush into effective operation. The age of steam power and of machinery was introduced. But for two generations, from 1830 to 1890, there was a singular uniformity in the principles of technology which were regulating the structure of society and the usages of business.

The conclusion to be drawn from this survey is a momentous one. Our sociological theories, our political philosophy, our practical maxims of business, our political economy, and our doctrines of education, are derived from an unbroken tradition of great thinkers and of practical examples, from the age of Plato in the fifth century before Christ to the end of the last century. The whole of this tradition is warped by the vicious assumption that each generation will substantially live amid the conditions governing the lives of its fathers and will transmit those conditions to mould with equal force the lives of its children. We are living in the first period of human history for which this assumption is false.

Of course in the past, there were great catastrophes: for example, plagues, floods, barbarian invasions. But, if such catastrophes were warded off, there was a stable, well-known condition of civilized life. This assumption subtly pervades the premises of political economy, and has permitted it to confine attention to a simplified edition of human nature. It is at the basis of our conception of the reliable business man, who has mastered a technique and never looks beyond his contracted horizon. It colours our political philosophy and our educational theory, with their overwhelming emphasis on past experience. The note of recurrence dominates the wisdom of the past, and still persists in many forms even where explicitly the fallacy of its modern application is admitted. The point is that in the past the time-span of important change was considerably longer than that of a single human life. Thus mankind was trained to adapt itself to fixed conditions.

Today this time-span is considerably shorter than that of human life, and accordingly our training must prepare individuals to face a novelty of conditions. But there can be no preparation for the unknown. It is at this point that we recur to the immediate topic, Foresight. We require such an understanding of the present conditions, as may give us some grasp of the novelty which is about to produce a measurable influence on the immediate future. Yet the doctrine, that routine is dominant in any society that is not collapsing, must never be lost sight of. Thus the grounds, in human nature and in the successful satisfaction of purpose, these grounds for the current routine must be understood; and at the same time the sorts of novelty just entering into social effectiveness have got to be weighed against the old routine. In this way the type of modification and the type of persistence exhibited in the immediate future may be foreseen.

SECTION IV. It is now time to give some illustrations of assertions already made. Consider our main conclusions that our traditional doctrines of sociology, of political philosophy, of the practical conduct of large business, and of political economy are largely warped and vitiated by the implicit assumption of a stable unchanging social system. With this assumption it is comparatively safe to base reasoning upon a simplified edition of human nature. For well-known stimuli working under well-known conditions produce well-known reactions. It is safe then to assume that human nature, for the purpose in hand, is adequately described in terms of some of the major reactions to some of the major stimuli. For example, we can all remember our old friend, the economic man.

The beauty of the economic man was that we knew exactly what he was after. Whatever his wants were, he knew them and his neighbours knew them. His wants were those developed in a well-defined social system. His father and grandfather had the same wants, and satisfied them in the same way. So whenever there was a shortage, everyone—including the economic man himself—knew what was short, and knew the way to satisfy the consumer. In fact, the consumer knew what he wanted to consume. This was the demand. The producer knew how to produce the required articles, hence the supply. The men who got the goods onto the spot first, at the cheapest price, made their fortunes; the other producers were eliminated. This was healthy competition. This is beautifully simple and with proper elaboration is obviously true. It expresses the dominant truth exactly so far as there are stable well-tried conditions. But when we are concerned with a social system which in important ways is changing, this simplified conception of human relations requires severe qualification.

It is, of course, common knowledge that the whole trend of political economy during the last thirty or forty years has been away from these artificial simplifications. Such sharp-cut notions as 'the economic man', 'supply and demand', 'competition', are now in process of dilution by a close study of the actual reactions of various populations to the stimuli which are relevant to modern commerce. This exactly illustrates the main thesis. The older political economy reigned supreme for about a hundred years from the time of Adam Smith, because in its main assumptions it did apply to the general circumstances of life as led, then and for innumerable centuries in the past. These circumstances were then already passing away. But it still remained a dominant truth that in commercial relations men were dominated by well-conditioned reactions to completely familiar stimuli.

In the present age, the element of novelty which life affords is too prominent to be omitted from our calculations. A deeper knowledge of the varieties of human nature is required to determine the reaction, in its character and its strength, to those elements of novelty which each decade of years introduces into social life. The possibility of this deeper knowledge constitutes the Foresight under discussion.

Another example which concerns sociological habits, and thence business relations and the shifting values of property, is to be seen in the history of cities. Throughout the whole span of civilization up to the present moment, the growth of condensed aggregates of humans, which we call cities, has been an inseparable accompaniment of the growth of civilization. There are many obvious reasons, the defence of accumulated wealth behind city walls, the concentration of materials requisite for manufacture, the concentration of power in the form of human muscles and, later, in the form of available heat energy, the ease of mutual intercourse required for business relations, the pleasure arising from a concentration of æsthetic and cultural opportunities, the advantages of a concentration of governmental and other directing agencies, administrative. legal, and military.

But there are disadvantages in cities. As yet no civilization has been self-supporting. Each civilization is born, it culminates, and it decays. There is a widespread testimony that this ominous fact is due to inherent biological defects in the crowded life of cities. Now, slowly and at first faintly, an opposite tendency is showing itself. Better roads and better vehicles at first induced the wealthier classes to live on the outskirts of the cities. The urgent need for defence had also vanished. This tendency is now spreading rapidly downwards. But a new set of conditions is just showing itself. Up to the present time, throughout the eighteenth and nineteenth centuries, this new tendency placed the homes in the immediate suburbs, but concentrated manufacturing activity, business relations. government, and pleasure, in the centres of the cities. Apart from the care of children, and periods of sheer rest, the active lives were spent in the cities. In some ways, the concentration of such activities was even more emphasized, and the homes were pushed outwards even at the cost of the discomfort of commuting. But, if we examine the trend of technology during the past generation, the reasons for this concentration are largely disappearing. Still more, the reasons for the choice of sites for cities are also altering. Mechanical power can be transmitted for hundreds of miles, men can communicate almost instantaneously by telephone, the chiefs of great organizations can be transported by airplanes, the cinemas can produce plays in every village, music, speeches, and sermons can be broadcast. Almost every reason for the growth of cities, concurrently with the growth of civilization, has been profoundly modified.

What then is to be the future of cities, three hundred years hence, a hundred years hence, or even thirty years hence? I do not know. But I venture a guess:—that those who are reasonably fortunate in this foresight will make their fortunes, and that others will be ruined by mistakes in calculation.

My second point that the reasons for the choice of sites for cities have also been modified is illustrated by recent changes in my own country, England. The first effect of the new industrial age of the eighteenth and nineteenth centuries was to concentrate population round the coalfields. Thus the central portion of England on its northern edge has become one huge city, disguised under different names for its various regional parts. But the novel conditions are shifting population and manufactures to the south of England, near to the great southern ports which look towards the Mediterranean, the South Atlantic Ocean, and the Panama Canal. They are the best ports, with the easiest navigation, and with uncrowded land around them. At present the transmission of electric power is one of the major pre-occupations of the government of England.

The effect of new technologies on the sites of cities, and on transformations of cities, is one of the fundamental problems which must enter into all sociological theories, including the forecasting of business relations. We must not exaggerate the importance of these particular examples. They are just two examples selected from a whole situation which can be analysed into innumerable examples with the same moral. I mean nothing so absurd as that all industrialists should meditate on the future of cities. The topic may be quite irrelevant to the future activities of most of them. Also I am ignorant as to how much Political Economy they should study.

But we are faced with a fluid, shifting situation in the immediate future. Rigid maxims, a rule-of-thumb routine, and caste-iron particular doctrines will spell ruin. The business of the future must be controlled by a somewhat different type of men to that of previous centuries. The type is already changing, and has already changed so far as the leaders are concerned. The Business Schools of Universities are concerned with spreading this newer type throughout the nations by aiming at the production of the requisite mentality.

SECTION V. I will conclude this chapter by a sketch of the Business Mind of the future. In the first place it is fundamental that there be a power of conforming to routine, of supervising routine, of constructing routine, and of understanding routine both as to its internal structure and as to its external purposes. Such a power is the bedrock of all practical efficiency. But for the production of the requisite Foresight, something more is wanted. This extra endowment can only be described as a philosophic power of understanding the complex flux of the varieties of human societies: for instance, the habit of noting varieties of demands on life, of serious purposes, of frivolous amusements. Such instinctive grasp of the relevant features of social currents is of supreme importance. For example, the time-span of various types of social behaviour is of the essence of their effect on policy. A widespread type of religious interest, with its consequent modes of behaviour, has a dominant life of about a hundred years, while a fashion of dress survives any time between three months and three years. Methods of agriculture change slowly. But the scientific world seems to be on the verge of far-reaching biological discoveries. The assumption of slow changes in agriculture must therefore be scanned vigilantly. This example of time-spans can be generalized. The quantitative aspect of social changes is of the essence of business relations. Thus the habit of transforming observation of qualitative changes into quantitative estimates should be a characteristic of business mentality.

I have said enough to show that the modern commercial mentality requires many elements of discipline, scientific and sociological. But the great fact remains that details of relevant knowledge cannot be foreseen. Thus even for mere success, and apart from any question of intrinsic quality of life, an unspecialized aptitude for eliciting generalizations from particulars and for seeing the divergent illustration of generalities in diverse circumstances is required. Such a reflective power is essentially a philosophic habit: it is the survey of society from the standpoint of generality. This habit of general thought, undaunted by novelty, is the gift of philosophy, in the widest sense of that term.

SECTION VI. But the motive of success is not enough. It produces a short-sighted world which destroys the sources of its own prosperity. The cycles of trade depression which afflict the world warn us that business relations are infected through and through with the disease of short-sighted motives. The robber barons did not conduce to the prosperity of Europe in the Middle Ages, though some of them died prosperously in their beds. Their example is a warning to our civilization. Also we must not fall into the fallacy of thinking of the business world in abstraction from the rest of the community. The business world is one main part of the very community which is the subject-matter of our study. The behaviour of the community is largely dominated by the business mind. A great society is a society in which its men of business think greatly of their functions. Low thoughts mean low behaviour, and after a brief orgy of exploitation low behaviour means a descending standard of life. The general greatness of the community, qualitatively as well as quantitatively, is the first condition for steady prosperity, buoyant, self-sustained, and commanding credit. The Greek philosopher who laid the foundation of all our finer thoughts ended his most marvellous dialogue with the reflection that the ideal state could never arrive till philosophers are kings. Today, in an age of democracy, the kings are the plain citizens pursuing their various avocations. There can be no successful democratic society till general education conveys a philosophic outlook.

Philosophy is not a mere collection of noble sentiments. A deluge of such sentiments does more harm than good. Philosophy is at once general and concrete, critical and appreciative of direct intuition. It is not—or, at least, should not be—a ferocious debate between irritable professors. It is a survey of possibilities and their comparison with actualities. In philosophy, the fact, the theory, the alternatives, and the ideal, are weighed together. Its gifts are insight and foresight, and a sense of the worth of life, in short, that sense of importance which nerves all civilized effort. Mankind can flourish in the lower stages of life with merely barbaric flashes of thought. But when civilization culminates, the absence of a coordinating philosophy of life, spread throughout the community, spells decadence, boredom, and the slackening of effort.

Every epoch has its character determined by the way its populations react to the material events which they encounter. This reaction is determined by their basic beliefs—by their hopes, their fears, their judgments of what is worth while. They may rise to the greatness of an opportunity, seizing its drama, perfecting its art, exploiting its adventure, mastering intellectually and physically the network of relations that constitutes the very being of the epoch. On the other hand, they may collapse before the perplexities confronting them. How they act depends partly on their courage, partly on their intellectual grasp. Philosophy is an attempt to clarify those fundamental beliefs which finally determine the emphasis of attention that lies at the base of character.

Mankind is now in one of its rare moods of shifting its outlook. The mere compulsion of tradition has lost its force. It is our business—philosophers, students, and practical men—to re-create and reenact a vision of the world, including those elements of reverence and order without which society lapses into riot, and penetrated through and through with unflinching rationality. Such a vision is the knowledge which Plato identified with virtue. Epochs for which, within the limits of their development, this vision has been widespread are the epochs unfading in the memory of mankind.

Our discussion has insensibly generalized itself. It has passed beyond the topic of Commercial Relations to the function of a properly concrete philosophy in guiding the purposes of mankind.

PART II

COSMOLOGICAL

Chapter VII

LAWS OF NATURE

SECTION I. THE PREVIOUS part of this book dealt with the influence exerted by the Platonic and Christian doctrines of the human soul upon the sociological development of the European races. In this second part of the book, I shall deal with the influence of scientific ideas upon European culture, and with the more general cosmological ideas thus generated and presupposed.

It would be useless to attempt a history of science within this compass. Accordingly, I shall confine myself to the most general ideas at the base of the whole development of science. I mean the concepts of Speculation and of Scholarship, and the various notions of the Order of Nature, and of Nature itself. In short, my topic is 'Cosmologies, Ancient and Modern', together with the variety of methods, speculative and scholarly, employed in their production. Special developments of learning will only be cited in order to exemplify the specializations of general ideas amid changing epochs of Western Culture.

Modern Europe and America have derived their civilization from the races whose countries border the Eastern Mediterranean. In the earlier chapters, Greece and Palestine were the regions providing the initial formulations of the ideas concerning the essence of human nature. When we examine the history of science, to these two countries we must add Egypt. These three countries are the direct ancestors of our modern civilization.

Of course there is a long tale of civilization behind them. Mesopotamia, Crete, Phœnicia, and India, China, also contributed. But whatever of scientific or religious value has passed into modern life, finally reached us through the mediation of these three countries, Egypt, Greece, Palestine. Of these countries, Egypt provided the mature technology, arising from three thousand years of secure civilization, Palestine provided the final religious cosmology, Greece provided the clear-cut generalizations leading to philosophy and science. This logical lucidity also tinges the remaining legacy from Greece, its art and imaginative literature. Every Greek statue expresses the welding of beauty to regularity of geometrical form: every Greek play investigates the interweaving of physical circumstances arising from the Order of Nature with states of mind which issue from the urge of the Moral Order.

'Canst thou by searching find out God?' is good Hebrew, but it is bad Greek. The effort to comprehend the great fact which procures the order in the Universe urged Greek thinkers to that culmination when Plato and Aristotle defined the complex of general ideas forming the imperishable origin of Western thought. The work was only accomplished just in time. In the very lifetime of Aristotle the political and cultural barriers collapsed; and the subsequent Hellenistic development at Alexandria and elsewhere was the joint enterprise of Greeks, Egyptians, Semites, and the mixed races of Syria and Asia Minor. The untroubled faith in lucidity within the depths of things, to be captured by some happy glance of speculation, was lost forever. Duller men were content with limited accuracy and constructed special sciences: thicker intellects gloried in the notion that the foundations of the world were laid amid impenetrable fog. They conceived God in their own image, and depicted him with a positive dislike of efforts after understanding beyond assigned methodologies. Satan acquired an intellectual character, and fell by reason of an indecent desire to understand his Creator. It was the downfall of Greece.

SECTION II. The progress of mankind proceeds by devious paths. The shift from the bright Hellenic age, whose final period was centred in Athens, to the Hellenistic age, with Alexandria as its intellectual capital, corresponds to a new direction of constructive genius. The special sciences were founded. Their principles were defined, their methods were determined, appropriate deductions were elicited. Learning was stabilized. It was furnished with methodologies, and was handed over to University professors of the modern type. Doctors of Medicine, Mathematicians, Astronomers, Grammarians, Theologians, for more than six hundred years dominated the schools of Alexandria, issuing text-books, treatises, controversies, and dogmatic definitions. Literature was replaced by Grammar, and Speculation by the Learned Tradition.

These men conventionalized learning. But they secured it. Their work survived two great religious revolutions, the rise of Christianity, and the rise of Mahometanism. It provided both these religions with their philosophical theologies. It fitted them out with heresies and with orthodoxies.

In the Western Roman Empire, the Christian Church. armed with Hellenistic thought, captured the intellects of the victorious barbarians and civilized Western Europe up to the Arctic Ocean. Along the south of the Mediterranean the Mahometan conquerors carried Hellenistic thought, as coloured by the mentalities of Arabs, Jews, and Persians, through Africa into Spain. From Spain, the Mahometan and Jewish versions made contact with the Christian version of Alexandrian culture. This fusion produced the brilliant culmination of Christian Scholasticism in the thirteenth century; and, in the seventeenth century, Spinoza.

The note of Hellenism is delight, speculation, discoursive literature: the note of Hellenistic Alexandria is concentration, thoroughness, investigation of the special types of order appertaining to special topics. The great Alexandrians were either right or wrong: Euclid either did, or did not make his text-book of Geometry logically coherent: the Ptolemaic doctrine of the heavens is true or false: Athanasius is directly opposed to Arius: and Cyril to Nestorius. The nearest analogues to the Alexandrian theological debates are the modern debates among mathematical physicists on the nature of the atom. The special topics differ slightly; but the methods and the men are identical.

It is unmeaning bluntly to ask of Plato, whether he be right or wrong. in the same exact sense in which we frame the question about the Alexandrians. When any eminent scholar has converted Plato into a respectable professor, by providing him with a coherent system, we quickly find that Plato in a series of Dialogues has written up most of the heresies from his own doctrines. It is as though Ptolemy had emitted the speculations of Aristarchus, and as though Athanasius had suggested the profanities of Arius.

1 am not alluding to the mere fact that men change their opinions, with the advance of age, or with the advance or decay of knowledge. The important point is the way in which opinions are held, and the weight attached to particular modes of statement. St. Augustine changed his opinions. He not only published for all ages the tragic intensity of feeling which the conversion involved, but also he devoted himself to exact statements of his new doctrines. He remained a Platonist, and his interest in the doctrine of Grace was a Platonic interest in the exact expression how finite human life can participate in the Divine Perfections. He performed an immense service to civilization by providing Western Europe with accurate definitions on great topics just before the oncoming of the Barbarians. He secured that western Christianity should persist as a civilizing influence, and not degenerate into hereditary superstition of the Abyssinian type. But his attitude to his own doctrines was very different from that of Plato. Consider some of Plato's phrases about his own ideas: "If, then, Socrates, we find ourselves in many points unable to make our discourse of the generation of gods and the universe in every way wholly consistent and exact, you must not be surprised. Nay, we must be well content if we can provide an account not less likely than another's; we must remember that I who speak, and you who are

my audience, are but men and should be satisfied to ask for no more than the likely story."[1]

Again: —"Perhaps they may be in a difficulty; and if this is the case, there is a possibility that they may accept a suggestion of ours respecting the nature of essence, having nothing of their own to offer."[2]

Can we imagine Augustine urbanely approaching Pelagius with 'a suggestion of ours respecting the nature of Grace?' It is quite true that passages can be quoted from Plato, more particularly from *The Laws,* which would justify all the persecution of atheists that has disgraced Europe. But the passages quoted above give the general tone of the *Dialogues,* in their handling of the precise expression of speculative notions.

SECTION III. In many ways Aristotle and Epicurus foreshadow the transition from Hellenic speculation to the exact scholarship of Alexandria. In both of them we find an effort towards system, explicitly stated and exactly phrased. Of course, Lucretius is our main authority for the Epicurean doctrines.

If we merely knew that great schools of exact scientific investigation had arisen in the succeeding generation, undoubtedly modem critical scholarship would have assigned to Aristotle's influence the honour of their origination. We can imagine the contrast which would have been drawn between the barrenness of mere speculation and the fruitfulness of Aristotle's power of detailed observation.

Unfortunately, cold fact points in exactly the opposite direction. In the first place Aristotle himself derived his own sources of thought from Plato's theoretical activity. He dissected fishes with Plato's thoughts in his head. He systematized the welter of Platonic suggestions, and in the course of his work he modified, improved, and spoilt. But he did introduce into sciences other

1. The *Timæus,* A. E. Taylor's translation.
2. The *Sophia,* Jowett's translation.

than Astronomy the much-needed systematic practice of passing beyond theory to direct observation of details. Unfortunately this was the one aspect of his life which never had any direct influence on any succeeding epoch.

Again, in point of fact the Alexandrian culture derived directly from Plato. Its thought was through and through Platonic both in science and theology. But it was not for nothing that Alexandria was situated in a land of old, secure technology. There were crafts and learned professions with traditions of detailed procedure stretching back for thousands of years. The schools of Alexandria were thronged with sons of priests, sons of metallurgists, sons of makers of implements for irrigation and agriculture, sons of land-surveyors. It is no wonder that the first emergence of modern scholarship studied in a modern university, took place when Platonic speculation was transferred to a land of old professional activity.

Undoubtedly the chasm between Hellenic mentality and mediæval scholastic learning was due to many influences accumulating their effects through a period of a thousand years. But the greatest gap in the transition is the first one, when the capital of Mediterranean learning was transferred from Athens to Alexandria. The general type of the cultural development of Western Civilization was then predetermined. How science should be developed: How mathematics should evolve: How religion, Jewish, Christian, Mahometan, should shape its various theologies. The modern world is primarily Alexandrian; and only for a short period of about a hundred years, to be placed somewhere between the Council of Constance and the Sack of Rome in 1527, did the Athenian tone of mind prevail: perhaps also earlier in the Italy of the Augustan epoch. The difference between the two, namely the Hellenic and the Hellenistic types of mentality, may be roughly described as that between speculation and scholarship. For progress, both are necessary. But, in fact, on the stage of history they are apt to appear as antagonists. Speculation, by entertaining alternative theories, is superficially sceptical, disturbing to established modes of prejudice. But it obtains its urge from a deep ultimate faith, that through and through the nature of things is penetrable by reason. Scholarship, by its strict attention to accepted methodologies, is superficially conservative of belief. But its tone of mind leans towards a fundamental negation. For scholars the reasonable topics m the world are penned in isolated regions, *this* subject-matter or *that* subject-matter. Your thoroughgoing scholar resents the airy speculation which connects his own patch of knowledge with that of his neighbour. He finds his fundamental concepts interpreted, twisted, modified. He has ceased to be king of his own castle, by reason of speculations of uncomfortable generality, violating the very grammar of his thoughts. Pope Adrian the Sixth exhibited himself as a typical scholar by remarking that in Luther's theological works so many errors could be found that any tyro could point them out.

New directions of thought arise from flashes of intuition bringing new material within the scope of scholarly learning. They commence as the sheer ventures of rash speculation. They may fortunately obtain quick acceptance, or they may initiate a quarrel of scholars from which all tinge of speculation has faded. Pope Leo the Tenth voiced the vanishing Athenian epoch when he characterized the Lutheran disputes as a quarrel of monks.

Pure speculation, undisciplined by the scholarship of detailed fact or the scholarship of exact logic, is on the whole more useless than pure scholarship, unrelieved by speculation. The proper balance of the two factors in progressive learning depends on the character of the epoch in question and on the capacities of particular individuals. Also it is a curious fact, somewhat lost sight of in Greek thought, that, notwithstanding the law of the Golden Mean between contrasted components, yet a certain excessiveness seems a necessary element in all greatness. In some direction or other we must devote ourselves beyond what would be warranted by the analysis of pure reason.

One aspect of the adventure of ideas is this story of the interplay of speculation and scholarship, a strife sustained through the ages of progress. This history discloses the happy balance attained in periods of culminating greatness, and it also exhibits the tinge of excessiveness in all such peaks of achievement. Thereby it gives the reason for the tragic transience of supreme moments in human life.

SECTION IV. The notion of Law, that is to say, of some measure of regularity or of persistence or of recurrence, is an essential element in the urge towards technology, methodology, scholarship, and speculation. Apart from a certain smoothness in the nature of things, there can be no knowledge, no useful method, no intelligent purpose. Lacking an element of Law, there remains a mere welter of details with no foothold for comparison with any other such welter, in the past, in the future, or circumambient in the present. But the expression of this notion of Law with due accuracy, and with due regard to what in fact is presupposed in human purposes, is a matter of extreme difficulty. Analogously to the histories of all the more general ideas, the notion of Law has entered into the explicit consciousness of various epochs under every variety of specialization, arising from its coalescence with other components in the popular cosmology.

The difficulty in all such notions of supreme generality is that conscious attention is not naturally directed to any factor which is a 'matter of course' in experience. Attention is rivetted upon 'news', and 'news' involves some aroma of capriciousness. It is useless to recur to periods of human history which lie beyond the reach of direct evidence. But anthropologists report the almost universal prevalence of tribal ceremonies having reference to the succession of the yearly seasons, more particularly to the Spring, the Harvest, and Mid-winter. Undoubtedly, as we view them now, there is a reference to agriculture in such celebrations. Now agriculture marks the first decisive step towards modern civilization. Its introduction marks the arrival of a stage of high grade reflection upon the course of events. It requires a forecast of the course of nature months ahead. Many an ape-man must have snatched up a stone wherewith to hit somebody, either another man or other animal, on the head, without any reflection upon the course of nature beyond the next few minutes. Also he might notice that some stones are better than others as lethal weapons, and he might even help them out by chipping them. He is then approaching civilization. But he—or more probably, she—has crossed the great divide, when he puts seeds into a patch of earth and waits for a season.

It is obvious that seasonal ceremonies must extend backwards in time far beyond the introduction of agriculture. The differences between the seasons impose differences of behaviour upon all living things, vegetables and animals alike. The seasonal urge towards change of habit, hibernation or migration, must have begotten some expression of emotional restlessness. The interest of agriculture comes in when we consider the later interpretation of the seasonal ceremonies in which the tribe had been indulging for countless ages. Civilization did not start with a social contract determining modes of behaviour. Its earliest effort was the slow introduction of ideas explanatory of modes of behaviour and of inrushes of emotion which already dominated their lives. Undoubtedly ideas modified the practice. But in the main practice precedes thought; and thought is mainly concerned with the justification or the modification of a pre-existing situation.

Now, apart from the practice of agriculture, animal habits are mainly based on the massive recurrence of the seasons, heat and frost, rain and drought, day and night. There was stolid recurrent matter of fact, with accompanying rhythms of emotion and ritual. Vagrant questions may have disturbed exceptional minds. But there was little to provoke tribal interest in explanation. There must have been some instances to provoke attention, because there was, in fact, among some tribes of our ancestors, a drift towards better ways of life. But I am seeking to determine the dividing line after which the curiously quick acceleration of civilized thought may conceivably have arisen. In the earlier stage the convenient unit of time is of the order of a hundred thousand years. In the later phases it shortens up to ten thousand years, to five thousand years, to one thousand years, to a hundred years.

Probably there was a concurrence of many causes. But among such causes the introduction of agriculture must be given a high place for its effectiveness in quickening progress. It at once introduced the capriciousness of the weather as a major topic of tribal interest. Also it provoked attention to the mystery of germination, and to the dependence of vegetable growth upon the seasonal phases. It compelled the tribe to descend from passive acquiescence in a general matter of course towards active interest in the details. It led to a serach for precautions. and discovery requires understanding. Of course, as we all know, the novel situation did not require every tribe to advance. Also the masses of mankind are always liable to reach some stable level of custom, and to halt progress there. But human life had then reached a stage at which obvious problems were presented to the more active minds, wherever such existed.

We inherit legends, weird, horrible, beautiful, expressing in curious, specialized ways the interweaving of law and capriciousness in the mystery of things. It is the problem of good and evil. Sometimes the law is good and the capriciousness evil; sometimes the law is iron and evil and the capriciousness is merciful and good. But from savage legends up to Hume's civilized Dialogues on Natural religion, with the conversation between Job and his friends as an intermediate between the two, the same problem is discussed. Science and technology are based upon law. Human behaviour exhibits custom mitigated by impulse. What exactly do we mean by the notion of the Laws of Nature?

SECTION V. At the present time, there are prevalent four main doctrines concerning the Laws of Nature: the doctrine of Law as immanent, the doctrine of Law as imposed, and the doctrine of Law as observed order of succession, in other words, Law as mere description, and lastly the later doctrine of Law as conventional interpretation. It will be convenient first to discuss these four alternative doctrines from the standpoint of today. We shall then be in a better position to understand the chequered history of the notion in civilized thought.

By the doctrine of Law as immanent it is meant that the order of nature expresses the characters of the real things which jointly compose the existences to be found in nature. When we understand the essences of these things, we thereby know their mutual relations to each other. Thus, according as there are common elements in their various characters, there will necessarily be corresponding identities in their mutual relations. In other words, some partial identity of pattern in the various characters of natural things issues in some partial identity of pattern in the mutual relations of those things. These identities of pattern in the mutual relations are the Laws of Nature. Conversely, a Law is explanatory of some community in character pervading the things which constitute Nature. It is evident that the doctrine involves the negation of 'absolute being.' It presupposes the essential interdependence of things.

There are some consequences to this doctrine. In the first place, it follows that scientists are seeking for explanations and not merely for simplified descriptions of their observations. In the second place the exact conformation of nature to any law is not to be expected. If all the things concerned have the requisite common character, then the pattern of mutual relevance which expresses that character will be exactly illustrated. But in general we may expect that a large proportion of things do possess the requisite character and a minority do not possess it. In such a case, the mutual relations of these things will exhibit lapses when the law fails to obtain illustration. In so far as we are merely interested in a confused result of many instances, then the law can be said to have a statistical character. It is now the opinion of physicists that most of the laws of physics, as known in the nineteenth century, are of this character.

Thirdly, since the laws of nature depend on the individual characters of the things constituting nature, as the things change, then correspondingly the laws will change. Thus the modern evolutionary view of the physical universe should conceive of the laws of nature as evolving concurrently with the things constituting the environment. Thus the conception of the Universe as evolving subject to fixed, eternal laws regulating all behaviour should be abandoned. Fourthly, a reason can now be produced why we should put some limited trust in induction. For if we assume an environment largely composed of a sort of existences whose natures we partly understand, then we have some knowledge of the laws of nature dominating that environment. But apart from that premise and apart from the doctrine of immanent Law, we can have no knowledge of the future. We should then acknowledge blank ignorance, and not make pretences about probability.

Fifthly, the doctrine of Immanent Law is untenable unless we can construct a plausible metaphysical doctrine according to which the characters of the relevant things in nature are the outcome of their interconnections, and their interconnections are the outcome of their characters. This involves some doctrine of Internal Relations.

Finally, the doctrine of Immanence is through and through a rationalistic doctrine. It is explanatory of the possibility of understanding nature.

SECTION VI. The doctrine of Imposed Law adopts the alternative metaphysical doctrine of External Relations between the existences which are the ultimate constituents of nature. The character of each of these ultimate things is thus conceived as its own private qualification. Such an existent is understandable in complete disconnection from any other such existent: the ultimate truth is that it requires nothing but itself in order to exist. But in fact there is imposed on each such existent the necessity of entering into relationships with the other ultimate constituents of nature. These imposed behaviour patterns are the Laws of Nature. But you cannot discover the natures of the relata by any study of the Laws of their relations. Nor, conversely, can you discover the laws by inspection of the natures.

The explanation of the doctrine of Imposition both suggests a certain type of Deism, and conversely it is the outcome of such a Deistic belief if already entertained. For example, we know from Newton's own statements that this was exactly how the Deistic problem presented itself to him. He definitely stated that the correlated modes of behaviour of the bodies forming the solar system required God for the imposition of the principles on which all depended. He was certainly doubtful, indeed more than doubtful, as to whether the Law of Gravity was the ultimate statement of principles imposed by God. But he certainly thought that the conception of the solar system exhibited in his Principia was sufficiently ultimate to make obvious the necessity of a God imposing Law. Newton was certainly right to this extent, that the whole doctrine of Imposition is without interest apart from the correlative doctrine of a transcendant imposing Deity. This is also a Cartesian doctrine.

The doctrine of Imposition very naturally follows from Descartes' notion of 'substance'. Indeed the phrase "requiring nothing but itself in order to exist" occurs in his *Principles of Philosophy.* The whole Cartesian apparatus of Deism, substantial materialism, and imposed law, in conjunction with the reduction of physical relations to the notion of correlated motions with mere spatio-temporal character, constitutes the simplified notion of Nature with which Galileo, Descartes, and Newton finally launched modern science on its triumphant career. If success be a guarantee of truth, no other system of thought has enjoyed a tithe of such success since mankind started on its job of thinking. Within three hundred years it has transformed human life, in its intimate thoughts, its technologies, its social behaviour, and its ambitions.

It follows from the Deism, which is part of the whole conception, that the Laws of Nature will be exactly obeyed. Certainly, what God meant he did. When he said, Let there be light, there was *light* and not a mere imitation or a statistical average. Thus the statistical notion, though it may explain some facts of our confused perception, is not applicable to the ultimate, imposed laws.

But even before Descartes, it was the implicit belief in some form of imposition, with its consequent exactness, that constituted the motive force in scientific research. Why should educated men have believed that there was anything to find out? Suppose that the doctrine of immanence had prevailed in Europe and in Mahometan Asia. Why should men assume that there were definite laws which even beyond the limits of meticulous observation underlie the apparent capriciousness of physical details? There are certain grand obvious uniformities, Day follows Night, and again relapses into Night, the Mountains endure, and Birth proceeds. But these grand regularities are shot through and through with details apparently capricious. The very savages saw that. and tremblingly worshipped malignant demons. But civilized men. who understand the doctrine of immanence, should draw the conclusion that the dominance of common traits of character throughout the constituents of nature is only very partial. There is no reason why it should be otherwise. A restless search for detailed explanation is futile, based upon no approach to probability. If in the past men had believed thus, today there would be no science. And even today, how little do we know about physiology. Also an individual electron is a rare bird whose behaviour is unpredictable: our information about electrons mostly concerns flocks numbering millions. What reason is there to expect success if we seek to push the reign of law one step further towards minute detail? Indeed, physicists in their recent researches have disclosed a novel illustration of capriciousness. These men, trained in the Positivist doctrine, have at once suggested the uselessness of further search for 'law'. Unless the psychology of mental behaviour still include some traces derived from the notion of Deistic imposition, even today the progress of science would cease by reason of the failure of hope. A considerable proportion of present-day philosophy is devoted to the endeavour by means of subtle argument to evade this plain inexorable conclusion.

Lastly apart from some notion of imposed Law, the doctrine of immanence provides absolutely no reason why the universe should not be steadily relapsing into lawless chaos. In fact, the Universe, as understood in accordance with the doctrine of Immanence, should exhibit itself as including a stable actuality whose mutual implication with the remainder of things secures an inevitable trend towards order. The Platonic 'persuasion' is required.

SECTION VII. Of the three earlier theories, there remains the Positivist doctrine concerning Law, namely, that a Law of Nature is merely an observed persistence of pattern in the observed succession of natural things: Law is then merely Description. There is an attractive simplicity about this doctrine. The two preceding doctrines lead us to the dubieties of metaphysics, such as the doctrine of internal relations or the existence and nature of God. But this third doctrine evades all such difficulties.

It presupposes that we have direct acquaintance with a succession of things. This acquaintance is analysable into a succession of things observed. But our direct acquaintance consists not only in distinct observations of the distinct things in succession, but also it includes a comparative knowledge of the successive observations. Acquaintance is thus cumulative and comparative. The laws of nature are nothing else than the observed identities of pattern persisting throughout the series of comparative observations. Thus a law of nature says something about things observed and nothing more.

The pre-occupation of science is then the search for simple statements which in their joint effect will express everything of interest concerning the observed recurrences. This is the whole tale of science, *that* and nothing more. It is the great Positivist doctrine, largely developed in the first half of the nineteenth century, and ever since growing in influence. It tells us to keep to things observed, and to describe them as simply as we can. This is all we can know. Laws are statements of observed facts. This doctrine dates back to Epicurus, and embodies his appeal to the plain man, away from metaphysics and mathematics. The observed facts of clear experience are understandable, and nothing else. Also 'understanding' means 'simplicity of description.'

Without doubt this Positivist doctrine contains a fundamental truth about scientific methodology. For example, consider the greatest of all scientific generalizations, Newton's Law of Gravitation: —Two particles of matter attract each other with a force directly proportional to the product of their masses and inversely proportional to the square of their distance. The notion of 'force' refers to the notion of the addition of a component to the vector acceleration of either particle. It also refers to the notion of the masses of the particles. Again the notion of mass is also explicitly referred to in the statement. Thus the mutual spatial relations of the particles, and their individual masses, are required for the Law. To this extent the Law is an expression of the presumed characters of the particles concerned. But the form of the Law, namely the product of the masses and the inverse square of the distance, is purely based upon description of observed fact. A large part of Newton's *Principia* is devoted to a mathematical investigation proving that the description is adequate for his purposes; it collects many details under one principle. Newton himself insisted upon this very point. He was not speculating: he was not explaining. Whatever your cosmological doctrines may be, the motions of the planets and the fall of the stones, so far as they have been directly measured, conform to his Law. He is enunciating a formula which expresses observed correlations of observed facts.

Without the shadow of a doubt, all science bases itself upon this procedure. It is the first rule of scientific method,—Enunciate observed correlations of observed fact. This is the great Baconian doctrine, namely, Observe and observe, until finally you detect a regularity of sequence. The scholastics had trusted to metaphysical dialectic giving them secure knowledge about the nature of things, including the physical world, the spiritual world, and the existence of God. Thence they deduced the various laws. immanent and imposed, which reigned throughout Nature.

Another difference between Scholasticism and the Moderns is in respect to criticism and reliance upon authority. But this distinction has been overstressed and misunderstood. The Scholastics were intensely critical, but they were critical within a different sphere of thought from that occupying the Moderns. Again modern scientists rely upon authority, but they rely upon different authorities from those to whom the Scholastics appealed. Undoubtedly the later Scholastics were uncritical in their appeal to their chosen authority, Aristotle, especially and most unfortunately in regard to his physics. The moderns push their criticism further. But the Scholastics and the modern Scientists are alike scholars of the Alexandrian type. They have the same sort of merit and the same sort of defect. Also, the sort of person who was a scholastic doctor in a mediaeval university, today is a scientific professor in a modern university. Again the Scholastics differed among themselves in opinion widely. The earlier set were not even Aristotelians, the later set were not all Thomists. Analogously, modern scientists differ among themselves, about details and about the general doctrine of the Laws of Nature.

Within the sphere of dialectic debate, the Scholastics were supremely critical. They trusted Aristotle because they could derive from him a coherent system of thought. It was a criticized trust. Unfortunately,—they did not reflect that some of his main ideas depended upon his direct acquaintance with experienced fact. They trusted to the logical coherence of the system as a guarantee of the unrestricted relevance of his primary notions. They thus accepted his confusion—when there was confusion—of superficial aspects with fundamental principles of widest generality. Their method for the furtherance of natural knowledge was endless debate, unrelieved by recurrence to direct observation. Unfortunately also their instrument of debate, Aristotelian Logic, was a more superficial weapon than they deemed it. Automatically it kept in the background some of the more fundamental topics for thought. Such topics are the quantitative relations examined in mathematics, and the complex possibilities of multiple relationship within a system. All these topics, and others, were kept in the background by Aristotelian logic.

Fortunately the scholastic age of Alexandrian scholarship dominated Europe for centuries, and bestowed upon civilization priceless treasures of thought. It was an age of immense progress. But a scholarly age works within rigid limitations. Fortunately, a revival of Hellenism overwhelmed the Hellenistic unity of the Middle Age. Plato arose as if from his tomb. Vagrant speculation and direct observation broke up the scholarly system. New interests, new Gods, prevailed. The new basis for thought was the report upon facts, directly observed, directly employed. Fortunately, in the subsidence of the Italian Renaissance of the fifteenth century, the drama of the transference of culture from Athens to Alexandria was again repeated. Europe gradually entered upon a new scholarly age. The modern historian appeared, the modern critical literature appeared, the modern man of science appeared, modern technology appeared. The old Egyptian metallurgists, the Semitic mathematicians and the mediaeval scholastics were avenged.

But modern scholarship and modern science reproduce the same limitations as dominated the bygone Hellenistic epoch, and the bygone Scholastic epoch. They canalize thought and observation within predetermined limits, based upon inadequate metaphysical assumptions dogmatically assumed. The modern assumptions differ from older assumptions, not wholly for the better. They exclude from rationalistic thought more of the final values of existence. The intimate timidity of professionalized scholarship circumscribes reason by reducing its topics to triviality, for example, to bare sensa and to tautologies. It then frees itself from criticism by dogmatically handing over the remainder of experience to an animal faith or a religious mysticism, incapable of rationalization. The world will again sink into the boredom of a drab detail of rational thought, unless we retain in the sky some reflection of light from the sun of Hellenism.

Chapter VIII

COSMOLOGIES

Section I. At the close of the previous chapter we were left with four antagonistic schools of thought regarding the analysis of the notion of Law, The School of Immanence, The School of Imposition, The Positivist School of Observation, that is to say, of mere Description, and finally the School of Conventional Interpretation. We find that each of these schools could produce grave reasons in confirmation of its own doctrine.

There is no greater hindrance to the progress of thought than an attitude of irritated party-spirit. Urbanity, the urbanity of Plato and, if we may trust his *Dialogues,* the urbanity of Athenian society, were part of the intellectual genius of those times. The vicious antagonisms of subsequent theologians, some centuries later, hid from them considerations which they ought never to have forgotten, and have hidden from us the metaphysical genius of their own contributions to thought.

We will recommence by scanning the history of these doctrines of Natural Law, with the view of determining their exact points of divergence, and the measure of conciliation of which they are capable. In the previous chapter Plato's urbane preface to a philosophical suggestion was quoted. The suggestion itself is now relevant to the present lecture:—

"My suggestion would be, that anything which possesses any sort of power to affect another, or to be affected by another even for a moment, however trifling the cause and however slight and momentary the effect, has real existence; and I hold that the definition of being is simply power."[1]

In the subsequent conduct of the dialogue Plato rises to the height of his genius as a metaphysician. But he also wrestles with the difficulty of making language express anything beyond the familiarities of daily life. It is misleading to study the history of ideas without constant remembrance of the struggle of novel thought with the obtuseness of language.

Also it is interesting to notice that, according to Plato, the distinguishing mark of the Philosopher in contrast to the Sophist is his resolute attempt to reconcile conflicting doctrines, each with its own solid ground of support. In the history of ideas the doctrine *of* Speculation is at least as important as the doctrines *for* Speculation.

SECTION II. But, to return to Plato's suggestion—"and I hold that the definition of being is simply power."

This statement can be construed in terms of the notion of imposed law, namely, that it is an external imposition on each existent, that it be correlated with determinate causal action on other such existents. But such an interpretation neglects the exact wording, Plato says that it is the *definition* of being that it exert power and be subject to the exertion of power. This means that the essence of being is to be implicated in causal action on other beings. It is the doctrine of Law as immanent. Further, a few sentences later he proceeds: —"... being, as being known, is acted on by knowledge, and is therefore in motion, for that which is in a state of rest cannot be acted upon as we affirm… Can we imagine being to be devoid of life and mind, and to remain in awful unmeaningness an everlasting fixture?"

Notice that in this argument, that which is not acted upon is a fixture. Plato denies that being can be conceived "in awful

1. *Sophist*, 247, Jowett's translation.

unmeaningness an everlasting fixture." It is therefore acted upon. This agrees with his primary definition, that 'being' is the agent in action, and the recipient of action. Thus, in these passages Plato enunciates the doctrine that 'action and reaction' belong to the essence of being: though the mediation of 'life and mind' is invoked to provide the medium of activity. This notion of a medium, connecting the eternality of being with the fluency of becoming, takes many shapes in Plato's *Dialogues.* Very probably, indeed almost certainly, passages inconsistent with this doctrine can be found in the *Dialogues.* For the moment, the interesting fact is that in these passages in this Dialogue we find a clear enunciation of the doctrine of Law as immanent.

The early, naïve trend of Semitic monotheism, Jewish and Mahometan, is towards the notion of Law imposed by the fiat of the One God. Subsequent speculation wavers between these two extremes, seeking their reconciliation. In this, as in most other matters, the history of Western thought consists in the attempted fusion of ideas which in their origin are predominantly Semitic. The modern scholar, with his tinge of speculation, is an Egyptian employing his wisdom upon his Hellenic and Semitic heritage.

In this instance, the extremes of the two doctrines of Law lead on the one hand to the extreme monotheistic doctrine of God, as essentially transcendent and only accidentally immanent, and on the other hand to the pantheistic doctrine of God, as essentially immanent and in no way transcendent.

Plato in the *Timæus* affords an early instance of this wavering between the two doctrines of Law, Immanence and Imposition. In the first place, Plato's cosmology includes an ultimate creator, shadowy and undefined, imposing his design upon the Universe. Secondly, the action and reaction of the internal constituents is—for Plato—the self-sufficient explanation of the flux of the world:—"Nothing was given off from it, nothing entered it,—there was nothing but itself."

We have here been examining the basic notion of the initial cosmology which dominated the world, Pagan, Christian, and Mahometan, before the rise of the modern period. It was modified by Aristotle, by the Alexandrians, by the Scholastics. But this fusion of the doctrines of Imposition and Immanence, with adjustments this way or that way, is the great conception which reigned supreme till the beginning of the seventeenth century.

SECTION III. But Greek thought provided a rival cosmology, in the shape of the Atomic theory, as adumbrated by Democritus, systematized by Epicurus, and as finally explained in Epic shape by Lucretius. According to Lucretius the world is an interminable shower of atomic particles, streaming through space, swerving, intermingling, disentangling their paths, recombining them. For this doctrine qualitative differences are merely the statistical expression of geometrical patterns of intermingled paths, the outcome of swerving, combined with a finite number of diversities of shape.

Plato and Lucretius both appeal to geometry, Plato to the regular solids, and Lucretius to the shapes of paths, and unspecified shapes of atoms. In this respect, their general attitude has been sustained by modern science. It seems necessary however for Epicurus to treat space and motion with the metaphysical naïvete exhibited later in Newton's *Principia.* Plato's doctrine of space, as stated in the *Timæus,* has a superior metaphysical subtlety; although the Platonic doctrine of a Receptacle, intrinsically devoid of any geometrical form, has some analogy to the doctrine of the 'Void' in Lucretius. It is probable however that if Lucretius had possessed the penetration to explain Epicurus further, he would have found it necessary to endow his Void with exactly those geometrical forms which Plato denied to his Receptacle considered in abstraction, and which Aristotle denied to his Matter in abstraction.

Plato's cosmology tends to a fusion of the doctrines of Imposition and Immanence; the Atomic Theory of Epicurus lends itself most readily to a fusion of the doctrines of Imposition and of Description.

The reason for this distinction between the two cosmologies is that for Plato behaviour is a function of the various characters of the things concerned—the intelligent activities of indwelling souls, and the geometric necessities of the indwelling shapes. But for Epicurus the paths of the atoms are derived from no necessities of their natures. It is intrinsic to their natures that they partake of spatial relations and are moveable. But the special path of a special atom seems to be a fact entirely extrinsic to its nature. The modern wave-theory of the atom sides with Plato rather than with Democritus: Newtonian dynamics sides with Democritus against Plato. Some passages of Lucretius surreptitiously introduce the doctrine of immanence. What Lucretius mainly cared about was the reign of law as opposed to the capricious intervention of demons and gods, to be coaxed by superstition.

As to the paths of the atoms, two views are possible. One theory can conceive them as imposed, and imposition requires a trancendent God as imposer. This is practically the cosmology adopted by Newton. The Newtonian forces, whatever their ultimate mathematical formulation, are nothing else than the imposed conditions provided by God. This point of view was the working formula of the eighteenth century. God made his appearance in religion under the frigid title of the First Cause, and was appropriately worshipped in white-washed churches.

Another theory as to the paths can be adopted by the Positivist School of Mere Description. For this reason, the atomic theory, of the Lucretian type, has always been a favorite first principle of cosmology with this School of Thought. The paths of the molecules can be ascribed to mere chance. They are random distributions, each path being entirely disconnected from any other path, and each continuation of one path being unconditioned by the earlier portion of the same path.

Thus the world, as we know it, exhibits for our confused perception an involution of paths and a concatenation of circumstances which have arisen entirely by chance. We can describe what has happened, but with that description all possibility of knowledge ends.

Lucretius wavers between the notion of imposed law and the notion of chance. For example: —"This point too we wish you to apprehend: when bodies are borne downwards sheer through void by their own weights, at quite uncertain times and uncertain spots they push themselves a little from their course: you just and only just can call it a change of inclination. If they were not used to swerve, they would all fall down, like drops of rain, through the deep void, and no clashing would have been begotten nor blow produced among the first-beginnings [i.e. the atoms]: thus nature never would have produced aught."[2]

But he rigidly limits his suggestion of chance:—[3]

"But lest you haply suppose that living things alone are bound by these conditions, such a law keeps all things within their limits."

The objection to the extreme Positivist doctrine at once suggests itself, that the enormous aspect of regular evolution through vast regions embracing the remotest star-galaxies, and through vast periods of time, is an unlikely product of mere chance.

There are two answers to this objection. In the first place, there is plenty of time and plenty of space. We are dealing with all space, from infinity to infinity, we are dealing with all time from eternity to eternity, and we are dealing with the unbounded wealth of all existence, to be comprehended in terms of no finite number. In any finite region of space and time, with its finite cargo of atoms, any pre-conceived arrangement of paths, however simple or however complex, is equally unlikely, indeed there is an infinite probability against it. But we are not dealing with a pre-conceived concept,

2. Book II, lines 216-224. Translated by H. A. J. Monro, published separately in Bohn's series, by G. Bell and Sons, Ltd.: Cf. also Cyril Bailey's translation, *Lucretius on the Nature of Things*, Oxford University Press, 1929.

3. Cf. Book II, lines 718, 719.

we observe what in fact is the case in a limited region. Something must be the case, and what we have observed is what in fact has been the case. There is nothing pre-conceived, and thus there is no question of infinite improbability. It is true that expectations float through our minds, but they are vague memories of what in fact has happened, combined with suggestions as to the more detailed analysis of past fact. The fact in the past is neither probable nor improbable, it is what in fact took place within the ambit of our observation.

The second answer takes the same point of view as that derived from the doctrine of immanence. There is no need—indeed there is not the slightest reason—to exaggerate the order in the spatio-temporal region under our observation. In the remote regions and epochs we have only intelligence of very general aspects of order. That is all we know. In the present epoch we have more detail, but our observation is rough, inaccurate, and sporadic. Again, that is all we know. We must not ascribe, we must not expect, one step beyond our direct knowledge. The Positivist has no foothold on which he can rely for speculation beyond the region of direct observation.

SECTION IV. The great Positivist school of thought, whose epic is the poem of Lucretius, at the present time reigns supreme in the domain of science. Its aim is to confine itself to fact, with a discard of all speculation. Unfortunately, among all the variant schools of opinion, it is the one which can least bear confrontation with the facts. It has never been acted on. It can never be acted on, for it gives no foothold for any forecast of the future around which purpose can weave itself.

But before confronting Positivism with the practice of mankind, it is interesting to note that atomism has taken on a new form of modern thought. Epistemology has arisen, in its function of a critic of all pretensions to knowledge. Today, the question, How do we know, takes precedence of the question,—What do we know.

Again, the doctrine of atomism reappears. The atomism of Democritus in the science of Cosmology is replaced by the atomism of Hume in the science of Epistemology. Epicurus enunciates the doctrine that the ultimate elements of the physical universe are physical atoms, showering through space with paths associated in complexes. Hume enunciates the doctrine that the ultimate elements, subjectively given in the activity of knowing, are the impressions of sensation, showering through the stream of experience, associated as memories, provocative of emotions and reflexions, and expectations. But for Hume, each impression is a distinct existence arising in soul from unknown causes. Epicurus bases himself upon an epistemology closely allied to that of Hume.

Positivism has seized on Hume's atomism, with Hume himself as its leader. The task of science is explained to be merely the formulation of observed identities of pattern persistent and recurrent in each stream of experience. But since Hume is dealing with subjective experience, he can add a corollary not open to the more objective doctrine of Epicurus. Hume adds that we expect the recurrences observed in the past, also to recur in the future. At this stage, Hotspur's question arises in our mind, "But will they come, when you do call for them?" To this question Hume, following the example of Glendower, returns no answer. It is an observed fact in the past that expected recurrences have recurred. But Positivistic science is solely concerned with observed fact, and must hazard no conjecture as to the future. If observed fact be all we know, then there is no other knowledge. Probability is relative to knowledge. There is no probability as to the future within the doctrine of Positivism.

Of course most men of science, and many philosophers, use the Positivistic doctrine to avoid the necessity of considering perplexing fundamental questions—in short, to avoid metaphysics—, and then save the importance of science by an implicit recurrence to their metaphysical persuasion that the past does in fact condition the future.

Indeed, as Hume pointed out, human life cannot be carried on without this persuasion. In this way the Positivistic doctrine of today bases itself on some form of atomism, objective or subjective, and deduces that the sole occupation of science is to elaborate simple descriptions of things observed.

There is a curious misconception that somehow the mathematical mysteries of Statistics help Positivism to evade its proper limitation to the observed past. But statistics tell you nothing about the future unless you make the assumption of the permanence of statistical form. For example, in order to use statistics for prediction, assumptions are wanted as to the stability of the mean, the mode, the probable error, and the symmetry or skewness of the statistical expression of functional correlation. Mathematics can tell you the consequences of your beliefs. For example, if your apple is composed of a finite number of atoms, mathematics will tell you that the number is odd or even. But you must not ask mathematics to provide you with the apple, the atoms, and the finiteness of their number. There is no valid inference from mere possibility to matter of fact, or, in other words, from mere mathematics to concrete nature.

SECTION V. It is now time to confront the Positivist doctrine with the facts of the History of Science. We want to discover the type of purpose exhibited in the practices of men of science. In order to avoid the suspicion of biased selection, consider the last discovery, which at the time of writing this chapter, has occupied a leading position in American newspapers. I mean the discovery of the new planet by the Lowell Observatory in Arizona. The final interpretation of this discovery is irrelevant: Nature, even in the act of satisfying anticipation, often provides a surprise. The story is typical of the previous discovery of Neptune, and of many discoveries of the faint members of double stars, and of the famous empirical term in the formula for the moon's motion.

The recent discovery is based upon the observed deviations of the orbits of the planets Uranus and Neptune from the calculated order. This calculation embraces the effect produced by all the previously known bodies of the solar system upon the motions of these two planets, assuming the Law of Gravitation. But their observed motions deviate slightly from their orbits as thus calculated. There is however no difficulty in producing a mathematical formula which describes the observed deviation. Such a formula will be of the most elementary mathematical character. It will consist of a few terms involving trigonometrical sines and cosines, with certain numerical components defining their periods, with other numerical components defining their amplitudes, and other numerical components defining their epochs—or in modern popular phraseology, their 'zero times'. Altogether a description of charming simplicity, which would have delighted Plato by its exemplification of his most daring speculations as to the future of mathematics.

Every Positivist must have been completely satisfied. A simple description had been evolved which fitted the observed facts. They could now relapse into their unexplained persuasion that in the future these formulæ would continue to describe the motions of Uranus and Neptune. Positivism had exhausted its message. But astronomers were not satisfied. They remembered the Law of Gravitation. Percy Lowell calculated the direction and magnitude of the vector component of acceleration, directed to an imaginary point moving round the sun in an elliptic path, even more remote than the orbit of Neptune. He succeeded in choosing his assumed path, so that the magnitude of the acceleration varies as the inverse square of the distance between Neptune and the moving point. A new description had been discovered, requiring some complex mathematics to connect it with the successive positions of Uranus, but conforming to the general form of Newton's Law. There has been a gain in generality, pleasing if you cherish a virtuosity in descriptions. But we have forgotten the main interest: —We have only got to look in the sky, towards Percy Lowell's moving point, and we shall see a new planet. Certainly we shall not. All that any person has seen is a few faint dots on photographic plates, involving the intervention of photography, excellent telescopes, elaborate apparatus, long exposures and favourable nights. The new explanation is now involved in the speculative extension of a welter of physical laws, concerning telescopes, light, and photography, laws which merely claim to register observed facts. It is involved in the speculative application of such laws to particular circumstances within the observatories, for which circumstances these laws are not concurrently verified. The result of this maze of speculative extensions is to connect the deviations of Uranus and Neptune with the dots on the photographic plates.

This narrative, framed according to the strictest requirements of the Positivist Theory, is a travesty of the plain facts. The civilized world has been interested at the thought of the newly discovered planet, solitary and remote, for endless ages circling the sun and adding its faint influence to the tide of affairs. At last it is discovered by human reason, penetrating into the nature of things and laying bare the necessities of their interconnection. The speculative extensions of laws, baseless on the Positivist theory, are the obvious issue of speculative metaphysical trust in the material permanences, such as telescopes, observatories, mountains, planets, which are behaving towards each other according to the necessities of the universe, including theories of their own natures. The point is, that speculative extension beyond direct observation spells some trust in metaphysics, however vaguely these metaphysical notions may be entertained in explicit thought. Our metaphysical knowledge is slight, superficial, incomplete. Thus errors creep in. But, such as it is, metaphysical understanding guides imagination and justifies purpose. Apart from metaphysical presupposition there can be no civilization.

There is a moral to be drawn as to the method of science. All scientific progress depends on first framing a formula giving a general description of observed fact. Lowell worked with such a formula in front of him, namely, the simple mathematical expression for the deviations. At one stage, the method of all discovery conforms to the Positivist doctrine. There can be no doubt that, with this restriction of meaning, the Positivist doctrine is correct.

Certain branches of science halt for centuries in this stage. Then their votaries embrace the unguarded Positivist doctrine. There is however a motive of unrest which urges scientists beyond mere satisfaction with the simple description, beyond even the *general,* description. It is the desire to obtain the *explanatory* description which may justify the speculative extension of Laws, beyond actual, particular instances of observation.

This urge towards explanatory description provides the interplay between science and metaphysics. The doctrines of metaphysics are modified, so as to be capable of providing the explanation, and the explanations of science are framed in terms of the popular metaphysics lingering in the imaginations of these scientists.

One aspect of the history of thought from the time of Plato to the present day is the struggle between metaphysicians and Positivists over the interpretation of the Laws of Nature. The Greeks, as distinguished from the Alexandrians, are to be looked on as the discoverers of ideas, rather than their systematizers. Thus it is not surprising, that the attitude of Plato on this topic is not as clearly defined as the preceding quotations might imply. In some of his Dialogues his attention is fixed on the distinction between the eternal world of ideas, completely open to the understanding, and the fluent world disclosed by the senses which fails to participate with any exact clarity in the eternal forms. To that extent the sensible world is closed to the understanding. Its history is reduced to matter of fact, incapable of complete rationalization. It is but a short step from the Plato who composed the myth of the shadows on the wall of the cave to the full Positivist doctrine of Hume [i.e. the 'Hume' of the *Treatise],* Mill, Comte and Huxley. The main distinction between Plato in this mood and the Moderns—

and it is a great distinction—is that the Platonic emphasis on the eminent reality of the eternal world of ideas must be replaced by the nominalism of most of these moderns.

But in his later Dialogues Plato's interest is concentrated on cosmology; and, as the quotations show, his final judgment, or the decay of his old age, leads him to an intermediate position between the doctrines of Immanent Law, and of Imposed Law.

SECTION VI. It was Plato in his later mood who put forward the suggestion, "and I hold that the definition of being is simply power." This suggestion is the charter of the doctrine of Immanent Law.

The next important landmark in the history of this doctrine is provided by the theological Alexandrians, some four to six hundred years later. It is customary to undervalue theology in a secular history of philosophical thought. This is a mistake, since for a period of about thirteen hundred years the ablest thinkers were mostly theologians.

The theologians of Alexandria were greatly exercised over the immanence of God in the world. They considered the general question, how the primordial Being, who is the source of the inevitable recurrence of the world towards order, shares his nature with the world. In some sense he is a component in the natures of all fugitive things. Thus, an understanding of the nature of temporal things involves a comprehension of the immanence of the Eternal Being. This doctrine effects an important reconciliation between the doctrines of Imposed Law and Immanent Law. For, with this doctrine, the necessity of the trend towards order does not arise from the imposed will of a transcendent God. It arises from the fact, that the existents in nature are sharing in the nature of the immanent God.

This doctrine, in any clear form, is not Platonic, though it is a natural modification from Plato's own doctrine. But in the *Timæus,* Plato provides a soul of this world who definitely is not the ultimate creator. By this notion, Plato prepared the way for the Gnostics with their fantastic machinery of emanations, and for the Arians. In the *Timæus* the doctrine can be read as an allegory. In that case it was Plato's most unfortunate essay in mythology. The World-Soul, as an emanation, has been the parent of puerile metaphysics, which only obscures the ultimate question of the relation of reality as permanent with reality as fluent: the mediator must be a component in common, and not a transcendent emanation.

The Western doctrine of Grace, derived from St. Augustine, leans heavily towards the notion of a wholly transcendent God imposing his partial favours on the world. Indeed, Calvin's rigid version of the same doctrine suggests the Manichean doctrine of a wholly evil material world partially rescued by God's arbitrary selection. For Calvinistic thought the physical order of the world was an arbitrary imposition of God's will. Indeed the Augustinian doctrine takes on diverse aspects according as it is derived from the will of a transcendent God, or the nature of an immanent God.

This unquestioned belief in order, with this chequered history,—Plato and Epicurus, the Gnostics, the Alexandrian theologians, the rationalists of Antioch and Mopsuetia, the Manicheans, Augustine, Calvin,—finally started the first phase of the modern world in the sixteenth century with the unquestioning presupposition that there is an order of nature which lies open in every detail to human understanding.

This belief can be traced back to the initiation of Plato and the Jewish prophets. But, in all probability, it is more than any of them clearly formulated or consistently believed. Lucretius gives the clearest formulation of the doctrine of an exact detailed order of nature. But even he has to make everything depend upon swervings of atoms which take place "at no fixed part of space and no fixed time."

SECTION VII. The conclusion of the seventeenth century marks a new stabilization of cosmological doctrine for the next two hundred years. For the moment the extreme Positivistic doctrine was eliminated. But, curiously enough, the three great figures, Newton, Leibniz, Locke, then dominating the world of thought, gave three diverse interpretations of the Platonic and Lucretian problems.

Newton's position was the more useful as a justification of the methodology required for the state of science, then and in the immediate future. He held the most simple-minded version of the Lucretian doctrine of the Void, the most simple-minded version of the Lucretian doctrine of material atoms, and the most simple-minded version of Law imposed by Divine decree. His only approach to any metaphysical penetration arises from his way of connecting the Void with the Sensorium of the Divine Nature. His cosmology is very easy to understand and very hard to believe. Pragmatically it experienced a supreme justification, for two centuries. Thus its truth was pragmatically established, for the same period. His doctrine will stand for all time as a clear and distinct system of ideas, with large applications. Any cosmology must be capable of interpreting this system and of expressing its limitations.

The monads of Leibniz constitute another version of an atomic doctrine of the universe. It is true that Newton adopted without question some of the main positions of the Cartesian physics. But Newton was entirely innocent of the subjectivist bias of thought introduced by Descartes. Newton found himself knowing a lot of things, as interpreted in Cartesian fashion; and he successfully introduced a systematization of this knowledge, thus interpreted. But Descartes, before he attacked the problem of physics, asked the momentous questions,—How do l know, and How can I divest my knowledge of doubtful interpretation? The final issue of this subjective train of thought after a century of philosophizing is given by Hume's mental atomism, already mentioned in this chapter.

Leibniz was acutely conscious of this problem of the criticism of knowledge. Thus he approached the problem of cosmology from the subjective side, whereas Lucretius and Newton approach it from the objective point of view. They implicitly ask the question, What does the world of atoms look like to an intellect surveying it? What would such an intellect say about the spectacle of an atomic universe? The answer is contained in the Epic of Lucretius and the *Principia* of Newton, immortal works.

But Leibniz answered another question. He explained what it must be like to be an atom. Lucretius tells us what an atom looks like to others, and Leibniz tells us how an atom is feeling about itself. In this account Leibniz wrestles with a difficulty which infects modern cosmologies, a difficulty which Plato, Aristotle, Lucretius, and Newton entirely ignore—perhaps because they would have declared it to be founded upon a mistake. Descartes, as is usual with the founders of new schools of thought, exactly balanced himself between the old way the new way of which he was the founder. The modern outlook arises from the slow influence of Aristotle's Logic, during a period of two thousand years. Also Aristotle's Logic is founded upon an analysis of the simplest form of a verbal sentence. For example, the sentence 'This water is hot' attributes the character of high temperature to the particular mass of water in the particular bathtub. The quality of 'being hot' is an abstraction. Many different things can be hot, and we can think of being hot without thinking of any particular thing in a bathtub which is hot. But in the real physical world, the quality of 'being hot' can only appear as a characteristic of concrete things which *are* hot.

Again, still keeping to the point of view derived from Aristotelian Logic, if we ask for a complete account of a real particular thing in the physical world, the adequate answer is expressed in terms of a set of these abstract characteristics, which are united into an individualized togetherness which is the real thing in question.

This answer is beautifully simple. But it entirely leaves out of account the interconnections between real things. Each substantial thing is thus conceived as complete in itself, without any reference to any other substantial thing. Such an account of the ultimate atoms, or of the ultimate monads, or of the ultimate subjects enjoying experience, renders an interconnected world of real individuals unintelligible. The universe is shivered into a multitude of disconnected substantial things, each thing in its own way exemplifying its private bundle of abstract characters which have found a common home in its own substantial individuality. But substantial thing cannot call unto substantial thing. A substantial thing can acquire a quality, a credit—but real landed estate, never. In this way, Aristotle's doctrines of Predication and of Primary Substance have issued into a doctrine of the conjunction of attributes and of the disjunction of primary substances.

All modern epistemologies, all modern cosmologies, wrestle with this problem. There is, for their doctrine, a mysterious reality in the background, intrinsically unknowable by any direct intercourse. In the foreground of direct enjoyment, there is the play and interplay of various qualities diversifying the surface of the substantial unity of the solitary individual in question.

But one characteristic of each experiencing subject is a mysterious impulse to interpret its private world of enjoyed qualifications as indicating and symbolically defining a complex of communication between ultimate realities. Yet, according to the doctrine of these modern cosmologies, the how, or the why, of such communication must forever lie beyond reason: for reason can only discern the set of qualities constituting the nature of an individual substance.

Such has been the long slow influence of Aristotelian Logic upon cosmological theory. Leibniz was the first, and by far the greatest philosopher, who both accepted the modern doctrine and frankly faced its difficulty. He boldly excepted God from the scope of the doctrine. God and each individual monad were in communication. Thus there is, on his doctrine, an indirect communication between monads by the mediation of God. But each monad independently develops its own experience according to its character which is imposed on it aboriginally by communication with God. This Leibnizian doctrine of Law by pre-established harmony is an extreme example of the doctrine of imposition, capable in some ways of being mitigated by the notion of the immanence of God. But no rea.mn can be given by the supreme monad, God, is exempted from the common fate of isolation. Monads, according to this doctrine, are windowless for each other. Why have they windows towards God, and Why has God windows towards them?

It is interesting to enquire how the ancient cosmologists—Plato and Lucretius—evaded this difficulty.

In the first place it must be acknowledged that in Plato's *Dialogues* many unguarded statements, and many trains of thought, can be found which in themselves would lead straight to the modern difficulty. In fact, in this respect Aristotle's Logic can be found in germ in Plato. But in the ancient cosmologies, including Aristotle's own doctrine of matter, another train of thought can be found, which is in fact an emphatic doctrine of real communication. Plato's doctrine of the real Receptacle [ύποδοχ́η and χώρα], and Epicurus' doctrine of the real Void [τό χενόν], differ in some details. But both doctrines are emphatic assertions of a real communication between ultimate realities. This communication is not accidental. It is part of the essential nature of each physical actuality that it is itself an element qualifying the Receptacle, and that the qualifications of the Receptacle enter into its own nature. In itself, with the various actualities abstracted from it, the Receptacle participates in no forms, according to Plato. But he designates it as 'the fostermother of all becoming'. Later in the same Dialogue he calls it 'a natural matrix for all things'. It receives its forms by reason of its inclusion of actualities, and in a way not to be abstracted from those actualities. The Receptacle, as discussed in the *Timæus,* is the way in which Plato conceived the many actualities of the physical world as components in each other's natures. It is the doctrine of the immanence of Law, derived from the mutual immanence of actualities. It is Plato's doctrine of the medium of intercommunication.[4]

Thus finally we can understand that the Receptacle, according to Plato, the Void, according to Lucretius, and God, according to Leibniz, play the same part in cosmological theory. Also in his general scholium, Newton definitely connects the Lucretian Void with the Leibnizian God. For he calls Empty space the 'sensorium of God'. We have here a formidable display of men of diverse genius, Plato and Aristotle, Epicurus and Lucretius, Newton and Leibniz. The modern cosmologies are all detailed variations of the great types which we have discussed. They revolve round the diverse notions of Law, the diverse notions of the communication between real individuals, the diverse notions of the mediating basis in virtue of which. such communication is attained. One other problem, derivative from these general principles, but of major importance for human life is the doctrine of the status of the spirit of man in the scheme of things.

This more special problem of cosmological theory was the theme of the former part of this book. Its important influence upon the course of human history was illustrated. But it must not be thought that the more general problem of cosmology lies outside the scope of practical interest. The directions of human activities in various epochs, and the clashings of such directions

4. On this topic, it is interesting to note the extreme difficulty of determining, whether or no Descartes held to the doctrine of *one* individual corporeal substance with *many* modal diversities of motion, or to the doctrine of many diverse individual corporeal substances essentially connected by extensive relations. Almost all his phrases are ambiguous on this point, with the exception of Principle LX, Part I, of his *Principles of Philosophy*. Here he unambiguously speaks of *every corporeal substance*, thus—at least in this place—deciding for a multiplicity of such substances. Either alternative leads him into difficulties.

in the same epoch, are the outcome of rough and ready solutions of the problem of cosmology, popularized throughout masses of mankind. Millions of men have marched to battle fiercely nerved by intense faith in Law imposed by the will of inflexible Allah, Law sharing out to each human his inevitable fate, Law sharing out to each faithful Mahometan either victory, or death and Paradise. Millions of Buddhists have shunned the intrinsic evils of such fierce Mahometan emotion relying on the impersonal immanence of Law, made clear to them by the doctrines of the Buddha. Millions of humans have shaped their lives according to the compromise between these two doctrines due to the Platonism of Christianity.

Finally, the restless modern search for increased accuracy of observation and for increased detailed explanation is based upon unquestioning faith in the reign of Law. Apart from such faith, the enterprise of science is foolish, hopeless.

SECTION VIII. The most recent of the four doctrines of the Laws of Nature still remains for discussion—The Doctrine of Conventional Interpretation. This doctrine certainly expresses the procedure by which free speculation passes into an interpretation of Nature. We elaborate a system of ideas, in detachment from any direct, detailed observation of matter of fact. For example, such detachment from detailed observation seems, on the surface, to be characteristic of Plato's *Dialogues.* They do not bear the aspect of patient induction from the facts. They are dominated by speculation and dialectics. Also Mathematics has developed, especially in recent years, by a speculative interest in types of order, without any determination of particular entities illustrative of those types. But Nature has subsequently been interpreted in terms of such mathematical laws. The conclusion seems to be, that Nature is patient of interpretation in terms of Laws which happen to interest us.

Yet another consideration supports this point of view. There is an element of arbitrary choice in our interpretation of the geometrical character of the physical world. Mathematicians have proved that any region which exemplifies metrical geometry of the Euclidean type, also exemplifies metrical geometry of the Elliptic type, and also metrical geometry of the Hyperbolic type. Further, if we start with any one of the three types, we can prove that both the remaining types are severally exemplified in the same subject-matter.

But it is an entire misconception, which has been entertained even by some mathematicians, to deduce that this mathematical truth has any bearing upon the notion of the Laws of Nature as arbitrary convention. For in the three metrical geometries as applying to the same subject-matter, the definitions of distance are different. Thus mathematicians have proved that if there be a metrical geometry of the Euclidean type, then with another definition of distance, and hence with another definition of congruence, there is a metrical geometry of the elliptic type also applying to the same subject-matter. There are three diverse systems of relationship within the subject-matter, so related that if one be present then the others are present. Also, of course, the description of one set of relationships can be achieved, though very clumsily, in terms of any one of the other two sets. There is nothing 'conventional' in this, except the obvious fact that we can direct attention to any selected group of facts. Of course the question remains, What set of geometrical relationships are we referring to, when we say that we have walked thirty miles and are tired? Are they thirty Euclidean miles, or thirty Elliptic miles, or thirty Hyperbolic miles? Here the standard of reference can be the same in both cases, namely, the interval between two assigned marks fixed securely in Washington, D. C.

Again there is yet another geometrical ambiguity. For keeping to the same type of geometry—Euclidean, say, but either of the other two would serve equally well-keeping to Euclidean geometry, there are an infinite number of different alternative ways of defining distance so as to produce alternative systems of Euclidean geometry. Thus granting that one Euclidean system holds, an infinite number of other Euclidean systems also hold. Thus when a friend says that he has motored a hundred miles to see us, we should enquire what particular geometrical system of metrics he has adopted. And he had not settled the question by merely answering Euclidean. Also the differences are not necessarily slight. A thousand miles between particular towns on one system may be two miles on another system. It follows that every legislature should anxiously settle the metric system that it means to adopt. This question has nothing to do with the difference between miles and kilometers, or with mere imperfections of measurement. That is a much slighter point.

It is fairly obvious that, apart from minor inaccuracies of perception, we all do in fact adopt the same system. It is a fact of nature that a distance of thirty miles is a long walk for any one. There is no convention about that. Thus the appeal to geometry can be dismissed when we are discussing the question of the conventionality of the Laws of Nature.

SECTION IX. But the analogy of Geometry suggests an important reflection. It is well-known that Geometry can be developed without any reference to measurement,—and thus without any reference to distance, and without any reference to numerical coordinates for the indication of points. Geometry, developed in this fashion has been termed 'Non-metrical Projective Geometry'. Elsewhere[5] I have termed it, 'the science of cross-classification'. Aristotle's science of classification into genera, and species, and sub-species, is the science of mutually exclusive classification. It develops Plato's suggestion of a science of 'Division'.

Projective Geometry is only one example of a science of cross-classification. Other such sciences have not been developed, partly

5. *The Axioms of Projective Geometry*, Cambridge Tracts in Mathematics, No. 4, Cambridge University Press, 1906. The reference is to Chapter I, Section 3.

because no obvious applications have obtruded themselves, and partly because the abstract interest of such sciences have not engaged the interest of any large group of mathematicians. For example, in *Principia Mathematica*,[6] Section 93, 'On the Inductive Analysis of the Field of a Relation', is a suggestion for another science of that type. Indeed the whole of Vol. I is devoted to the initiation of non-numerical quasi-geometrical sciences, together with a technique for their elaboration. The subsequent parts of the book specialize on those more special mathematical sciences which involve number and quantity.

This reference to *Principia Mathematica* has been made to remind ourselves that numerical relations derived from measurements constitute the subject-matter of a very special development of mathematics. This development has as yet constituted the only really important part of mathematics, except for the impressive disclosure of the extent to which ordinary Geometry is independent of measurement and number.

It follows that there are an indefinite number of purely abstract sciences, with their laws, their regularities, and their complexities of theorems—all as yet undeveloped. We can hardly avoid the conclusion that Nature in her procedures illustrates many such sciences. We are blind to such illustration because we are ignorant of the type of regularities to look for. In such cases, we may dimly sense a sort of familiarity attached to novel circumstances, without any notion how to proceed in the analysis of the vague feeling.

There is thus a certain amount of convention as to the emergence into human consciousness of sorts of Laws of Natures. The order of emergence depends upon the abstract sciences which civilized mankind have in fact chosen to develop.

But such 'convention' should not be twisted to mean that any facts of nature can be interpreted as illustrating any laws that we like to assign.

---

6. Cambridge University Press, 1910.

SECTION X. This discussion of the possible variety of types of Laws of Nature draws attention to a three-fold distinction which it is important to keep in mind during philosophic discussion. There are: (i) our direct intuitions which we enjoy prior to all verbalization: (ii) our literary modes of verbal expression of such intuitions, together with the dialectic deductions from such verbal formulæ: (iii) the set of purely deductive sciences, which have been developed so that the network of possible relations with which they deal are familiar in civilized consciousness.

The sciences under the heading (iii) direct attention for the exploration of the recesses of experience, and also assist in providing the verbal formulæ belonging to the heading (ii). The chief danger in philosophy is that the dialectic deductions from inadequate formulæ should exclude direct intuitions from explicit attentions. In fact the abstract sciences tend to correct the evil effects of the inadequacy of language, and the consequent dangers of a logic which presupposes linguistic adequacy.

Chapter IX

SCIENCE AND PHILOSOPHY

SECTION I. IN ONE sense, Science and Philosophy are merely different aspects of one great enterprise of the human mind. We will dwell upon their cooperation in the task of raising humanity above the general level of animal life. At this low, animal level, flashes of æsthetic insight, of technological attainment, of sociological organization, of affectionate feeling, display themselves. Nightingales, beavers, ants, the kindly nurture of the young, all witness to the existence of this level of life in the animal world. Of course all these modes of functioning are carried to an immeasurably higher level among mankind. In human beings these various modes of functioning exhibit more variety of adaptation to special circumstances, they are more complex, and they are more interwoven with each other. But without question, among animals they are there, plainly demonstrated to our observation.

Among living things on this planet, so far as direct evidence reaches, Science and Philosophy belong to men alone. They are both concerned with the understanding of individual facts as illustrations of general principles. The principles are understood in the abstract, and the facts are understood in respect to their embodiment of the principles.

For example, animals seem quite familiar with the habit of bodies to fall down. They show no surprise at such an occurrence, and they often knock things over. But quite early in the history of modem European science we find Aristotle formulating the law that there is a tendency for material bodies to seek the centre of the

Earth. This law was almost certainly not a discovery of Aristotle's. It was a reigning commonplace of Greek thought, although not accepted unanimously. But it is plainly set forth in his writings, and it is beside our point to indulge further in archæological conjectures. This scientific law seems rather antiquated to us, and in fact not quite true. It is over special. and yet requires severe limitation before the quantitative measurements bear out its statements with any exactness. We shall find that the subsequent history of this law and of its successive modifications throws great light upon the relative functions of Science and Philosophy.

But let us first examine Aristotle's Law, which is one of the earlier doctrines of that Western Science whose history stretches from Thales of Miletus, alive at the date 600 B.C., to the present day. Roughly speaking, it is a history of about twenty-five hundred years. Of course there were anticipations in Egypt, Mesopotamia, India, and China. But modern science, urged onward by the curiosity of the human spirit, permeated with criticism, and divorced from hereditary superstitions, had its birth with the Greeks; and among the Greeks Thales was the earliest exponent known to us.

In this general characterization science and philosophy are not discriminated. But the word 'curiosity' somewhat trivializes that inward motive which has driven men. In the greater sense, in which it is here used, 'curiosity' means the craving of reason that the facts discriminated in experience be understood. It means the refusal to be satisfied with the bare welter of fact, or even with the bare habit of routine. The first step in science and philosophy has been made when it is grasped that every routine exemplifies a principle which is capable of statement in abstraction from its particular exemplifications. The curiosity, which is the gadfly driving civilization from its ancient safeties, is this desire to state the principles in their abstraction. In this curiosity there is a ruthless element which in the end disturbs. We are American, or French, or English; and we love our modes of life, with their beauties and tendernesses. But curiosity drives us to an attempt to define civilization; and in this generalization we soon find that we have lost our beloved America, our beloved France, and our beloved England. The generality stands with a cold impartiality, where our affections cling to one or other of the particulars.

An examination of Aristotle's Law of Gravitation exemplifies this abstractive process inherent in science. The Law involves a classification of the things around us. There are the heavy bodies with the property of tending downwards, and there are the other elements such as flames, with the intrinsic nature that they tend upwards though they are component things on the Earth's surface. These upward moving things tend to their proper place which is the heavens. The stars and planets form yet a third class of things which by their own nature are in the heavens, things which are ingenerable and incorruptible. In this classification of the components of physical nature yet a fourth component remains over, in its character unique and thus the only member of its class. This component is the Earth, the centre of the Universe, by reference to which all these other types of being are defined.

In this classification of the various components of physical nature Aristotle has given to Science and Philosophy its first sweeping analysis of the facts of physical nature. You will notice that the classification proceeds entirely by reference to function, quite in the modern spirit. In the place of an uninterpreted swamp, pestilential with mystery and magic, he sets before our understanding a majestic, coordinated scheme, lucid to the understanding and based upon the obvious, persistent facts of our experience. In the generality of its scope, it is equally philosophic and scientific, and later on it provided the physical background for the Christian scheme of salvation. Its overthrow, eighteen hundred years later, was resisted equally by Luther and the Church of Rome. As an example of a majestic inductive generalization, appealing to the obvious facts. and neglecting the welter of minor differences, Aristotle's general conception of the physical universe remains unsurpassed. For every feature in it, there is an appeal to observation; and for every observation to which appeal is made, there is the possibility of its indefinite repetition. With Aristotle and Epicurus, the science of modern civilization reached adolescence.

SECTION II. There is a clear-cut obviousness about Aristotle's doctrines which is entirely lacking to Plato's cosmology. Of course neither Plato, nor Aristotle, originated his own particular line of thought. There was a history behind them of three or four generations of thinkers, back to the dim figures of Thales and Pythagoras, and even beyond them. Also Aristotle worked for twenty years in the Academy of Plato, and derived ideas from that active, speculative group of thinkers, to whom the modern world owes its speculation, its criticism, its deductive and inductive sciences, and the civilization of its religious concepts. They were the narrow channel through which passed the confused traditions of Egypt, Mesopotamia, Syria, and of the sea-borne Greek civilization. From this Academy and its Aristotelian off-shoot, there emerged the various lines of thought which the subsequent schools of Alexandria turned into the first phase of modern science, natural and humane. Undoubtedly the world then lost picturesqueness. For prophets were superseded by professors. In other words, as the movement has penetrated into habits of thought, intuitive conviction has wilted in the face of criticism. But amid all the limitations of humanity, wandering dazed in the abundant universe, knowledge has re-conditioned human life, and has made possible that virtue which requires such measure of intellectual analysis.

Between them, Plato and Aristotle succeed in illustrating the chief connections between science and philosophy. The emphasis of science is upon observation of particular occurrences, and upon inductive generalization, issuing in wide classifications of things according to their modes of functioning, in other words according to the laws of nature which they illustrate. The emphasis of philosophy is upon generalizations which almost fail to classify by reason of their universal application. For example, all things are involved in the creative advance of the Universe, that is, in the general temporality which affects all things, even if at all times they remain self. identical. Thus the consideration of time does not lead to classification in the same direct way in which the consideration of weight led Aristotle to his four-fold classification.

Now Plato had already emphasized the importance of this Aristotelian notion of classification, that is to say, of 'division' as he called it. Perhaps indeed he invented the method. It would have been quite in accordance with his clear-cut intellectual subtlety to have done so. We find in his dialogues the first explicit formulations of the science of Logic. But his applications of the method are feeble in the extreme, from the point of view of the advancement of natural science. Whereas Aristotle in his life's work seized upon the general notion of classification, he gave a masterly analysis of the complexities inherent in the mutual relation of classes. He also applied his theoretical doctrine to the immense material to be collected by direct observation in the fields of zoology, physics, sociology. Indeed we must trace to him nearly all our special sciences, both the natural sciences, and those concerning the activities of the spirit of mankind. He is the origin of the striving towards an accurate analysis of each given situation which in the end has created modern European Science. We can see in the labours of his life, the first clear example of a philosophic intuition passing into a scientific method.

SECTION III. This transition from philosophic intuitions to scientific methods is in fact the whole topic of this chapter. A philosophic system, viewed as an attempt to coordinate all such intuitions, is rarely of any direct importance for particular sciences. Each such science in tracing its ideas backward to their basic notions stops at a half-way house. It finds a resting place amid notions which for its immediate purposes and for its immediate methods it need not analyse any further. These basic notions are a specialization from the philosophic intuitions which form the background of the civilized thought of the epoch in question. They are intuitions which, apart from their use in science, ordinary language rarely expresses in any defined accuracy, but habitually presupposes in its current words and expressions. For example, the words 'tables', 'chairs', 'rocks', presuppose the scientific notion of material bodies, which has governed natural science from the seventeenth century to the end of the nineteenth.

But, even from the point of view of the special sciences, philosophic systems with their ambitious aims at full comprehensiveness. are not useless. They are the way in which the human spirit cultivates its deeper intuitions. Such systems give life and motion to detached thoughts. Apart from these efforts at coordination, detached thoughts would flash out in idle moments, illuminate a passing phase of reflection, and would then perish and be forgotten. The scope of an intuition can only be defined by its coordination with other notions of equal generality. Even the discordance of competing philosophic systems is a factor essential for progress. The history of European thought, even to the present day, has been tainted by a fatal misunderstanding. It may be termed The Dogmatic Fallacy. The error consists in the persuasion that we are capable of producing notions which are adequately defined in respect to the complexity of relationship required for their illustration in the real world. Canst thou by searching describe the Universe? Except perhaps for the simpler notions of arithmetic, even our more familiar ideas, seemingly obvious, are infected with this incurable vagueness. Our right understanding of the methods of intellectual progress depends on keeping in mind this characteristic of our thoughts. The notions employed in every systematic topic require enlightenment from the perspective of every standpoint. They must be criticized from the standpoint of their own internal consistency within that topic, and from the standpoint of other topics of analogous generality, and from the standpoint of so-called philosophic topics with a wider range.

During the mediaeval epoch in Europe, the theologians were the chief sinners in respect to dogmatic finality. During the last three centuries, their bad preeminence in this habit passed to the men of science. Our task is to understand how in fact the human mind can successfully set to work for the gradual definition of its habitual ideas. It is a step by step process, achieving no triumphs of finality. We cannot produce that final adjustment of well-defined generalities which constitute a complete metaphysics. But we can produce a variety of partial systems of limited generality. The concordance of ideas within any one such system shows the scope and virility of the basic notions of that scheme of thought. Also the discordance of system with system, and success of each system as a partial mode of illumination, warns us of the limitations within which our intuitions are hedged. These undiscovered limitations are the topics for philosophic research.

This doctrine of the limitations to which our best ideas are subject is illustrated by that very notion of material bodies which has just been mentioned. That notion is so obvious that it has haunted language so far as we can trace history backwards. Finally in the seventeenth century it was given a new precision for the purposes of physical science. Also physical science, thus re-conditioned, proved an overwhelming success for three centuries. It has transformed thought, and has transformed the physical activities of mankind. It seemed that at last mankind had achieved the fundamental notion for all practical purposes, and that beyond it in the way of generality there lay mere aimless speculation. But in the twentieth century this great notion, as shaped for use by Galileo and Newton, has completely collapsed so far as concerns its use as a fundamental notion for physical science. In the modern science, it is a limited notion confined to special purposes.

This collapse of nineteenth century dogmatism is a warning that the special sciences require that the imaginations of men be stored with imaginative possibilities as yet unutilized in the service of scientific explanation. The nearest analogy is to be seen in the history of some species of animal, or plant, or microbe, which lurks for ages as an obscure by-product of nature in some lonely jungle, or morass, or island. Then by some trick of circumstance it escapes into the outer world and transforms a civilization, or destroys an empire or the forests of a continent. Such is the potential power of the ideas which live in the various systems of philosophy.

Of course in this action, and reaction, between science and philosophy either helps the other. It is the task of philosophy to work at the concordance of ideas conceived as illustrated in the concrete facts of the real world. It seeks those generalities which characterize the complete reality of fact, and apart from which any fact must sink into an abstraction. But science makes the abstraction, and is content to understand the complete fact in respect to only some of its essential aspects. Science and Philosophy mutually criticize each other, and provide imaginative material for each other. A philosophic system should present an elucidation of concrete fact from which the sciences abstract. Also the sciences should find their principles in the concrete facts which a philosophic system presents. The history of thought is the story of the measure of failure and success in this joint enterprise.

SECTION IV. Plato's contribution to the basic notions connecting Science and Philosophy, as finally settled in the later portion of his life. has virtues entirely different from that of Aristotle, although of equal use for the progress of thought. It is to be found by reading together the *Theætetus,* the *Sophist,* the *Timæus,* and the fifth and tenth books of the *Laws;* and then by recurrence to his earlier work, the *Symposium.* He is never entirely self-consistent, and rarely explicit and devoid of ambiguity. He feels the difficulties, and expresses his perplexities. No one could be perplexed over Aristotle's classifications; whereas Plato moves about amid a fragmentary system like a man dazed by his own penetration.

A few main doctrines stand out and they are of priceless importance for science, in the largest sense of that term. As to their coordination into a system, he is undogmatic and can only tell 'the most likely tale'. Indeed, in his seventh Epistle[1] he denounces the notion that a final system can be verbally expressed. His later thought circles round the interweaving of seven main notions namely, The Ideas, The Physical Elements, The Psyche, The Eros, The Harmony, The Mathematical Relations, The Receptacle. These notions are as important for us now, as they were then at the dawn of the modern world, when civilizations of the old type were dying. From their point of view the Athenians were right to condemn Socrates. After the coalescence of Greek and Semitic thought the old order of life was doomed. Western Civilization acquired a new intellectuality, clarified, humanized, moralized.

Considering the Ideas by themselves, Plato points out that any selections are either compatible for joint exemplification, or are incompatible. It thus follows, as he notes, that the determinations of compatibilities and incompatibilities are the key to coherent thought, and to the understanding of the world in its function as the theatre for the temporal realization of ideas. The Aristotelian Logic is only a specialized derivative from this general notion.

Plato then passes on to the agency whereby ideas obtain efficiency in the creative advance. As he conceives them in abstraction, he finds ideas to be static, frozen, and lifeless. They obtain 'life and motion' by their entertainment in a living intelligence. Such a living intelligence with its 'gaze fixed upon ideas' was what Plato termed a Psyche, a word we can translate as 'soul'. We must, however, be careful to divest the associations of the English word from the accretions due to centuries of Christianity. He conceives of a basic Psyche whose active grasp of ideas conditions impartially the whole process of the Universe. This is the Supreme Craftsman, on whom depends that degree of orderliness which the world exhibits. There is a perfection in this Psyche, which Plato finds out of his power to explain. There are also

1. Cf. 341, C.

finite souls of varying grades, including human souls, all playing their part in conditioning nature by the inherent persuasiveness of ideas.

But the notion of mere knowledge, that is to say, of mere understanding, is quite alien to Plato's thought. The age of professors had not yet arrived. In his view, the entertainment of ideas is intrinsically associated with an inward ferment, an activity of subjective feeling, which is at once immediate enjoyment, and also an appetition which melts into action. This is Plato's Eros, which he sublimates into the notion of the soul in the enjoyment of its creative function, arising from its entertainment of ideas. The word Eros means 'Love', and in *The Symposium* Plato gradually elicits his final conception of the urge towards ideal perfection. It is obvious that he should have written a companion dialogue which might have been named The Furies, dwelling on the horrors lurking within imperfect realization. Plato, although he neglected to write this missing dialogue, did not overlook the confusion and disorder in Nature. He expressly denies omnipotence to his Supreme Craftsman. The influence of the entertainment of ideas is always persuasive, and can only produce such order as is possible. However, on this point he wavers, and sometimes writes as if the Craftsman were disposing the world according to his supreme will.

This notion of an excellence, partly attained and partly missed, raises another problem which greatly exercised Greek thought at the time of Plato. The problem can take many special forms. In what does beauty consist, for example, the beauty of a musical melody, the beauty of a statue, or of a building such as the Parthenon? Also, there is that other form of beauty, which is rightness of conduct. Probably, in this naïve shape, the question has no answer; since 'The Good' is an ultimate qualification not to be analysed in terms of any things more final than itself. But an analogous question can be asked, to which Greek thought was unanimous as to its answer. To what sort of things does the concept apply, and in particular what sort of conditions are requisite for its evocation? The Greek answer to this latter pair of questions was that beauty belonged to composite things, and that the composition is beautiful when the many components have obtained in some sense their proper proportions. This was the Greek doctrine of Harmony, in respect to which neither Plato not Aristotle ever waver.

In respect to Harmony, the Greeks made a discovery which is a landmark in the history of thought. They found out that exact Mathematical Relationships, as they exist in Geometry and in the numerical proportions of measurements, are realized in various outstanding examples of beautiful composition. For instance Archytas discovered that, other circumstances being equal, the note given out by a stretched string depends on the length of the string, and that beautiful compositions of notes correspond to certain simple laws as to the proportional lengths of the strings. Also they investigated the dependence of the beauty of architecture upon the preservation of the proper proportions in the various dimensions. This was an immense discovery, the dependence of the qualitative elements in the world upon mathematical relations. The facts had gradually accumulated through thousands of years. The early Babylonians knew that the qualitative fact of the succession of seasons depended upon the lapse of definite numbers of days. In fact, they constructed very creditable calendars. But the Greeks, with their power of generalization, grasped the full law of the interweaving of qualitative fact with geometrical and quantitative composition. They had the genius to be astonished.

Plato drew the conclusion that the key to the understanding of the natural world, and in particular of the physical elements, was the study of mathematics. There is good reason to believe that the greater part of the studies of his Academy was devoted to mathematics. The mathematicians of the succeeding generation, and indeed of the next two hundred years, ending with the astronomers Ptolemy and Hipparchus, are the product of the systematic tradition shaped by the example and the doctrine of

Plato. Of course the Academy inherited the Pythagorean tradition of Mathematics.

Thus with Plato and Aristotle, a new epoch commences. Science acquires the cleansing of logical and mathematical lucidity. Aristotle established the importance of scientific classification into species and genera; Plato divined the future scope of applied mathematics. Unfortunately, later on, the explicit development of Plato's doctrines has been exclusively in the hands of religious mystics, of literary scholars, and of literary artists. Plato, the mathematician, for long intervals disappeared from the explicit Platonic tradition.

The notions of Harmony and of Mathematical Relations are only special exemplifications of a yet more general philosophic concept, namely, that of the general interconnectedness of things, which transforms the manifoldness of the many into the unity of the one. We speak in the singular of *The* Universe, of Nature, of φύσις; which can be translated as Process. There is the one all-embracing fact which is the advancing history of the one Universe. This community of the world, which is the matrix for all begetting, and whose essence is process with retention of connectedness,—this community is what Plato terms The Receptacle [ὑποδοχή]. In our effort to divine his meaning, we must remember that Plato says that it is an obscure and difficult concept, and that in its own essence the Receptacle is devoid of all forms. It is thus certainly not the ordinary geometrical space with its mathematical relations. Plato calls his Receptacle, 'The foster-mother of all becoming'. He evidently conceived it as a necessary notion without which our analysis of Nature is defective. It is dangerous to neglect Plato's intuitions. He carefully varies his phrases in referring to it, and implies that what he says is to be taken in its most abstract sense. The Receptacle imposes a common relationship on all that happens, but does not impose what that relationship shall be. It seems to be a somewhat more subtle notion than Aristotle's 'matter' which, of course. is not the 'matter' of Galileo and Newton. Plato's Receptacle may be conceived as the necessary community within which the course of history is set, in abstraction from all the particular historical facts. I have directed attention to Plato's doctrine of The Receptacle because, at the present moment, physical science is nearer to it than at any period since Plato's death. The space-time of modern mathematical physics, conceived in abstraction from the particular mathematical formulæ which applies to the happenings in it, is almost exactly Plato's Receptacle. It is to be noted that mathematical physicists are extremely uncertain as to what these formulæ are exactly, nor do they believe that any such formulæ can be derived from the mere notion of space-time. Thus, as Plato declares, space-time in itself is bare of all forms.

SECTION V. In the preceding sketch only one incidental generalization, selected from one topic comprised in the enormous labours of Aristotle's life, has been brought forward. Aristotle was at once a man of science, a philosopher, a literary critic, and a student of political theory. This particular classification of the things constitutive of the visible universe has been dwelt upon because it is an almost perfect example of a scientific induction satisfying all the conditions insisted on by the modern philosophy of science. It was a generalization from observed fact, and could be confirmed by repeated observation. In its day—and its day lasted for eighteen hundred years—it was extremely useful; and now that it is dead, it is stone-dead, an archæological curiosity. This is the fate of scientific generalizations, so long as they are considered in relation to their strict scientific purpose. Towards the end of its long life, the doctrine lost its utility and turned into an obstructive agency.

The Platonic group of notions which have been considered have none of the merits of the Aristotelian set. In fact, they are philosophic, and in the narrow sense are not scientific. They suggest no detailed observation. Indeed it has always been a reproach to Plato that he diverted interest from observation of the particular facts. So far as concerns political theory, and in particular jurisprudence, this accusation is certainly untrue, and arises, from the habit of concentrating interest on his Dialogues in proportion to their literary brilliance. Nevertheless the assertion is undoubtedly true in respect to physical science. But Plato had another message. Where Aristotle said 'observe' and 'classify', the moral of Plato's teaching is the importance of the study of mathematics. Of course, neither of them was so stupid as to dissuade from observation or, on the other hand, to deny the utility of mathematics. Probably Aristotle thought that the mathematical knowledge of his day was about as much as was wanted for the purposes of physical science. Any further progress could only minister to an unpractical curiosity about subtle abstractions.

An intense belief that a knowledge of mathematical relations would prove the key to unlock the mysteries of the relatedness within Nature was ever at the back of Plato's cosmological speculations. In one passage he reprobates the swinish[2] ignorance of those who have failed to study the doctrine of proportions incapable of expression as numerical ratios. He evidently feels that the chance of some subtle elucidation of the nature of Harmony is being crassly lost. His own speculations as to the course of nature are all founded upon the conjectural application of some mathematical construction. So far as I can remember, in every case he made a sensible shot which, in fact, went wide of the mark.

Although the *Timæus* was widely influential, yet for about eighteen hundred years after their epoch, it seemed that Aristotle was right and Plato wrong. Some mathematical formulæ were interwoven with scientific ideas, but no more than would have been perfectly familiar to Aristotle apart from what were in his day the latest refinements. The cosmological scheme of the active scientists was in fact that of Aristotle. But Plato's divination exemplifies another important function for philosophy. It evokes interest in topics as yet remote from our crude understanding

2. ὑηνός cf. *Laws*, Bk. VII, 819 D.

of the interplay of natural forces. The science of the future depends for its ready progress upon the antecedent elucidation of hypothetical complexities of connection, as yet unobserved in nature. Plato's mathematical speculations have been treated as sheer mysticism by scholars who follow the literary traditions of the Italian Renaissance. In truth, they are the products of genius brooding on the future of intellect exploring a world of mystery.

Greeks, Egyptians, Arabs, Jews, and Mesopotamians advanced the science of mathematics beyond the wildest dreams of Plato. Unfortunately this side of Plato's interest was notably absent among the Christian populations. I believe it to be true that no Christian made any original contribution to mathematical science before the revival of science at the time of the Renaissance. Pope Silvester II—Gerbert, who reigned in the year 1000 A.D.—studied mathematics. But he added nothing. Roger Bacon proclaimed the importance of mathematics and named contemporary mathematicians. In the thirteenth and fourteenth centuries the University of Oxford cherished mathematics. But none of these mediaeval Europeans advanced the subject. An exception must be made in favour of Leonardo of Pisa who flourished at the beginning of the thirteenth century. He was the first Christian to make an advance in the science which in its early history illustrates the cultural union of the Hellenistic Greeks with the Near East. But, subject to this qualification, sixteenth-century mathematics was entirely based upon non-Christian sources. Among the Christians mathematics and magic were confused. The Pope himself hardly escaped. We can hardly hope for a better illustration of the curious limitations of epochs and schools of civilization. It is especially interesting in view of the dominant influence of Plato upon Christian thought.

But the Platonic doctrine of the interweaving of Harmony with mathematical relations has been triumphantly vindicated.

The Aristotelian classifications based upon qualitative predicates have a very restricted application apart from the introduction of mathematical" formulæ. Indeed, Aristotelian Logic, by its neglect of mathematical notions, has done almost as much harm as good for the advancement of science. We can never get away from the questions: —How much,—In what proportions,—and In what pattern of arrangement with other things. The exact laws of chemical proportions make all the difference; CO will kill you, when CO_2 will only give you a headache. Also CO_2 is a necessary element for the dilution of oxygen in the atmosphere; but too much or too little is equally harmful. Arsenic deals out either health or death, according to its proportions amid a pattern of circumstances. Also when the health-giving proportion of CO_2 to free oxygen has been obtained, a rearrangement of these proportional quantities of carbon and oxygen into carbon monoxide and free oxygen will provide a poisonous mixture. In Political Economy, the Law of Diminishing Returns points to the conditions for the maximum efficiency of a dose of capital. In fact, there is hardly a question to be asked which should not be fenced round with qualifications as to how much, and as to what pattern of circumstances. Aristotelian Logic, apart from the guardianship of mathematics, is the fertile matrix of fallacies. It deals with propositional forms only adapted for the expression of high abstractions, the sort of abstractions usual in current conversation where the presupposed background is ignored.

But it is evident that even the appeal to mathematics is too narrow, at least if mathematics is taken to mean those branches hitherto developed. The general science of mathematics is concerned with the investigation of patterns of connectedness, in abstraction from the particular relata and the particular modes of connection. It is only in some special branches of mathematics that notions of quantity and number are dominant themes. The real point is that the essential connectedness of things can never be safely omitted. This is the doctrine of the thoroughgoing relativity which infects the universe and which makes the totality of things as it were a Receptacle uniting all that happens.

The Greek doctrine of Composition and Harmony has been vindicated by the progress of thought. Yet the vivid fancy of the Greeks was also apt to invest each factor in the Universe with an independent individuality, for example, the self-sufficient realm of ideas which dominated Plato's earlier thought, and which intermittently intrudes into his later Dialogues. But we must not blame the Greeks for this excess of individualization. All language witnesses to the same error. We habitually speak of stones, and planets, and animals, as though each individual thing could exist, even for a passing moment, in separation from an environment which is in truth a necessary factor in its own nature. Such an abstraction is a necessity of thought, and the requisite background of systematic environment can be presupposed. That is true. But it also follows that, in the absence of some understanding of the final nature of things, and thus of the sorts of backgrounds presupposed in such abstract statements, all science suffers from the vice that it may be combining various propositions which tacitly presuppose inconsistent backgrounds. No science can be more secure than the unconscious metaphysics which tacitly it presupposes. The individual thing is necessarily a modification of its environment, and cannot be understood in disjunction. All reasoning, apart from some metaphysical reference, is vicious.

SECTION VI. Thus the Certainties of Science are a delusion. They are hedged around with unexplored limitations. Our handling of scientific doctrines is controlled by the diffused metaphysical concepts of our epoch. Even so, we are continually led into errors of expectation. Also, whenever some new mode of observational experience is obtained the old doctrines crumble into a fog of inaccuracies.

Our coordinated knowledge, which in the general sense of the term is Science, is formed by the meeting of two orders of experience. One order is constituted by the direct, immediate discriminations of particular observations. The other order is constituted by our general way of conceiving the Universe. They will be called, the Observational Order, and the Conceptual Order. The first point to remember is that the observational order is invariably interpreted in terms of the concepts supplied by the conceptual order. The question as to the priority of one or the other is, for the purpose of this discussion, academic. We inherit an observational order, namely types of things which we do in fact discriminate; and we inherit a conceptual order, namely a rough system of ideas in terms of which we do in fact interpret. We can point to no epoch in human history, or even in animal history, at which this interplay began. Also it is true that novel observations modify the conceptual order. But equally, novel concepts suggest novel possibilities of observational discrimination.

The history of thought cannot be understood unless we take account of a grave weakness in the observational order. Observational discrimination is not dictated by the impartial facts. It selects and discards, and what it retains is rearranged in a subjective order of prominence. This order of prominence in observation is in fact a distortion of the facts. Thus we have to rescue the facts as they are from the facts as they appear. We have to rescue the facts in the discard, and we have to discard the subjective order of prominence which is itself a fact of observation. For example, consider the observed facts in early stages of civilization. The observed fact was a flat Earth with the arched dome of the Sky. Even to the contemporaries of Pope Silvester the antipodes were inconceivable, and his reputed belief in them did no credit to the old wizard of a Pope.

Again we view the sky at noon on a fine day. It is blue, flooded by the light of the Sun. The direct fact of observation is the sun as the sole origin of light, and the bare heavens. Conceive the myth of Adam and Eve in the Garden on the first day of human life. They watch the sunset, the stars appear:—

'And, Lo!, creation widened to man's view'.

The excess of light discloses facts and also conceals them. It distorts the facts for human observation. It is one task of speculation to urge observation beyond the boundaries of its delusive completeness, and to urge the doctrines of science beyond their delusive air of finality.

We can now briefly characterize the history of the transformation of mediaeval cosmology into our modern standpoint. The effective agency in this transformation has a history of about eighteen hundred years entirely divorced from physical observation. It is a history of abstract thought, namely, of the development of mathematics. The interest, which was the motive in its development, was the interest in the coordination of theoretical notions and in the theoretical constructions arising from the domination of such notions. Yet, if many modern philosophers and men of science could have had their way, they would have been dissuading Greeks, Jews, and Mahommedans from such useless studies, from such pure abstractions for which no foresight could divine the ghost of an application. Luckily they could not get at their ancestors.

SECTION VII. The services to mankind rendered by the Newtonian System of Nature are incalculable. It combines ideas derived from Plato, Aristotle, and Epicurus, into a consistent scheme of thought which elucidates an incredible number of observed facts. Thereby it has enabled men to obtain a new command over Nature. Where we formerly obeyed, we now direct. But at last the Newton cosmology has broken down.

The story of the breakdown extends over more than a century. For by far the greater part of that period men of science were quite unaware that the ideas which they were introducing, slowly, one after the other, were finally to accumulate into a body of thought inconsistent with the Newtonian ideas dominating their thoughts and shaping their modes of expression. The story commences with the wave-theory of light and ends with the wave-theory of matter. It finally leaves us with the philosophic question, What are the concrete facts which exhibit this mathematical attribute of wave-vibration?

The story in detail is the history of modern physics, which lies beyond the scope of this discussion. We merely require to understand the contrast between the most general notions respectively underlying Newtonian physics and modern physics. Newtonian physics is based upon the independent individuality of each bit of matter. Each &tone is conceived as fully describable apart from any reference to any other portion of matter. It might be alone in the Universe, the sole occupant of uniform space. But it would still be that stone which it is. Also the stone could be adequately described without any reference to past or future. It is to be conceived fully and adequately as wholly constituted within the present moment.

This is the full Newtonian concept, which bit by bit was given away, or dissolved, by the advance of modern physics. It is the thoroughgoing doctrine of 'simple location' and of 'external relations'. There was some divergence of opinion as to the external relations. Newton himself was inclined to construe them in terms of shock and of stress between contiguous bodies. But his immediate followers, such as Roger Cotes, added the notion of force at a distance. But either alternative was wholly and completely a fact in the present, namely. the fact of that external relation between two bits of matter either contiguous or distant. The opposed doctrine of internal relations has been distorted by reason of its description in terms of language adapted to the presupposition of external relations of the Newtonian type. Even its adherents, such as F. H. Bradley for instance, fall into this pitfall. It must be remembered that just as the relations modify the natures of the relata, so the relata modify the nature of the relation. The relationship is not a universal. It is a concrete fact with the same concreteness as the relata. The notion of the immanence of the cause in the effect illustrates this truth. We have to discover a doctrine of nature which expresses the concrete relatedness of physical functionings and mental functionings, of the past with the present, and also expresses the concrete composition of physical realities which are individually diverse.

Modern physics has abandoned the doctrine of Simple Location. The physical things which we term stars, planets, lumps of matter, molecules, electrons, protons, quanta of energy, are each to be conceived as modifications of conditions within space-time, extending throughout its whole range. There is a focal region, which in common speech is where the thing is. But its influence streams away from it with finite velocity throughout the utmost recesses of space and time. Of course, it is natural, and for certain purposes entirely proper, to speak of the focal region, thus modified, as the thing itself situated there. But difficulties arise if we press this way of thought too far. For physics, the thing itself is what it does, and what it does is this divergent stream of influence. Again the focal region cannot be separated from the external stream. It obstinately refuses to be conceived as an instantaneous fact. It is a state of agitation. only differing from the so-called external stream by its superior dominance within the focal region. Also we are puzzled how to express exactly the existence of these physical things at any definite moment of time. For at every instantaneous point-event, within or without the focal region, the modification to be ascribed to this thing is antecedent to, or successive to, the corresponding modification introduced by that thing at another point-event. Thus if we endeavor to conceive a complete instance of the existence of the physical thing in question, we cannot confine ourselves to one part of space or to one moment of time. The physical thing is a certain coordination of spaces and times and of conditions in those spaces at those times, this coordination illustrating one exemplification of a certain general rule, expressible in terms of mathematical relations. Here we have returned to a fundamental Platonic doctrine.

Again, with the denial of simple location we must admit that within any region of space-time the innumerable multitude of these physical things are in a sense superposed. Thus the physical fact at each region of space-time is a composition of what the physical entities throughout the Universe mean for that region. But a complete existence is not a composition of mathematical formulæ, mere formulæ. It is a concrete composition of things illustrating formulæ. There is an interweaving of qualitative and quantitative elements. For example, when a living body assimilates food, the fact cannot be *merely* that one mathematical formula assimilates another mathematical formula. The fact cannot be merely that the equality of two and three with five assimilates the fact of the equality of thrice three with nine, nor can the number eleven assimilate the number sixteen. Any of these mathematical notions may be illustrated, but the fact is more than the formulæ illustrated.

SECTION VIII. The final problem is to conceive a complete [παντελής] fact.[3] We can only form such a conception in terms of fundamental notions concerning the nature of reality. We are thrown back upon philosophy. Centuries ago Plato divined the seven main factors interwoven in fact: —The Ideas, The Physical Elements, The Psyche, The Eros, The Harmony, The Mathematical Relations, The Receptacle. All philosophical systems are endeavours to express the interweaving of these components. Of course, it is most unscholarly to identify our modern notions with these archaic thoughts of Plato. For us everything has a subtle difference. But for all these differences, human thought is now

3. Cf. *Sophist*, 248E, τῷ παντελῶς. Here παντελῶς is often wrongly translated by 'absolute'. For Plato's reference to 'absolute' and 'relative' cf. *Sophist*, 255 C.

endeavouring to express analogous elements in the composition of nature. It only dimly discerns, it misdescribes, and it wrongly associates. But always there remain the same beacons that lure. Systems, scientific and philosophic, come and go. Each method of limited understanding is at length exhausted. In its prime each system is a triumphant success: in its decay it is an obstructive nuisance. The transitions to new fruitfulness of understanding are achieved by recurrence to the utmost depths of intuition for the refreshment of imagination. In the end—though there is no end—what is being achieved, is width of view, issuing in greater opportunities. But opportunity leads upwards or downwards. In unthinking Nature 'natural selection' is a synonym for 'waste'. Philosophy should now perform its final service. It should seek the insight, dim though it be, to escape the wide wreckage of a race of beings sensitive to values beyond those of mere animal enjoyment.

Chapter X

THE NEW REFORMATION

SECTION I. THE THEME of this chapter can be introduced by directing attention to a contrast. Protestant Christianity, so far as concerns the institutional and dogmatic forms in which it flourished for three hundred years as derived from Luther, Calvin, and the Anglican Settlement, is shewing all the signs of a steady decay. Its dogmas no longer dominate: its divisions no longer interest: its institutions no longer direct the patterns of life. That is one side of the contrast.

The other side is that the religious, spirit as an effective element in the affairs of men has just [April, 1931] obtained one of its most signal triumphs. In India the forces of violence and strife, between rulers and people, between races, between religions, between social grades,—forces threatening to overwhelm with violence hundreds of millions of mankind—these forces have for the moment been halted by two men acting with the moral authority of religious conviction, the Mahatma Gandhi and the Viceroy of India [Lord Irwin].

They may fail. More than two thousand years ago, the wisest of men proclaimed that the divine persuasion is the foundation of the order of the world, but that it could only produce such a measure of harmony as amid brute forces it was possible to accomplish. This, I suggest, is a plain anticipation by Plato of a doctrine of Grace. seven hundred years before the age of Pelagius and Augustine.

But the dramatic halt effected by Gandhi and the Viceroy, requiring as it does an effective response from uncounted millions in India, in England, in Europe, and America, witnesses that the religious motive, I mean the response to the divine persuasion, still holds its old power, even more than its old power, over the minds and the consciences of men. In this response the protestant populations of the British Empire, and importantly, though more remotely, that of the United States, have sustained their part. We stand at a moment when the course of history depends upon the calm reasonableness arising from a religious public opinion. An initial triumph has already been gained.

There is the contrast, decay and survival. We have to estimate what has decayed, and what has survived. My thesis is that a new Reformation is in full progress. It is a reformation; but whether its issue be fortunate or unfortunate depends largely on the actions of comparatively few men, and notably upon the leaders of the protestant clergy.

I do not hold it to be possible, or even desirable, that identity of detailed belief can be attained. But it is possible that amid diversities of belief, arising from differences of stress exhibited in metaphysical insight and from differences of sympathetic intuition respecting historical events,—that it is possible, amid these differences, to reach a general agreement as to those elements, in intimate human experience and in general history, which we select to exemplify that ultimate theme of the divine immanence, as a completion required by our cosmological outlook. In other words, we may agree as to the qualitative aspects of religious facts, and as to their general way of coordination in metaphysical theory, while disagreeing in various explanatory formulations.

The problem, however, is not nearly so simple as this exordium suggests. We are dealing with a topic, complex and many-sided. It comprises the deliverances of the understanding as it harmonizes our deepest intuitions. It comprises emotional responses to formulations of thought and to modes of behaviour. It comprises the direction of purposes and the modifications of behaviour. It cuts into every aspect of human existence. So far as concerns religious problems, simple solutions are bogus solutions. It is written, that he who runs, may read. But it is not said, that he provides the writing.

For religion is concerned with our reactions of purpose and emotion due to our personal measure of intuition into the ultimate mystery of the universe. We must not postulate simplicity. The witness of history and of common sense tells us that systematic formulations are potent engines of emphasis, of purification, and of stability. Christianity would long ago have sunk into a noxious superstition, apart from the Levantine and European intellectual movement, sustained from the very beginning until now. This movement is the effort of Reason to provide an accurate system of theology. Indeed, in outlying districts where this effort at rationalization died away, the religion has in fact sunk into the decrepitude of failure.

SECTION II. Thus the attack of the liberal clergy and laymen, during the eighteenth and nineteenth centuries, upon systematic theology was entirely misconceived. They were throwing away the chief safeguard against the wild emotions of superstition. A civilized religion should aim at the training of such emotions as naturally arise from a civilized rational criticism of the metaphysical intuitions powerfully influential in great epochs of human history, The appeal to history is the appeal to summits of attainment beyond any immediate clarity in our own individual existence. rt is an appeal to authority. The appeal to reason is the appeal to that ultimate judge, universal and yet individual to each, to which all authority must bow. History has authority so far, and exactly so far, as it admits of some measure of rational interpretation.

Thus an attack upon systematic thought is treason to civilization. Yet the great minds who laid the foundations of our modern mentality—John Locke, for example—had reason for their dissatisfaction with the traditional dogmatic theology, though they partially misconceived the grounds upon which they should base their attitude. Their true enemy was the doctrine of dogmatic finality, a doctrine which flourished and is flourishing with equal vigour throughout Theology, Science, and Metaphysics. The methodology of rational thought from the Greeks to our own times has been vitiated by this fundamental misconception. These errors are not confined to religious thought. They have infected all departments. Their total effect has been to introduce in each age a dogmatic sense of finality. The emphasis of certainty has been wrongly placed, and with equal error dogmatic rejection.

From the very beginning of critical thought, we find the distinction between topics susceptible of certain knowledge, and topics about which only uncertain opinions are available. The dawn of this distinction, explicitly entertained, is the dawn of modern mentality. It introduces criticism. Such a notion hardly enters into any book of the Bible, either in the mind of Jehovah, or of any of his worshippers. The first effect of this new distinction was very unfortunate. For it was much too simple-minded, and the area of certainty was misconceived. For example, we find Plato in his old age advocating religious persecution, and justifying himself by the importance of the topic and the certainty of his own demonstrations.[1]

I suggest that the development of systematic theology should be accompanied by a critical understanding of the relation of linguistic expression to our deepest and most persistent intuitions. Language was developed in response to the excitements of practical actions. It is concerned with the prominent facts. Such facts are those seized upon by consciousness for detailed examination, with the view of emotional response leading to immediate purposeful action. These prominent facts are the variable facts,—the appearance of a tiger, of a clap of thunder, or of a spasm of pain. They are the facts entering into experience by the medium of our

1. Cf. Plato's *Laws*, Book X.

sense-organs. Hence the sensationalist doctrine concerning the data which are the origin of experience.

But the prominent facts are the superficial facts. They vary because they are superficial; and they enter into conscious discrimination because they vary. There are other elements in our experience, on the fringe of consciousness, and yet massively qualifying our experience. In regard to these other facts, it is our consciousness that flickers, and not the facts themselves. They are always securely there, barely discriminated, and yet inescapable. For example, consider our derivation from our immediate past of a quarter of a second ago. We are continuous with it, we are the same as it, prolonging its affective tone, enjoying its data. And yet we are modifying it, deflecting it, changing its purposes, altering its tone, reconditioning its data with new elements.

We reduce this past to a perspective, and yet retain it as the basis of our present moment of realization. We are different from it, and yet we retain our individual identity with it. This is the mystery of personal identity, the mystery of the immanence of the past in the present, the mystery of transcience. All our science, all our explanations require concepts originating in this experience of derivation. In respect to such intuitions, language is peculiarly inadequate. Our powers of analysis, and of expression, flicker with our consciousness. It is not true that there is a definite area of human consciousness, within which there is clear discrimination and beyond which mere darkness. Nor is it true that elements of experience are important in proportion to their clarity in consciousness.

The appeal to history gains its importance by reason of this complex character of human experience. Metaphysics and theology alike require it. The requisite evidence cannot be gained by mere acts of direct introspection conducted at one epoch by a few clear-sighted individuals. If a flood of oblivion should overwhelm human memory, we could in this way of introspection recover the multiplication table. But not much else. In each age of the world, the actions of men and their interpretations of feelings, motives, and purposes, throw light upon the recesses of their experience. In this elucidation of what it means to live, to act, and feel, age differs from age. In the discrimination of this historical evidence, there is required a criticism founded upon taste, and a criticism founded upon logical analysis and inductive probability.

The two grounds of criticism, æsthetic and logical, are welded together in the final judgment of reason as to the comparison of historical periods, one with the other. Each age deposits its message as to the secret character of the nature of things. Civilizations can only be understood by those who are civilized. And they have this property, that the appropriation of them in the understanding unveils truths concerning our own natures. It has been said that the great dramatic tragedies in their representations before audiences act as a purification of the passions. In the same way, the great periods of history act as an enlightenment. They reveal ourselves to ourselves.

SECTION III. Christianity bases itself upon an intensive study of the significance of certain historical occasions scattered irregularly within a period of about twelve hundred years, from the earlier Hebrew prophets and historians to the stabilization of western theology by Augustine. The story wanders around the shores of the Eastern Mediterranean, from the Palestine of the prophets to the Athens of Plato: it culminates in Galilee and Jerusalem: the main interest then fluctuates uncertainly backwards and forwards between Antioch, Ephesus, Egypt, Rome, Constantinople and Africa. When Augustine died at Hippo in the year 430, the religion of the European races was in its main outlines settled. All its capacities for variant forms were already inherent in it. The Papal Church, the Eastern Church, Wycliffe and Huss, Luther and Calvin, Archbishop Cranmer, Jonathan Edwards and John Wesley, Erasmus, Ignatius Loyola, the Socinians, George Fox, and the Vatican Council could with equal right appeal to history. The conclusion to be drawn from the appeal entirely depends upon the value-judgments guiding your selection, and upon the metaphysical presuppositions dictating your notions of a coherent theology. The appeal is to the actions, thoughts, emotions, and institutions, which great persons and great occasions had made effective on the shores of the Mediterranean within that earlier period of time.

In this appeal to history we must remember the gaps in time between the extant written Gospels and the events which they relate: the discordances in accounts, the translations of tradition from language to language, the suspicious passages: also the seeming indifference to direct historical evidence, notably in the case of St. Paul, who retired to Arabia when we should have expected him to have recourse to the disciples who had seen his Lord. I mention these latter points, upon which whole libraries have been written, merely to draw the unquestioned conclusion that any modem reformation of the religion must first concentrate upon the moral and metaphysical intuitions scattered throughout the whole epoch. This conclusion is a commonplace of modem thought.

I suggest, with the diffidence due to my entire lack of expertness in the literature of this immense stretch of history, that even now there is room for a new appeal to the lesson to be derived from it. In this chapter I shall deal wholly in general principles. My personal conclusions as to the details of reconstruction have none of the importance to be ascribed to scholarship. Also to speak with complete candour, I cannot place any of the events within that period as out of scale in type of happenings with analogous occurrences elsewhere. I do hold, however, that the culminating points of the period embody the greatest advances in the expression of moral and intellectual intuitions which mark the growth of recent civilization.

The period as a whole begins in barbarism and ends in failure. The failure consisted in the fact that barbaric elements and the defects in intellectual comprehension had not been discarded, but remained as essential elements in the various formulations of Christian theology, orthodox and heretical alike. Also the later Protestant Reformation was, in this respect, an even more complete failure, in no way improving Catholic theology. The Quakers perhaps form a minor exception to this statement. But George Fox lived a hundred years after the age of Luther. The issue of these failures is the tragic history of Christianity.

SECTION IV. I suggest that in the whole period there are three culminating phases which, in theological language, constitute its threefold revelation. The first and the last phases were primarily intellectual with a sufficient background of moral insight. The middle phase, which forms the driving power of the religion, is primarily an exhibition in life of moral intuition, with a sufficiency of intellectual insight to give an articulate expression of singular beauty. The three phases are bound together as intellectual discovery,—then exemplification,—finally metaphysical interpretation. The discovery and the exemplification are historically independent.

The first phase is constituted by Plato's publication of his final conviction, towards the end of his life,[2] that the divine element in the world is to be conceived as a persuasive agency and not as a coercive agency. This doctrine should be looked upon as one of the greatest intellectual discoveries in the history of religion. It is plainly enunciated by Plato, though he failed to coordinate it systematically with the rest of his metaphysical theory. Indeed, Plato always failed in his attempts at systematization, and always succeeded in displaying depth of metaphysical intuition—the greatest metaphysician, the poorest systematic thinker. The alternative doctrine, prevalent then and now, sees either in the many gods or in the one God, the final coercive forces wielding the thunder. By a metaphysical sublimation of this doctrine of God as the supreme agency of compulsion, he is transformed into the one

2. Cf. The *Sophist* and the *Timæus*.

supreme reality, omnipotently disposing a wholly derivative world. Plato wavered inconsistently between these diverse conceptions. But he does finally enunciate without qualification the doctrine of the divine persuasion, by reason of which ideals are effective in the world and forms of order evolve.

The second phase is the supreme moment in religious history, according to the Christian religion. The essence of Christianity is the appeal to the life of Christ as a revelation of the nature of God and of his agency in the world. The record is fragmentary, inconsistent, and uncertain. It is not necessary for me to express any opinion as to the proper reconstruction of the most likely tale of historic fact. Such a procedure would be useless, without value, and entirely out of place in this book. But there can be no doubt as to what elements in the record have evoked a response from all that is best in human nature. The Mother, the Child, and the bare manger: the lowly man, homeless and self-forgetful, with his message of peace, love, and sympathy: the suffering, the agony, the tender words as life ebbed, the final despair: and the whole with the authority of supreme victory.

I need not elaborate. Can there be any doubt that the power of Christianity lies in its revelation in act, of that which Plato divined in theory?

The third phase is again intellectual. It is the first period in the formation of Christian theology by the schools of thought mainly associated with Alexandria and Antioch. The originality and value of their contribution to the thought of the world has been greatly underestimated. This is partly their own fault. For they persisted in declaring that they were only stating the faith once delivered to the saints; whereas in fact they were groping after the solution of a fundamental metaphysical problem, although presented to them in a highly special form.

These Christian theologians have the distinction of being the only thinkers who in a fundamental metaphysical doctrine have improved upon Plato. It is true that this period of Christian theology was Platonic. But it is also true that Plato is the originator of the heresies and of the feeblest side of Christian Theology. When Plato is faced with the problem of expressing the relationship of God to the World, and of the relation to the World of those Ideas which it is in God's nature to contemplate, Plato's answer is invariably framed in terms of mere dramatic imitation. When Plato turns to the World, after considering God as giving life and motion to the ideas by the inclusion of them in the divine nature, he can find only second-rate substitutes and never the originals. For Plato there is a derivative second-rate God of the World, who is a mere Icon, that is to say an image. Also when he looks for the ideas, he can only find, in the World, imitations. Thus the World, for Plato, includes only the image of God, and imitations of his ideas, and never God and his ideas.

Plato has definite reasons for this gap between the transient world and the eternal nature of God. He is avoiding difficulties, although he only achieves the feeblest of solutions. What metaphysics requires is a solution exhibiting the plurality of individuals as consistent with the unity of the Universe, and a solution which exhibits the World as requiring its union with God, and God as requiring his union with the World. Sound doctrine also requires an understanding how the Ideals in God's nature, by reason of their status in his nature, are thereby persuasive elements in the creative advance. Plato grounded these derivations from God upon his will; whereas metaphysics requires that the relationships of God to the World should lie beyond the accidents of will, and that they be founded upon the necessities of the nature of God and the nature of the World.

These problems came before the Christian theologians in highly special forms. They had to consider the nature of God. On this topic, there can be no doubt that the Arian solution, involving a derivative Image, is orthodox Platonism, though it be heterodox Christianity. The accepted solution of a multiplicity in the nature of God, each component being unqualifiedly Divine, involves a doctrine of mutual immanence in the divine nature. I am not in any way venturing upon a decision upon the correctness of the original assumption of this multiplicity. The point is the recourse to a doctrine of mutual immanence.

Again, the theologians had also to construct a doctrine of the person of Christ. And again they rejected the doctrine of an association of the human individual with a divine individual, involving responsive imitations in the human person. They decided for the direct immanence of God in the one person of Christ. They also decided for some sort of direct immanence of God in the World generally. This was their doctrine of the third person of the Trinity. I am not making any judgment about the details of their theology, for example, about the Trinitarian doctrine. My point is that in the place of Plato's solution of secondary images and imitations, they demanded a direct doctrine of immanence. It is in this respect that they made a metaphysical discovery. They pointed out the way in which Platonic metaphysics should develop, if it was to give a rational account of the role of the persuasive agency of God.

Unfortunately, the theologians never made this advance into general metaphysics. The reason for this check was another unfortunate presupposition. The nature of God was exempted from all the metaphysical categories which applied to the individual things in this temporal world. The concept of him was a sublimation from its barbaric origin. He stood in the same relation to the whole World as early Egyptian or Mesopotamian kings stood to their subject populations. Also the moral characters were very analogous. In the final metaphysical sublimation, he became the one absolute, omnipotent, omniscient source of all being, for his own existence requiring no relations to anything beyond himself. He was internally complete. Such a conception fitted on very well to the Platonic doctrine of subordinate derivations. The final insistence, after much wavering, on the immanence of God was therefore all the more a fine effort of metaphysical imagination on the part of the theologians of the early Christian ages. But their general concept of the Deity stopped all further generalization. They made no effort to conceive the World in terms of the metaphysical categories by means of which they interpreted God, and they made no effort to conceive God in terms of the metaphysical categories which they applied to the World. For them, God was eminently real, and the World was derivatively real. God was necessary to the World, but the World was not necessary to God. There was a gulf between them.

The worst of a gulf is, that it is very difficult to know what is happening on the further side of it. This has been the fate of the God of traditional theology. It is only by drawing the long bow of mysticism that evidences for his existence can be collected from our temporal World. Also the worst of unqualified omnipotence is that it is accompanied by responsibility for every detail of every happening. This whole topic is discussed by Hume in his famous Dialogues.

SECTION V. I am suggesting that Protestant theology should develop as its foundation an interpretation of the Universe which grasps its unity amid its many diversities. The interpretation to be achieved is a reconciliation of seeming incompatibilities. But these incompatibilities are not hypothetical. They are there on the stage of history, undoubted and claiming interpretation. There stand in the public view the persuasiveness of the eternal ideals, the same today as when realized in the Founder of Christianity, and the compulsoriness of physical nature, which passes and yet remains, and the compulsoriness of that realized urge toward social union, such as the Roman Empire, which was then, and is now as it were a dream. Nature changes and yet remains. The ideals declare themselves as timeless: and yet they pass on, as it were the flicker of a brightness.

It is the business of philosophical theology to provide a rational understanding of the rise of civilization, and of the tenderness of mere life itself, in a world which superficially is founded upon the clashings of senseless compulsion. I am not disguising my belief that in this task, theology has largely failed. The notion of the absolute despot has stood in the way. The doctrine of Grace has been degraded, and the doctrines of the Atonement ·are mostly crude. The defect of the liberal theology of the last two hundred years is chat it has confined itself to the suggestion of minor, vapid reasons why people should continue to go to church in the traditional fashion.

The last book in the Bible illustrates the barbaric elements which have been retained to the undoing of Christian intuition. In itself and apart from its bearing upon religious sentiment, it is one of the finest examples of imaginative literature as it stands translated in King James's Bible. Also, as an historical document, whether its origin be Christian or Jewish, it is of priceless value for the understanding of strains of thought prevalent when the Christian religion was in process of formation. Finally, the book only states, more pointedly and more vividly, ideas spread throughout the Old Testament and the New Testament, even in the Gospels themselves. Yet it is shocking to think that this book has been retained for the formation of religious sentiment, while the speech of Pericles, descriptive of the Athenian ideal of civilization, has remained neglected in this connection. What I am advocating can be symbolized by this shift in the final book of the authoritative collection of religious literature, namely, the replacement of the book of the Revelation of St. John the Divine by the imaginative account given by Thucydides of the Speech of Pericles to the Athenians. Neither of them is history: St. John never received just that revelation, nor did Pericles ever make just that speech.

SECTION VI. There remains for discussion one final question. I wish to emphasize the importance that, amid many divergencies of interpretation, the leaders of religious thought should today concentrate upon the Christian tradition and more particularly upon its historical origins. In the case of the more conservative schools of thought such advice is, of course, unnecessary, and indeed impertinent. But it is a question for discussion why the more radical schools should not cut entirely free from any appeal to the past, and concentrate entirely upon the contemporary world and contemporary examples. The summary answer is that in so far as such an appeal to tradition can be made with complete honesty, without any shadow of evasion, there is an enormous gain in popular effectiveness.

Civilization is constituted out of four elements, (I) Patterns of Behaviour, (2) Patterns of Emotion, (3) Patterns of Belief, and (4) Technologies. We can at once dismiss Technologies as beyond our topic, though all four constitutive elements interact upon each other. Also patterns of behaviour are in the long run sustained or modified by patterns of emotion and patterns of belief. It is the primary business of religion to concentrate upon emotion and belief.

Now, so far as concerns beliefs of a general character, it is much easier for them to destroy en1otion than to generate it. In any survey of the adventure of ideas nothing is more surprising than the ineffectiveness of novel general ideas to acquire for themselves an appropriate emotional pattern of any intensity. Profound flashes of insight remain ineffective for centuries, not because they are unknown, but by reason of dominant interests which inhibit reaction to that type of generality. The history of religion is the history of the countless generations required for interest to attach itself to profound ideas. For this reason religions are so often more barbarous than the civilizations in which they flourish.

This faintness of impress of general ideas upon the human mind has another effect. It is difficult even for acute thinkers to understand the analogies between ideas expressed in diverse phraseologies and illustrated by different sorts of examples. Desperate intellectual battles have been fought by philosophers who have expressed the same idea in different ways. For both these reasons, if you want to make a new start in religion, based upon ideas of profound generality, you must be content to wait a thousand years. Religions are like species of animals: they do not originate from special creations.

Finally, if there be any truth in the contention that dogmatic finality of verbal expression is a mistaken notion, there is an enormous advantage in keep together, with common modes of procedure, religious opinions of analogous types. They can learn from each other, borrow from each other, and individuals can make imperceptible transitions. Above all, they can learn to understand each other and to love.

Must 'religion' always remain as a synonym for 'hatred'? The great social ideal for religion is that it should be the common basis for the unity of civilization. In that way it justifies its insight beyond the transient clash of brute forces.

This discussion has concentrated upon three culminating phases, the thought of Plato, the life of Christ, and the first formative period of Christian theology. But this whole period of twelve centuries, with its legendary antecedents and its modern successors, is required to complete the tale of the Christian religion. The story is wholly concerned with the interplay of ideas belonging to different levels of insight. The religious spirit is always in process of being explained away, distorted, buried. Yet, since the travel of mankind towards civilization, it is always there.

The task of Theology is to show how the World is founded on something beyond mere transient fact, and how it issues in something beyond the perishing of occasions. The temporal World is the stage of finite accomplishment. We ask of Theology to express that element in perishing lives which is undying by reason of its expression of perfections proper to our finite natures. In this way we shall understand how life includes a mode of satisfaction deeper than joy or sorrow.

PART III

PHILOSOPHICAL

Chapter XI

OBJECTS AND SUBJECTS

. . . Τὸ παρὸν εχάστω πάθος, εξ ων αί αίσθήσεις χαί αί χάτα ναύτας γίγνονται . . . *Theaetetus*, 179 C.

§1. *Prefatory.*—When Descartes, Locke, and Hume undertake the analysis of experience, they utilize those elements in their own experience which lie clear and distinct, fit for the exactitude of intellectual discourse. It is tacitly assumed, except by Plato, that the more fundamental factors will ever lend themselves for discrimination with peculiar clarity. This assumption is here directly challenged.

§2. *Structure of Experience.*—No topic has suffered more from this tendency of philosophers than their account of the object-subject structure of experience. In the first place, this structure has been identified with the bare relation of knower to known. The subject is the knower, the object is the known. Thus, with this interpretation, the object-subject relation is the known-knower relation. It then follows that the more clearly any instance of this relation stands out for discrimination, the more safely we can utilize it for the interpretation of the status of experience in the universe of things. Hence Descartes' appeal to clarity and distinctness.

This deduction presupposes that the subject-object relation is the fundamental structural pattern of experience. I agree with this presupposition, but not in the sense in which subject-object is identified with knower-known. I contend that the notion of mere knowledge is a high abstraction, and that conscious discrimination itself is a variable factor only present in the more elaborate examples of occasions of experience. The basis of experience is emotional. Stated more generally, the basic fact is the rise of an affective tone originating from things whose relevance is given.

§3. *Phraseology.*—Thus the Quaker word 'concern', divested of any suggestion of knowledge, is more fitted to express this fundamental structure. The occasion as subject has a 'concern' for the object. And the 'concern' at once places the object as a component in the experience of the subject, with an affective tone drawn from this object and directed towards it. With this interpretation the subject-object relation is the fundamental structure of experience.

Quaker usages of language are not widely spread. Also each phraseology leads to a crop of misunderstandings. The subject-object relation can be conceived as Recipient and Provoker, where the fact provoked is an affective tone about the status of the provoker in the provoked experience. Also the total provoked occasion is a totality involving many such examples of provocation. Again this phraseology is unfortunate; for the word 'recipient' suggests a passivity which is erroneous.

§4. *Prehensions.*—A more formal explanation is as follows. An occasion of experience is an activity, analysable into modes of functioning which jointly constitute its process of becoming. Each mode is anlysable into the total experience as active subject, and into the thing or object with which the special activity is concerned. This thing is a datum, that is to say, is describable without reference to its entertainment in that occasion. An object is anything performing this function of a datum provoking some special activity of the occasion in question. Thus subject and object are relative terms. An occasion is a subject in respect to its special activity concerning an object; and anything is an object in respect to its provocation of some special activity within a subject. Such a mode of activity is termed a 'prehension'. Thus a prehension involves three factors. There is the occasion of experience within which the prehension is a detail of activity; there is the datum whose relevance provokes the origination of this prehension; this datum is the prehended object; there is the subjective form, which is the affective tone determining the effectiveness of that prehension in that occasion of experience. How the experience constitutes itself depends on its complex of subjective forms.

§5. *Individuality.*—The individual immediacy of an occasion is the final unity of subjective form, which is the occasion as an absolute reality. This immediacy is its moment of sheer individuality, bounded on either side by essential relativity. The occasion arises from relevant objects, and perishes into the status of an object for other occasions. But it enjoys its decisive moment of absolute self-attainment as emotional unity. As used here the words 'individual' and 'atom' have the same meaning, that they apply to composite things with an absolute reality which their components lack. These words properly apply to an actual entity in its immediacy of self-attainment when it stands out as for itself alone, with its own affective self-enjoyment. The term 'monad' also expresses this essential unity at the decisive moment, which stands between its birth and its perishing. The creativity of the world is the throbbing emotion of the past hurling itself into a new transcendent fact. It is the flying dart, of which Lucretius speaks, hurled beyond the bounds of the world.

§6. *Knowledge.*—All knowledge is conscious discrimination of objects experienced. But this conscious discrimination, which is knowledge, is nothing more than an additional factor in the subjective form of the interplay of subject with object. This interplay is the stuff constituting those individual things which make up the sole reality of the Universe. These individual things are the individual occasions of experience, the actual entities.

But we do not so easily get rid of knowledge. After all, it is knowledge that philosophers seek. And all knowledge is derived from, and verified by, direct intuitive observation. I accept this axiom of empiricism as stated in this general form. The question then arises how the structure of experience outlined above is directly observed. In answering this challenge I remind myself of the old advice that the doctrines which best repay critical examination are those which for the longest period have remained unquestioned.

§7. *Sense-Perception.*—The particular agelong group of doctrines which I have in mind is: (1) that all perception is by the mediation of our bodily sense-organs, such as eyes, palates, noses, ears, and the diffused bodily organization furnishing touches, aches, and other bodily sensations; (2) that all percepta are bare sensa, in patterned connections, given in the immediate present; (3) that our experience of a social world is an interpretative reaction wholly derivative from this perception; (4) that our emotional and purposive experience is a reflective reaction derived from the original perception, and intertwined with the interpretative reaction and partly shaping it. Thus the two reactions are different aspects of one process, involving interpretative, emotional, and purposive factors. Of course, we are all aware that there are powerful schools of philosophy which explicitly reject this doctrine. Yet I cannot persuade myself that this rejection has been taken seriously by writers belonging to the schools in question. When the direct question as to things perceived arises, it seems to me that the answer is always returned in terms of sensa perceived.

§8. *Perceptive Functions.*—In the examination of the sensationalist doctrine, the first question to be asked concerns the general definition of what we mean by those functions of experience which we term 'perceptions'. If we define them as those experiential functions which arise directly from the stimulation of the various bodily sense-organs, then argument ceases. The traditional doctrine then becomes a mere matter of definition of the use of the word 'perception'. Indeed, having regard to long-standing usage, I am inclined to agree that it may be advisable for philosophers to confine the word 'perception' to this limited meaning. But the point on which I am insisting is that this meaning *is* limited, and that there is a wider meaning with which this limited use of the term 'perception' has been tacitly identified.

§9. *Objects.*—The process of experiencing is constituted by the reception of entities, whose being is antecedent to that process, into the complex fact which is that process itself. These antecedent entities, thus received as factors into the process of experiencing, are termed 'objects' for that experiential occasion. Thus primarily the term 'object' expresses the relation of the entity, thus denoted, to one or more occasions of experiencing. Two conditions must be fulfilled in order that an entity may function as an object in a process of experiencing: (1) the entity must be *antecedent,* and (2) the entity must be experienced in virtue of its antecedence; it must be *given.* Thus an object must be a thing received, and must not be either a *mode* of reception or a thing *generated* in that occasion. Thus the process of experiencing is constituted by the reception of objects into the unity of that complex occasion which is the process itself. The process creates itself, but it does not create the objects which it receives as factors in its own nature.

'Objects' for an occasion can also be termed the 'data' for that occasion. The choice of terms entirely depends on the metaphor which you prefer. One word carries the literal meaning of 'lying in the way of', and the other word carries the literal meaning of 'being given to'. But both words suffer from the defect of suggesting that an occasion of experiencing arises out of a passive situation which is a mere welter of many data.

§10. *Creativity.*—The exact contrary is the case. The initial situation includes a factor of activity which is the reason for the origin of that occasion of experience. This factor of activity is what I have called 'Creativity'. The initial situation with its creativity can be termed the initial phase of the new occasion. It can equally well be termed the 'actual world' relative to that occasion. It has a certain unity of its own, expressive of its capacity for providing the objects requisite for a new occasion, and also expressive of its conjoint activity whereby it is essentially the primary phase of a new occasion. It can thus be termed a 'real potentiality'. The 'potentiality' refers to the passive capacity, the term 'real' refers to the creative activity, where the Platonic definition of 'real' in the *Sophist* is referred to. This basic situation, this actual world, this primary phase, this real potentiality—however you characterise it—as a whole is active with its inherent creativity, but in its details it provides the passive objects which derive their activity from the creativity, of the whole. The creativity is the actualization of potentiality, and the process of actualization is an occasion of experiencing. Thus viewed in abstraction objects are passive, hut viewed in conjunction they carry the creativity which drives the world. The process of creation is the form of unity of the Universe.

§11. *Perception.*—In the preceding sections, the discovery of objects as factors in experience was explained. The discussion was phrased in terms of an ontology which goes beyond the immediate purpose, although the status of objects cannot be understood in the absence of some such ontology explaining their function in experience, that is to say, explaining why an occasion of experience by reason of its nature requires objects.

The objects are the factors in experience which function so as to express that that occasion originates by including a transcendent universe of other things. Thus it belongs to the essence of each occasion of experience that it is concerned with an otherness transcending itself. The occasion is one among others, and including the others which it is among. Consciousness is an emphasis upon a selection of these objects. Thus perception is consciousness analysed in respect to those objects selected for this emphasis. Consciousness is the acme of emphasis.

It is evident that this definition of perception is wider than the narrow definition based upon sense-perception, sensa. and the bodily sense-organs.

§12. *Non-Sensuous Perception.*—This wider definition of perception can be of no importance unless we can detect occasions of experience exhibiting modes of functioning which fall within its wider scope. If we discover such instances of non-sensuous perception, then the tacit identification of perception with sense-perception must be a fatal error barring the advance of systematic metaphysics.

Our first step must involve the clear recognition of the limitations inherent in the scope of sense-perception. This special mode of functioning essentially exhibits percepta as *here, now, immediate,* and *discrete.* Every impression of sensation is a distinct existence, declares Hume; and there can be no reasonable doubt of this doctrine. But even Hume clothes each impression with force and liveliness. It must be distinctly understood that no prehension, even of bare sensa, can be divested of its affective tone, that is to say, of its character of a 'concern' in the Quaker sense. Concernedness is of the essence of perception.

Gaze at a patch of red. In itself as an object, and apart from other factors of concern, this patch of red, as the mere object of that present act of perception, is silent as to the past or the future. How it originates, how it will vanish, whether indeed there was a past, and whether there will be a future, are not disclosed by its own nature. No material for the interpretation of sensa is provided by the sensa themselves, as they stand starkly, barely, present and immediate. We *do* interpret them; but no thanks for the feat is due to them. The epistemologies of the last two hundred years are employed in the tacit introduction of alien considerations by the uncritical use of current forms of speech. A copious use of simple literary forms can thus provide a philosophy delightful to read, easy to understand, and entirely fallacious. Yet the usages of language do prove that our habitual interpretations of these barren sensa are in the main satisfying to common sense, though in particular instances liable to error. But the evidence on which these interpretations are based is entirely drawn from the vast background and foreground of non-sensuous perception with which sense-perception is fused, and without which it can never be. We can discern no clean-cut sense-perception wholly concerned with present fact.

In human experience, the most compelling example of non-sensuous perception is our knowledge of our own immediate past. I am not referring to our memories of a day past, or of an hour past, or of a minute past. Such memories are blurred and confused by the intervening occasions of our personal existence. But our immediate past is constituted by that occasion, or by that group of fused occasions, which enters into experience devoid of any perceptible medium intervening between it and the present immediate fact. Roughly speaking, it is that portion of our past lying between a tenth of a second and half a second ago. It is gone, and yet it is here. It is our indubitable self, the foundation of our present existence. Yet the present occasion while claiming self-identity, while sharing the very nature of the bygone occasion in all its living activities, nevertheless is engaged in modifying it, in adjusting it to *other* influences, in completing it with *other* values, in deflecting it to *other* purposes. The present moment is constituted by the influx of *the other* into that self-identity which is the continued life of the immediate past within the immediacy of the present.

§13. *Illustration.*—Consider a reasonably rapid speaker enunciating the proper name 'United States'. There are four syllables here. When the third syllable is reached, probably the first is in the immediate past; and certainly during the word 'States' the first syllable of the phrase lies beyond the immediacy of the present. Consider the speaker's own occasions of existence. Each occasion achieves for him the immediate sense-presentation of sounds, the earlier syllables in the earlier occasions, the word 'States' in the final occasion. As mere sensuous perception, Hume is right in saying that the sound 'United' as a mere sensum has nothing in its nature referent to the sound 'States', yet the speaker is carried from

'United' to 'States', and the two conjointly live in the present, by the energizing of the past occasion as it claims its self-identical existence as a living issue in the present. The immediate past as surviving to be again lived through in the present is the palmary instance of non-sensuous perception.

The Humian explanation, involving the 'association of ideas', has its importance for this topic. But it is not to the point for this example. The speaker, a citizen of the United States and therefore dominated by an immense familiarity with that phase, may in fact have been enunciating the phrase 'United Fruit Company'—a corporation which, for all its importance, he may not have heard of till half a minute earlier. In his experience the relation of the later to the earlier parts of this phrase is entirely the same as that described above for the phrase 'United States'. In this latter example it is to be noted that while association would have led him to 'States', the fact of the energizing of the immediate past compelled him to conjoin 'Fruit' in the immediacy of the present. He uttered the word 'United' with the non-sensuous anticipation of an immediate future with the sensum 'Fruit', and he then uttered the word 'Fruit' with the non-sensuous perception of the immediate past with the sensum 'United'. But, unfamiliar as he was with the United Fruit Company, he had no association connecting the various words in the phrase 'United Fruit Company'; while, patriot as he was, the orator had the strongest association connecting the words 'United' and 'States'. Perhaps, indeed, he was the founder of the Company, and also invented the name. He then uttered the mere sounds 'United Fruit Company' for the first time in the history of the English language. There could not have been the vestige of an association to help him along. The final occasion of his experience which drove his body to the utterance of the sound 'Company' is only explicable by his concern with the earlier occasions with their subjective forms of intention to procure the utterance of the complete phrase. Also, in so far as there was consciousness, there was direct observation of the past with its intention finding its completion in the present fact. This is an instance of direct intuitive observation which is incapable of reduction to the sensationalist formula. Such observations have not the clear sharp-cut precision of sense-perception. But surely there can be no doubt about them. For instance, if the speaker had been interrupted after the words 'United Fruit', he might have resumed his speech with the words 'I meant to add the word Company'. Thus during the interruption, the past was energizing in his experience as carrying in itself an unfulfilled intention.

§14. *Conformation of Feeling.*—Another point emerges in this explanation, namely, the doctrine of the continuity of nature. This doctrine balances and limits the doctrine of the absolute individuality of each occasion of experience. There is a continuity between the subjective form of the immediate past occasion and the subjective form of its primary prehension in the origination of the new occasion. In the process of synthesis of the many basic prehensions modifications enter. But the subjective forms of the immediate past are continuous with those of the present. I will term this doctrine of continuity, the Doctrine of Conformation of Feeling.

Suppose that for some period of time some circumstance of his life has aroused anger in a man. How does he now know that a quarter of a second ago he was angry? Of course, he remembers it; we all know that. But I am enquiring about this very curious fact of memory, and have chosen an overwhelmingly vivid instance. The mere word 'memory' explains nothing. The first phase in the immediacy of the new occasion is that of the conformation of feelings. The feeling as enjoyed by the past occasion is present in the new occasion as datum felt, with a subjective form conformal to that of the datum. Thus if A be the past occasion, D the datum felt by A with subjective form describable as A angry, then this feeling—namely, A feeling D with 1oubjective form of anger—

is initially felt by the new occasion B with the same subjective form of anger. The anger is continuous throughout the successive occasions of experience. This continuity of subjective form is the initial sympathy of B for A. It is the primary ground for the continuity of nature.

Let us elaborate the consideration of the angry man. His anger is the subjective form of his feeling some datum D. A quarter of a second later he is, consciously, or unconsciously, embodying his past as a datum in the present, and maintaining in the present the anger which is a datum from the past. In so far as that feeling has fallen within the illumination of consciousness, he enjoys a non-sensuous perception of the past emotion. He enjoys this emotion both objectively, as belonging to the past, and also formally as continued in the present. This continuation is the continuity of nature. I have labored this point, because traditional doctrines involve its denial.

Thus non-sensuous perception is one aspect of the continuity of nature.

§15. *Hume's Doctrine of Custom.*—Hume appeals to a doctrine of force and liveliness as an essential factor in an impression of sensation. This doctrine is nothing but a special case of the doctrine of subjective forms. Again he holds that the force and liveliness of one occasion of experience enter into the character of succeeding occasions. The whole doctrine of 'custom' depends on this assumption. If the occasions be entirely separate, as Hume contends, this transition of character is without any basis in the nature of things. What Hume, in his appeal to memory, is really doing is to appeal to an observed immanence of the past in the future, involving a continuity of subjective form.

With this addition, every argument of Part III of Hume's *Treatise* can be accepted. But the conclusion follows that there is an observed relation of causation between such occasions. The general character of this observed relation explains at once memory and personal identity. They are all different aspects of the doctrine of the immanence of occasions of experience. The additional conclusion can also be derived, that in so far as we apply notions of causation to the understanding of events in nature, we must conceive these events under the general notions which apply to occasions of experience. For we can only understand causation in terms of our observations of these occasions. This -appeal to Hume has the sole purpose of illustrating the common-sense obviousness of the present thesis.

§16. *The Flux of Energy.*—An occasion of experience which includes a human mentality is an extreme instance, at one end of the scale, of those happenings which constitute nature. As yet this discussion has fixed attention upon this extreme. But any doctrine which refuses to place human experience outside nature, must find in descriptions of human experience factors which also enter into the descriptions of less specialized natural occurrences. If there be no such factors, then the doctrine of human experience as a fact within nature is mere bluff, founded upon vague phrases whose sole merit is a comforting familiarity. We should either admit dualism. at least as a provisional doctrine, or we should point out the identical elements connecting human experience with physical science.

The science of physics conceives a natural occasion as a locus of energy. Whatever else that occasion may be, it is an individual fact harboring that energy. The words electron, proton, photon, wave-motion, velocity, hard and soft radiation, chemical elements, matter, empty space, temperature, degradation of energy, all point to the fact that physical science recognizes qualitative differences between occasions in respect to the way in which each occasion entertains its energy.

These differences are entirely constituted by the flux of energy, that is to say, by the way in which the occasions in question have inherited their energy from the past of nature, and in which they are about to transmit their energy to the future. The discussion of the Poynting Flux of Energy is one of the most fascinating chapters of Electrodynamics. Forty-seven years ago, when a young graduate student, I first heard of it in a lecture delivered by Sir J. J. Thomson. It was then a new discovery recently published by Poynting. But its father was the great Clerk-Maxwell who had expounded all the requisite principles. The sole conclusion with which we are concerned is that energy has recognizable paths through time and space. Energy passes from particular occasion to particular occasion. At each point there is a flux, with a quantitative flow and a definite direction.

This is a conception of physical nature in terms of continuity. In fact, the concept of continuity was dominant in Clerk-Maxwell's thought. But the alternative concept of distinguishable individualities has again emerged into importance in the more recent physics. Electrons and protons and photons are unit charges of electricity; also there are the quanta of the flux of energy. These contrasted aspects of nature, continuity and atomicity, have a long history in European thought, reaching back to the origin of science among the Greeks. The more probable conclusion is that neither can be dispensed with, and that we are only witnessing that modern phase of the contrast which is relevant to the present stage of science.

§17. *Mind and Nature Compared.*—The doctrine of human experience which I have outlined above, also for its own purposes preserves a doctrine of distinguishable individualities which are the separate occasions of experience, and a doctrine of continuity expressed by the identity of subjective form inherited conformally from one occasion to the other. The physical flux corresponds to the conformal inheritance at the base of each occasion of experience. This inheritance, in spite of its continuity of subjective form, is nevertheless an inheritance from definite individual occasions. Thus, if the analogy is to hold, in the account of the general system of relations binding the past to the present, we should expect a doctrine of quanta, where the individualities of the occasions are relevant, and a doctrine of continuity where the conformal transference of subjective form is the dominating fact.

The notion of physical energy, which is at the base of physics, must then be conceived as an abstraction from the complex energy, emotional and purposeful, inherent in the subjective form of the final synthesis in which each occasion completes itself. It is the total vigor of each activity of experience. The mere phrase that 'physical science is an abstraction', is a confession of philosophic failure. It is the business of rational thought to describe the more concrete fact from which that abstraction is derivable.

§18. *Personality.*—In our account of human experience we have attenuated human personality into a genetic relation between occasions of human experience. Yet personal unity is an inescapable fact. The Platonic and Christian doctrines of the Soul, the Epicurean doctrine of a Concilium of subtle atoms, the Cartesian doctrine of Thinking Substance, the Humanitarian doctrine of the Rights of man, the general Common Sense of civilized mankind,—these doctrines between them dominate the whole span of Western thought. Evidently there is a fact to be accounted for. Any philosophy must provide some doctrine of personal identity. In some sense there is a unity in the life of each man, from birth to death. The two modem philosophers who most consistently reject the notion of a self-identical Soul-Substance are Hume and William James. But the problem remains for them, as it does for the philosophy of organism, to provide an adequate account of this undoubted personal unity, maintaining itself amidst the welter of circumstance.

§19. *Plato's Receptacle.*—In mathematical studies, where there is a problem to be solved it is a sound method to generalize, so as to divest the problem of details irrelevant to the solution. Let us therefore give a general description of this personal unity, divesting it of minor details of humanity. For this purpose it is impossible to improve upon a passage from one of Plato's Dialogues. I summarize it with the insertion of such terms as 'personal unity', 'events', 'experience', and 'personal identity', for two or three of its own phrases: —"In addition to the notions of the welter of events and of the forms which they illustrate, we require a third term, personal unity. It is a perplexed and obscure concept. We must conceive it the receptacle, the foster-mother as I might say, of the becoming of our occasions of experience. This personal identity is the thing which receives all occasions of the man's existence. It is there as a natural matrix for all transitions of life, and is changed and variously figured by the things that enter it; so that it differs in its character at different times. Since it receives all manner of experiences into its own unity, it must itself be bare of all forms. We shall not be far wrong if we describe it as invisible, formless, and all-receptive. It is a locus which persists, and provides an emplacement for all the occasions of experience. That which happens in it is conditioned by the compulsion of its own past, and by the persuasion of its immanent ideals."

You will have recognized that in this description I have been adapting from Plato's *Timæus*[1], with the slightest of changes. But this is not Plato's description of the Soul. It is his doctrine of the Receptacle [υποδοχή] or Locus [χώρα] whose sole function is the imposition of a unity upon the events of Nature. These events are together by reason of their community of locus, and they obtain their actuality by reason of emplacement within this community.

§20. *Immanence.*—This is at once the doctrine of the unity of nature, and of the unity of each human life. The conclusion follows that our consciousness of the self-identity pervading our

1. I have used A. E. Taylor's translation, with compression and changes of phrase.

life-thread of occasions, is nothing other than knowledge of a special strand of unity within the general unity of nature. It is a locus within the whole, marked out by its own peculiarities, but otherwise exhibiting the general principle which guides the constitution of the whole. This general principle is the object-to-subject structure of experience. It can be otherwise stated as the vector-structure of nature. Or otherwise, it can be conceived as the doctrine of the immanence of the past energizing in the present.

This doctrine of immanence is practically that doctrine adumbrated by the Hellenistic Christian theologians of Egypt. But they applied the doctrine only to the relation of God to the World, and not to all actualities.

§21. *Space and Time.*—The notion of Space-Time represents a compromise between Plato's basic Receptacle, imposing no forms, and the Actual World imposing its own variety of forms. This imposition of forms is subject to the perspective elimination required by incompatibilities of affective tone. Geometry is the doctrine of loci of intermediaries imposing perspective in the process of inheritance. In geometry this doctrine is restricted to its barest generalities of coordination prevailing for this epoch of the Universe. These generalities solely concern the complex of serial relations persistently illustrated in the connection of events.

Our perception of this geometrical order of the Universe brings with it the denial of the restriction of inheritance to mere personal order. For personal order means one-dimensional serial order. And space is many-dimensional. Spatiality involves separation by reason of the diversity of intermediate occasions, and also it involves connection by reason of the immanence involved in the derivation of present from past. There is thus an analogy between the transference of energy from particular occasion to particular occasion in physical nature and the transference of affective tone, with its emotional energy, from one occasion to another in any human personality. The object-to-subject structure of human experience is reproduced in physical nature by this vector relation of particular to particular. It was the defect of the Greek analysis of generation that it conceived it in terms of the bare incoming of novel abstract form. This ancient analysis failed to grasp the real operation of the antecedent particulars imposing themselves on the novel particular in process of creation. Thus the geometry exemplified in fact was disjoined from their account of the generation of fact.

§22. *The Human Body.*—But this analogy of physical nature to human experience is limited by the fact of the linear seriality of human occasions within any one personality and of the many-dimensional seriality of the occasions in physical Space-Time.

In order to prove that this discrepancy is only superficial. it now remains for discussion whether the human experience of direct inheritance provides any analogy to this many-dimensional character of space. If human occasions of experience essentially inherit in one-dimensional personal order, there is a gap between human occasions and the physical occasions of nature.

The peculiar status of the human body at once presents itself as negating this notion of strict personal order for human inheritance. Our dominant inheritance from our immediately past occasion is broken into by innumerable inheritances through other avenues. Sensitive nerves, the functionings of our viscera, disturbances in the composition of our blood, break in upon the dominant line of inheritance. In this way, emotions, hopes, fears, inhibitions, sense-perceptions arise, which physiologists confidently ascribe to the bodily functionings. So intimately obvious is this bodily inheritance that common speech does not discriminate the human body from the human person. Soul and body are fused together. Also this common identification has survived the scientific investigation of physiologists, who are apt to see more body than soul in human beings.

But the human body is indubitably a complex of occasions which are part of spatial nature. It is a set of occasions miraculously coordinated so as to pour its inheritance into various regions within the brain. There is thus every reason to believe that our sense of unity with the body has the same original as our sense of unity with our immediate past of personal experience. It is another case of non-sensuous perception, only now devoid of the strict personal order.

But physiologists and physicists are equally agreed that the body inherits physical conditions from the physical environment according to the physical laws. There is thus a general continuity between human experience and physical occasions. The elaboration of such a continuity is one most obvious task for philosophy.

§23. *Dualism.*—This discussion has begged attention to a complex argument. I will conclude it by drawing attention to a general question which is relevant.

Is this discussion to be looked upon as another example of *The Revolt against Dualism?* We have all read with high appreciation Professor Lovejoy's brilliant book in criticism of this revolt. Now superficially the position which I have here put forward is certainly an instance of the revolt which he criticizes. But in another sense, I have endeavored to put forward a defence of dualism, differently interpreted. Plato, Descartes, Locke, prepared the way for Hume; and Kant followed upon Hume. The point of this discussion is to show an alternative line of thought which evades Hume's deduction from philosophical tradition, and at the same time preserves the general trend of thought received from his three great predecessors. The dualism in the later Platonic dialogues between the Platonic 'souls' and the Platonic 'physical' nature, the dualism between the Cartesian 'thinking substances' and the Cartesian 'extended substances', the dualism between the Lockian 'human understanding' and the Lockian 'external things' described for him by Galileo and Newton-all these kindred dualisms are here found within each occasion of actuality. Each occasion has its physical inheritance and its mental reaction which drives it on to its self-completion. The world is not merely physical, nor is it merely mental. Nor is it merely *one* with many subordinate phases. Nor it is merely a complete fact, in its essence static with the illusion of change. Wherever a vicious dualism appears, it is by reason of mistaking an abstraction for a final concrete fact.

The universe is dual because, in the fullest sense, it is both transient and eternal. The universe is dual because each final actuality is both physical and mental. The universe is dual because each actuality requires abstract character. The universe is dual because each occasion unites its formal immediacy with objective otherness. The universe is *many* because it is wholly and completely to be analysed into many final actualities—or in Cartesian language, into many *res verae.* The Universe is *one,* because of the universal immanence. There is thus a dualism in this contrast between the unity and multiplicity. Throughout the universe there reigns the union of opposites which is the ground of dualism.

Chapter XII

PAST, PRESENT, FUTURE

SECTION I. THE DOCTRINE of the immanence of past occasions in the occasions which are future, relatively to them, has been sufficiently discussed in the previous chapter. The past has an objective existence in the present which lies in the future beyond itself. But the sense in which the future can be said to be immanent in occasions antecedent to itself, and the sense in which contemporary occasions are immanent in each other, are not so evident in terms of the doctrine of the subject-object structure of experience. It will be simpler first to concentrate upon the relation of the future to the present. It is evident that the future certainly is something for the present. The most familiar habits of mankind witness to this fact. Legal contracts, social understandings of every type, ambitions, anxieties, railway time-tables. are futile gestures of consciousness apart from the fact that the present bears in its own realized constitution relationships to a future beyond itself. Cut away the future, and the present collapses, emptied of its proper content. Immediate existence requires the insertion of the future in the crannies of the present.

Here again the habits of a literary training with its long-range forecast and back-cast of critical thought exercise an unfortunate effect upon philosophy. We think of the future in time-spans of centuries. or of decades, or of years, or of days. We dwell critically upon the mass of fables termed history. As a result we conceive ourselves as related to past or to future by a mere effort of purely abstract imagination, devoid of direct observation of particular fact. If we admit this conclusion. there is no real evidence that there was a past, or that there will be a future. Our ignorance on this point is complete. All that we can observe consists of conceptual persuasions in the present. Such is the outcome of the literary habit of dwelling upon the long future or upon the long past. Literature preserves the wisdom of the human race; but in this way it enfeebles the emphasis of first-hand intuition. In considering our direct observation of past, or of future, we should confine ourselves to time-spans of the order of magnitude of a second, or even of fractions of a second.

SECTION II. If we keep ourselves to this short-range intuition, assuredly the future is not nothing. It lives actively in its antecedent world. Each moment of experience confesses itself to be a transition between two worlds, the immediate past and the immediate future. This is the persistent delivery of common-sense. Also this immediate future is immanent in the present with some degree of structural definition. The difficulty lies in the explanation of this immanence in terms of the subject-object structure of experience. In the present, the future occasions, as individual realities with their measure of absolute completeness, are non-existent. Thus the future must be immanent in the present in some different sense to the objective immortality of the individual occasions of the past. In the present there are no individual occasions belonging to the future. The present contains the utmost verge of such realized individuality. The whole doctrine of the future is to be understood in terms of the account of the process of self-completion of each individual actual occasion.

This process can be shortly characterized as a passage from re-enaction to anticipation. The intermediate stage in this transition is constituted by the acquisition of novel content, which is the individual contribution of the immediate subject for the re-shaping of its primary phase of re-enaction into its final phase of anticipation. This final phase is otherwise termed the 'satisfaction,' since it marks the exhaustion of the creative urge for that individuality. This novel content is composed of positive conceptual prehensions, that is to say, of conceptual feelings. These conceptual feelings become integrated with the physical prehensions of antecedent occasions, and thus yield propositions concerning the past. These propositions are again integrated and re-integrated with each other and with conceptual feelings, and yield other propositions.

Finally propositions emerge concerning the constitution of the immediate subject. It belongs to the essence of this subject that it pass into objective immortality. Thus its own constitution involves that its own activity in *self*-formation passes into its activity of *other*-formation. It is by reason of the constitution of the present subject that the future will embody the present subject and will re-enact its patterns of activity. But the future individual occasions are non-existent. The sole immediate actuality is the constitution of the present subject which embodies its own necessity for objective immortality beyond its own immediacy of self-formation. This objective immortality is a stubborn fact for the future, involving its pattern of perspective re-enaction.

The final phase of anticipation is a propositional realization of the essence of the present-subject, in respect to the necessities which it lays upon the future to embody it and to re-enact it so far as compatibility may permit. Thus the self-enjoyment of an occasion of experience is initiated by an enjoyment of the past as alive in itself and is terminated by an enjoyment of itself as alive in the future. This is the account of the creative urge of the universe as it functions in each single individual occasion. In this sense, the future is immanent in each present occasion, with its particular relations to the present settled in various degrees of dominance. But no future individual occasion is in existence. The anticipatory propositions all concern the constitution of the present occasion and the necessities inherent in it. This constitution necessitates that there be a future, and necessitates a quota of contribution for re-enaction in the primary phases of future occasions.

The point to remember is that the fact that each individual occasion is transcended by the creative urge, belongs to the essential constitution of each such occasion. It is not an accident which is irrelevant to the completed constitution of any such occasion.

In the formation of each occasion of actuality the swing over from re-enaction to anticipation is due to the intervening touch of mentality. Whether the ideas thus introduced by the novel conceptual prehensions be old or new, they have this decisive result, that the occasion arises as an effect facing its past and ends as a cause facing its future. In between there lies the teleology of the Universe.

If the mental activity involves no introduction of ideal novelty, the data of the conceptual feelings are merely eternal objects already illustrated in the initial phase of re-enaction. In that case, the re-integration with the primary phase merely converts the initial conformal reception into the anticipation of preservation of types of order and ·of patterns of feeling already dominant in the inheritance. There is a reign of acquiescence. In this way, a region of such occasions assumes the aspect of passive submission to imposed laws of nature. But when there is conceptual novelty made effective by its re-iteration and by the added emphasis on it throughout a chain of coordinated occasions, we have the aspect of an enduring person with a sustained purpose originated by that person and made effective in that person's environment. Thus in this case the anticipation of kinship with the future assumes the form of purpose to transform concept into fact. In either case, whether or no there be conceptual novelty, the subjective forms of the conceptual prehensions constitute the drive of the Universe, whereby each occasion precipitates itself into the future.

SECTION III. It is now possible to determine the sense in which the future is immanent in the present. The future is immanent in the present by reason of the fact that the present bears in its own essence the relationships which it will have to the future. It thereby includes in its essence the necessities to which the future must conform. The future is there in the present, as a general fact belonging to the nature of things. It is also there with such general determinations as it lies in the nature of the particular present to impose on the particular future which must succeed it. All this belongs to the essence of the present, and constitutes the future, as thus determined, an object for prehension in the subjective immediacy of the present. In this way each present occasion prehends the general metaphysical character of the universe, and thereby it prehends its own share in that character. Thus the future is to the present as an object for a subject. It has an objective existence in the present. But the objective existence of the future in the present differs from the objective existence of the past in the present. The various particular occasions of the past are in existence, and are severally functioning as objects for prehension in the present. This individual objective existence of the actual occasions of the past, each functioning in each present occasion, constitutes the causal relationship which is efficient causation. But there are no actual occasions in the future, already constituted. Thus there are no actual occasions in the future to exercise efficient causation in the present. What is objective in the present is the necessity of a future of actual occasions, and the necessity that these future occasions conform to the conditions inherent in the essence of the present occasion. The future belongs to the essence of present fact, and has no actuality other than the actuality of present fact. But its particular relationships to present fact are already realized in the nature of present fact.

SECTION IV. It is the definition of contemporary events that they happen in causal independence of each other. Thus two contemporary occasions are such that neither belongs to the past of the other. The two occasions are not in any direct relation to efficient causation. The vast causal independence of contemporary occasions is the preservative of the elbow-room within the Universe. It provides each actuality with a welcome environment for irresponsibility. 'Am I my brother's keeper?'

expresses one of the earliest gestures of self-consciousness. Our claim for freedom is rooted in our relationship to our contemporary environment. Nature does provide a field for independent activities. The understanding of the Universe requires that we conceive in their proper relations to each other the various roles, of efficient causation, of teleological self-creation, and of contemporary independence. This adequate conception requires also understanding of perspective elimination, and of types of order dominating vast epochs, and of minor endurances with their own additional modes of order diversifying each larger epoch within which they find themselves.

The mutual independence of contemporary occasions lies strictly within the sphere of their teleological self-creation. The occasions originate from a common past and their objective immortality operates within a common future. Thus indirectly, *via* the immanence of the past and the immanence of the future, the occasions are connected. But the immediate activity of self-creation is separate and private, so far as contemporaries are concerned.

There is thus a certain indirect immanence of contemporary occasions in each other. For if A and B be contemporaries, and C be in the past of both of them, then A and B are each in a sense immanent in C, in the way in which the future can be immanent in its past. But C is objectively immortal in both A and B. Thus, in this indirect sense, A is immanent in B, and B is immanent in A. But the objective immortality of A does not operate in B, nor does that of B operate in A. As individual complete actualities, A is shrouded from B, and B is shrouded from A. It is not wholly true that two contemporaries A and B enjoy a common past. In the first place, even if the occasions in the past of A be identical with the occasions in the past of B, yet A and B by reason of their difference of status, enjoy that past under a difference of perspective elimination. Thus the objective immortality of the past in A differs from the objective immortality of that same past in B. Thus two contemporary occasions, greatly remote from each other, are in effect derived from different pasts.

Again, according to the notions of time recently developed in modem physics, if A and B are contemporaries and P is contemporary with A, then it is not necessarily true that P is contemporary with B. It is possible that P may be earlier than B, or that it may be later than B. Thus even the occasions in the past of A are not wholly identical with those in the past of B. When A and B are neighbouring, then this distinction between their pasts may be negligible. But when they are remote from each other, the distinction may be of major importance.

It follows from this discussion that in so far as the relevant environment is dominated by any uniform type of coordination, any occasion will experience its past as 'anticipating' the prolongation of that type of order into the future beyond that past. But this future includes the occasion in question and its contemporary environment. In this way there is an indirect immanence of its contemporary world in that occasion; not in respect to its particular individual occasions, but as the general substratum for that relation of order. This type of order will both relate the various parts of the contemporary world among themselves, and will also relate these parts to the occasion in question. But the parts of the contemporary world will only belong to the experience of the occasion in their function of relata for this type of order. This is the general explanation why the contemporary world should be perceived as the field of the uniform spatial relations. It gives no reason why any special system of relationships should dominate this epoch. But the explanation does give a reason why some system of uniform relations should dominate our perceptions of the contemporary world. Also the intrinsic activity has been lost. The contemporary world enters into experience as the passive subject of relations and qualities.

SECTION V. The actualities of the Universe are processes of experience, each process an individual fact. The whole Universe is the advancing assemblage of these processes. The Aristotelian doctrine, that all agency is confined to actuality, is accepted. So also is the Platonic dictum that the very meaning of existence is 'to be a factor in agency', or in other words 'to make a difference'. Thus, 'to be something' is to be discoverable as a factor in the analysis of some actuality. It follows that in one sense everything is 'real', according to its own category of being. In this sense the word 'real' can only mean that some sound or mark is a word with a denotation. But the term 'realization' refers to the actual entities which include the entity in question as a positive factor in their constitutions. Thus though everything is real, it is not necessarily realized in some particular set of actual occasions. But it is necessary that it be discoverable somewhere, realized in some actual entity. There is not anything which has failed in some sense to be realized, physically or conceptually. The term 'real' can also mark the differences arising in the contrast between physical and conceptual realization.

SECTION VI. Any set of actual occasions are united by the mutual immanence of occasions, each in the other. To the extent that they are united they mutually constrain each other. Evidently this mutual immanence and constraint of a pair of occasions is not in general a symmetric relation. For, apart from contemporaries, one occasion will be in the future of the other. Thus the earlier will be immanent in the later according to the mode of efficient causality, and the later in the earlier according to the mode of anticipation, as explained above. Any set of occasions, conceived as thus combined into a unity, will be termed a nexus. The unity of such a nexus may be of a trivial description, if the various occasions are dispersed through the Universe, each with a widely different status from the other. When the unity of the nexus is of dominating importance, nexus of different types emerge, which may be respectively termed Regions, Societies, Persons, Enduring Objects, Corporal Substances, Living Organisms, Events, with other analogous terms for the various shades of complexity of which Nature is capable. It will be sufficient in the next chapter to indicate a few of these special types of nexus.

SECTION VII. We think of Constraint and Freedom in terms of the values realized in connection with them, and also in terms of the antithesis between them. But there is another way of considering them. We can ask what there is in the physical nature of things constituting the physical realization either of freedom, or of constraint, or of a compatible association of both in a suitable pattern. In fact we do habitually interpret human history in terms of freedom and constraint. Apart from the realization of this antithesis in physical occurrences, the history of civilized humanity is a meaningless succession of events, involving a play of emotions concernedwith concepts entirely irrelevant to the physical facts.

The causal independence of contemporary occasions is the ground for the freedom within the Universe. The novelties which face the contemporary world are solved in isolation by the contemporary occasions. There is complete contemporary freedom. It is not true that whatever happens is immediately a condition laid upon everything else. Such a conception of complete mutual determination is an exaggeration of the community of the Universe. The notions of 'sporadic occurrences' and of 'mutual irrelevance' have a real application to the nature of things. Again the perspective imposed by incompatibilities of subjective form in another way provides for freedom. The antecedent environment is not wholly efficacious in determining the initial phase of the occasion which springs from it. There are factors in the environment which are eliminated from any function as explicit facts in the new creation. The running stream purifies itself, or perhaps loses some virtue which in happier circumstances might have been retained. The initial phase of each fresh occasion represents the issue of a struggle within the past for objective existence beyond itself. The determinant of the struggle is the supreme Eros incarnating itself as the first phase of the individual subjective aim in the new process of actuality. Thus in any two occasions of the Universe there are elements in either one which are irrelevant to the constitution of the other. The forgetfulness of this doctrine leads to an over-moralization in the view of the nature of things. Fortunately there are a great many things which do not much matter, and we can have them how we will. The opposite point of view has been the nursery of fanaticism, and has tinged history with ferocity.

SECTION VIII. The understanding of the Universe, in terms of the type of metaphysic here put forward, requires that the various roles of efficient causation, of teleological self-creation, of perspective elimination, of contemporary independence, of the laws of order dominating vast epochs, and of the minor endurances within each epoch, be conceived in their various relations to each other. Another summary expression of this type of understanding is contained in the phrases, Constraint and Freedom, Survival and Destruction, Depth of Feeling and Triviality of Feeling, Conceptual realization and physical realization, Appearance and Reality. Any account of the Adventure of Ideas is concerned with Ideas threading their way among the alternatives presented by these various phrases.

When we examine the structure of the epoch of the Universe in which we find ourselves, this structure exhibits successive layers of types of order, each layer introducing some additional type of order within some limited region which shares in the more general type of order of some larger environment. Also this larger environment in its turn is a specialized region within the general epoch of creation as we know it. Each one of these regions, with its dominant set of ordering relations, can either be considered from the point of view of the mutual relations of its parts to each other, or it can be considered from the point of view of its impact, as a unity, upon the experience of an external percipient. There is yet a third mode of consideration which combines the other two. The percipient may be an occasion within the region, and may yet grasp the region as one, including the percipient itself as a member of it.

A region, analysed in the first way, is thereby conceived as subject to certain Laws of Nature, which laws are its dominant set of ordering relations. In the second mode of consideration, synthesis replaces analysis. The region in question assumes the guise of an enduring unity, of which the essence is a certain complex internal character. This essential character, as it appears in the second approach, is nothing other than the set of Laws of Nature reigning within the region, as they appear in the first approach. Either mode of approach simply lays stress upon the dominant identity of character pervading the concrete connexity of the many occasions constituting the region. The unity of the region is two-fold: —first, by reason of the sheer connexity arising from the mutual immanence of the various occasions included in it, and secondly, by reason of a pervasive identity of character whereby the various parts play an analogous role in any external occasion. Thus the region with its Laws of Nature is a synonym for the enduring substance with its Essential Character.

Chapter XIII

THE GROUPING OF OCCASIONS

SECTION I. THE GROUPING of Occasions is the outcome of some common function performed by those occasions in the percipient experience. The grouped occasions then acquire a unity; they become, for the experience of the percipient, one thing which is complex by reason of its divisibility into many occasions, or into many subordinate groups of occasions. The subordinate groups are then complex unities, each belonging to the same metaphysical category of existence as the total group. This characteristic, namely divisibility into groups of analogous type of being, is the general notion of extensiveness. The peculiar relationships (if any) diffused systematically between the extensive groups of an epoch constitute the system of geometry prevalent in that epoch.

The general common function exhibited by any group of actual occasions is that of mutual immanence. In Platonic language, this is the function of belonging to a common Receptacle. If the group be considered merely in respect to this basic property of mutual immanence, however otherwise lacking in common relevance, then—conceived as exemplifying this general connectedness—the group is termed a Nexus.

Thus the term Nexus does not presuppose any special type of order, nor does it presuppose any order at all pervading its members other than the general metaphysical obligation of mutual immanence. But in fact the teleology of the Universe, with its aim at intensity and variety, produces epochs with various types of order dominating subordinate nexus interwoven with each other. A nexus can spread itself both spatially and temporally. In other words, it can include sets of occasions which are contemporary with each other, and it can include sets which are relatively past and future. If the nexus be purely spatial, then it will include no pair of occasions such that one of the pair is antecedent to the other. The mutual immanence between the occasions of the nexus will then be of the indirect type proper to contemporary occasions. It is for this reason that the notion of externality dominates our intuition of space. If the nexus be purely temporal, then it will include no pair of contemporary occasions. It is to be a mere thread of temporal transition from occasion to occasion. The idea of temporal transition can never be wholly disengaged from that of 'causation'. This latter notion is merely a special way of considering direct immanence of the past in its future.

SECTION II. The notion of the contiguity of occasions is important. Two occasions, which are not contemporary, are contiguous in time when there is no occasion which is antecedent to one of them and subsequent to the other. A purely temporal nexus of occasions is continuous when, with the exception of the earliest and the latest occasions, each occasion is contiguous with an earlier occasion and a later occasion. The nexus will then form an unbroken thread in temporal or serial order. The first and the last occasions of the thread will, of course, only enjoy a one-sided contiguity with the thread.

Spatial contiguity is more difficult to define. It requires a reference to the temporal dimension. It can be defined by the aid of the doctrine that no two contemporary occasions are derived from a past wholly in common. Thus if A and B be two contemporary occasions, the past of A includes some occasions not belonging to the past of B, and that of B includes occasions not belonging to the past of A Then A and B are contiguous when there is no occasion (i) contemporary with both A and B, and (ii) such that its past includes all occasions, each belonging both to the past of A and the past of B. The particular form of this definition is of no great importance. But the principle that the inter-relations of the present are derived from a reference to the past is fundamental. It gives the reason why the contemporary world is experienced as a display of lifeless substances passively illustrating imposed characters.

Anyhow contiguity, temporal and spatial, is definable in terms of the doctrine of immanence. By the aid of the notion of contiguity, the notion of a region can be defined as denoting a nexus in which certain conditions of contiguity are preserved. The logical details of such a definition are irrelevant to this discussion.

So far we have been considering various species of nexus, whose sole principle of unity is derived from the bare fact of mutual immanence. We will term this genus of nexus, the genus whose species are discriminated by differences of bare extensive pattern. More briefly, it will be termed the *Genus* of *Patterned Nexus.* Every nexus belongs to some species of this genus, if we abstract from the qualitative factors which are interwoven in its patterns.

SECTION III. We now pass on to the general notion of a *Society.* This notion introduces the general consideration of types of order, and the genetic propagation of order. The definition depends upon taking into account factors which are omitted in the analysis of the Genus of Patterned Nexus.

A Society is a nexus which 'illustrates' or 'shares in', some type of 'Social Order'. 'Social Order' can be defined[1] as follows: —'A nexus enjoys "social order" when (i) there is a common element of form illustrated in the definiteness of each of its included actual entities, and (ii) this common element of form arises in each member of the nexus by reason of the conditions imposed upon it by its prehensions of some other members of the nexus, and (iii) these prehensions impose that condition of reproduction

1. Cf. *Process and Reality*, Part I, Ch. III, Sect. II.

by reason of their inclusion of positive feelings involving[2] that common form. Such a nexus is called a "society", and the common form is the "defining characteristic" of that society'.

Another rendering[3] of the same definition is as follows: —'The point of a "society" as the term is here used, is that it is self-sustaining; in other words, that it is its own reason. Thus a society is more than a set of [actual] entities to which the same class-name applies: that is to say, it involves more than a merely mathematical conception of 'order'. To constitute a society, the class-name has got to apply to each member, by reason of genetic derivation from other members of that same society. The members of the society are alike because, by reason of their common character, they impose on other members of the society the conditions which lead to that likeness.'

It is evident from this description of the notion of a 'Society', as here employed, that a set of mutually contemporary occasions cannot form a complete society. For the genetic condition cannot be satisfied by such a set of contemporaries. Of course a set of contemporaries may belong to a society. But the society, as such, must involve antecedents and subsequents. In other words, a society must exhibit the peculiar quality of endurance. The real actual things that endure are all societies. They are not actual occasions. It is the mistake that has thwarted European metaphysics from the time of the Greeks, namely, to confuse societies with the completely real things which are the actual occasions. A society has an essential character, whereby it is the society that it is, and it has also accidental qualities which vary as circumstances alter. Thus a society, as a complete existence and as retaining the same metaphysical status, enjoys a history expressing its changing reactions to changing circumstances[4]. But an actual occasion has

2. In the original, *Process and Reality*, 'of that' in place of 'involving'.
3. Cf. *Process and Reality*, Part II, Ch. III, Sect. II.
4. This notion of 'society' has analogies to Descartes' notion of 'substance', cf. Descartes' *Principles of Philosophy*, Part I, Principles LI-LVII.

no such history. It never changes. It only becomes and perishes. Its perishing is its assumption of a new metaphysical function in the creative advance of the universe.

The self-identity of a society is founded upon the self-identity of its defining characteristic, and upon the mutual immanence of its occasions. But there is no definite nexus which is the nexus underlying that society, except when the society belongs wholly to the past. For the realized nexus which underlies the society is always adding to itself, with the creative advance into the future. For example, the man adds another day to his life, and the earth adds another millennium to the period of its existence. But until the death of the man and the destruction of the earth, there is no determinate nexus which in an unqualified sense is either the man or the earth.

SECTION IV. Though there is no one nexus which can claim to be the society, so long as that society is in existence, there is a succession of nexus each of which is the whole realized society up to that stage of its exis1ence. The extensive patterns of various members of such a succession for a given society may be different. In such a case the extensive patterns, so far as they differ, cannot be any element in the defining characteristic of the society. But the extensive patterns of the various nexus of the succession may be identical, or at least they may have in common some feature of their pattern. In this case the common pattern, or the common feature, can be one element in the defining characteristic of the society in question.

The simplest example of a society in which the successive nexus of its progressive realization have a common extensive pattern is when each such nexus is purely temporal and continuous. The society, in each stage of realization, then consists of a set of contiguous occasions in serial order. A man, defined as an enduring percipient, is such a society. This definition of a man is exactly what Descartes means by a thinking substance. It will be remembered that in his *Principles of Philosophy* [Part I, Principle XXI; also *Meditation* III]

Descartes states that endurance is nothing else than successive re-creation by God. Thus the Cartesian conception of the human soul and that here put forward differ only in the function assigned to God. Both conceptions involve a succession of occasions, each with its measure of immediate completeness.

Societies of the general type, that their realized nexus are purely temporal and continuous, will be termed 'personal'. Any society of this type may be termed a 'person'. Thus, as defined above, a man is a person.

But a man is more than a serial succession of occasions of experience. Such a definition may satisfy philosophers—Descartes, for example. It is not the ordinary meaning of the term 'man'. There are animal bodies as well as animal minds; and in our experience such minds always occur incorporated. Now an animal body is a society involving a vast number of occasions, spatially and temporally coordinated. It follows that a 'man', in the full sense of ordinary usage, is not a 'person' as here defined. He has the unity of a wider society, in which the social coordination is a dominant factor in the behaviours of the various parts.

Also, when we survey the living world, animal and vegetable, there are bodies of all types. Each living body is a society, which is not personal. But most of the animals, including all the vertebrates, seem to have their social system dominated by a subordinate society which is 'personal'. This subordinate society is of the same type as 'man', according to the personal definition given above, though of course the mental poles in the occasions of the dominant personal society do not rise to the height of human mentality. Thus in one sense a dog is a 'person', and in another sense he is a non-personal society. But the lower forms of animal life, and all vegetation, seem to lack the dominance of any included personal society. A tree is a democracy. Thus living bodies are not to be identified with living bodies under personal dominance. There is no necessary connection between 'life' and 'personality'. A 'personal' society need not be 'living', in the general sense of the term; and a 'living' society need not be 'personal'.

SECTION V. The Universe achieves its values by reason of its coordination into societies of societies, and in societies of societies of societies. Thus an army is a society of regiments, and regiments are societies of men, and men are societies of cells, and of blood, and of bones, together with the dominant society of personal human experience, and cells are societies of small physical entities such as protons, and so on, and so on. Also all of these societies presuppose the circumambient space of social physical activity.

It is evident that the previous definition of 'society' has been phrased so as to suggest an over-simplified concept of the meaning For the notion of a defining characteristic must be construed to include the notion of the coordination of societies. Thus there are societies at different levels. For instance, the army is a society at a level different from that of a regiment, and similarly for a regiment and a man. Nature is a complex of enduring objects, functioning as subordinate elements in a larger spatial-physical society. This larger society is for us the natural universe. There is however no reason to identify it with the boundless totality of actual things.

Also each of these enduring objects, such as tables, animal bodies, and stars, is itself a subordinate universe including subordinate enduring objects. The only strictly personal society of which we have direct discriminative intuition is the society of our own personal experiences. We also have a direct, though vaguer, intuition of our derivation of experience from the antecedent functioning of our bodies, and a still vaguer intuition of our bodily derivation from external nature.

Nature suggests for our observation gaps, and then as it were withdraws them upon challenge. For example, ordinary physical bodies suggest solidity. But solids turn to liquids, and liquids to gases. And from the gas the solid can again be recovered. Also the most solid of solids is for certain purposes a viscous fluid. Again impenetrability is a difficult notion. Salt dissolves in water, and can be recovered from it. Gases interfuse in liquids. Molecules arise from a patterned interfusion of atoms. Food interfuses with the body, and produces an immediate sense of diffused bodily vigour. This is especially the case with liquid stimulants. Thus the direct immediate experience of impenetrability loses upon challenge its sharp-cut status.

SECTION VI. Another gap is that between lifeless bodies and living bodies. Yet the living bodies can be pursued down to the edge of lifelessness. Also the functionings of inorganic matter remain intact amid the functionings of living matter. It seems that, in bodies that are obviously living, a coordination has been achieved that raises into prominence some functionings inherent in the ultimate occasions. For lifeless matter these functionings thwart each other, and average out so as to produce a negligible total effect. In the case of living bodies the coordination intervenes, and the average effect of these intimate functionings has to be taken into account.

Those activities in the self-formation of actual occasions which, if coordinated, yield living societies are the intermediate mental functionings transforming the initial phase of reception into the final phase of anticipation. In so far as the mental spontaneities of occasions do not thwart each other, but are directed to a common objective amid varying circumstances, there is life. The essence of life is the teleological introduction of novelty, with some conformation of objectives. Thus novelty of circumstance is met with novelty of functioning adapted to steadiness of purpose.

Life may ·characterize a set of occasions diffused throughout a society, though not necessarily including all, or even a majority of, the occasions of that society. The common element of purpose which characterizes these various occasions must be reckoned as one element of the determining characteristic of the society. It is evident that according to this definition no single occasion can be called living. Life is the coordination of the mental spontaneities throughout the occasions of a society.

But apart from life a high grade of mentality in individual occasions seems to be impossible. A personal society, itself living and dominantly influencing a living society wider than itself, is the only type of organization which provides occasions of high-grade mentality. Thus in a man, the living body is permeated by living societies of low-grade occasions so far as mentality is concerned. But the whole is coordinated so as to support a personal living society of high-grade occasions. This personal society is the man defined as a person. It is the soul of which Plato spoke.

How far this soul finds a support for its existence beyond the body is: —another question. The everlasting nature of God, which in a sense is non-temporal and in another sense is temporal, may establish with the soul a peculiarly intense relationship of mutual immanence. Thus in some important sense the existence of the soul may be freed from its complete dependence upon the bodily organization.

But it is to be noticed that the personality of an animal organism may be more or less. It is not a mere question of having a soul or of not having a soul. The question is, How much, if any? Any tendency to a high-grade multiple personality would be self-destructive by the antagonism of divergent aims. In other words, such multiple personality is destructive of the very essence of life, which is conformation of purpose.

Chapter XIV

APPEARANCE AND REALITY

SECTION I. THE OBJECTIVE content of an occasion of experience sorts itself out under two contrasted characters—Appearance and Reality. It is to be noticed that this is not the only dichotomy exhibited in experience. There are the physical and the mental poles, and there are the objects prehended and the subjective forms of the prehensions. In fact this final pair of opposites, Appearance and Reality, is not quite so fundamental metaphysically as the other two pairs.

In the first place the division between appearance and reality does not cover the whole of experience. It only concerns the objective content, and omits the subjective form of the immediate occasion in question. In the second place, its importance is negligible except in the functionings of the higher phases of experience, when the mental functionings have achieved a peculiar complexity of synthesis with the physical functionings. But in these higher phases, the contrast Appearance and Reality dominates those factors of experience which are discriminated in consciousness with peculiar distinctness. Thus the foundation of metaphysics should be sought in the understanding of the subject-object structure of experience, and in the respective roles of the physical and mental functionings.

Unfortunately the superior dominance in consciousness of the contrast 'Appearance and Reality' has led metaphysicians from the Greeks onwards to make their start from the more superficial characteristic. This error has warped modem philosophy to a greater extent than ancient or mediaeval philosophy. The warping has taken the form of a consistent reliance upon sensationalist perception as the basis of all experiential activity. It has had the effect of decisively separating 'mind' from 'nature', a modern separation which found its first exemplification in Cartesian dualism. But it must be remembered that this modern development was only the consistent carrying out of principles already present in the older European philosophy. It required two thousand years for the full implication of those principles to dawn upon men's minds in the seventeenth and the eighteenth centuries after Christ.

SECTION II. The distinction between 'appearance and reality' is grounded upon the process of self-formation of each actual occasion. The objective content of the initial phase of reception is the real antecedent world, as given for that occasion. This is the 'reality' from which that creative advance starts. It is the basic fact of the new occasion, with its concordances and discordances awaiting coordination in the new creature. There is nothing there apart from the real agency of the actual past, exercising its function of objective immortality. This is reality, at that moment, for that occasion. Here the term 'reality' is used in the sense of the opposite to 'appearance'.

The intermediate phase of self-formation is a ferment of qualitative valuation. These qualitative feelings are either derived directly from qualities illustrated in the primary phase, or are indirectly derived by their relevance to them. These conceptual feelings pass into novel relations to each other, felt with a novel emphasis of subjective form. The ferment of valuation is integrated with the physical prehensions of the physical pole. Thus the initial objective content is still there. But it is overlaid by, and intermixed with, the novel hybrid prehensions derived from integration with the conceptual ferment. In the higher types of actual occasions, propositional feelings are now dominant. This enlarged objective content obtains a coordination adapting it to the enjoyments and purposes fulfilling the subjective aim of the new occasion.

The mental pole has derived its objective content alike by abstraction from the physical pole and by the immanence of the basic Eros which endows with agency all ideal possibilities. The content of the objective universe has passed from the function of a basis for a new individuality to that of an instrument for purposes. The individual process is now feeling its own completion: — Cogito, ergo sum. And in Descartes' phraseology, 'cogitatio' is more than mere intellectual understanding.

This difference between the objective content of the initial phase of the physical pole and the objective content of the final phase, after the integration of physical and mental poles, constitutes 'appearance' for that occasion. In other words, 'appearance' is the effect of the activity of the mental pole, whereby the qualities and coordinations of the given physical world undergo transformation. It results from the fusion of the ideal with the actual: —The light that never was, on sea or land.

SECTION III. There can be no general metaphysic principles which determine how in any occasion appearance differs from the reality out of which it originates. The divergencies between reality and appearance depend on the type of social order dominating the environment of the occasion in question. All our information on this topic, direct and inferential, concerns this general epoch of the Universe and, more particularly, animal life on the surface of the Earth.

In respect to the occasions which compose the societies of inorganic bodies or of the so-called empty spaces, there is no reason to believe that in any important way the mental activities depart from functionings which are strictly conformal to those inherent in the objective datum of the first phase. Thus no novelty is introduced. The perspective elimination is effected according to the 'laws of nature' inherent in the epoch. This composition of activities constitutes the laws of physics. There is no effective 'appearance'.

But the case is very different for the high-grade occasions which are components in the animal life on the Earth's surface. Each animal body is an organ of sensation. It is a living society which may include in itself a dominant 'personal' society of occasions. This 'personal' society is composed of occasions enjoying the individual experiences of the animals. It is the soul of man. The whole body is organized, so that a general coordination of mentality is finally poured into the successive occasions of this personal society. Thus in the constitutions of these occasions, appearance is sufficiently coordinated to be effective. Also consciousness arises in the subjective forms in these experiences of the higher animals. It arises peculiarly in connection with the mental functions, and has to do primarily with their product. Now appearance is one product of mentality. Thus in our conscious perceptions appearance is dominant. It possesses a clear distinctness, which is absent from our vague massive feeling of derivation from our actual world. Appearance has shed the note of derivation. It lives in our consciousness as the world presented to us for our enjoyment and our purposes. It is the world in the guise of a subject-matter for an imposed activity. The occasion has gathered the creativity of the Universe into its own completeness, abstracted from the real objective content which is the source of its own derivation.

This status of 'appearance' in the constitution of experience is the reason for the disastrous metaphysical doctrine of physical matter passively illustrating qualities, and devoid of self-enjoyment. As soon as clarity and distinctness are made the test of metaphysical importance, an entire misapprehension of the metaphysical status of appearance is involved.

SECTION IV. When the higher functionings of mentality are socially stabilized in an organism, appearance merges into reality. To take the most conspicuous example, consider the personal succession of experiences in the life of a human being. The present occasion in this personal life inherits with peculiar dominance the antecedent experiences in this succession. But these antecedent experiences include the 'appearances' as in those occasions. These antecedent appearances are part of the real functioning of the real actual world as it stands in the primary phase of the immediately present occasion. It is a real fact of nature that the world has appeared thus from the standpoint of these antecedent occasions of the personal life. And more generally dropping the special case of personality, the objective reality of the past, as it now functions in the present, in its day was appearance. They may be strengthened in emphasis, embroidered upon, and otherwise modified by the novel appearances of the new occasion. In this way, there is an intimate, inextricable fusion of appearance with reality, and of accomplished fact with anticipation. In truth, we have been describing the exact situation which human experience presents for philosophic analysis.

We are apt to think of this fusion from the point of view of the higher grades of human beings. But it is a fusion proceeding throughout nature. It is the essential mode in which novelty enters into the functionings of the world.

SECTION V. It is a mistake to suppose that, at the level of human intellect, the role of mental functionings is to add subtlety to the content of experience. The exact opposite is the case. Mentality is an agent of simplification; and for this reason appearance is an incredibly simplified edition of reality. There should be no paradox in this statement. A moment's introspection assures one of the feebleness of human intellectual operations, and of the dim massive complexity of our feelings of derivation. The point for discussion is how in animal experience this simplification is effected.

The best example of this process of simplification is afforded by the perception of a social nexus as a unity, characterized by qualities derived from its individual members and their interconnections. With some elimination, the defining characteristic of the nexus is directly perceived to be qualifying that nexus as a unity. It often happens that in this perception of the nexus as thus qualified there is a wavering between the ascription of the quality to the group as one, and to its individual components as many. Thus, the orchestra is loud as one entity, and also in virtue of the perceived loudness of the individual members with their musical instruments. The transference of the characteristic from the individuals to the group as one can be explained by the mental operations. There is the conceptual entertainment of the qualities illustrated by the individual actualities. The qualities shared by many individuals are fused into one dominating impression. This dominating prehension is integrated with the nexus, or with some portion of it, perceived as a unity illustrating that quality. The association of a nexus as one with a quality will, for the experient subject, be in general a mode of exemplification which differs from the mode in which the respective individuals illustrate it. The discipline of a regiment inheres in the regiment in a different mode from its inherence in the individual soldiers. This difference of mode of illustration may be more or less evident. But it is there. It gives another reason for the aspect of the passive inherence of quality in substance. The composite group illustrates its qualities passively. The activity belongs to the individual actualities. This whole question of the transference of quality from the many individuals to the nexus as one is discussed at length in *Process and Reality,* Part Ill, Chapter III, Section IV, where it is termed 'Transmutation'. Obviously the transmuted percept belongs to Appearance. But as it occurs in animal experience, it belongs to appearance merged with reality. For it is inherited from the past. It is thus a fact of nature that the world so appears. It is a structural relationship of animate nature on the Earth's surface. In all Appearance there is an element of Transmutation.

SECTION VI. For animal life on Earth by far the most important example of Transmutation is afforded by Sense-Perception. No doctrine of sense-perception can neglect the teaching of physiology.

The decisive factor in sense-perception is the functioning of the brain, and the functioning of the brain is conditioned by the antecedent functionings of the other parts of the animal body. Given requisite bodily functionings, the sense-perception results. The activities. of nature external to the animal body are irrelevant as to their details, so long as they have the general character of supporting the existence of the total animal organism. The human body is the self-sufficient organ of human sense-perception.

There are external events, such as the transmission of light or the movements of material bodies which respectively are the normal modes of exciting sense-percepts of particular types. But in the first place these external events are only the normal modes. A diet of drugs will do equally well, though its issue in perception is not so definitely to be predicted. Thus no one type of external event is necessarily associated with one type of sense-percept. Hardly any percept is strictly normal. Gross illusions are plentiful, and some element of illusion almost universal. An ordinary looking-glass produces illusive percepts in almost every room.

Secondly, confining ourselves to the normal modes of excitation, the only important factor in the external event is how it affects the functionings of the surface of the body. How the light enters the eye, and a normal healthy state of the body, are the only important factors in normal visual sensation. The light may have come from a nebula distant by a thousand light-years, or it may have its origin in an electric lamp two feet off and have suffered a complex arrangement of reflections and refractions. Nothing matters except how it enters the eye, as to its composition, its intensity, and its geometric ordering. The body is supremely indifferent as to the past history of its exciting agents, and requires no certificate of character. The peculiar bodily excitement is all that matters.

The conclusion is that the direct information to be derived from sense-perception wholly concerns the functionings of the animal body. The sense of unity with the body does in fact dominate our sense-experiences. But the bodily organization is such as finally to promote a wholesale transmutation of sensa, inherited from antecedent bodily functionings, into characteristics of regions with well-marked geometrical relations to the geometrical structures of these functionings. In this transmutation the experient occasion in question belongs to the personal succession of occasions which is the soul of the animal. The bodily functionings and the nexus relevant to them by geometrical relationship are immanent in the experient occasion. The qualitative inheritance from the individual occasions implicated in these functionings is transmuted into the characteristics of regions conspicuously indicated by their geometrical connections. This doctrine is plainly indicated in the analysis of optical vision, where the image occupies the region indicated by geometrical relations within the eyes. It is more obscurely evident in the case of other species of sensa.

It is to be remembered also that along the personal succession of the soul's experiences, there is an inheritance of sense-perception from the antecedent members of the personal succession. Also incipient sense-percepta may be forming themselves in the nerve-routes, or in the neighbouring regions of the brain. But the final synthesis, with its production of appearance, is reserved for the occasions belonging to the personal soul.

SECTION VII. The question of the proper description of the species of qualities termed 'sensa' is important. Unfortunately the learned tradition of philosophy has missed their main characteristic, which is their enormous emotional significance. The vicious notion has been introduced of mere receptive entertainment, which for no obvious reason by reflection acquires an affective tone. The very opposite is the true explanation. The true doctrine of sense-perception is that the qualitative characters of affective tones inherent in the bodily functionings are transmuted into the characters of regions. These regions are then perceived as associated with those character-qualities, but also these same qualities are shared by the subjective forms of the prehensions. This is the reason of the definite æsthetic attitude imposed by sense-perception. The pattern of sensa characterizing the object—that is, those sensa in that pattern of contrast—enters also into the subjective form of the prehension. Thus art is possible. For not only can the objects be prescribed, but also the corresponding affective tones of their prehensions. This is the æsthetic experience so far as it is based upon sense-perception.

SECTION VIII. Another point to be noticed is that in sense-perception a region in the contemporary world is the substratum supporting the sensa. It is the region straightaway in such-and-such a direction. But this geometrical relation of being 'straight-away in such-and-such a direction' is defined by the operations of the brain. It has nothing to do with any physical transmission from the substrate region to the grain. To judge from some descriptions of perception in terms of modern scientific theories, it might be concluded that we perceive along the track of a ray of light. There is not the slightest warrant for such a notion. The track of light in the world external to the animal body is irrelevant. The coloured region is perceived straight-away in such-and-such a direction. This is the fundamental notion of 'straightness'.

It therefore becomes necessary for the self-consistency of this doctrine to enquire whether the dominant structure of geometrical relations includes a determination of straightness. The theory requires that a prehension of a nexus within the brain as exhibiting straightness in the mutual relations of its parts should thereby determine the prolongation of those relations into regions beyond the brain. In simpler language, a segment of a straight line as prehended within the brain should necessarily determine its prolongation externally to the body, irrespective of the particular characters of the external events. The possibility of 'Transmutation' involving the 'Projection' of sensa is then secured.

I have discussed this question elsewhere[1], and have given a definition of straight lines—and, more generally, of flatness—which satisfies the requirements. The necessity thereby avoided. The notions of straightness and of congruence, and thence of distance, can be derived from those underlying a uniform systematic non-metrical geometry.

It may be noticed in passing that, if straightness depends upon measurement, there can be no perception of straightness in the unmeasured. The notion of 'straight in front' must then be meaningless.

SECTION IX. In this way, the inheritance from the past is precipitated upon the present. It becomes sense-perception, which is the 'appearance' of the present.

The 'mutual immanence' of contemporary occasions to each other is allied to the immanence of the future in the present, though it presents some features of its own. This immanence exhibits a symmetrical relation of causal independence. In human experience, the prehensions of the contemporary world exhibit themselves as sense-perceptions, effected by means of the bodily organs of sensation. The subjective forms of these sense-perceptions involve conscious discrimination, with varying degrees of clarity and distinctness. Indeed sense-perceptions can exhibit themselves as clear and distinct in consciousness to a degree unrivalled by any other type of prehension. The result is that all attempts at an exact systematic doctrine of the nature of things seeks its most obvious verification in the conformity of its theory with sense-perception. The unfortunate effect has been, that all direct observation has been identified with sense-perception. This assumption has been criticized in Chapter XI.

1. Cf. *Process and Reality*, Part IV, Chapters III, IV, and V. The required definition is given in Chapter III, and the theory of the projection of sensa is discussed in Chapters IV and V.

But sense-perception, as conceived in the isolation of its ideal purity, never enters into human experience. It is always accompanied by so-called 'interpretation'. This 'interpretation' does not seem to be necessarily the product of any elaborate train of intellectual cogitation. We find ourselves 'accepting'[2] a world of substantial objects, directly presented for our experience. Our habits, our states of mind, our modes of behaviour, all presuppose this 'interpretation'. In fact the concept of mere sensa is the product of high-grade thinking. It required Plato to frame the myth of the Shadows in the Cave, and it required Hume to construct the doctrine of pure sensationalist perception. Yet even animals share in some 'interpretation'. There is every evidence that animals enjoy a sensationalist experience. Dogs smell, eagles see, and noises attract the attention of most of the higher animals. Also their consequent modes of behaviour suggest their immediate assumption of a substantial world around them. In fact the hypothesis of a mere sensationalist perception does not account for our direct observation of the contemporary world. There is some other factor present, which is equally primitive with our perception of sensa. This factor is provided by the immanence of the past in the immediate occasion whose percipience is under discussion. The immanence of the past in this percipient occasion cannot be fully understood apart from due attention to the doctrine of the immanence of the future in the past. Thus the past as an objective constituent in the experience of the percipient occasion carries its own prehension of the future beyond itself. This prehension survives objectively in the primary phase of the percipient. Accordingly there is an indirect prehension of contemporary occasion, *via* the efficient causation, from which they arise. For

2. Cf. '*Perception*', by H. H. Price, especially Chapter VI, '*Perceptual Assurance, Perceptual Acceptance*'. Published by Methuen, London, 1932. Price in his valuable work gives to sense-perception a more fundamental rale in experience than my doctrine allows to it. Cf. also Santayana's doctrine of 'Animal Faith'.

the immediate future of the immediate past constitutes the set of contemporary occasions for the percipient. Also these prehensions of immediate past and of immediate future operate dominantly in their experience of their respective subjects. Thus the prehension of contemporary occasions is the prehension of those occasions in so far as they are conditioned by the occasions in the immediate past of the prehending subject. Thus the present is perceivable in so far as it is conditioned by the efficient causation from the past of the perceiver. The great dominant relationships, fundamental for the epochal order of nature, thereby stand out with overwhelming distinctness. These are the general, all-pervasive, obligations of perspective. Such relationships are what we term the spatial relationships as perceivable from the standpoint of the observer.

But the particular occasions of the contemporary world, each with its own individual spontaneity, are veiled from the observer. In this respect, the contemporary world in the experience of the percipient shares the characteristics of the future. The relevant environment, which is the immediate past of the human body, is peculiarly sensitive to its geometrical experiences and to the synthesis of its qualitative prehensions with these experiences of geometrical relations. In this way, there is a basis in fact for the association of derivates from significant regions in the past with the geometrical representatives of those regions in the present. [Cf. *Process and Reality.* Part III, Chap. III. Section IV. and Part IV, Chs. IV and V.]

The conclusion is that the contemporary world is not perceived in virtue of its own proper activity, but in virtue of activities derived from the past, the past which conditions it and which also conditions the contemporary percipient. These activities are primarily in the past of the human body, and more remotely in the past of the environment within which the body is functioning. This environment includes those occasions dominantly conditioning the perceived contemporary regions. This theory of the perception of contemporaries allows for our habitual belief that we perceive the contemporary world with a general qualitative relevance to the essences of the occasions making up its various regions; and also with a bias of qualitative distortion due to the functioning of the animal body of the percipient.

One distortion stands out immediately. Each actual occasion is in truth a process of activity. But the contemporary regions are mainly perceived in terms of their passive perspective relationship to the percipient and to each other. They are thus perceived merely as passive recipients of the qualities with which in sense-perception they are associated. Hence the false notion of a substratum with vacuously inherent qualities. Here the term 'vacuous' means 'devoid of any individual enjoyment arising from the mere fact of realization in that context'. In other words, the substratum with its complex of inherent qualities is wrongly conceived as bare realization, devoid of self-enjoyment, that is to say, devoid of intrinsic worth. In this way, the exclusive reliance on sense-perception promotes a false metaphysics. This error is the result of high-grade intellectuality. The instinctive interpretations which govern human life and animal life presuppose a contemporary world throbbing with energetic values. It requires considerable ability to make the disastrous abstraction of our bare sense-perceptions from the massive insistency of our total experiences. Of course, whatever we can do in the way of abstraction is for some purposes useful—provided that we know what we are about.

Chapter XV

PHILOSOPHIC MIND

SECTION I. IN THIS final chapter of Part III my aim is a discussion of some methods which can usefully be employed in the pursuit of speculative philosophy. In illustration, and as a subsidiary aim, I shall refer to some doctrines of my own[1], and to some comments upon them. In this chapter the 'transient aspect of nature will be mainly emphasized.

So far as concerns methodology, the general issue of the discussion will be that theory dictates method, and that any particular method is only applicable to theories of one correlate species. An analogous conclusion holds for the technical terms. This close relation of theory to method partly arises from the fact that the relevance of evidence depends on the theory which is dominating the discussion. This fact is the reason why dominant theories are also termed 'working hypotheses'.

An example is afforded when we interrogate experience for direct evidence of the interconnectedness of things. If we hold with Hume, that the sole data originating reflective experience are impressions of sensation, and also if we also admit with him the obvious fact that no one such impression by its own individual nature discloses any information as to another such impression, then on that hypothesis the direct evidence for interconnectedness vanishes. Again, if we hold the Cartesian doctrine of substantial

1. Cf. *Process and Reality*, subsequently cited under the abbreviation *P. R.* Also, *Science and The Modern World*, cited as *S. M. W.*

souls with many adventures of experience, and of substantial material bodies, then on that hypothesis the relations between two occasions of experience qualifying one soul are no evidence as to the connectedness of two such occasions respectively qualifying two different souls, and are no evidence as the connectedness of a soul and a material body, and are no evidence as to the connectedness of two occasions of agitation of one material body, or of two such occasions respectively belonging to different material bodies. But if we hold, as for example in *Process and Reality,* that all final individual actualities have the metaphysical character of occasions of experience, then on that hypothesis the direct evidence as to the connectedness of one's immediate present occasion of experience with one's immediately past occasions, can be validly used to suggest categories applying to the connectedness of all occasions in nature. A great deal of confused philosophical thought has its origin in obliviousness to the fact that the relevance of evidence is dictated by theory. For you cannot prove a theory by evidence which that theory dismisses as irrelevant. This is also the reason that in any science which has failed to produce any theory with a sufficient scope of application, progress is necessarily very slow. It is impossible to know what to look for, and how to connect the sporadic observations. Philosophical discussion in the absence of a theory has no criterion of the validity of evidence. For example, Hume assumes that his doctrine of association holds for all types of impressions of sensation and of ideas of them indiscriminately. This assumption is part of his theory. In divorce from the theory, a separate appeal to experience is required for each type of impression, for example, tastes, sounds, sights, etc., and likewise, not only for the association of tastes *inter se* and of sounds *inter se,* but for the association of tastes with sounds, and so on for every possible type, and for every possible conjunction of types.

To sum up this preface, every method is a happy simplification. But only truths of a congenial type can be investigated by any one method, or stated in the terms dictated by the method. For every simplification is an over-simplification. Thus the criticism of a theory does not start from the question, True or false? It consists in noting its scope of useful application and its failure beyond that scope. It is an unguarded statement of a partial truth. Some of its terms embody a general notion with a mistaken specialization, and others of its terms are too general and require discrimination of their possibilities of specialization.

SECTION II. Philosophy is a difficult subject, from the days of Plato to the present time haunted by subtle perplexities. The existence of such perplexities arising from the common obviousness of speech is the reason why the topic exists. Thus the very purpose of philosophy is to delve below the apparent clarity of common speech. In this connection, it is only necessary to refer to Socrates. Another illustration is to be found in the *Sophist,* where Plato states that 'not-being' is a form of 'being'. This statement is at once an extreme instance of the breakdown of language, and the enunciation of a profound metaphysical truth which lies at the foundation of this discussion.

SECTION III. Speculative Philosophy can be defined[2] as the endeavour to frame a coherent, logical, necessary system of general ideas in terms of which every element of our experience can be interpreted. Here 'interpretation' means that each element shall have the character of a particular instance of the general scheme.

Thus speculative philosophy embodies the method of the 'working hypothesis'. The purpose of this working hypothesis for philosophy is to coordinate the current expressions of human experience, in common speech, in social institutions, in actions, in the principles of the various special sciences, elucidating harmony and exposing discrepancies. No systematic thought has made progress apart from some adequately general working hypothesis, adapted to its special topic. Such an hypothesis directs

2. Cf. *P. R.* Pt. I, Ch. I, Sect. I.

observation, and decides upon the mutual relevance of various types of evidence. In short, it prescribes method. To venture upon productive thought without such an explicit theory is to abandon oneself to the doctrines derived from one's grandfather.

In the preliminary stages of knowledge a haphazard criterion is all that is possible. Progress is then very slow, and most of the effort is wasted. Even an inadequate working hypothesis with some conformation to fact is better than nothing. It coordinates procedure.

The advance of any reasonably developed science is twofold. There is the advance of detailed knowledge within the method prescribed by the reigning working hypothesis; and there is the rectification of the working hypothesis dictated by the inadequacies of the current orthodoxy.

Sometimes it is necessary for a science to entertain concurrently two—or more—working hypotheses, each with its own success and its own failure. Such hypotheses are contradictory as stated; and science awaits their conciliation by the production of a working hypothesis with a wider sweep. When a new working hypothesis is proposed, it must be criticized from its own point of view. For example, it is futile to object to the Newtonian dynamics that, on the Aristotelian system, the loose things on the earth's surface must be left behind by the earth's motion.

Philosophy has been afflicted by the dogmatic fallacy, which is the belief that the principles of its working hypotheses are clear, obvious, and irreformable. Then, as a reaction from this fallacy, it has swayed to the other extreme which is the fallacy of discarding method. Philosophers boast that they uphold no system. They are then a prey to the delusive clarities of detached expressions which it is the very purpose of their science to surmount. Another type of reaction is to assume, often tacitly, that if there can be any intellectual analysis it must proceed according to some one discarded dogmatic method, and thence to deduce that intellect is intrinsically tied to erroneous fictions. This type is illustrated by the anti-intellectualism of Nietzsche and Bergson, and tinges American Pragmatism.

SECTION IV. A method is a way of dealing with data, with evidence. What are the evidences to which philosophy appeals?

It is customary to contrast the objective approach of the ancient Greeks with the subjective approach of the moderns, initiated by Descartes, and further emphasized by Locke and Hume.

But, whether we be ancient or modern, we can only deal with things, in some sense, experienced. The Greeks dealt with things that they thought they experienced, and Hume merely asked, What do we experience? This is exactly the question which Plato and Aristotle thought that they were answering.

To speak of anything, is to speak of something which, by reason of that very speech, is in some way a component in that act of experience. In some sense or other, it is thereby known to exist. This is what Plato pointed out when he wrote, "Not-being is itself a sort of being."

Speech consists of noises, or visible shapes, which elicit an experience of things other than themselves. In so far as vocables fail to elicit a stable coordination of sound-character, or shape-character, to meaning, those vocables fail to function as speech. And in so far as some meaning is not in some sense directly experienced, there is no meaning conveyed. To point at nothing is not to point.

To speak of the same thing twice is to demonstrate that the being of that thing is independent of either singular act of speech, unless we believe that the two acts presuppose each other or are both presupposed by the thing spoken of. If we cannot speak of the same thing twice, knowledge vanishes taking philosophy with it. Thus, since speech can be repeated, things spoken of have a determined being in abstraction from the occasion of experience which includes that act of speech.

The difference between ancients and moderns is that the ancients asked what have we experienced, and the moderns asked what can we experience. But in both cases, they asked about things transcending the act of experience which is the occasion of asking.

SECTION V. The translation of Hume's question from 'What *do* we experience' to 'What *can* we experience' makes all the difference, though in his 'Treatise' Hume makes the transition, time and again, without explicit comment. For modern epistemology the latter form of the question—with its substitution of *can* for *do*—is accompanied by the implicit presupposition of a method, namely that of placing ourselves in an introspective attitude of attention so as to determine the *given* components of experience in abstraction from our private way of subjective reaction, by reflexion, conjecture, emotion, and purpose.

In this attitude of strained attention, there can be no doubt as to the answer. The data are the patterns of sensa provided by the sense organs. This is the sensationalist doctrine of Locke and Hume. Later, Kant has interpreted the patterns as forms introduced by the mode of reception provided by the recipient. Here Kant introduces the Leibnizian notion of the self-development of the experiencing subject. Thus for Kant the data are somewhat narrower than for Hume: they are the sensa ·devoid of their patterns. Hume's general analysis of the consequences of this doctrine stands unshaken. So also does his final reflection, that the philosophic doctrine fails to justify the practice of daily life. The justification of this procedure of modern epistemology is twofold, and both of its branches are based upon mistakes. The mistakes go back to the Greek philosophers. What is modern, is the exclusive reliance upon them.

SECTION VI. The first error is the assumption of a few definite avenues of communication with the external world, the five sense-organs. This leads to the pre-supposition that the search for the data is to be narrowed to the question, what data are directly provided by the activity of the sense-organs-preferably the eyes. This doctrine of sense-organs has a vague, general truth, very important for practical affairs. In particular all exact scientific observation is derived from such data. The scientific categories of thought are obtained elsewhere.

But the living organ of experience is the living body as a whole. Every instability of any part of it—be it chemical, physical, or molar imposes an activity of readjustment throughout the whole organism. In the course of such physical activities human experience has its origin. The plausible interpretation of such experience is that it is one of the natural activities involved in the functioning of such a high-grade organism. The actualities of nature must be so interpreted as to be explanatory of this fact. This is one *desideratum* to be aimed at in a philosophic scheme.

Such experience seems to be more particularly related to the activities of the brain. But how far an exact doctrine can be based upon this presumption lies beyond our powers of observation. We cannot determine with what molecules the brain begins and the rest of the body ends. Further, we cannot tell with what molecules the body ends and the external world begins. The truth is that the brain is continuous with the body, and the body is continuous with the rest of the natural world. Human experience is an act of self-origination including the whole of nature, limited to the perspective of a focal region[3], located within the body, but not necessarily persisting in any fixed coordination with a definite part of the brain.

SECTION VII. The second error is the presupposition that the sole way of examining experience is by acts of conscious introspective analysis. Such a doctrine of the exclusive primacy of introspection is already discredited in psychology. Each occasion of experience has its own individual pattern. Each occasion lifts some components into primacy and retreats others into a background enriching the total enjoyment. The attitude of introspection shares this characteristic with all other experiential occasions. It lifts the clear-cut data of sensation into primacy, and cloaks the

3. Cf. *P. R.* Pt. II, Ch. III, especially Sects. IV-XI, and Pt. IV, Chs. IV and V.

vague compulsions and derivations which form the main stuff of experience. In particular it rules out that intimate sense of derivation from the body, which is the reason for our instinctive identification of our bodies with ourselves.

In order to discover some of the major categories under which we can classify the infinitely various components of experience, we must appeal to evidence relating to every variety of occasion. Nothing can be omitted, experience drunk and experience sober, experience sleeping and experience waking, experience drowsy and experience wide-awake, experience self-conscious and experience self-forgetful, experience intellectual and experience physical, experience religious and experience sceptical, experience anxious and experience care-free, experience anticipatory and experience retrospective, experience happy and experience grieving, experience dominated by emotion and experience under self-restraint, experience in the light and experience in the dark, experience normal and experience abnormal.

SECTION VIII. We have now reached the heart of our topic. What is the store-house of that crude evidence on which philosophy should base its discussion, and in what terms should its discussion be expressed?

The main sources of evidence respecting this width of human experience are language, social institutions, and action, including thereby the fusion of the three which is language interpreting action and social institutions.

Language delivers its evidence in three chapters, one on the meanings of words, another on the meanings enshrined in grammatical forms, and the third on meanings beyond individual words and beyond grammatical forms, meanings miraculously revealed in great literature.

Language is incomplete and fragmentary, and merely registers a stage in the average advance beyond ape-mentality. But all men enjoy flashes of insight beyond meanings already stabilized in etymology and grammar. Hence the role of literature, the role of the special sciences, and the role of philosophy: —in their various ways engaged in finding linguistic expressions for meanings as yet unexpressed.

As a special example, consider the line and a half of poetry in which Euripides[4] compresses the main philosophical problems which have tortured European thought from his day to the present: —"Zeus, whether thou are Compulsion of Nature or Intelligence of Mankind, to thee I prayed." Consider the ideas involved, 'Zeus', 'necessity [compulsion] of nature', 'intelligence of mankind', 'prayer'. These lines have survived the ages with a modern appeal vivid as when first they thrilled an Athenian audience. The biographer[5] of a modern statesman cites them to express the solemnity of the spectacle of life passing into religious emotion. Yet Hume would be able to find no 'impression of sensation' from which to derive 'Zeus', or 'compulsion', or 'intelligence', or the would-be 'persuasiveness' which we term 'prayer'. John Morley himself selected the quotation in spite of his own positivistic bias which should trivialize these meanings. Also, perhaps even for their original author, the lines represent a triumph of dramatic intuition over temperamental scepticism.

The common practice, interpreted by the common language of mankind, tells the same tale. A statesman, or a president of a business corporation, assumes the 'compulsion of recent events' [ἀνάγκη φύσεως] as laying down inexorable conditions for the future. He frames a 'policy' upon this assumption and advises that it be 'acted on', thereby also assuming that the imposed conditions leave room for the effectiveness of 'choice' and 'intelligence' [νοῦς]. He assumes alternatives in contrast to the immediate fact. He conceives an ideal, to be attained or to be missed. He conceives

4. *Trojan Women*, 886-7.

5. Cf. John Morley's *Life of Gladstone*, Ch. X.

such ideals as effective in proportion as they are entertained. He praises and he blames by reason of this belief.

In the world, there are elements of order and disorder, which thereby presuppose an essential interconnectedness of things. For disorder shares with order the common characteristic that they imply many things interconnected.

Each experient enjoys a perspective apprehension of the world, and equally is an element in the world by reason of this very prehension, which anchors him to a world transcending his own experience. For, it belongs to the nature of this perspective derivation, that the world thus disclosed proclaims its own transcendence of that disclosure. To every shield, there is another side, hidden.

Thus an appeal to literature, to common language, to common practice, at once carries us away from the narrow basis for epistemology provided by the sense-data disclosed in direct introspection. The world within experience is identical with the world beyond experience, the occasion of experience is within the world and the world is within the occasion. The categories have to elucidate this paradox of the connectedness of things: —the many things, the one world without and within.

SECTION IX. European philosophy is founded upon Plato's dialogues, which in their methods are mainly an endeavour to elicit philosophic categories from a dialectic discussion of the meanings of language taken in combination with shrewd observation of the actions of man and of the forces of nature.

But in one dialogue, the *Sophist,* Plato explicitly considers the methods of philosophy. One of his conclusions is to point out the limitations of common speech. Mere dialectic, uncriticized, is a fallacious instrument, the mark of the *Sophist.* For example, Plato insists that not-being is itself a form of being. Thus in philosophy linguistic discussion is a tool, but should never be a master. Language is imperfect both in its words and in its forms. Thus we discover two main errors to which philosophic method is liable, one is the uncritical trust in the adequacy of language, and the other is the uncritical trust in the strained attitude of introspection as the basis for epistemology.

But since the life-time of Plato nearly two and a half thousand years have intervened, including the continuous activity of European philosophic thought, pagan, Christian, secular. It is widely held that a stable, well-known philosophic vocabulary has been elaborated, and that in philosophic discussion any straying beyond its limits introduces neologisms, unnecessary and therefore to be regretted.

This alleged fact requires examination. In the first place, if the allegation be true, it is very remarkable. It decisively places philosophy apart from the more special sciences. Modern mathematics, most secure and authoritative of sciences, is largely written in verbal and symbolic phrases which would have been unintelligible eighty years ago. In modern physics the old words, where they are still used, convey different meanings, and the new words are abundant. But it is futile to make a catalogue of the sciences accompanied by this refrain. The conclusion is obvious to the most cursory inspection.

SECTION X. Undoubtedly, philosophy is dominated by its past literature to a greater extent than any other science. And rightly so. But the claim that it has acquired a set of technical terms sufficient for its purposes, and exhaustive of its meanings, is entirely unfounded. Indeed its literature is so vast, and the variations of its schools of thought so large, that there is abundant evidence of most excusable ignorance respecting verbal usages.

A recent instance illustrates the vagueness of philosophical terminology. Logic is, by far, that branch of philosophy best sytematized with the aid of a stable technical language. Consider the terms Judgment and Proposition. I am not writing a preface to Logic, so I will confine myself to the assertion that there is considerable variation in the usages of these terms among logicians.

Also we may well ask whether there are not subtle variations of meaning stretching far beyond the competence of the two-term vocabulary,—Judgment, Proposition. For example, Mr. Joseph[6] has been examining Mr. W. E. Johnson's use of the term Proposition in his well-known Logical Treatise. Mr. Joseph finds twenty distinct meanings. It is to be remembered that we are here referring to two of the most acute of modern logicians. Whether Mr. Joseph has rightly interpreted Mr. Johnson's phrases is not to the point. If Mr. Joseph has found twenty distinct, though allied, meanings closely connected with the term Proposition, there are twenty such meanings, even though for the moment their divergencies may seem unimportant to Mr. Johnson or to Mr. Joseph. Importance depends on purpose and on point of view. So at any moment twenty new terms may be required by some advance in the subtlety of logical theory. Again, if Mr. Johnson has employed twenty distinct meanings, it is because they were relevant to his argument, even though his argument may require further completion by reason of their unnoted distinction.

It is safe to affirm that this situation can be repeated over every technical term in philosophy.

SECTION XI. Another illustration, in which my use of the words[7] Prehension, Feeling, Satisfaction, is partly concerned, can be drawn from the terms expressive of the connectedness of things. For this topic, the reigning philosophical term is the word Relation. There are various controversies about relations which need not be explicitly referred to. But there is one discussion which illustrates our immediate topic.

It is generally held that relations are universals, so that A can have the same relation to B as C has to D. For example 'loving', 'believing', 'between', 'greater than', are relations. There can be no objection to this doctrine. For it is a mere definition. Universals which require two or more particulars for their illustration need some term to indicate them, and Relation is the word chosen.

6. Cf. *Mind*, Vols. 36, 37, New Series.
7. Cf. *S. M. W.*, Ch.IV and *passim* and *P.R.* Part I, Ch. II and *passim*.

But with this meaning to the term, a relation cannot signify the actual connectedness of the actual individual things which constitute the actual course of history. For example, New York lies between Boston and Philadelphia. But the connectedness of the three towns is a real particular fact on the earth's surface involving a particular part of the eastern seaboard of the United States. It is not the universal 'between'. It is a complex actual fact which, among other things, exemplifies the abstract universal 'betweenness'.

This consideration is the basis of Bradley's objection that relations do not relate. Three towns and an abstract universal are not three connected towns. A doctrine of connectedness is wanted. Bradley[8] writes 'Is there, in the end, such a thing as a relation which is merely *between* terms? Or, on the other hand, does not a relation imply an underlying unity and an inclusive whole?'

Bradley's 'inclusive whole' is the connectedness of which we are in search. Throughout this chapter *[loc. cit.]* Bradley uses the term Feeling to express the primary activity at the basis of experience. It is experience itself in its origin and with the minimum of analysis. The analysis of Feeling can never disclose anything lying beyond the essence of the occasion of experience. Hence Bradley terms it 'non-relational'. There are of course grave differences between my own doctrine and that of Bradley. This was a reason[9] for expounding my point of view in some independence of Bradley, with due acknowledgement. Surely the proper method of choosing technical terms is to adopt terms from some outstanding exposition of an analogous doctrine. It throws an interesting light on the belief in a well-understood technical phraseology reigning in philosophy, that an accomplished philosopher censured in

8. Cf. *Essays on Truth and Reality*, Ch. VI, *On our Knowledge of Immediate Experience, Appendix*, p. 193.
   The page references are to the Oxford edition of 1914. Also cf. *Appendix to Ch. VI, passim*, and Supplementary Note to the same.
9. Cf. *P. R. passim.*

print, my use of the word Feeling as being in a sense never before employed in philosophy.

I may add that William James also employs the word in much the same sense in his Psychology. For example in the first chapter he writes, "Sensation is the feeling of first things". And in the second chapter he writes, "In general, this higher consciousness about things is called Perception, the mere inarticulate feeling of their presence is Sensation, so far as we have it at all. To some degree we seem able to lapse into this inarticulate feeling at moments when our attention is entirely dispersed." It is interesting to make a few citations from Bradley, illustrating my general adherence to his doctrine of Feeling, as expressed in his Chapter. "In my general feeling at any moment there is more than the objects before me, and no perception of objects will exhaust the sense of a living emotion."[10]

In accordance with this doctrine of Bradley's, I analyze a feeling [or prehension] into the 'datum', which is Bradley's 'object before me', into the 'subjective form' which is Bradley's 'living emotion', and into the 'subject' which is Bradley's 'me'. My reason for using the term 'subjective form' is that I stretch its meaning beyond 'emotion'. For example consciousness, if it be present. is an element in the subjective form. This is, of course, a grave divergence from Bradley. Subjective form is the character assumed by the subject by reason of some prehended datum.

But on the whole I conform to Bradley's conception of the function of subjective form. For example, "These puzzles are insoluble unless that which I feel, and which is not an object before me, is present and active. This felt element is used and it must be used in the constitution of that object which satisfies me".[11]

From my point of view there is an ambiguity in this statement, but I adhere to either alternative meaning.

---

10. Bradley, p. 159.
11. P. 161.

The component of feeling 'which is not an object before me' is the subjective form. If Bradley is stating that the subjective forms of feelings determine the process of integration, I entirely agree. The result, as Bradley states, is the 'satisfaction' which is the final feeling terminating the unrest of the creative process.

Bradley, however, may mean by his phrase "that which I feel, and which is not an object before me" what I term a "negative prehension". Such a prehension is active *via* its contribution of its subjective form to the creative process. but it dismisses its 'object' from the possibility of entering into the datum of the final satisfaction. This final complex datum will be what Bradley calls "that object that satisfies me". Again I agree.

The doctrine of the 'living emotion' which necessarily clothes each concrete exhibition of the subject-object situation is far older than Bradley. We find its germ in Plato, who insists that the whole character is conformed to the adequate knowledge. He implicitly refuses to abstract the 'living emotion' from the bare intellectual perception, and thereby identifies virtue with knowledge. The advance in psychology has added to our conscious discrimination, but it has not altered the fact that inevitably perception is clothed with emotion.

The historical importance of the doctrine is stated by George Foot Moore[12]:—"Civilization develops only where considerable numbers of men work together for common ends. Such unity is brought about, not so much by community of bare ideas as by community of the feelings by which ideas are 'emotionalized' and become beliefs and motives."

The conventionalized abstractions prevalent in epistemological theory are very far from the concrete facts of experience. The word 'feeling' has the merit of preserving this double significance of

12. In the *Prefatory Note to Emotion as the Basis of Civilization*, by J. H. Denison, New York, 1928 (Scribner's): a work of importance.

subjective form and of the apprehension of an object. It avoids the *disjecta membra* provided by abstraction.[13]

SECTION XII. Thus an occasion of human experience is one illustration of the required doctrine of connectedness.

Bradley's authority can be quoted in support. He writes:[14] "At every moment my stage of experience, whatever else it is, is a whole of which I am immediately aware. It is an experienced non-relational unity of many in one." Here Bradley by 'non-relational' apparently means that experience is not a relation of an experient to something external to it, but is itself the 'inclusive whole' which is the required connectedness of 'many in one'.

In this I thoroughly agree, holding that the connectedness of things is nothing else than the togetherness of things in occasions of experience. Of course, such occasions are only rarely occasions of human experience.

Curiously enough Hume also agrees. For his only togetherness of the stream of impressions of sensation, which in his doctrine are distinct existences at distinct times, lies in the 'gentle force' of association which must lie wholly within an occasion of experience. This is also one aspect of Kant's doctrine, that the occasions of experience provide the forms of connectedness.

Of course there are important differences between all these doctrines. But they agree in their general principle—to look on occasions of experience as the ground of connectedness.

SECTION XIII. Also Leibniz can find no other connectedness between reals except that lying wholly within the individual experiences of the monads, including the Supreme Monad. He employed the terms 'perception' and 'apperception' for the lower and higher ways in which one monad can take account of

---

13. The genetic description of the process of 'emotionalization' is considered in my '*Symbolism, Its Meaning and Effect*' and also in *P.R.* Pt. II, Ch. VIII, and throughout Pt. III.

14. *Loc. cit.*, p.175

another, namely for ways of awareness. But these terms are too closely allied to the notion of consciousness which in my doctrine is not a necessary accompaniment. Also they are all entangled in the notion of representative perception which I reject. But there is the term[15] 'apprehension' with the meaning of 'thorough understanding'. Accordingly, on the Leibnizian model, I use the term 'prehension' for the general way in which the occasion of experience can include, as part of its own essence, any other entity, whether another occasion of experience or an entity of another type. This term is devoid of suggestion either of consciousness or of representative perception. Feelings are the positive type of prehensions. In positive prehensions the 'datum' is preserved as part of the final complex object which 'satisfies' the process of self-formation and thereby completes the occasion.

This nomenclature has been made up to conform to the condition, that, as a theory develops, its technical phraseology should grow out of the usages of the great masters who laid its foundations. The immediate verbal usages at any moment prevalent in any school of philosophy are but a small selection from the total vocabulary of the philosophic tradition. This is rightly the case having regard to the variations of doctrine.

The current usage can express the doctrine of the reigning school of thought and of certain accredited variations from it. The demand that an alternative doctrine with other roots in the historic tradition should confine itself to this selection of terms amounts to the dogmatic claim that certain preliminary assumptions should never be revised. Only those schools of thought are to be allowed which can be expressed in the sacred terms. What can reasonably be asked, is that each doctrine should ground its vocabulary on its own proper tradition. If this precaution has been taken, an outcry as to neologisms is a measure of unconscious dogmatism.

---

15. This term is used by L. T. Hobhouse, *Theory of Knowledge*, Chs. I and II.

SECTION XIV. The main method of philosophy in dealing with its evidence is that of descriptive generalization. Social institutions exemplify a welter of characteristics. No fact is merely such-and-such. It exemplifies many characters at once, all rooted in the specialities of its epoch. Philosophic generalization seizes on those characters of abiding importance, dismissing the trivial and the evanescent. There is an ascent from a particular fact, or from a species, to the genus exemplified.

It is to be noted that the converse procedure is impossible. There can be no descent from a mere genus to a particular fact, or to a species. For facts and species are the product of the mingling of genera. No genus in its own essence indicates the other genera with which it is compatible. For example, the notion of a backbone does not indicate the notions of suckling the young or of swimming in water. Thus no contemplation of the genus vertebrate, taken by itself, can suggest mammals or fishes, even as abstract possibilities. Neither the species nor the instance are to be discovered by the genus alone, since both include forms not 'given' by the genus. A species is a potential mingling of genera, and an individual instance involves, among other things, an actual mingling of many species. A syllogism is a scheme for demonstration of ways of mingling.

Thus the business of Logic is not the analysis of generalities but their mingling.[16]

Philosophy is the ascent to the generalities with the view of understanding their possibilities of combination. The discovery of new generalities thus adds to the fruitfulness of those already known. It lifts into view new possibilities of combination.

SECTION XV. Even the dim apprehension of some great principle is apt to clothe itself with tremendous emotional force. The welter of particular actions arising out of such complex feelings with their core of deep intuition are in primitive times

16. Cf. Plato's *Sophist*, 253.

often brutish and nasty. Finally civilized language provides a whole group of words, each embodying the general idea under its own specialization. If we desire to reach the generality common to these various specializations, we must gather together the whole group of words with the hope of discerning their common element. This is a necessary procedure for the purpose of philosophical generalization. The premature use of one familiar word inevitably limits the required generalization by importing the familiar special connotation of that word.

For example,[17] let the working hypothesis be that the ultimate realities are the events in their process of origination. Then each event, viewed in its separate individuality, is a passage between two ideal termini, namely, its components in their ideal disjunctive diversity passing into these same components in their concrele togetherness. There are two current doctrines as to this process. One is that of the external Creator, eliciting this final togetherness out of nothing. The other doctrine is that it is a metaphysical principle belonging to the nature of things, that there is nothing in the Universe other than instances of this passage and components of these instances. Let this latter doctrine be adopted. Then the word Creativity expresses the notion that each event is a process issuing in novelty. Also if guarded in the phrases Immanent Creativity, or Self-Creativity, it avoids the implication of a transcendent Creator. But the mere word Creativity suggests Creator, so that the whole doctrine acquires an air of paradox, or of pantheism. Still it does convey the origination of novelty. The word Concrescence is a derivative from the familiar Latin verb, meaning 'growing together'. It also has the advantage that the participle 'concrete' is familiarly used for the notion of complete physical reality. Thus Concrescence is useful to convey the notion of many things acquiring complete complex unity. But it fails to suggest the creative novelty involved. For example, it omits the notion of the individual character

17. Cf. *P. R. passim*, where the second of the doctrines stated below is developed.

arising in the concrescence of the aboriginal data. The event is not suggested as 'emotionalized', that is, as with its 'subjective form'.

Again the term 'together' is one of the most misused terms in philosophy. It is a generic term illustrated by an endless variety of species. Thus its use as though it conveyed one definite meaning in diverse illustrations is entirely sophistical. Every meaning of 'together' is to be found in various stages of analysis of occasions of experience. No things are 'together' except in experience; and no things *are,* in any sense of 'are', except as components in experience or as immediacies of process which are occasions in self-creation.

SECTION XVI. Thus to arrive at the philosophic generalization which is the notion of a final actuality conceived in the guise of a generalization of an act of experience, an apparent redundancy of terms is required. The words correct each other. We require[18] 'together', 'creativity', 'concrescence', 'prehension', 'feeling', 'subjective form', 'data', 'actuality', 'becoming', 'process'.

SECTION XVII. At this stage of the generalization a new train of thought arises. Events become and perish. In their becoming they are immediate and then vanish into the past. They are gone; they have perished; they are no more and have passed into not-being. Plato terms[19] them things that are 'always becoming and never really are'. But before he wrote this phrase, Plato had made his great metaphysical generalization, a discovery which forms the basis of the present discussion. He wrote in the *Sophist,* not-being is itself a form of being. He only applied this doctrine to his eternal forms. He should have applied the same doctrine to the things that perish. He would then have illustrated another aspect of the method of philosophic generalization. When a general idea has been obtained, it should not be arbitrarily limited to the topic of its origination.

In framing a philosophic scheme, each metaphysical notion should be given the widest extension of which it seems capable. It is

18. Cf. *P. R. passim,* also *S. M. W.*

19. Cf. *Timæus.*

only in this way that the true adjustment of ideas can be explored. More important even than Occam's doctrine of parsimony—if it be not another aspect of the same—is this doctrine that the scope of a metaphysical principle should not be limited otherwise than by the necessity of its meaning.

Thus we should balance Aristotle's—or, more rightly, Plato's—doctrine of becoming by a doctrine of perishing. When they perish. occasions pass from the immediacy of being into the not-being of immediacy. But that does not mean that they are nothing. They remain 'stubborn fact': —

Pereunt et imputantur.

The common expressions of mankind fashion the past for us in three aspects,—Causation, Memory, and our active transformation of our immediate past experience into the basis of our present modification of it. Thus 'perishing' is the assumption of a role in a transcendent future. The not-being of occasions is their 'objective immortality'. A pure physical prehension is how an occasion in its immediacy of being absorbs another occasion which has passed into the objective immortality of its not-being. It is how the past lives in the present. It is causation. It is memory. It is perception of derivation. It is emotional conformation to a given situation, an emotional continuity of past with present. It is a basic element from which springs the self-creation of each temporal occasion. Thus perishing is the initiation of becoming. How the past perishes is how the future becomes.

PART IV

CIVILIZATION

Chapter XVI

TRUTH

SECTION I. TRUTH AND Beauty are the great regulative properties in virtue of which Appearance justifies itself to the immediate decision of the experient subject. The justification determines its status in the immediate occasion. The subjective form of the prehension can include immediate emphasis or attenuation, and it can include purpose of prolongation into the future or purpose of exclusion. Truth and Beauty are the ultimate grounds for emphasis and for prolongation. Of course the present can be sacrificed to the future, so that Truth or Beauty in the future can be the reason for the immediate attenuation of either.

SECTION II. Truth is a qualification which applies to Appearance alone. Reality is just itself, and it is nonsense to ask whether it be true or false. Truth is the conformation of Appearance to Reality. This conformation may be more or less, also direct or indirect. Thus Truth is a generic quality with a variety of degrees and modes. In the Law-Courts, the wrong species of Truth may amount to perjury. For example, a portrait may be so faithful as to deceive the eye. Its very truthfulness then amounts to deception. A reflexion in a mirror is at once a truthful appearance and a deceptive appearance. The smile of a hypocrite is deceptive, and that of a philanthropist may be truthful. But both of them were truly smiling.

SECTION III. The notion of Truth can be generalized, so as to avoid any explicit reference to Appearance. Two objects may be such that (I) neither may be a component of the other, and (2) their composite natures may includes a common factor, although in the full sense of the term their 'essences' are different. The two objects can then be said to have a truth-relation to each other. The examination of one of them can disclose some factor belonging to the essence of the other. In other words, an abstraction can be made and some elements of the complete pattern can be omitted. The partial pattern thus obtained will be said to be abstracted from the original. A truth-relation will be said to connect the objective contents of two prehensions when one and the same identical partial pattern can be abstracted from both of them. They each exhibit this same partial pattern, though their omitted elements involve the differences which belong to their diverse individualities. Plato uses the term 'participation' [μέθεξις] to express the relation of a composite fact to some partial pattern which it illustrates. Only he limits the notion of the partial pattern to some purely abstract pattern of qualitative elements, to the exclusion of the notion of concrete particular realities as components in a composite reality. This limitation is misleading. Thus we will speak of a pattern as possibly including concrete particulars among its patterned elements. With this enlargement of meaning, we can say that two objective contents are united in a truth-relation when they severally participate in the same pattern. Either illustrates what in part the other is. Thus they interpret each other. But if we ask what is meant by 'truth'. we can only answer that there is a truth-relation when two composite facts participate in the same pattern. Then knowledge about one of the facts involves knowledge about the other, so far as the truth-relation extends.

The truth-relation as realized in experience always involves some element of Appearance. For the separate prehensions of the two composite facts have been integrated so that the two objects stand in the unity of a contrast with each other. There is an intuition of a limited identity of pattern involved in the contrast of the diverse essences. In virtue of this identity there is a transference of subjective form from the feeling of one object to that of the other. What is appropriate to one is appropriate to the other. The intuitive recognition of 'that is so' is the subjective form including in itself justification of its own transference from the object on one side of the contrast to the object on the other side.

In this way one object as a real fact obtains a re-adjustment of the relative values of its factors by reason of its analogies to another object. In other words, it becomes a real fact tinged with Appearance. By itself, its factors would not be felt in those proportions. To know the truth partially is to distort the Universe. For example, the savage who can only count up to ten enormously exaggerates the importance of the small numbers, and so do we whose imaginations fail when we come to millions. It is an erroneous moral platitude, that it is necessarily good to know the truth. The minor truth may beget the major evil. And this major evil may take the form of the major error. Henri Poincare points out that instruments of precision, used unseasonably, may hinder the advance of science. For example, if Newton's imagination had been dominated by the errors in Kepler's Laws as disclosed by modern observation, the world might still be waiting for the Law of Gravitation. The Truth must be seasonable.

SECTION IV. The two conspicuous examples of the truth-relation in human experience are afforded by propositions and by sense-perception. A proposition is the abstract possibility of some specified nexus of actualities realizing some eternal object, which may either be simple, or may be a complex pattern of simpler objects. The realization may (I) concern the complete nexus with its component occasions in assigned functions, or (2) it may concern the individual realization of the eternal object by some or all, of the component occasions, or (3) it may concern the joint realization by some unspecified subordinate nexus. All of these alternatives merely concern the possibility of propositions of the various types, so important for the purposes of Formal Logic.

But for the present discussion we need simply consider the broad fact that a proposition is the abstract possibility of an assigned nexus illustrating an assigned pattern.

No verbal sentence merely enunciates a proposition. It always includes some incitement for the production of an assigned psychological attitude in the prehension of the proposition indicated. In other words, it endeavours to fix the subjective form which clothes the feeling of the proposition as a datum. There may be an incitement to believe, or to doubt, or to enjoy, or to obey. This incitement is conveyed partly by the grammatical mood and tense of the verb, partly by the whole suggestion of the sentence, partly by the whole content of the book, partly by the material circumstances of the book, including its cover, partly by the names of the author and of the publisher. In the discussion of the nature of a proposition, a great deal of confusion has been introduced by confusing this psychological incitement with the proposition itself.

A proposition is a notion about actualities, a suggestion, a theory, a supposition about things. Its entertainment in experience subserves many purposes. It is an extreme case of Appearance. For actualities which are the logical subjects are conceived in the guise of illustrating the predicate. The unconscious entertainment of propositions is a stage in the transition from the Reality of the initial phase of experience to the Appearance of the final phase. In the lowest types of actualities in whose processes propositions hardly arise, there is practically no Appearance differentiating the final and initial phases.

It is more important that a proposition be interesting than that it be true. This statement is almost a tautology. For the energy of operation of a proposition in an occasion of experience is its interest, and is its importance. But of course a true proposition is more apt to be interesting than a false one. Also action in accordance with the emotional lure of a proposition is more apt to be successful if the proposition be true. And apart from action, the contemplation of truth has an interest of its own. But, after all this explanation and qualification, it remains true that the importance of a proposition lies in its interest. Nothing illustrates better the danger of specialist sciences than the confusion due to handing over propositions for theoretical consideration by logicians, exclusively. The truth of a proposition lies in its truth-relation to the nexus which is its logical subject. A proposition is true when the nexus does in reality exemplify the pattern which is the predicate of the proposition. Thus in the analysis of the various component factors involved the proposition, if true, seems to be identical with the nexus. For there are the same actual occasions and the same eternal objects involved. But in all analysis there is one supreme factor which is apt to be omitted, namely, the mode of togetherness. The nexus includes the eternal object in the mode of realization. Whereas in the true proposition the togetherness of the nexus and the eternal object belongs to the mode of abstract possibility. The eternal object is then united to the nexus as a mere 'predicate'. Thus a nexus and a proposition belong to different categories of being. Their identification is mere nonsense. It is the nonsense of the same sort as the fashionable identification of physical fact with formula: of pure mathematics.

Propositions, like everything else except experience in its own immediacy, only exist as entertained in experience. It is the peculiar function of the mental pole that the objective content of its prehensions only exists in the mode of possibility. But matter of fact essentially involves a mental pole. Thus in the analysis of an actual occasion, we necessarily find components belonging to the mode of possibility. The most conspicuous example of truth and falsehood arises in the comparison of existences in the mode of possibility with existences in the mode of actuality.

SECTION V. For animals on this Earth, sense-perception is the culmination of Appearance. The sensa derived from bodily activities in the past are precipitated upon the regions in the contemporary world. The note of hypothesis, the note of mere suggested possibility is eliminated. The regions appear to the percipient as in their own right associated with the sensa. The Appearance now is, that the sensa qualify the regions.

The question then arises, Do the sensa in fact qualify the regions? The answer depends on what is meant by 'in fact', and what is meant by 'qualification'. It is here that the notion of truth and falsehood applies to sense-perception. But in the realm of truth there are many mansions; and we have to analyse the types of truth and of falsehood which sense-perception is capable of.

In the first place, the primary status of the sensa as qualifications of affective tone must be kept in mind. They are primarily inherited as such qualifications and then by 'transmutation' are objectively perceived as qualifications of regions. The immense æsthetic importance of sensa is due to this status of sensa. For the sensum as a factor in the datum of a prehension imposes itself as a qualification of the affective tone which is the subjective form of that prehension. Thus a pattern of affective tone is conformally produced by a pattern of sensa as datum. Now when a region appears as red in sense-perception, the question arises whether red is qualifying in any dominant manner the affective tones of the actualities which in fact make up the region.

If so, there is in this sense a truth-relation between the reality of the region and its appearance for the contemporary percipient. For example, if the light has undergone reflexions in a mirror, the appearance of the region behind the mirror affords no ground for conjecture as to the affective tones of its component actualities.

This notion of the sensa as qualifications of affective tone is a paradox for philosophy, though it is fairly obvious to common sense. A red-irritation is prevalent among nerve-racked people and among bulls. The affective tone of perception of a green woodland in spring can only be defined by the delicate shades of the green. It is a strong æsthetic emotion with the qualification of green in springtime. The intellect fastens on smell as a datum: the animal experiences it as a qualification of his subjective feelings. Our developed consciousness fastens on the sensum as datum: our basic animal experience entertains it as a type of subjective feeling. The experience starts as that smelly feeling, and is developed by mentality into the feeling of that smell.

We can also observe qualifications of moods hovering on the verge of becoming sensa, in fact functioning as sensa for the infant, and being dismissed from that category by the developed intellect of the grown-up person. For example, the emotional moods of the mother nursing the infant, moods of love, or gaiety, or depression, or irritation, are directly perceived on the mother's face by the infant, and are responded to. It certainly is in the highest degree improbable that the subtle trains of thought by which our epistemologists obtain their knowledge should have occurred to speechless infants, or to dogs and horses. Direct perceptions of such moods in these cases must enter on equal terms with the other sensa. But in respect to the perception of such moods, the animal body functions vary differently from its functionings in the conveyance of sensa. Hence for the educated intellect there is a distinction of type.

But in any case the infant feels its mother's cheerfulness as a datum, and feels it conformally, with that affective tone. The datum is derived from the past, the immediate past. It is precipitated upon that present region occupied by the nexus of occasions which constitute the complex fact of the mother's existence, body and soul. For the infant, the Appearance includes the qualification of cheerfulness. And in this respect it may have—it often does have—to the contemporary real mother a truth-relation in the fullest sense of the term 'truth'.

SECTION VI. The relation of sense-perception to contemporary occasions can also exemplify another type of truth-relation between Appearance and Reality.

The sense-perception may result from the normal functioning of the healthy animal body. The consequent inheritance from the antecedent occasions of the personal soul may likewise share in this healthy normality. Also the particular body and soul in question may share in that conformation of their reactions to those main external activities of fluent energy which is normally required for the preservation of that species of animal. Given these conditions of normality, the resulting appearance will be that proper to that species of animal under circumstances of that type. This is a fact of nature, and the Appearance expresses the issue of a Law of Nature, belonging to that cosmic epoch and to those more special conditions within that epoch. This is a truth-relation between Appearance and Reality of a more indirect character than the first sort of truth-relation. It is wider, vaguer, and more diffuse in its reference. We have perceived what well-conditioned individuals of our own type would perceive under those circumstances.

SECTION VII. Within any type of truth-relation a distinction arises. The Reality functions in the past, the Appearance is perceived in the present. On a moonless night, the faintly luminous stretch of the sky which is the Milky Way is an Appearance of the contemporary world, namely, it is a great region within the 'Receptacle' of that world as it appears. But the Reality whose functioning issues in that Appearance, is a flux of light-energy travelling through the utmost depths of space and, to our imaginations, through illimitable time.

Beyond that Milky Way as it stands in sight, at a finite ill-defined distance, a barrier separating us from the contemporary space beyond: —Does that remote activity of the transference of light-energy still persist as a contemporary fact? Perhaps the occasions whose interconnections constitute that distant region have changed the ordering of their goings-on. Stars flare out in a few days, and in a few years, their light has died. The Appearance of the contemporary regions has its truth-relations to the past, and its truth-relations to contemporary Reality. These latter truth-relations can only be estimated by an imaginative leap, which has as its basis for justification the truth-relations to the past and our experience of the stability of the types of order involved.

Perhaps in the mutual immanence of occasions, although the antecedence and the consequence,—the past, the present and the future—still hold equally for physical and mental poles, yet the relations of the mental poles to each other are not subject to the same laws of perspective as are those of the physical poles. Measureable time and measureable space are then irrelevant to their mutual connections. Thus in respect to some types of Appearance there may be an element of immediacy in its relations to the mental side of the contemporary world. Other types of Appearance, such as the located sensa in sense-perception, may depend on the time and space which express the perspective arising in the mutual immanence of the physical poles.

If such be the case, some types of Appearance will have a more direct relation than others to contemporary Reality.

SECTION VIII. There is a third type of truth-relation which is even vaguer and more indirect than the second type considered above. It may be termed the type of 'symbolic truth'. This species of truth may be included under the second type, as an extreme instance of it. But on the whole, it is clearer to consider it as a distinct species.

The relation of Appearance to Reality, when there is symbolic truth, is that for certain sets of percipients the prehension of the Appearance leads to the prehension of the Reality, such that the subjective forms of the two prehensions are conformal. There is however no direct causal relation between the Appearance and the Reality; so that in no direct sense is the Appearance the cause of the Reality, or the Reality the cause of the Appearance. A set of adventitious circumstances has brought about this connection between those Appearances and those Realities as prehended in the experiences of those percipients. In their own natures the Appearances throw no light upon the Realities, nor do the Realities upon the Appearances, except in the experiences of a set of peculiarly conditioned percipients. Languages and their meanings are examples of this third type of truth. There is an indirect truth-relation of the sounds or of the visual marks on paper to the propositions conveyed. We are confining the discussion to the relation of written or spoken sentences to propositions. There is a right and a wrong use of any particular language among the group of people who are properly conditioned. Also, having regard to the æsthetics of literature, language not only conveys objective meaning, but also involves a conveyance of subjective form.

Music, ceremonial clothing, ceremonial smells, and ceremonial rhythmic visual appearances, also have symbolic truth, or symbolic falsehood. In these latter instances, the conveyance of objective meaning is at a minimum, while the conveyance of suitable subjective form is at its height. Music provides an example when it interprets some strong sentiment, patriotic, martial, or religious, by providing the emotion which the votaries dumbly feel ought to be attached to the apprehension of national life, or of the clash of nations, or of the activities of God. Music elicits some confused feeling into distinct apprehension. It performs this service, or disservice, by introducing an emotional clothing which changes the dim objective reality into a clear Appearance matching the subjective form provided for its prehension.

There is then the vague truth-relation, *via* community of subjective form, between the music and the resulting Appearance. There is also the truth-relation between the Appearance and the Reality—the Reality of National Life, or of Strife between nations, or of the Essence of God. This complex fusion of truth-relations, with their falsehoods intermixed, constitutes the indirect interpretative power of Art to express the truth about the nature of things. Of course a somewhat gross, almost vulgar, instance has been given, for the sake of easy explanation. But the delicate inner truth of Art is mostly of this sort.

SECTION IX. This discussion suggests an illustrative digression on the origins of socially diffused habits of behaviour and of habits of interpretation, among human beings. An idea arises from the antecedent establishment of modes of human functioning which are germane to it. In the infancy of its incarnation in human history, it lurks in the penumbra of consciousness, undiscriminated and unexpressed. For the historian in later ages it discloses itself by the dim growth of the sense of importance attached to those functionings of the tribe which dimly elicit its discrimination. But soon an inversion takes place. These modes of functioning are interpreted by some restless intellects of the tribe. The behaviour patterns then, in addition to their own intrinsic value for tribal life, take on the role of an apparatus of expression. They become linked to an intellectual construction. The behaviour patterns, with their entwined emotions, evoke the apprehension of the construction. Conversely, the entertainment of the construction constitutes an urge towards the modes of behaviour. In this way, the ceremonies with their output of emotion become the mode of expression for the ideas; and the ideas become an interpretation of the ceremonies. This is the account of the primitive origination of the linkage of an idea to an apparatus of expression.

The linkage between an idea and its expression has been desribed above as being 'interpretation'. Some analysis of this concept of 'interpretation' has now to be made. Two behaviour patterns mutually interpret each other, only when some common factor of experience is realized in the enactment of either pattern. The common factor constitutes the reason for the transition from one pattern to the other pattern. Each pattern interprets the other as expressive of that common factor. Here a behaviour-pattern is merely another phrase for a mode of experience. Thus, in this sense, the entertainment of a myth is one behaviour-pattern, and a tribal dance, or a Court ceremonial, is another behaviour pattern.

SECTION X. But after all, it is the blunt truth that we want. The final contentment of our aims requires something more than vulgar substitutes, or subtle evasions, however delicate. The indirections of truth can never satisfy us. Our purposes seek their main justification in sheer matter-of-fact. AU the rest is addition, however important, to this foundation. Apart from blunt truth, our lives sink decadently amid the perfume of hints and suggestions.

The blunt truth that we require is the conformal correspondence of clear and distinct Appearance to Reality. In human experience, clear and distinct Appearance is primarily sense-perception. The blunt truth required for sense-perception is the truth of the first type, already partially discussed in Section V of this Chapter. In that section the doctrine was developed that the prehension of a sensum, as an apparent object qualifying a region, involved for that prehension a subjective form also involving that sensum as a factor. We enjoy the green foliage of the spring greenly: we enjoy the sunset with an emotional pattern including among its elements the colours and the contrasts of the vision. It is this that makes Art possible: it is this that procures the glory of perceived nature. For if the subjective form of reception be not conformal to the objective sensa, then the values of the percept would be at the mercy of the chance makeup of the other components in that experience. For example, in the intuition of a multiplicity of three or four objects, the mere number imposes no subjective form. It is merely a condition regulating some pattern of effective components. In abstraction from those components, mere triplicity can dictate no subjective form for its prehension. But green can. And there lies the difference between the sensa and the abstract mathematical forms.

The steady values derived from sense-perception, which are there even when disregarded and even when jarring with other emotions, exist because the sensa themselves enter into the subjective forms of their physical prehensions.

SECTION XI. The point to be decided is whether the green meadow in springtime, as it appears to us, in any direct way conforms to the happenings within the region of the meadow, and more particularly within the regions of the blades of grass. Have we any grounds for the belief that in some way things really are in those regions as our senses perceive those regions? In the first place, such conformation evidently cannot arise from the necessities of nature. The delusive perceptions prove that. Double vision, and images due to reflexion and refraction of light, show that the appearance of regions may be quite irrelevant to the happenings within regions. Appearances are finally controlled by the functionings of the animal body. These functionings and the happenings within the contemporary regions are both derived from a common past, highly relevant to both. It is thereby pertinent to ask, whether the animal body and the external regions are not attuned together, so that under normal circumstances, the appearances conform to natures within the regions.

The attainment of such conformation would belong to the perfection of nature in respect to the higher types of its animal life. There is no necessity about it. Evidently there is failure, interference, and only partial adjustment. But we have to ask whether nature does not contain within itself a tendency to be in tune, an Eros urging towards perfection. This question cannot be discussed without passing beyond the narrow grounds of the truth-relation.

Chapter XVII

BEAUTY

SECTION I. BEAUTY IS the mutual adaptation of the several factors in an occasion of experience. Thus in its primary sense Beauty is a quality which finds its exemplification in actual occasions: or put conversely, it is a quality in which such occasions can severally participate. There are gradations in Beauty and in types of Beauty.

"Adaptation" implies an end. Thus Beauty is only defined when the aim of the 'adaptation' has been analysed. This aim is twofold. It is in the first place, the absence of mutual inhibition among the various prehensions, so that the intensities of subjective form, which naturally and properly—or in one word, conformally—arise from the objective contents of the various prehensions, do not inhibit each other. When this aim is secured, there is the minor form of beauty, the absence of painful clash, the absence of vulgarity. In the second place, there is the major form of Beauty. This form presupposes the first form, and adds to it the condition that the conjunction in one synthesis of the various prehensions introduces new contrasts of objective content with objective content. These contrasts introduce new conformal intensities of feelings natural to each of them, and by so doing raise the intensities of conformal feeling in the primitive component feelings. Thus the parts contribute to the massive feeling of the whole, and the whole contributes to the intensity of feeling of the parts. Thus the subjective forms of these prehensions are severally and jointly interwoven in patterned contrasts. In other words, the perfection of Beauty is defined as being the perfection of Harmony; and the perfection of Harmony is defined in terms of the perfection of Subjective Form in detail and in final synthesis. Also the perfection of Subjective Form is defined in terms of 'Strength'. In the sense here meant, Strength has two factors, namely, variety of detail with effective contrast, which is Massiveness, and Intensity Proper which is comparative magnitude without reference to qualitative variety. But the maximum of intensity proper is finally dependent upon massiveness.

SECTION II. In order to understand this definition of Beauty, it is necessary to keep in mind three doctrines which belong to the metaphysical system in terms of which the World is being interpreted in these chapters. These three doctrines respectively have regard to the mutual relations (a) between the objective content of a prehension and the subjective form of that prehension, and (b) between the subjective forms of various prehensions in the same occasion, and (c) between the subjective form of a prehension and the spontaneity involved in the subjective aim of the prehending occasion. These doctrines are interconnected; but each of them introduces a principle which is not made explicit by the other two. They will now be successively explained: —

(a) It is held that every qualitative factor in the Universe is primarily a qualification of subjective form, so that the infinite variety of qualities involves the possibility of an infinite variety of subjective forms exemplifying those qualities. This does not mean that the subjective forms exemplifying various qualities are all equally prominent in human consciousness. Consciousness is a variable uncertain element which flickers uncertainly on the surface of experience. But it is part of the doctrine that the qualitative content of the object prehended enters into the qualities exemplified in the subjective form of that prehension. This is the general principle underlying (I) the doctrine of conformal[1] feelings, constituting the primary phase of the occasion, and (2)

1. Cf. Part III, above, and *Process and Reality, passim*, as indexed.

the doctrine of the qualitative valuations forming the activities of the mental pole, and (3) the doctrine of the valuations involved in the Primordial Nature of God, here also termed the Eros of the Universe. It follows that the subjective form of a prehension is partly dictated by the qualitative element in the objective content of that prehension. There is in fact initial conformation. It has been repeatedly stated above that this is what makes Art possible. Also the factor of compulsive determinism in the Universe depends on this principle.

This doctrine of conformation only holds for the qualitative side of the content of the objective datum. It follows that two exceptions arise to the more general statement that subjective form conforms to the objective datum. Both exceptions arise when abstraction has reached its extreme limit. The extremity of abstraction from all qualitative elements reduces pattern to bare mathematical form—for example, triplicity or the abstract relationship of sets of numbers, such as the squareness of the number four. Such forms by their very natures cannot qualify subjective form. For example, there is not a squareness of emotion. Thus, except in an indirect fashion—such as the qualitative feelings of smoothness of a sphere, of spikeyness of a square, of amplitude of a volume—, the doctrine of conformation does not apply to mathematical pattern. Here pure mathematics in its strictest modern sense is in question.

Again the notion of an actual occasion—that is, of individual actuality—can be entertained in abstraction from any qualitative or mathematical components which in any sense are realized in its essence, either as objective data, or as subjective forms, or as relations between prehensions. A particular actuality can also be abstracted from the mode of its initial indication. so that in a later phase of experience it is entertained[2] as a bare *'It'*. Only the qualitative components of an actuality in the datum can pass into

2. Cf. *The Concept of Nature*, Chapter I, and *Process and Reality*, Part II, Section III, Chapter IX, and Part III, Chapter IV.

the subjective form. The only actuality implicated in the subjective form is the immediate occasion in process of self-formation. The subjective form is that immediate subject in that state of subjective feeling. In the sense in which an actuality can be indicated as a bare *It* for objective prehension—in that sense it does not enter into the subjective form of the prehension.

(b) The second doctrine expresses the unity of the immediate occasion in process of formation. The subjective forms are merely contributions to the one fact which is the subjective feeling of the one occasion. There is a certain distribution among the various prehensions, by reason of the fact that each part of the total objective datum dictates its conformal qualitative reproduction in the subjective form. In so far as identical qualities occur in diverse objective data, then the efficiency of that quality in the subjective form must be dictated by a process of integration, and also by compatibility with the other qualitative feelings. Thus the distribution of subjective form among the separate prehensions refers primarily to the conformal origins of subjective form derived from the various components of the total objective datum.

(c) The third doctrine expresses the final autonomy of the process. This process of the synthesis of subjective forms derived conformally is not settled by the antecedent fact of the data. For these data in their own separate natures do not carry any regulative principle for their synthesis. The regulative principle is derived from the novel unity which is imposed on them by the novel creature in process of constitution. Thus the immediate occasion from the spontaneity of its own essence must supply the missing determination for the synthesis of subjective form. Thus the future of the Universe, though conditioned by the immanence of its past, awaits for its complete determination the spontaneity of the novel individual occasions as in their season they come into being.

SECTION III. A distinction must now be made between two meanings of the term Beauty. There is the primary meaning which has been given in Section I of this chapter. This is Beauty realized in actual occasions which are the completely real things in the Universe. But in the analysis of an occasion, some parts of its objective content may be termed Beautiful by reason of their conformal contribution to the perfection of the subjective form of the complete occasion. This secondary sense of the term Beauty is more accurately to be considered as a definition of the term 'Beautiful'. The Beauty realized in an occasion depends both on the objective content from which that occasion originates and also on the spontaneity of the occasion. The objective content is 'beautiful' by reason of the Beauty that would be realized in that occasion by a fortunate exercise of its spontaneity. In the same way any part of the objective content is 'beautiful' in a still more indirect sense, capable of slight variations in meaning. It may be beautiful by reason of the Beauty that would be realized by a fortunate association with other data combined with a fortunate exercise of spontaneity by the occasion prehending it. But such supreme fortune is an ideal, not for this world. By the term 'beautiful' we usually mean the presupposition of the sort of objective environment which in that general social setting may be presupposed, and the sort of spontaniety which may be hoped for from the percipient occasions in question. We may be thinking of artists, or of cultivated men of the modern world, or of the ruck of mankind in a given city at a given time. But in all its senses, 'beautiful' means the inherent capability for the promotion of Beauty when functioning as a datum in a percipient occasion. When 'Beauty' is ascribed to any component in a datum, it is in this secondary sense.

SECTION IV. In the initial definition of Beauty, the notion of 'perfection' was tacitly introduced. The 'perfection' of subjective form means the absence from it of component feelings which mutually inhibit each other so that neither rises to the strength proper to it. But there are two meanings to 'inhibition' which must be carefully distinguished, since only one of them involves a derogation from perfection. Complete inhibition is an example of the finiteness of subjective form. It does not derogate from 'perfection'. There is then 'perfection' in its kind—that is to say, in its type of finiteness with such-and-such exclusions. But then the completely inhibited component subjective feeling is not properly a component of that subjective form. It is merely what would have been a component under other conditions. This sense of inhibition will be termed 'anæsthesia'.

The other meaning of inhibition—the meaning which derogates from perfection—involves the true active presence of both component feelings. In this case there is a third feeling of mutual destructiveness, so that one or other—or both—of the component feelings fails to attain the strength properly belonging to the prehension of the datum from which it arises. This is the feeling of evil in the most general sense, namely physical pain or mental evil, such as sorrow, horror, dislike. This type of inhibition will be termed 'æsthetic destruction'. Æsthetic destruction is a positive component in subjective form, and is inconsistent with perfection. The subjective experience of æsthetic destruction will be termed a 'discordant feeling'. Such a feeling is a factor in the subjective form of the percipient occasion. The more intense the discordant feeling, the further the retreat from perfection. A complex datum is 'objectively discordant' when among the type of percipients in question it will normally produce discordant feelings.

It follows from this discussion that in the definition of Beauty a distinction has been overlooked. The subjective feelings which are of the type of an emotional experience of æsthetic destruction must be excepted—or rather, as we shall find, belong to a class requiring special treatment. 'Perfection', properly so called, requires the exclusion of feelings of this class. On further consideration we shall find that always there are imperfect occasions better than occasions which realize some given type of perfection. There are in fact higher and lower perfections, and an imperfection aiming at a higher type stands above lower perfections. The most material and the most sensuous enjoyments are yet types of Beauty.

Progress is founded upon the experience of discordant feelings. The social value of liberty lies in its production of discords. There are perfections beyond perfections. All realization is finite, and there is no perfection which is the infinitude of all perfections. Perfections of diverse types are among themselves discordant. Thus the contribution to Beauty which can be supplied by Discord—in itself destructive and evil—is the positive feeling of a quick shift of aim from the tameness of outworn perfection to some other ideal with its freshness still upon it. Thus the value of Discord is a tribute to the merits of Imperfection.

SECTION V. A consideration of ancient Greek civilization illustrates ,the value of discordance. The race was awakened into progress by a great ideal of perfection. This ideal was an immense advance upon the ideals which the surrounding civilizations had produced. It was effective and realized in a civilization which attained its proper beauty in human lives to an extent not surpassed before or since. Its art, its theoretic sciences, its modes of life, its literature, its philosophic schools, its religious rituals, all conspired to express every aspect of this wonderful ideal. Perfection was attained, and with the attainment inspiration withered. With repetition in successive generations, freshness gradually vanished. Learning and learned taste replaced the ardour of adventure. Hellenism was replaced by the Hellenistic epoch in which genius was stifled by repetition. We can imagine the fate of the Mediterranean civilization if it had been spared the irruptions of Barbarians and the rise of two new religions, Christianity and Mahometanism: —For two thousand years the Greek art-forms lifelessly repeated: The Greek schools of philosophy, Stoic, Epicurean, Aristotelian, Neo-Platonic, arguing with barren formulæ: Conventional histories: A stabilized Government with the sanctity of ancient ceremony, supported by habitual pieties: Literature without depth: Science elaborating details by deductions from unquestioned premises: Delicacies of feeling without robustness of adventure.

This is no fancy picture. Despite all storms, something of this sort did happen to the Byzantine Empire for a thousand years; and despite the inroad of a new religion, Buddhism, and despite Tartar invasions, something of this sort did happen to the vast Chinese Empire for a thousand years. The Chinese and the Greeks both achieved certain perfections of civilization—each worthy of admiration. But even perfection will not bear the tedium of indefinite repetition. To sustain a civilization with the intensity of its first ardour requires more than learning. Adventure is essential, namely, the search for new perfections.

SECTION VI. There is nothing to be astonished at in this conclusion. Spontaneity, originality of decision, belongs to the essence of each actual occasion. It is the supreme expression of individuality: its conformal subjective form is the freedom of enjoyment derived from the enjoyment of freedom. Freshness, zest, and the extra keenness of intensity arise from it. In a personal succession of occasions the upward path towards an ideal of perfection, with the end in sight, gives a thrill keener than any prolonged halt in a stage of attainment with the major variations completely tried out. Thus the wise advice is, Not to rest too completely in any continued realization of the same perfection of type. Each occasion in a society of occasions, and more particularly each occasion in a personal society, seeks this zest by finding some contrast between the Appearance resulting from the operations of the mental pole and the inherited Realities of the physical pole. When spontaneity is at its lowest, in practice negligible, the final trace of its operation is found in alternations backwards and forwards between alternative modes. This is the reason for the predominant importance of wave-transmission in physical nature.

But—considering occasions at their highest, with effective exercise of mental originality—the preservation of zest, after the attainment of a stage of perfection, first requires the exploration of all variations which do not introduce discordances into the type of perfection attained. The variation of styles and of decorative detail in mediaeval Gothic architecture may serve as an illustration. But such variations are easily exhausted. Bolder adventure is needed—the adventure of ideas, and the adventure of practice conforming itself to ideas. The best service that ideas can render is gradually to lift into the mental poles the ideal of another type of perfection which becomes a program for reform. An illustration of this is the service of Christianity by its introduction of new ideals for the social life of mankind. In other words, the ideal of a new society derived from a new defining characteristic is introduced.

SECTION VII. The doctrine has been stated that the experience of destruction is in itself evil; in fact that it constitutes the meaning of evil. We find now that this enunciation is much too simple-minded. Qualifications have to be introduced, though they leave unshaken the fundamental position that 'destruction as a dominant fact in the experience' is the correct definition of evil.

The intermingling of Beauty and Evil arises from the conjoint operation of three metaphysical principles: —(1) That all actualization is finite; (2) That finitude involves the exclusion of alternative possibility; (3) That mental functioning introduces into realization subjective forms conformal to relevant alternatives excluded from the completeness of physical realization.

The result is that the concerns of the actual world are deflected from harmony of feeling by the divergent tonalities introduced from the mental poles. The new occasion, even apart from its own spontaneous mentality, is thus confronted by basic disharmony in the actual world from which it springs. This is fortunate. For otherwise actuality would consist in a cycle of repetition, realizing only a finite group of possibilities. This was the narrow, stuffy doctrine of some ancient thinkers.

In an individual experience there are three ways of dealing with this disharmony of the world as given for initial prehension. Two of these ways have been discussed under the general term 'inhibition'. One way is termed 'Anæsthesia', and is the way of mere negative prehension. The other way is by positive realization with the positive feeling of discordance. In this case, the elimination of the sheer incompatibility is accompanied by a positive feeling of acute disruption of affective tone. This experience is the prehension of a qualitative datum which also imposes itself conformally on the subjective form. The third way depends on another principle, that a readjustment of the relative intensities of incompatible feelings can in some cases reduce them to compatibilities. This possibility arises when the clash in affective tones is a clash of intensities, and is not a sheer logical incompatibility of qualities. Thus two systems of prehensions may each be internally harmonious; but the two systems in the unity of one experience may be discordant, when the two intensities of their subjective forms are comparable in magnitude. There may be a discordance in feeling *this* as much as *that,* or in feeling *that* as much as *this.* But if one be kept at a lower intensity in the penumbra of feeling, it may act as a background to the other, providing a sense of massiveness and variety. This is the habitual state of human experience, a vast undiscriminated, or dimly discriminated background, of low intensity, and a clear foreground. This third way of eliminating discordance may be termed the method of 'reduction to a background'. Alternatively, it can equally well be termed the method of 'raising to a foreground'. For the avoidance of anæsthesia may come by the percipient occasion so functioning as to increase the intensity of subjective tone belonging to the prehension of one of the two systems.

Yet a fourth way now discloses itself, and this way is the explanation of the second and third ways for all occasions of experience where mentality has been developed into its higher activities. The second and the third ways, when they are not in truth this fourth way, are examples of the low type of mental functionings termed[3] 'physical purposes'. This fourth way is by spontaneity of the occasion so directing its mental functionings

3. Cf. *Process and Reality*, Part III, Ch. V, Sections VII, VIII.

as to introduce a third system of prehensions, relevant to both the inharmonious systems. This novel system is such as radically to alter the distribution of intensities throughout the two given systems, and to change the importance of both in the final intensive experience of the occasion. This way is in fact the introduction of Appearance, and its use to preserve the massive qualitative variety of Reality from simplification by negative prehensions.

Appearance preserves this variety by concentrating on itself the intensities properly derived from Reality in the background. It is a procedure of simplification. For example, in Appearance the one Region supersedes the many individual occasions which compose it. Also qualities widely spread throughout the occasions in Reality are in Appearance inherent either in Regions occupied by these occasions, or in Regions having some definite association with such Regions. The Reality is in the background as explanatory of the procedures by which its rich variety has been saved. Also the variety of affective tone is now transferred to Appearance, with that amount of transformation which saves its compatibility. There is massive feeling transferred to Appearance, either of Harmony, or of Discords, or of Vulgarity, or of utter Commonplaceness. Appearance raises into a distinctness of feeling, factors which can be generalized for salvation from the welter of Fact. In this way, it emphasizes for individual experience widespread qualities of feeling. Massiveness of subjective form is somewhat at variance with the intensity of individual feelings. The variety of individual intensities thwart each other by their diversities of objects. Appearance combines massiveness with intensity by unifying the diversities of objects. It simplifies the objects and precipitates upon the simplification the qualitative contents of the given world. It saves intensities and massiveness at the cost of eliciting vivid experiences of affective tones, good and bad. It makes possible the height of Beauty and height of Evil; because it saves both from a tame elimination or a tame scaling down.

SECTION VIII. We can now consider more closely the grounds of Harmony and the grounds for the positive feeling of its destruction. It must be remembered that just as there is a positive integral feeling of Harmony lost, so there is a positive integral feeling of Harmony attained. There is not only the fact of details in experience allowing each other: beyond that there is the positive feeling of the whole as Harmonious. Analogously there is the positive feeling of the whole as discordant. Either feeling as the case may be. The Harmony is felt as such, and so is the Discord. Now Harmony is more than logical compatibility, and Discord is more than logical incompatibility. Logicians are not called in to advise artists. The key to the explanation is the understanding of the prehension of individuality. This is the feeling of each objective factor as an individual *'It'* with its own significance. The emotional significance of an object as *'It'*. divorced from its qualitative aspects at the moment presented, is one of the strongest forces in human nature. It is at the base of family affection, and of the love of particular possessions. This trait is not a pecularity of mankind alone. A dog smells in order to find out if the person in question is that *It* to which its affections cling. The room, or stable, may be full of odours, many of them for a dog sweeter. But he is not smelling for the pleasure of that smell, but to discover that *It* who claims his whole affection. An analogous substitute may deceive, but when discovered never does as well. The analogy may claim affection. But the original *It* commands a poignancy of feeling. This type of interest is at the base of much in archæology—an inscribed stone, executed at the command of and under the very eyes of Sennacherib. A really admirable replica by a modern workman lacks interest, except for certain purposes of scholarship. The worship of relics touches upon the pathology of such concerns.

Undoubtedly the emotional value of particular individuality arises from the generalization of emotions, so as to get rid of their mere sensory elements. Such generalized emotional qualities are love, admiration, the feeling of exquisiteness, the feeling of worth, hate, horror, the general feeling of association, that is of particular objects entwined with one's own existence. The successive immanence of occasion after occasion in the life of the soul will in the present occasion of that life include the cumulation of the successive prehensions of some particular object. In the various prehensions of it new qualities secure prominence, original qualities are present with some difference. There is thus a gradual elimination of the more special types of quality, which vary and fluctuate, from conformal effectiveness in the tone of the final prehensions. Generalized aromas take their place—the basic feelings of lifelong devotion, of lifelong repulsion, or of æsthetic excellence. Thus the indication of that *It,* partly by its status in the pattern of experience and partly by its immediate exhibition of minor qualities, produces a strong sharp-cut emotional tone of dominating significance. The significance is not merely for the general complex of subjective form in the immediate percipient. It is also reflected back onto the original objective *It.* Thus the *It* which is indicated by minor details of a status and quality is finally prehended in Appearance as *It* with its permanent character.

For epistemology of the sensationalist school, this final prehension is construed as an interpretation of original sense-impressions. But in this final prehension there is no logical train, inductive or deductive. The percipient directly integrates antecedent real functionings of that object in antecedent occasions of the soul's life. The so-called 'interpretation' is the conflation of real history, and is not a top-dressing of conjecture. The notion of purely qualitative sense-impressions as the origin of experience has no warrant in direct intuition.

For the understanding of Harmony and Discord it is essential to remember that strength of experience, in massiveness and in intensity, depends upon the substratum of detail being composed of significant individuals. Appearance has been constituted fortunately when it has simplified the welter of occasions, individually insignificant, into a few significant individual things. It has 'interpreted' the world in terms of factors received from the world—so that each factor of interpretation can be substantiated by direct intuition—if only consciousness can analyse so far. Such is fortunate experience. It derives its strength from the concurrence of significant individual objects, and its own existence adds to the significance of those objects. This is the enjoyment of Harmony, and a factor in this enjoyment is the intuition that the future, where its objective immortality lies, is increasing the grounds for Harmony. Destruction is absent.

But there can be intense experience without Harmony. In this event, there is Destruction of the significant characters of individual objects. When the direct feeling of such Destruction dominates the whole, there is the immediate feeling of evil, and the anticipation of destructive or weakened data for the future. Harmony is bound up with the preservation of the individual significance of detail, and Discord consists in its destruction. In Discord there is always a frustration. But even Discord may be preferable to a feeling of slow relapse into general anæsthesia, or into tameness which is its prelude. Perfection at a low level ranks below Imperfection with higher aim.

A mere qualitative Harmony within an experience comparatively barren of objects of high significance is a debased type of Harmony, tame, vague, deficient in outline and intention. It is one property of a beautiful system of objects that as entertained in a succession of occasions adapted for its enjoyment, it quickly builds up a system of apparent objects with vigorous characters. The sculptures on the famous porch of the Cathedral at Chartres at once assume individual importance with definite character while performing their office as details in the whole. There is not a mere pattern of qualitative beauty. There are those statues, each with its individual beauty, and all lending themselves to the beauty of the whole. Enduring Individuality in the details is the backbone of strong experience.

Art at its highest exemplifies the metaphysical doctrine of the interweaving of absoluteness upon relativity. In the work of art the relativity becomes the harmony of the composition, and the absoluteness is the claim for separate individuality advanced by component factors. We also understand how Appearance leads to the Aristotelian doctrine of a substantial, enduring *It* with essential character. The point of view expresses important truth. Hence its obviousness. The æsthetic importance of this apparent individuality lies in its claim to attention. In so far as Appearance has a truth-relation to Reality such enduring individuality indicates a real society important for its control of the future. The claim to æsthetic attention thus represents the indirect importance of anticipation and purpose as factors in the immediate enjoyment of the immediate percipient. The danger of a street-crossing is for the pedestrian a regulative factor in the æsthetic values of the apparent scene. The concept of completely passive contemplation in abstraction from action and purpose is a fallacious extreme. It omits the final regulative factor in the æsthetic complex. But of course there are large diversities of action and large diversities of purpose. The final point is that the foundation of Reality upon which Appearance rests can never be neglected in the evaluation of Appearance.

Chapter XVIII

TRUTH AND BEAUTY

SECTION I. IT APPEARS from the discussion in the two previous chapters of this Part that Beauty is a wider, and more fundamental, notion than Truth. Of course both terms have been used here in a very generalized sense. Narrower usages are not marked off from the wider meanings, here employed, by anything except habitual presupposition respecting importance and triviality. Beauty is the internal conformation of the various items of experience with each other, for the production of maximum effectiveness. Beauty thus concerns the inter-relations of the various components of Reality, and also the inter-relations of the various components of Appearance, and also the relations of Appearance to Reality. Thus any part of experience can be beautiful. The teleology of the Universe is directed to the production of Beauty. Thus any system of things which in any wide sense is beautiful is to that extent justified in its existence. It may however fail in another sense, by inhibiting more Beauty than it creates. Thus the system, though in a sense beautiful, is on the whole evil in that environment. But Truth has a narrower meaning in two ways. First, Truth, in any important sense, merely concerns the relations of Appearance to Reality. It is the conformation of Appearance to Reality. But in the second place the notion of 'conformation' in the case of Truth is narrower than that in the case of Beauty. For the truth-relation requires that the two relata have some factor in common.

In itself, and apart from other factors, there seems to be no special importance about the truth-relation. There is the bare fact of a certain limited relationship of identity. There is nothing in such a fact which will necessarily dictate any corresponding type of subjective form within the percipient occasion. Still less is there any reason why such influence as a truth-relation does have upon subjective form should be in the direction of the promotion of Beauty. In other words, a truth-relation is not necessarily beautiful. It may not even be neutral. It may be evil. Thus Beauty is left as the one aim which by its very nature is self-justifying. The Discord in the Universe arises from the fact that modes of Beauty are various, and not of necessity compatible. And yet some admixture of Discord is a necessary factor in the transition from mode to mode. The objective life of the past and the future in the present is an inevitable element of disturbance. Discord may take the form of freshness or hope, or it may be horror or pain. In the higher types of mentality the note of displacement impresses its qualitative character upon subjective form with peculiar keenness: —welcome or antagonism. Wide purpose is in its own nature beautiful by reason of its contribution to the massiveness of experience. It increases the dimensions of the experient subject, adds to its ambit. Then the destruction of immediate realizations for the sake of purpose is, on the face of it, a sacrifice to Harmony.

SECTION II. Notwithstanding the possible unseasonableness of the truth-relation, the general importance of Truth for the promotion of Beauty is overwhelming. After all has been said, yet the truth-relation remains the simple, direct mode of realizing Harmony. Other ways are indirect, and indirectness is at the mercy of the environment. There is a blunt force about Truth, which in the subjective form of its prehension is akin to cleanliness—namely, the removal of dirt, which is unwanted irrelevance. The sense of directness which it carries with it, sustains the upstanding individualities so necessary for the beauty of a complex. Falsehood is corrosive.

Truth is various in its extent, its modes, and its relevance. But an apparent object, beautiful beyond the hope of antecedent imagination, as it functions in experience is realizing some hidden, penetrating Truth with a keenness beyond compare. The type of Truth required for the final stretch of Beauty is a discovery and not a recapitulation. The Truth that for such extremity of Beauty is wanted· is that truth-relation whereby Appearance summons up new resources of feeling from the depths of Reality. It is a Truth of feeling, and not a Truth of verbalization. The relata in Reality must lie below the stale presuppositions of verbal thought. The Truth of supreme Beauty lies beyond the dictionary meanings of words.

When Appearance has to Reality, in some important direct sense, a truth-relation, there is a security about the Beauty attained, that is to say, a pledge for the future.

From these functions of Truth in the service of Beauty, the realization of Truth becomes in itself an element promoting Beauty of feeling. Consciousness, with its dim intuitions, welcomes a factor so generally on the right side, so habitually necessary. The element of anticipation under the influence of Truth is in a deep sense satisfied, and thus adds a factor to the immediate Harmony. Thus Truth, in itself and apart from special reasons to the contrary, becomes self-justifying. It is accompanied by a sense of rightness in the deepest Harmony. But Truth derives this self-justifying power from its services in the promotion of Beauty. Apart from Beauty, Truth is neither good, nor bad.

SECTION III. Art is purposeful adaptation of Appearance to Reality. Now 'purposeful adaptation' implies an end, to be obtained with more or less success. This end, which is the purpose of art, is two-fold,—namely Truth and Beauty. The perfection of art has only one end, which is Truthful Beauty. But some measure of success has been reached, when either Truth or Beauty is gained. In the absence of Truth, Beauty is on a lower level, with a defect of massiveness. In the absence of Beauty, Truth sinks to triviality. Truth matters because of Beauty.

The relation of 'appearance' to 'reality' is such that in the final phase of experience ['satisfaction' or 'anticipation'] the reality of the primary phase is prehended with subjective form as though it participated in the qualitative characters of 'appearance'. When in fact the reality does so participate, the relation is truthful. When it does not so participate, the relation is falsifying.

Beauty, so far as concerns its exemplification in Appearance alone, does not necessarily involve the attainment of truth. Appearance is beautiful when the qualitative objects which compose it are interwoven in patterned contrasts, so that the prehensions of the whole of its parts produces the fullest harmony of mutual support. By this it is meant, that in so far as the qualitative characters of the whole and the parts pass into the subjective forms of their prehensions, the whole heightens the feelings for the parts, and the parts heighten the feelings for the whole, and for each other. This is harmony of feeling; and with harmony of feeling its objective content is beautiful.

It is evident that when appearance has obtained truth in addition to beauty, harmony in a wider sense has been produced. For in this sense, it also involves the relation of appearance to reality. Thus, when the adaptation of appearance to reality has obtained truthful Beauty, there is a perfection of art. That is to say, if there be art: for the result may be the slow outcome of nature. Such an outcome may be due to some wide universal purpose. But it will not be due to quick purposeful adaptation originated by finite creatures, the sort of adaptation usually termed art.

Goodness is the third member of the trinity which traditionally has been assigned as the complex aim of art—namely, Truth, Beauty, and Goodness. With the point of view here adopted, Goodness must be denied a place among the aims of art. For Goodness is a qualification belonging to the constitution of reality, which in any of its individual actualizations is better or worse. Good and evil lie in depths and distances below and beyond appearance. They solely concern inter-relations within the real world. The real world is good when it is beautiful. Art has essentially to do with perfections attainable by purposeful adaptation of appearance. With a larger view and a deeper analysis, some instance of the perfection of art may diminish the good otherwise inherent in some specific situation as it passes into its objective actuality for the future. Unseasonable art is analogous to an unseasonable joke, namely, good in its place, but out of place a positive evil. It is a curious fact that lovers of art who are most insistent on the doctrine of 'art for art's sake' are apt to be indignant at the banning of art for the sake of other interests. The charge of immorality is not refuted by pointing to the perfection of art. Of course it is true that the defence of morals is the battle-cry which best rallies stupidity against change. Perhaps countless ages ago respectable amœbæ refused to migrate from ocean to dry land—refusing in defence of morals. One incidental service of art to society lies in its adventurousness.

SECTION IV. It is a tribute to the strength of the sheer craving for freshness, that change, whose justification lies in aim at the distant ideal, should be promoted by Art which is the adaptation of immediate Appearance for immediate Beauty. Art neglects the safety of the future for the gain of the present. In so doing it is apt to render its Beauty thin. But after all, there must be some immediate harvest. The good of the Universe cannot lie in indefinite postponement. The Day of Judgment is an important notion: but that Day is always with us. Thus Art takes care of the immediate fruition, here and now; and in so doing is apt to lose some depth by reason of the immediate fruition at which it is aiming. Its business is to render the Day of Judgment a success, now. The effect of the present on the future is the business of morals. And yet the separation is not so easy. For the inevitable anticipation adds to the present a qualitative element which profoundly affects its whole qualitative harmony.

There is a paradox concerning morals to be added to the one concerning art. Morals consists in the aim at the ideal, and at its lowest it concerns the prevention of relapse to lower levels. Thus stagnation is the deadly foe of morality. Yet in human society the champions of morality are on the whole the fierce opponents of new ideals. Mankind has been afflicted with low-toned moralists, objecting to expulsion from some Garden of Eden. And in a way they are right. For after all we can aim at nothing except from the standpoint of a well-assimilated system of customs—that is, of *mores.* The fortunate changes are made 'Hand in hand, with wand'ring steps and slow'.

SECTION V. The factor in experience that renders Art possible is consciousness.[1] Of course consciousness, like everything else, is in a sense indefinable. It is just itself and must be experienced. But, also like other things, it is the emergent quality illustrated in the essence of a conjunction of circumstances. It is a qualitative aspect of that conjunction. We can ask therefore for an analysis of the details whose conjunction in experience issues in consciousness.

Consciousness is that quality which emerges into the objective content as the result of the conjunction of a fact and a supposition about that fact. It passes conformally from the complex object to the subjective form of the prehension. It is the quality inherent in the contrast between Actuality and Ideality, that is, between the products of the physical pole and the mental pole in experience. When that contrast is a feeble element in experience, then consciousness is there merely in germ, as a latent capacity. So far as the contrast is well-defined and prominent, the occasion includes

1. Cf. *P. R.*, Part II, Chapter VII, Section II, and Part III, Chapter II, Section IV, and Chapters IV and V.

a developed consciousness. That portion of experience irradiated by consciousness is only a selection. Thus consciousness is a mode of attention. It provides the extreme of selective emphasis. The spontaneity of an occasion finds its chief outlets, first in the direction of consciousness, and secondly in production of ideas to pass into the area of conscious attention. Thus consciousness, spontaneity, and art are closely interconnected. But that art which arises within clear consciousness is only a specialization of the more widely distributed art within dim consciousness or within the unconscious activities of experience.

Consciousness is the weapon which strengthens the artificiality of an occasion of experience. It raises the importance of the final Appearance relatively to that of the initial Reality. Thus it is Appearance which in consciousness is clear and distinct, and it is Reality which lies dimly in the background with its details hardly to be distinguished in consciousness. What leaps into conscious attention is a mass of presuppositions about Reality rather than the intuitions of Reality itself. It is here that the liability to error arises. The deliverances of clear and distinct consciousness require criticism by reference to elements in experience which are neither clear nor distinct. On the contrary. they are dim, massive, and important. These dim elements provide for art that final background of tone apart from which its effects fade. The type of Truth which human art seeks lies in the eliciting of this background to haunt the object presented for clear consciousness.

SECTION VI. The merit of Art in its service to civilization lies in its artificiality and its finiteness. It exhibits for consciousness a finite fragment of human effort achieving its own perfection within its own limits. Thus the mere toil for the slavish purpose of prolonging life for more toil or for mere bodily gratification, is transformed into the conscious realization of a self-contained end, timeless within time. The work of Art is a fragment of nature with the mark on it of a finite creative effort, so that it stands alone, an individual thing detailed from the vague infinity of its background. Thus Art heightens the sense of humanity. It gives an elation of feeling which is supernatural. A sunset is glorious, but it dwarfs humanity and belongs to the general flow of nature. A million sunsets will not spur on men towards civilization. It requires Art to evoke into consciousness the finite perfections which lie ready for human achievement.

Consciousness itself is the product of art in its lowliest form. For it results from the influx of ideality into its contrast with reality, with the purpose of reshaping the latter into a finite, select appearance. But consciousness having emerged from Art at once produces the new specialized art of the conscious animals—in particular human art. In a sense art is a morbid overgrowth of functions which lie deep in nature. It is the essence of art to be artificial. But it is its perfection to return to nature, remaining art. In short art is the education of nature. Thus, in its broadest sense, art is civilization. For civilization is nothing other than the unremitting aim at the major perfections of harmony.

SECTION VII. The human body is an instrument for the production of art in the life of the human soul. It concentrates upon those elements in human experience selected for conscious perception intensities of subjective form derived from components dismissed into shadow. It thereby enhances the value of that appearance which is the subject-matter for art. In this way the work of art is a message from the Unseen. It unlooses depths of feeling from behind the frontier where precision of consciousness fails. The starting-point for the highly developed human art is thus to be sought amid the cravings generated by the physiological functionings of the body. The origin of art lies in the craving for re-enaction. In some mode of repetition we need by our personal actions, or perceptions, to dramatize the past and the future, so as to relive the emotional life of ourselves, and of our ancestors. There is a biological law—which however must not be pressed too far—that in some vague sense the embryo in the womb reproduces in its life-history features of ancestors in remote geologic epochs. Thus art has its origin in ceremonial[2] evolutions from which issue play, religious ritual, tribal ceremonial, dance, pictures on caves, poetic literature, prose, music. In this list each member in its simpler forms enshrines some effort to reproduce a vivid experience flashed out among the necessities of daily life. But the secret of art lies in its freedom. The emotion and some elements of the experience itself are lived again divorced from their necessity. The strain is over, but the joy of intense feeling remains. Originally the intensity arose from some dire necessity; but in art it has outlived the compulsion which was its origin. If Odysseus among the shades could hear Homer chanting his Odyssey, he then re-enacted with free enjoyment the perils of his wanderings.

The arts of civilization now spring from many origins, physical and purely imaginative. But they are all sublimations, and sublimations of sublimations, of the simple craving to enjoy freely the vividness of life which first arises in moments of necessity. With a slight shift of the focus of our attention, Art can be described as a psychopathic reaction of the race to the stresses of its existence. From that point of view, Odysseus as he listened to Homer was evading the Furies. This psychopathic function of Art is lost when the conviction of Truth is absent. It is here that the concept of Art as the pursuit of Beauty is shallow. Art has a curative function in human experience when it reveals as in a flash intimate. absolute Truth regarding the Nature of Things. This service of Art is even hindered by trivial truths of detail. Such petty conformations place in the foreground the superficialities of sense-experience. Art performing this great service belongs to the essence of civilization. By the growth of such Art the adventure of mentality gains upon the physical basis of existence.

---

2. Cf. *Religion in the Making*, Ch. I, Section III.

Science and Art are the consciously determined pursuit of Truth and of Beauty. In them the finite consciousness of mankind is appropriating as its own the infinite fecundity of nature. In this movement of the human spirit types of institutions and types of professions are evolved. Churches and Rituals, Monasteries with their dedicated lives, Universities with their search for knowledge, Medicine, Law, methods of Trade—they all represent that aim at civilization, whereby the conscious experience of mankind preserves for its use the sources of Harmony.

Chapter XIX

ADVENTURE

SECTION I. THE NOTION of civilization is very baffling. We all know what it means. It suggests a certain ideal for life on this earth, and this ideal concerns both the individual human being and also societies of men. A man can be civilized, and a whole society can be civilized; although the senses are somewhat different in the two cases.

Yet civilization is one of those general notions that are very difficult to define. We pronounce upon particular instances. We can say *this* is civilized, or *that* is savage. Yet somehow the general notion is elusive. Thus we proceed by examples. During the last six centuries, the culture of Europe has guided itself by example. The Greeks and Romans at their best period have been taken as the standard of civilization. We have aimed at reproducing the excellencies of these societies—preferably the society of Athens in its prime.

These standards have served the Western races well. But the procedure has its disadvantages. It is backward looking, and it is limited to one type of social excellence. Today the world is passing into a new stage of its existence. New knowledge, and new technologies have altered the proportions of things. The particular example of an ancient society sets too static an ideal, and neglects the whole range of opportunity. It is really not sufficient to direct attention to the best that has been said and done in the ancient world. The result is static, repressive, and promotes a decadent habit of mind.

Also I suggest that the Greeks themselves were not backward looking, or static. Compared to their neighbours, they were singularly unhistorical. They were speculative, adventurous, eager for novelty. The most un-Greek thing that we can do, is to copy the Greeks. For emphatically they were not copyists.

Another danger in forming our notions of civilization is to concentrate exclusively upon passive, critical qualities concerned chiefly with the Fine Arts. Such qualities are an important element in a civilized society. But civilization is more than the appreciation of the Fine Arts. We must not tie it down to museums and studios.

I put forward as a general definition of civilization, that a civilized society is exhibiting the five qualities of Truth, Beauty, Adventure, Art, Peace.

Here by the last quality of Peace, I am not referring to political relations. I mean a quality of mind steady in its reliance that fine action is treasured in the nature of things.

It is impossible in the short space of five chapters to discuss all the various questions which are suggested by these notions. In this chapter I will concentrate upon a few points in philosophy and history which throw light upon the various functions of these elements in civilization.

SECTION II. From the three preceding chapters and with this short explanation as to Peace, let us assume for the moment that Truth, Beauty, and Peace are sufficiently obvious as to their meanings. We will now concentrate upon Adventure and Art as necessary elements in civilization. It is in respect to these two factors that prevalent concepts of civilization are weakest.

The foundation of all understanding of sociological theory—that is to say, of all understanding of human life—is that no static maintenance of perfection is possible. This axiom is rooted in the nature of things. Advance or Decadence are the only choices offered to mankind. The pure conservative is fighting against the essence of the universe. This doctrine requires justification. It is implicitly denied in the learned tradition derived from ancient thought.

The doctrine is founded upon three metaphysical principles. One principle is that the very essence of real actuality—that is, of the completely real—is *process.* Thus each actual thing is only to be understood in terms of its becoming and perishing. There is no halt in which the actuality is just its static self, accidently played upon by qualifications derived from the shift of circumstances. The converse is the truth.

The static notion, here rejected, is derived by two different paths from ancient thought. Plato in the earlier period of his thought, deceived by the beauty of mathematics intelligible in unchanging perfection, conceived of a super-world of ideas, forever perfect and forever interwoven. In his latest phase he sometimes repudiates the notion, though he never consistently banishes it from his thought. His later Dialogues circle round seven notions, namely—The Ideas, The Physical Elements, The Psyche, The Eros, The Harmony, The Mathematical Relations, The Receptacle. I mention them because I hold that all philosophy is in fact an endeavour to obtain a coherent system out of some modification of these notions. They largely explain themselves as to their general meanings, apart from any precise coordination. The Psyche is, of course, the Soul; the Eros is the urge towards the realization of ideal perfection. The Receptacle is expressly stated by Plato to be a difficult notion; so that we may safely put aside easy explanations of it. I explain it to myself as the conception of the essential unity of the Universe conceived as an actuality, and yet in abstraction from the 'life and motion' in which all actualities must partake. If we omit the Psyche and the Eros, we should obtain a static world. The 'life and motion', which are essentials in Plato's later thought, are derived from the operation of these two factors. But Plato left no system of metaphysics.

Thus in the modern development of these seven metaphysical notions, we should start from the notion of actuality as in its essence a process. This process involves a physical side which is the perishing of the past as it transforms itself into a new creation. It also involves a mental side which is the Soul entertaining ideas.

The Soul thereby by synthesis creates a new fact which is the Appearance woven out of the old and the new—a compound of reception and anticipation, which in its turn passes into the future. The final synthesis of these three complexes is the end to which its indwelling Eros urges the soul. Its good resides in the realization of a strength of many feelings fortifying each other as they meet in the novel unity. Its evil lies in the clash of vivid feelings, denying to each other their proper expansion. Its triviality lies in the anæsthesia by which evil is avoided. In this way through sheer omission, fewer, fainter feelings constitute the final Appearance. Evil is the half-way house between perfection and triviality. It is the violence of strength against strength.

Aristotle introduced the static fallacy by another concept which has infected all subsequent philosophy. He conceived of primary substances as the static foundations which received the impress of qualification. In the case of human experience, a modern version of the same notion is Locke's metaphor of the mind as an 'empty cabinet' receiving the impress of ideas. Thus for Locke the reality does not reside in the process but in the static recipient of process. According to the versions of Aristotle and Locke, one primary substance cannot be a component in the nature of another primary substance. Thus the interconnections of primary substances must be devoid of the substantial reality of the primary substances themselves. With this doctrine, the conjunction of actualities has, in various shapes, been a problem throughout modern philosophy—both for metaphysics and for epistemology. The· taint of Aristotelian Logic has thrown the whole emphasis of metaphysical thought upon substantives and adjectives, to the neglect of prepositions and conjunctions. This

Aristotelian doctrine is in this book summarily denied. The process is itself the actuality, and requires no antecedent static cabinet. Also the processes of the past, in their perishing, are themselves energizing as the complex origin of each novel occasion. The past is the reality at the base of each new actuality. The process is its absorption into a new unity with ideals and with anticipation, by the operation of the creative Eros.

SECTION III. I now pass to the second metaphysical principle. It is the doctrine that every occasion of actuality is in its own nature finite. There is no totality which is the harmony of all perfections. Whatever is realized in any one occasion of experience necessarily excludes the unbounded welter of contrary possibilities. There are always 'others', which might have been and are not. This finiteness is not the result of evil, or of imperfection. It results from the fact that there are possibilities of harmony which either produce evil in joint realization, or are incapable of such conjunction. This doctrine is a commonplace in the fine arts. It also is—or should be—a commonplace of political philosophy. History can only be understood by seeing it as the theatre of diverse groups of idealists respectively urging ideals incompatible for conjoint realization. You cannot form any historical judgment of right or wrong by considering each group separately. The evil lies in the attempted conjunction.

This principle of intrinsic incompatibility has an important bearing upon our conception of the nature of God. The concept of impossibility such that God himself cannot surmount it, has been for centuries quite familiar to theologians. Indeed, apart from it there would be difficulty in conceiving any determinate divine nature. But curiously enough, so far as I know, this notion of incompatibility has never been applied to ideals in the Divine realization. We must conceive the Divine Eros as the active entertainment of all ideals, with the urge to their finite realization, each in its due season. Thus a process must be inherent in God's nature, whereby his infinity is acquiring realization.

It is unnecessary to pursue theology further. But the point stands out that the conceptual entertainment of incompatibilities is possible, and so is their conceptual comparison. Also there is the synthesis of conceptual entertainment with physical realization. The idea conceptually entertained may be identical with the idea exemplified in the physical fact; or it may be different, compatible or incompatible. This synthesis of the ideal with the real is just what happens in each finite occasion.

Thus in every civilization at its culmination we should find a large measure of realization of a certain type of perfection. This type will be complex and will admit of variation of detail, this way or that. The culmination can maintain itself at its height so long as fresh experimentation within the type is possible. But when these minor variations are exhausted, one of two things must happen. Perhaps the society in question lacks imaginative force. Staleness then sets in. Repetition produces a gradual lowering of vivid appreciation. Convention dominates. A learned orthodoxy suppresses adventure.

The last flicker of originality is exhibited by the survival of satire. Satire does not necessarily imply a decadent society, though it flourishes upon the outworn features in the social system. It was characteristic that at the close of the silver age of Roman culture, shortly after the deaths of the younger Pliny and of Tacitus, the satirist Lucian was born. Again, at the close of the silver age of the Renaissance culture, during the eighteenth century, Voltaire and Edward

Gibbon perfected satire in their various styles. Satire was natural to the age as it neared the American Revolution, the French Revolution, and the Industrial Revolution. Again a new epoch arose, the first phase of modern industrialism. It flourished with consistent growth for a hundred and fifty years. Its central period has been termed the Victorian Epoch. Within that period, the European races created new methods of industry; they peopled North America; they developed trade with the old civilizations of Asia; they gave new directions to literature and to art; they refashioned their forms of government. The nineteenth century was an epoch of civilized advance—humanitarian, scientific, industrial, literary, political. But at length it wore itself out. The crash of the Great War marked its end, and marked the decisive turn of human life into some new direction as yet not fully understood. But the close of the epoch has been marked by the rise of satire—Lytton Strachey in England, Sinclair Lewis in the United States of America. Satire is the last flicker of originality in a passing epoch as it faces the onroad of staleness and boredom. Freshness has gone: bitterness remains. The prolongation of outworn forms of life means a slow decadence in which there is repetition without any fruit in the reaping of value. There may be high survival power. For decadence, undisturbed by originality or by external forces, is a slow process. But the values of life are slowly ebbing. There remains the show of civilization, without any of its realities.

There is an alternative to this slow decline. A race may exhaust a form of civilization without having exhausted its own creative springs of originality. In that case, a quick period of transition may set in, which may or may not be accompanied by dislocations involving widespread unhappiness. Such periods are Europe at the close of the Middle Ages, Europe during the comparatively long Reformation Period, Europe at the end of the eighteenth century. Also let us hope that our present epoch is to be viewed as a period of change to a new direction of civilization, involving in its dislocations a minimum of human misery. And yet surely the misery of the Great War was sufficient for any change of epoch.

These quick transitions to new types of civilization are only possible when thought has run ahead of realization. The vigour of the race has then pushed forward into the adventure of imagination, so as to anticipate the physical adventures of exploration. The world dreams of things to come, and then in due season arouses itself to their realization. Indeed all physical adventure which is entered upon of set purpose involves an adventure of thought regarding things as yet unrealized. Before Columbus set sail for America, he had dreamt of the far East, and of the round world, and of the trackless ocean. Adventure rarely reaches its predetermined end. Columbus never reached China. But he discovered America.

Sometimes adventure is acting within limits. It can then calculate its end, and reach it. Such adventures are the ripples of change within one type of civilization, by which an epoch of given type preserves its freshness. But, given the vigour of adventure, sooner or later the leap of imagination reaches beyond the safe limits of the epoch, and beyond the safe limits of learned rules of taste. It then produces the dislocations and confusions marking the advent of new ideals for civilized effort.

A race preserves its vigour so long as it harbours a real contrast between what has been and what may be; and so long as it is nerved by the vigour to adventure beyond the safeties of the past. Without adventure civilization is in full decay.

It is for this reason that the definition of culture as the knowledge of the best that has been said and done, is so dangerous by reason of its omission. It omits the great fact that in their day the great achievements of the past were the adventures of the past. Only the adventurous can understand the greatness of the past. In its day, the literature of the past was an adventure. Æschylus, Sophocles, Euripides were adventurers in the world of thought. To read their plays without any sense of new ways of understanding the world and of savouring its emotions is to miss the vividness which constitutes their whole value. But adventures are to the adventurous. Thus a passive knowledge of the past loses the whole value of its message. A living civilization requires learning; but it lies beyond it.

SECTION IV. The third metaphysical principle may be termed the principle of Individuality. It concerns the doctrine of Harmony; and its omission is, I think, the greatest gap in traditional discussions of that doctrine. Indeed, in recent times, with the predominance of the sensationalist doctrine of perception, modern views of the Harmony characterizing a great experience have reached their lowest point. This sensationalist doctrine concentrates attention upon a mere qualitative harmony within an experience comparatively barren of objects of high significance. The complex to which the term Harmony is applicable is conceived as a mere spatio-temporal pattern of sensa. The Harmony to be derived from such a complex belongs to a debased type—tame, vague, deficient in outline and intention. At the best, it can only excite by a sense of strangeness. At the worst, it fades into insignificance. It lacks any strong, exciting element capable of stirring the depths of feeling. Sense-perception, despite its prominence in consciousness, belongs to the superficialities of experience. It is here that the Aristotelian doctrine of primary substances has done some of its worst harm. For according to this doctrine no individual primary substance can enter into the complex of objects observed in any occasion of experience. The qualifications of the soul are thus confined to universals. According to the metaphysical system that I suggest to you, this Aristotelian doctrine is a complete mistake. The individual, real facts of the past lie at the base of our immediate experience in the present. They are the reality from which the occasion springs, the reality from which it derives its source of emotion, from which it inherits its purposes, to which it directs its passions. At the base of experience there is a welter of feeling, derived from individual realities or directed towards them. Thus for strength of experience we require to discriminate the component factors, each as an individual 'It' with its own significance.

Our lives are dominated by enduring things, each experienced as a unity of many occasions bound together by the force of inheritance. Each such individual endurance collects into its unity the shifting qualities of its many occasions. Perhaps it is the thing we love, or perhaps it is the thing we hate. There is a bare It—a real fact of the past, stretching into the present, which concentrates upon itself the wealth of emotion derived from its many occasions. Such enduring individualities, as factors in experience, control a wealth of feeling, an amplitude of purpose, and a regulative power to subdue into background the residue of things belonging to the immensity of the past. Surely, this is what Descartes must have meant by the *realitas objectiva* which, according to his doctrine, clings more or less to our perceptions.

A complex experience which includes conscious attention to such enduring individualities at once unlooses a wealth of feeling far beyond anything derived from patterns of sensa, merely as such. The great Harmony is the harmony of enduring individualities, connected in the unity of a background. It is for this reason that the notion of freedom haunts the higher civilizations. For freedom, in any one of its many senses, is the claim for vigorous self-assertion.

In considering the process which constitutes the existence of an occasion of experience, the perception of the enduring individuals must belong to the final Appearance wherein the occasion terminates. For in the primary phase, the past is initiating the process in virtue of the energizing of its diverse individual occasions. This is the Reality from which the new occasion springs. The process is urged onward by operation of the mental pole providing conceptual subject-matter for synthesis with the Reality. There finally emerges the Appearance, which is the transformed Reality after synthesis with the conceptual valuations. The Appearance is a simplification by a process of emphasis and combination. Thus the enduring individuals, with their wealth of emotional significance, appear in the foreground. In the background there lie a mass of undistinguished occasions providing the environment with its vague emotional tone. In a general sense, the Appearance is a work of Art, elicited from the primary Reality. In so far as the Appearance emphasizes connections and qualities of connections which in fact reside in the Reality, then the Appearance is truthful in its relation to Reality. But the Appearance may have effected connections, and have introduced qualities, which have no counterpart in Reality. In that case, the occasion of experience contains in itself a falsehood, namely the disconnection of its Appearance from its Reality. In any case, the Appearance is a simplification of Reality, reducing it to a foreground of enduring individuals and to a background of undiscriminated occasions. Sense-perception belongs to Appearance. It is interpreted as indicating enduring individuals, truthfully or otherwise.

Thus, the basis of a strong, penetrating experience of Harmony is an Appearance with a foreground of enduring individuals carrying with them a force of subjective tone, and with a background providing the requisite connection. Undoubtedly, the Harmony is finally a Harmony of qualitative feelings. But the introduction of the enduring individuals evokes from the Reality a force of already harmonized feelings which no surface show of sensa can produce. It is not a question of intellectual interpretation. There is a real conflation of fundamental feeling.

Thus civilization in its aim at fineness of feeling should so arrange its social relations, and the relations of its members to their natural environment, as to evoke into the experiences of its members Appearances dominated by the harmonies of forceful enduring things. In other words, Art should aim at the production of individuality in the component details of its compositions. It cannot trust to a mere composition of qualities. In that case, it becomes tame and vapid. It must create, so that in the experience of the beholder there appear Individuals as it were immortal by their appeal to the deep recesses of feeling. For this reason, it is hardly a paradox to say, that a great civilization interfused with Art presents the world to its members clothed with the Appearance of immortality. The Individuals it presents for Appearance belong equally to all time.

This is exactly what we find in great Art. The very details of its compositions live supremely in their own right. They make their own claim to individuality, and yet contribute to the whole. Each such detail receives an access of grandeur from the whole, and yet manifests an individuality claiming attention in its own right.

As an example, the sculpture and the tracery in a Gothic cathedral—Chartres for instance—subserve the harmony. They lead the eye upward to the vaulting above, and they lead the eye onward horizontally to the supreme symbolism of the altar. They claim attention by their beauty of detail. Yet they shun attention by guiding the eye to grasp the significance of the whole. Yet the sculpture and the tracery could not perform this service apart from their supreme individuality, evoking a wealth of feeling in their own right. Each detail claims a permanent existence for its own sake, and then surrenders it for the sake of the whole composition.

Again, the value of discord arises from this importance of the forceful individuality of the details. The discord enhances the whole, when it serves to substantiate the individuality of the parts. It brings into emphatic feeling their claim to existence in their own right. It rescues the whole from the tameness of a merely qualitative harmony.

Also the importance of truth now emerges. Truth of belief is important, both in itself and in its consequences. But above all, there emerges the importance of the truthful relation of Appearance to Reality. A grave defect in truth limits the extent to which any force of feeling can be summoned from the recesses of Reality. The falsehood thus lacks the magic by which a beauty beyond the power of speech to express can be called into being, as if by the wand of an enchanter. It is for these reasons that the civilization of a society requires the virtues of Truth, Beauty, Adventure and Art.

Chapter XX

PEACE

SECTION I. OUR DISCUSSIONS have concerned themselves with specializations in History, of seven Platonic generalities, namely, The Ideas, The Physical Elements, The Psyche, The Eros, The Harmony, The Mathematical Relations, The Receptacle. The historical references have been selected and grouped with the purpose of illustrating the energizing of specializations of these seven general notions among the peoples of Western Europe, driving them towards their civilization.

Finally, in this fourth and last Part of the book, those essential qualities, whose joint realization in social life constitutes civilization, are being considered. Four such qualities have, so far, been examined: —Truth, Beauty, Adventure, Art.

SECTION II. Something is still lacking. It is difficult to state it in terms that are wide enough. Also, where clearly distinguished and exposed in all its bearings, it assumes an air of exaggeration. Habitually it is lurking on the edge of consciousness, a modifying agency. It clings to our notion of the Platonic 'Harmony', as a sort of atmosphere. It is somewhat at variance with the notion of the 'Eros'. Also the Platonic 'Ideas' and 'Mathematical Relations' seem to kill it by their absence of 'life and motion'. Apart from it, the pursuit of 'Truth, Beauty, Adventure, Art' can be ruthless, hard, cruel; and thus, as the history of the Italian Renaissance illustrates, lacking in some essential quality of civilization. The notions of 'tenderness' and of 'love' are too narrow, important though they be. We require the concept of some more general quality, from which 'tenderness' emerges as a specialization. We are in a way seeking for the notion of a Harmony of Harmonies, which shall bind together the other four qualities, so as to exclude from our notion of civilization the restless egotism with which they have often in fact been pursued. 'Impersonality' is too dead a notion, and 'Tenderness' too narrow. I choose the term 'Peace' for that Harmony of Harmonies which calms destructive turbulence and completes civilization. Thus a society is to be termed civilized whose members participate in the five qualities—Truth, Beauty, Adventure, Art, Peace.

SECTION III. The Peace that is here meant is not the negative conception of anæsthesia. It is a positive feeling which crowns the 'life and motion' of the soul. It is hard to define and difficult to speak of. It is not a hope for the future, nor is it an interest in present details. It is a broadening of feeling due to the emergence of some deep metaphysical insight, unverbalized and yet momentous in its coordination of values. Its first effect is the removal of the stress of acquisitive feeling arising from the soul's preoccupation with itself. Thus Peace carries with it a surpassing of personality. There is an inversion of relative values. It is primarily a trust in the efficacy of Beauty. It is a sense that fineness of achievement is as it were a key unlocking treasures that the narrow nature of things would keep remote. There is thus involved a grasp of infinitude, an appeal beyond boundaries. Its emotional effect is the subsidence of turbulence which inhibits. More accurately, it preserves the springs of energy, and at the same time masters them for the avoidance of paralyzing distractions. The trust in the self-justification of Beauty introduces faith, where reason fails to reveal the details.

The experience of Peace is largely beyond the control of purpose. It comes as a gift. The deliberate aim at Peace very easily passes into its bastard substitute, Anæsthesia. In other words, in the place of a quality of 'life and motion', there is substituted their destruction. Thus Peace is the removal of inhibition and not its introduction. It results in a wider sweep of conscious interest. It enlarges the field of attention. Thus Peace is self-control at its widest,—at the width where the 'self' has been lost, and interest has been transferred to coordinations wider than personality. Here the real motive interests of the spirit are meant, and not the superficial play of discursive ideas. Peace is helped by such superficial width, and also promotes it. In fact it is largely for this reason that Peace is so essential for civilization. It is the barrier against narrowness. One of its fruits is that passion whose existence Hume denied, the love of mankind as such.

SECTION IV. The meaning of Peace is most clearly understood by considering it in its relation to the tragic issues which are essential in the nature of things. Peace is the understanding of tragedy, and at the same time its preservation.

We have seen that there can be no real halt of civilization in the indefinite repetition of a perfected ideal. Staleness sets in. And this fatigue is nothing other than the creeping growth of anæsthesia; whereby that social group is gradually sinking towards nothingness. The defining characteristics are losing their importance. There may be no pain or conscious loss. There is merely a slow paralysis of surprise. And apart from surprise, intensity of feeling collapses.

Decay, Transition, Loss, Displacement belong to the essence of the Creative Advance. The new direction of aim is initiated by Spontaneity, an element of confusion. The enduring Societies with their rise, culmination, and decay, are devices to combine the necessities of Harmony and Freshness. There is the deep underlying Harmony of Nature, as it were a fluid, flexible support; and on its surface the ripples of social efforts, harmonizing and clashing in their aims at ways of satisfaction. The lower types of physical objects can have a vast endurance of inorganic life. The higher types, involving animal life and the dominance of a personality primarily mental, preserve their zest by the quick succession of stages from birth, culmination, to death. As soon as high consciousness is reached, the enjoyment of existence is entwined with pain, frustration, loss, tragedy. Amid the passing of so much beauty, so much heroism, so much daring, Peace is then the intuition of permanence. It keeps vivid the sensitiveness to the tragedy; and it sees the tragedy as a living agent persuading the world to aim at fineness beyond the faded level of surrounding fact. Each tragedy is the disclosure of an ideal: —What might have been, and was not: What can be. The tragedy was not in vain. This survival power in motive force, by reason of appeal to reserves of Beauty, marks the difference between the tragic evil and the gross evil. The inner feeling belonging to this grasp of the service of tragedy is Peace—the purification of the emotions.

SECTION V. The deepest definition of Youth is, Life as yet untouched by tragedy. And the finest flower of youth is to know the lesson in advance of the experience. undimmed. The question here for discussion is how the intuition of Peace asserts itself apart from its disclosure in tragedy. Evidently observation of the earlier stages of personal life will afford the clearest evidence.

Youth is distinguished for its whole-hearted absorption in personal enjoyments and personal discomforts. Quick pleasure and quick pain, quick laughter and quick tears, quick absence of care, and quick diffidence, quick courage and quick fear, are conjointly characters of youth. In other words. immediate absorption in its own occupations. On this side, Youth is too chequered to be termed a happy period. It is vivid rather than happy. The memories of youth are better to live through, than is youth itself. For except in extreme cases, memory is apt to count the sunny hours. Youth is not peaceful in any ordinary sense of that term. In youth despair is overwhelming. There is then no tomorrow, no memory of disasters survived.

The short-sightedness of youth matches the scantiness of its experience. The issues of its action are beyond its ken, perhaps with literature supplying a delusory sense of knowledge. Thus generosity and cruelty are equally natural, by reason of the fact that their full effects lie beyond conscious anticipation.

All this is the veriest commonplace in the characterization of Youth. Nor does the modern wealth of social literature in any fundamental way alter the case. The reason for its statement here is to note that these features of character belong to all animals at all ages, including human beings at every stage of their lives. The differences only lie in relative proportions. Also the success of language in conveying information is vastly over-rated, especially in learned circles. Not only is language highly elliptical, but also nothing can supply the defect of first-hand experience of types cognate to the things explicitly mentioned. The general truth of Hume's doctrine as to the necessity of first-hand impressions is inexorable.

There is another side. Youth is peculiarly susceptible to appeals for beauty of conduct. It understands motives which presuppose the irrelevance of its own person. Such motives are understood as contributing to the magnification of its own interests. Its very search for personal experience thus elicits impersonality, self-forgetfulness. Youth forgets itself in its own ardour. Of course, not always. For it can fall in love. But the test of the better nature, so happily plentiful, is that love passes from selfishness to devotion. The higher forms of love break down the narrow self-regarding motives.

When youth has once grasped where Beauty dwells—with a real knowledge and not as a mere matter of literary phraseology in some poetic, scriptural, or psychological version—when youth has once grasped, its self-surrender is absolute. The vision may pass. It may traverse consciousness in a flash. Some natures may never permit it to emerge into attention. But Youth is peculiarly liable to the vision of that Peace, which is the harmony of the soul's activities with ideal aims that lie beyond any personal satisfaction.

SECTION VI. The vigour of civilized societies is preserved by the widespread sense that high aims are worthwhile. Vigorous societies harbour a certain extravagance of objectives, so that men wander beyond the safe provision of personal gratifications. All strong interests easily become impersonal, the love of a good job well done. There is a sense of harmony about such an accomplishment, the Peace brought by something worthwhile. Such personal gratification arises from aim beyond personality.

The converse tendency is at least equally noticeable; the egotistic desire for fame—'that last infirmity'—is an inversion of the social impulse, and yet presupposes it. The tendency shows itself in the trivialities of child-life, as well as in the career of some conqueror before whom mankind trembled. In the widest sense, it is the craving for sympathy. It involves the feeling that each act of experience is a central reality, claiming all things as its own. The world has then no justification except as a satisfaction of such claims. But the point is that the desire for admiring attention becomes futile except in the presence of an audience fit to render it. The pathology of feeling, so often exemplified, consists in the destruction of the audience for the sake of the fame. There is also, of course, the sheer love of command, finally devoid of high purpose. The complexity of human motive, the entwinement of its threads, is infinite. The point, which is here relevant, is that the zest of human adventure presupposes for its material a scheme of things with a worth beyond any single occasion. However perverted, there is required for zest that craving to stand conspicuous in this scheme of things as well as the purely personal pleasure in the exercise of faculties. It is the final contentment aimed at by the soul in its retreat to egoism, as distinct from anæsthesia. In this, it is beyond human analysis to detect exactly where the perversion begins to taint the intuition of Peace. Milton's phrase states the whole conclusion—'That last infirmity of noble mind'.

Fame is a cold, hard notion. Another half-way house between the extreme ecstasy of Peace and the extreme of selfish desire, is the love of particular individual things. Such love is the completion almost necessary for finite reality, and all reality is in some way finite. In the extreme of love, such as mother's love, all personal desire is transferred to the thing loved, as a desire for its perfection. Personal life has here evidently passed beyond itself, but with explicit, definite limitation to particular realities. It is partly based upon the importance of the individuality of details for the æsthetic value of objective appearance. This has been discussed before.[1] This aspect of personal love is simply a clinging to a condition for selfish happiness. There is no transcendence of personality.

But some closeness of status, such as the relation of parent to child or the relation of marriage, can produce the love of self-devotion where the potentialities of the loved object are felt passionately as a claim that it find itself in a friendly Universe. Such love is really an intense feeling as to how the harmony of the world should be realised in particular objects. It is the feeling as to what would happen if right could triumph in a beautiful world, with discord routed. It is the passionate desire for the beautiful result, in this instance. Such love is distracting, nerve-racking. But, unless darkened by utter despair, it involves deep feeling of an aim in the Universe, winning such triumph as is possible to it. It is the sense of Eros, hovering between Peace as the crown of Youth and Peace as the issue of Tragedy.

SECTION VII. The general health of social life is taken care of by formularized moral precepts, and formularized religious beliefs and religious institutions. All of these explicitly express the doctrine that the perfection of life resides in aims beyond the individual person in question.

It is a doctrine of great generality, capable of a large variety of specialization, not all of them mutually consistent. For example, consider the patriotism of the Roman farmers, in the full vigour of the Republic. Certainly Regulus did not return to Carthage, with the certainty of torture and death, cherishing any mystic notions of another life—either a Christian Heaven or a Buddhist Nirvana. He was a practical man, and his ideal aim was the Roman Republic

1. Ch. XVII, Sect. VIII, and Ch. XIX, Sect. IV.

flourishing in this world. But this aim transcended his individual personality; for this aim he entirely sacrificed every gratification bounded by such limits. For him there was something in the world which could not be expressed as sheer personal gratification—and yet in thus sacrificing himself, his personal existence rose to its full height. He may have been mistaken in his estimate of the worth of the Roman Republic. The point is that with that belief, he achieved magnificence by the sacrifice of himself.

In this estimate, Regulus has not in any way proved himself to be exceptional. His conduct showed heroism that is unusual. But his estimate of the worth of such conduct has evoked widest assent. The Roman farmers agreed; and generation after generation, amid all the changes of history, have agreed by the instinctive pulse of emotion as the tale is handed down.

Moral codes have suffered from the exaggerated claims made for them. The dogmatic fallacy has here done its worst. Each such code has been put out by a God on a mountain top, or by a Saint in a cave, or by a divine Despot on a throne, or, at the lowest, by ancestors with a wisdom beyond later question. In any case, each code is incapable of improvement; and unfortunately in details they fail to agree either with each other or with our existing moral intuitions. The result is that the world is shocked, or amused, by the sight of saintly old people hindering in the name of morality the removal of obvious brutalities from a legal system. Some *Acta Sanctorum* go ill with civilization.

The details of these codes are relative to the social circumstances of the immediate environment—life at a certain date on 'the fertile fringe' of the Arabian desert, life on the lower slopes of the Himalayan Mountains, life on the plains of China, or on the plains of India, life on the delta of some great river. Again the meaning of the critical terms is shifting and ambiguous, for example, the notions of ownership, family, marriage, murder, God. Conduct which in one environment and at one stage produces its measure of harmonious satisfaction, in other surroundings at another stage is destructively degrading. Each society has its own type of perfection, and puts up with certain blots, at that stage inevitable. Thus the notion that there are certain regulative notions, sufficiently precise to prescribe details of conduct, for all reasonable beings on Earth, in every planet, and in every star-system, is at once to be put aside. That is the notion of the one type of perfection at which the Universe aims. All realization of the Good is finite, and necessarily excludes certain other types.

But what these codes do witness to, and what their interpretation by seers of various races throughout history does witness to, is the aim at a social perfection. Such a realized fact is conceived as an abiding perfection in the nature of things, a treasure for all ages. It is not a romance of thought, it is a fact of Nature. For example, in one sense the Roman Republic declined and fell; in another sense, it stands a stubborn fact in the Universe. To perish is to assume a new function in the process of generation. Devotion to the Republic magnified the type of personal satisfactions for those who conformed their purposes to its maintenance. Such conformation of purpose to ideal beyond personal limitations is the conception of that Peace with which the wise man can face his fate, master of his soul.

SECTION VIII. The wide scope of the notion of 'society' requires attention. Transcendence begins with the leap from the actuality of the immediate occasion to the notion of personal existence, which is a society of occasions. In terms of human life, the soul is a society. Care for the future of personal existence, regret or pride in its past, are alike feelings which leap beyond the bounds of the sheer actuality of the present. It is in the nature of the present that it should thus transcend itself by reason of the immanence in it of the 'other'. But there is no necessity as to the scale of emphasis that this fact of nature should receive. It belongs to the civilization of consciousness, to magnify the large sweep of harmony.

Beyond the soul, there are other societies, and societies of societies. There is the animal body ministering to the soul: there are families, groups of families, nations, species, groups involving different species associated in the joint enterprise of keeping alive. These various societies, each in its measure, claim loyalties and loves. In human history the various responses to these claims disclose the essential transcendence of each individual actuality beyond itself. The stubborn reality of the absolute self-attainment of each individual is bound up with a relativity which it issues from and issues into. The analysis of the various strands of relativity is the analysis of the social structure of the Universe, as in this epoch.

Although particular codes of morality reflect, more or less imperfectly, the special circumstances of social structure concerned, it is natural to seek for some highly general principles underlying all such codes. Such generalities should reflect the very notions of the harmonizing of harmonies, and of particular individual actualities as the sole authentic reality. These are the principles of the generality of harmony, and of the importance of the individual. The first means 'order', and the second means 'love'. Between the two there is a suggestion of opposition. For 'order' is impersonal; and love, above all things, is personal. The antithesis is solved by rating types of order in relative importance according to their success in magnifying the individual actualities, that is to say, in promoting strength of experience. Also in rating the individual on the double basis, partly on the intrinsic strength of its own experience, and partly on its influence in the promotion of a high-grade type of order. These two grounds in part coalesce. For a weak individual exerts a weak influence. The essence of Peace is that the individual whose strength of experience is founded upon this ultimate intuition, thereby is extending the influence of the source of all order.

The moral code is the behaviour-patterns which in the environment for which it is designed will promote the evolution of that environment towards its proper perfection.

SECTION IX. The attainment of Truth belongs to the essence of Peace. By this it is meant, that the intuition constituting the realization of Peace has as its objective that Harmony whose interconnections involve Truth. A defect in Truth is a limitation to Harmony. There can be no secure efficacy in the Beauty which hides within itself the dislocations of falsehood.

The truth or falsehood of propositions is not directly to the point in this demand for Truth. Since each proposition is yoked to a contradictory proposition, and since of these one must be true and the other false, there are necessarily as many false as there are true propositions. This bare 'truth or falsehood' of propositions is a comparatively superficial factor affecting the discursive interests of the intellect. The essential truth that Peace demands is the conformation of Appearance to Reality. There is the Reality from which the occasion of experience springs—a Reality of inescapable, stubborn fact; and there is the Appearance with which the occasion attains its final individuality—an Appearance including its adjustment of the Universe by simplification, valuation, transmutation, anticipation. A feeling of dislocation of Appearance from Reality is the final destructive force, robbing life of its zest for adventure. It spells the decadence of civilization, by stripping from it the very reason for its existence.

There can be no necessity governing this conformation. Sense-perception, which dominates the appearance of things, in its own nature rearranges, and thus in a way distorts. Also there can be no mere blunt truth about the Appearance which it provides. In its own nature Sense-perception is an interpretation, and this interpretation may be completely misleading. If there were a necessary conformation of Appearance to Reality then Morality would vanish. There is no morality about the multiplication table, whose items are necessarily linked. Art would also be a meaningless term. For it presupposes the efficacy of purpose. Art is an issue of Adventure.

The question for discussion is whether there exists any factor in the Universe constituting a general drive towards the conformation of Appearance to Reality. This drive would then constitute a factor in each occasion persuading an aim at such truth as is proper to the special appearance in question. This concept of truth, proper to each special appearance, would mean that the appearance has not built itself up by the inclusion of elements that are foreign to the reality from which it springs. The appearance will then be a generalization and an adaptation of emphasis; but not an importation of qualities and relations without any corresponding exemplification in the reality. This concept of truth is in fact the denial of the doctrine of Appearance which lies on the surface of Kant's *Critique of Pure Reason.* It is a denial of his answer to the question,—How are synthetic *a priori* judgments possible? It is at least the introduction of guarding limitations, which Kant explicitly in that work does not introduce.

SECTION X. The answer to this question must issue from a survey of the factors in terms of which individual experience has been interpreted: —The antecedent World from which each occasion springs, a World of many occasions presenting for the new creature harmonies and discords: the easy road of Anæsthesia by which discordant factors are dismissed into irrelevance: the activity of the mental poles in building conceptual experience into patterns of feeling which rescue discords from loss: the spontaneity of the mental action and its persuasion by a sense of relevance: the selective nature of consciousness and its initial failure to discriminate the deeper sources of feeling: that there is no agency in abstraction from actual occasions, and that existence involves implication in agency: the sense of a unity of many occasions with a value beyond that of any individual occasion; for example, the soul, the complete animal, the social group of animals, the material body, the physical epoch: the aim at immediate individual contentment.

The justification for the suggestion derived from this group of factors must mainly rest upon their direct elucidation of first-hand experience. They are not, and should not be, the result of an argument. For all argument must rest upon premises more fundamental than the conclusions. Discussion of fundamental notions is merely for the purpose of disclosing their coherence, their compatibility, and the specializations which can be derived from their conjunction.

The above set of metaphysical notions rests itself upon the ordinary, average experience of mankind, properly interpreted. But there is a further set for which the appeal lies to occasions and modes of experience which in some degree are exceptional. It must be remembered that the present level of average waking human experience was at one time exceptional among the ancestors of mankind. We are justified therefore in appealing to those modes of experience which in our direct judgment stand above the average level. The gradual emergence of such modes, and their effect on human history, have been among the themes of this book in its appeal to history. We have found the growth of Art: its gradual sublimation into the pursuit of Truth and Beauty: the sublimation of the egoistic aim by its inclusion of the transcendent whole: the youthful zest in the transcendent aim: the sense of tragedy: the sense of evil: the persuasion towards Adventure beyond achieved perfection: the sense of Peace.

SECTION XI. The concept of Civilization, as developed up to this stage, remains inherently incomplete. No logical argument can demonstrate this gap. Such arguments are merely subsidiary helps for the conscious realization of metaphysical intuitions—*Non in dialectica complacuit Deo salvum facere populum suum.* This saying, quoted by Cardmal Newman,[2] should be the motto of every metaphysician. He is seeking, amid the dim recesses of his ape-like consciousness and beyond the reach of dictionary language, for the premises implicit in all reasoning. The speculative methods of metaphysics are dangerous, easily perverted. So is all Adventure; but Adventure belongs to the essence of civilization.

2. *Grammar of Assent.*

The incompleteness of the concept relates to the notion of Transcendence, the feeling essential for Adventure, Zest, and Peace. This feeling requires for its understanding that we supplement the notion of the Eros by including it in the concept of an Adventure in the Universe as One. This Adventure embraces all particular occasions but as an actual fact stands beyond any one of them. It is, as it were, the complement to Plato's Receptacle, its exact opposite, yet equally required for the unity of all things. In every way, it is contrary to the Receptacle. The Receptacle is bare of all forms: the Unity of Adventure includes the Eros which is the living urge towards all possibilities, claiming the goodness of their realization. The Platonic Receptacle is void, abstract from all individual occasions: The Unity of Adventure includes among its components all individual realities, each with the importance of the personal or social fact to which it belongs. Such individual importance in the components belongs to the essence of Beauty. In this Supreme Adventure, the Reality which the Adventure transmutes into its Unity of Appearance, requires the real occasions of the advancing world each claiming its due share of attention. This Appearance, thus enjoyed, is the final Beauty with which the Universe achieves its justification. This Beauty has always within it the renewal derived from the Advance of the Temporal World. It is the immanence of the Great Fact including this initial Eros and this final Beauty which constitutes the zest of self-forgetful transcendence belonging to Civilization at its height.

At the heart of the nature of things, there are always the dream of youth and the harvest of tragedy. The Adventure of the Universe starts with the dream and reaps tragic Beauty. This is the secret of the union of Zest with Peace: —That the suffering attains its end in a Harmony of Harmonies. The immediate experience of this Final Fact, with its union of Youth and Tragedy, is the sense of Peace. In this way the World receives its persuasion towards such perfections as are possible for its diverse individual occasions.

Epilogue

At this stage we conclude the consideration of that group of ideas that most directly contributed to the civilization of the behaviour-systems of human beings in their intercourse with each other. This improvement depended on the slow growth of mutual respect, sympathy, and general kindliness. All these feelings can exist with the minimum of intellectuality. Their basis is emotional, and humanity acquired these emotions by reason of its unthinking activities amid the course of nature.

But mentality as it emerges into coordinated activity has a tremendous effect in selecting, emphasizing, and disintegrating. We have been considering the emergence of ideas from activities, and the effect of ideas in modifying the activities from which they emerge. Ideas arise as explanatory of customs and they end by founding novel methods and novel institutions. In the preceding chapters we have watched instances of their transition from one to other of these two modes of functioning.